PLANNING MEDIA: STRATEGY AND IMAGINATION

William J. Donnelly

Prentice Hall
Upper Saddle River, New Jersey 07458

Acquisitions Editor: David Borkowsky
Marketing Manager: John Chillingworth
Senior Project Manager: Alana Zdinak
Production Editor: Andrea Mulligan, Benchmark Productions, Inc.
Cover Design: Bruce Kenselaar
Copy Editor: Benchmark Productions, Inc.
Manufacturing Buyer: Kenneth J. Clinton
Assistant Editor: Melissa Steffens
Editorial Assistant: Theresa Festa
Production Coordinator: David Cotugno

Cover Photo: Ron Fleming/Burnstein and Andriulli, Inc.

Printed in the United States of America

10 9 8 7 6 5 4 3

ISBN 0-13-567835-8

Prentice-Hall International (UK) Limited, London
Prentice-Hall of Australia Pty. Limited, Sydney
Prentice-Hall Canada Inc., Toronto
Prentice-Hall Hispanoamericana, S.A., Mexico
Prentice-Hall of India Private Limited, New Delhi
Prentice-Hall of Japan, Inc., Tokyo
Pearson Education Asia Pte. Ltd., Singapore
Editoria Prentice-Hall do Brasil, Ltda., Rio De Janeiro

Contents

Foreword: Creativity and Stewardship

DAVID K. BRAUN
VICE PRESIDENT, MEDIA SERVICES
KRAFT GENERAL FOODS, INC.

In one sense, this is a textbook on media planning, and a good one at that. It provides a comprehensive and thorough description of the media planning process, the requisite information for building an effective media plan, and the considerations that affect the eventual implementation of the plan. A student aspiring to join an advertising agency as a media planner could rely on this text as an excellent foundation for understanding how to produce effective work.

Planning Media is more than just a training manual on how to do media planning, however. As Bill acknowledges in his preface, "This is a book about thinking." It is full of philosophy and rich historical context, which make today's media planning approaches more understandable. Quite correctly, it presents media planning as a far more challenging and rewarding process than the number crunching stereotype with which it has so long been associated. Most of media's long-standing practitioners know this truth about media planning. Bill's book will help students to appreciate it also.

I was struck by how many times Bill refers to the act of "imaging." Most frequently, he asks the reader to imagine the connection between a particular communications medium (or an advertisement in it) and the consumer prospect for a brand's message. This is the essence of effective media planning. It is the question with which the media planner must begin his or her investigation, and it is the benchmark against which the process must be measured.

Creative conceptualization is the driver of successful media plans. Numbers are one of the tools we use to measure the efficiency of our concepts and to persuade others to believe in them. Even in this role, however, common-sense logic is often more persuasive than numbers.

It amazes me how often people think of media as science and numbers. Doing so can be a serious mistake for an advertiser. It's like looking through a telescope backward. A brand's advertising message is intended to alter consumer attitudes and behavior. In selecting the vehicle that will effectively deliver the brand's message to the consumer, we need to begin with the contextual aspects of the media vehicle: the editorial or programming Tissue that has attracted our consumer's interest in the first place. These are typically gut judgments that have little to do with the numbers that may be available.

At Kraft General Foods, we encourage our brand and agency people to explore alternative media by focusing initially only on concepts and ideas—communications connections in Donnelly's lexicon. This is where one can more clearly assess the power of the message to change consumer behavior. It matters very little that a particular medium has an efficient cost per thousand against a brand's demographic target group if that medium will not create an optimal context for the consumer to receive the brand's message.

One of the things I like most about Bill's book is its strong emphasis on "thinking" as distinguished from "quantifying." I believe the ingredients most important to an effective media plan are:

1. how tightly it is linked to the brand's marketing objectives and creative strategy, and
2. the insightful selection of media vehicles that can effectively "present" the message to the consumer.

These areas demand disciplined thinking and imagination. They establish the basic framework for the media plan. If they are done poorly, the plan can never be great.

In closing, let me say a few words about stewardship: For most advertisers, this is a key area of focus. Stewardship is the collection of activities devoted to ensuring that the brand actually receives the media value assumed in the plan. Here is where numbers have real value.

Stewardship actually begins in the media plan itself. When we translate the "communications connections" and concepts into specifics and document them with quantified measures, we establish the benchmarks for stewardship. Weekly GRP goals, flight dates, program specifications, editorial adjacencies in print, traffic locations in outdoor—all these define the currency by which media value is to be measured. Communications objectives like awareness levels, attitude shifts, and so on, are other measures by which to determine whether or not the plan is effective. Stewardship expectations are defined in the plan.

Measuring how well these quantified goals are achieved is the essential stewardship role as the plan is implemented. These measures can be correlated with market share and consumer purchases to validate (or refute) the media plan's basic assumptions. Consistent achievement reinforces conviction in the plan. Lack of achievement provides a sound basis for exploring different strategies. As such, stewardship provides useful raw material for the next media planning cycle. "Media science" becomes a catalyst for "media art," which is the key to developing superior media plans.

Bill's book is a refreshing view of media planning. It should prove increasingly valuable as the Confetti Generation unfolds.

Foreword

JOSEPH W. OSTROW
PRESIDENT AND CEO
CABLE TELEVISION ADVERTISING BUREAU

During twenty years as a World Wide Media Director—first, at Young & Rubicam and, then, at Foote Cone & Belding—I was often asked how to position the media function at an advertising agency. I often felt that it could all be solved if, like the military, we all had uniforms to wear—in effect, a dress code that symbolized what we did, and represented the right kind of image. Everyone in the field that I talked to about this agreed that the appropriate attire was a white coat. I found it difficult, however, to determine whether they meant a white coat as in a lab technician's attire, or a white coat as in an artist's smock. This divergence is, in many ways, what media planning is all about. Despite the singular focus of acting as an investment counselor to clients and providing the planning and execution guidance needed to make the proper media investments, the skill to do this well requires a combination of both art and science. This combination captures the nature of the diverse challenges that are available to anyone entering a career in the world of media planning or media buying.

All of us in this segment of marketing like to bathe in the glow of successfully helping clients invest their media funds. It is within this effort that we deal with the continuum of who, what, when, where, and why. Knowing how to do this is what Bill Donnelly's *Planning Media: Strategy and Imagination* is all about. The key skill is to be able to marry a knowledge of the role that media play in the lives of the clients' target audience or customers with an understanding of how best to utilize the various media that are available. This is what helps produce success for the investment of the marketing funds that go into purchasing media time or space. It should also explain why it is not unrealistic to say that there really is no such thing as a "bad" medium (assuming that it attracts an audience), but rather that what does exist is bad media usage.

The media function, be it media planning or buying, provides yet another set of satisfactions—namely, the "magic" of creating a selling bridge that results from bringing a new concept to the client and then getting the media to help you make it happen. You can actually become the fulcrum point in the triangle between client, consumer, and media. Innovating in these situations, whether it is based upon statistical analysis or based upon thinking "outside of the box," is one of the most rewarding parts of the media career experience.

The eclectic nature of these undertakings also makes this one of the most exciting, interesting, and rewarding professions. One day you are trying to appraise the potential for success of a new magazine, and on another you may be trying to cut a cost-effective deal with a television program producer.

Within this arena of challenges and rewards, Bill Donnelly has put together a marvelous text. He has provided both the salt and pepper, the yin and yang, the black and white, that goes into producing an algorithm for success in the media profession. I recommend that you read Bill's planning words, understand his analysis, structure, premises, and checklists. Most of all, appreciate the full richness of the basic idea that here we have a profession that is as broad or deep as you wish to make it, and is among the most challenging career options available.

Preface

This is a book about thinking.

The reasons for writing a book are often complex, and often poorly uderstood by the author. Nevertheless, it is fair to attempt to explain some of the reasons that dictate the style and content of a book that pretends, in part, to work as a textbook. Students should be alerted, at least, to what is included, what is left out, and how the book is intended to work.

The origins of this book are rooted in two experiences: The first is my experiences as a teacher of several different courses in the Media Planning Track at Temple University. The second is derived from my experiences as a Senior Vice President of Young & Rubicam responsible for developing innovative concepts in all media forms. What I feel I must teach naturally relates to what I wish had been taught.

I believe that the most important fact confronted by a teacher of media planning is that nearly 80 percent of the students enrolled in the course have no intentions of actively pursuing an advertising agency career, to say nothing of a media planner's career. These students have a right to expect that the media planning course contribute to their general liberal arts education. This requires that the course be more than an immersion experience in the technical details of a craft. Professional courses should relate to larger concepts while encouraging the development of critical thinking and prudent judgment. After all, universities are in the education business, not the training business.

After searching for a media planning textbook supportive of these goals, I concluded that most of the textbooks were trade manuals rather than educational texts. They focused more on the tools of the trade than on the thought patterns of analysis and judgment characteristic of the profession. More elaborate texts seemed to be so knotted up in statistical analysis as to be manuals for future research practitioners, rather than planning professionals.

It has long seemed to me that three things have been missing from our considerations of media planning at both the educational and professional levels. The first is a sense and articulation of process. There should be a natural progression from beginning to end of "the doing."

On the one hand, process and progression suggest that technical tools and issues should not be introduced up front and all at once. Rather, they should be introduced and discussed when they are appropriate to the thoughtful moment at hand. Consequently, media cost data, audience research, ratings, cost-per-thousand, and other purchasing data and formulas are found in part 4 of this text. They are tactical tools and considerations and should be addressed when our thought process is ready to conclude in executions.

On the other hand, process and progression also imply that a text should attempt to replicate the associative thoughts experienced by the best media planners at the various moments of analysis and judgment. Consequently, we not only follow the straight-line logic of the media planning process, but also reflect the consumer and marketing meaning planners are seeking to uncover during the process. The process of analyzing a situation and arriving at a strategy is, in fact, a dialogue between insight and judgment. We try to capture this experience of thought throughout parts 2 and 3 of this text before elaborating on executional options.

Second, we should not overlook the conceptual foundations of media planning. We should understand both why we are pursuing a process and why it works. The reasons should be more fundamental than "It is our job to best spend the available budget" and more satisfying than "This is how our predecessors have successfully performed this job." We should uncover the foundations of media planning in both social communications and marketing. We should also make the effort to spell out the connections between social communications and marketing throughout the process, rather than just state that the connections exist and leave it at that.

Finally, media planning is about people engaged in human communications and in the process of discovering the satisfaction of their wants and needs. Abstract, data driven, technical thinking is only a supportive tool in this context. Media are imaginative products, primarily accessible through the imagination, and only imaginative thought can penetrate the vitality of human activity. Imagination—its role, function, and utility—was simply nowhere to be found in the existing texts, nor in most discussions of media planning.

The most direct function of the imagination is to make things, people, and events present to us. What we will call the "cognitive imagination" makes it possible for us to make judgments based on the experiences of consumers and their relationships. The cognitive imagination enables us to emerge from a consideration of the numerically described evidence of the existence of motivations and relationships to the human truth whose only evidence is the story that contains it, and whose only proof is found in our recognition and acknowledgment. Aristotle understood this, and it is what Tennessee Williams meant when he wrote in a stage direction of *Cat on a Hot Tin Roof* that a play should be "a snare for the truth of human experience." That is how the imagination works and what the cognitive imagination does.

These issues of process, fundamental insight, and imagination are critical to media planning as a discipline contributing to a liberal arts education; but these same issues are important to professional progress, vitality, and creativity. These are the tools that will be required in abundance as we face a rapidly changing world, driven by multiple communications technologies. Growing data will, in fact, tell us less in the future because the audiences will be smaller and their experiences so disparate. Only well-grounded imaginative disciplines will provide the possibility of athletic penetration of these new markets, media dynamics, and consumers in the near future.

Some believe that the exponential growth of data and rapidly multiplying media can be confronted and managed only with the help of computers. For several decades, computers have been the characteristic technology of media planning, and computers have become the desktop tool of contemporary business. Any media planner should welcome the growing databases and the computer programs available for managing and analyzing the data.

The challenge facing the media planner today and tomorrow, however, is the same challenge which has always confronted the media planner. The challenge is to "see through the numbers" and discover the dynamics of consumer communications and purchasing behavior that the numbers symbolize and the data suggests. As databases and media vehicles proliferate, it becomes more difficult to comprehend the evidence and discover the connections. This growing challenge will put ever greater demands on the one faculty that offers us the possibility of athletic penetration of abstract data and communications experience. That faculty is the imagination, and it will be in ever greater demand as we are forced to ask ever more penetrating questions of the computers at our fingertips.

This effort, then, is intended to be both a textbook and a professional text. It should be a useful and dependable resource for media planning executives seeking creative solutions to marketing problems as well as a daily tour guide for students trying to learn how the system works. All authors are warned of the dangers of trying to write for two audiences at the same time. In this instance, however, I see no other way to do it. In a remarkable way, both students and working professionals need to learn many of the same things about process and imagination in media planning. As far as I can tell, I am the first to address these things in a book. I am prepared to be told that I have fallen short of my goals, but my goals are clear. They also explain the character of this book. I hope it works, for all our sakes.

Acknowledgments

This book would not exist except for two groups of people. First, the people of Young & Rubicam, who encouraged me, and their dozens of clients who put their money where my ideas were. Second, my students who taught me what needed to be articulated and had not been articulated before. I also thank David Marans of J. Walter Thompson, Barbara Zidovsky of A.C. Nielsen, and Bernard Golstein of Vitt Media International who identified, accumulated, and verified much of the research base. Finally, my wife and daughter who shared the cost in time and attention which a book demands.

Part 1

Basic Concepts and Skills

1

Conceptual Foundations of Media Planning

OVERVIEW

This chapter introduces the concepts basic to the foundations of media planning and explores the relationships between the mass media and consumer purchase decisions. Advertising works because the media have created a market. Media perform an intrinsic role in individual or group learning and motivation. Media planners are advertising investment analysts and counselors. Media planning is the art and science of making the delivery of advertising synchronous with the appropriate processes of society communicating.

IMPORTANCE OF MEDIA PLANNING

Media planning has evolved into a highly complex and intensely competitive part of advertising. At its simplest level, **media planning** is the process of choosing the vehicle of mass communication in which to place an advertiser's message, purchasing that time or space, and insuring that the advertising message runs as purchased. Until it does, the advertising message is not advertising.

Advertising agencies had their origins in the media function. Volney B. Palmer, often identified as having established the first advertising agency, was a media broker. He established his business in 1841 in Philadelphia to contract for extensive space in newspapers, and then resell this space to advertisers. The advertisers prepared their own ads, and Palmer was, in effect, paid by the publishers.[1]

In the 1870s, the new N. W. Ayer Agency, another Philadelphia company, offered advertisers a contract acknowledging that it operated as the advertiser's agent, not the media's, and agreed to share all of the agency's previously proprietary knowledge of publication rates and circulations.[2] The agency continued to be paid by publishers, however, through a system of discount rates.

The *Ladies Home Journal* first appeared in 1902. Cyrus H. K. Curtis, who founded the magazine, once explained his motives to a group of businessmen:

> The editor of the *Ladies Home Journal* thinks we publish it for the benefit of American women. This is an illusion, but a very proper one for him to have. The real reason, the publisher's reason, is to give you, who manufacture things American women want, a chance to tell them about your product.[3]

In this way, he described how advertising and publishing have been bound together since the Industrial Revolution. The agency function continued to be that of media broker throughout these early years. In fact, "national advertising, the advertising agency, and the publisher's commission to the agent appear to have come into existence together."[4]

The media function was still ascendant when agencies began preparing advertising copy in the 1890s in order to facilitate space sales. It wasn't until John E. Kennedy and Albert Lasker teamed up at the Lord & Thomas agency in 1905, and concluded that advertising was no longer just news but "salesmanship in print," that the "whole complexion of advertising for all America was changed."[5] From that point on, the creative star was ascendant and media descendant.

For generations after World War I, media planning was not perceived as a difficult process. Media practitioners only facilitated the delivery of the advertising message, and the process of media purchasing was no longer an esoteric and entrepreneurial craft. The fun, the excitement, and the challenge of the business were in creating advertising and, occasionally, the radio programs that broadcast the message.

By the mid-1960s, television had changed the environment. The necessity of using television radically escalated the costs of advertising. The consequence was a demand that greater emphasis be placed on demonstrating how media contributed to the achievement of marketing objectives. Products, outlets, competition, and media vehicles proliferated throughout the subsequent decades. Advertising budgets grew, and the process of reaching the consumer became more difficult. This evolution in marketing and communications had an impact on media planning and its perceived importance because that was where the advertising money was (Exhibit 1.1). Planners were required to become smarter and tougher, and media planning reemerged as an increasingly important part of agency service (Exhibit 1.2).

The bottom line is that every year over $140 billion is spent in buying advertising time and space. Furthermore, media costs represent 80 to 90 percent of any advertiser's budget. That is what makes the determinations involved in deciding how advertising messages will reach consumers so salient. Media planners are advertising investment counselors.

EXHIBIT 1.1 CONTINUING INCREASE IN AD EXPENDITURES

Annual spending on advertising in the United States and current estimates.

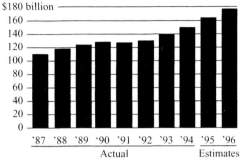

Source: McCann-Erickson USA

EXHIBIT 1.2

The cost per thousand (CPM) of reaching consumers through various media has increased dramatically from the base years 1982–1984.

Newspapers	+68%
Magazines	+83
Network TV	+63
Spot TV	+60
Network Radio	+31
Spot Radio	+34
Outdoor	+34
Direct Mail	+55

Source: McCann-Erickson Worldwide

Money focuses attention, and media planning is receiving a great deal more attention than it used to.[6] Media practitioners have often been observed jumping up and down on this trampoline of self-importance, having developed an acute case of sibling rivalry in a business populated with glamorous peers; but that is not our intention here.

MEDIA FUNCTION

Advertising is often defined as any message that has been paid for by an identified sponsor, has been sent through one or more mass media, and is directed to a specific group of individuals or organizations with the explicit purpose of aiding the sale or the purchase of a product, brand, or service. The job of media planning is to manage the sending of the advertiser's message through one or more mass media. More important to our conceptual understanding, however, is the fact that, by definition, there can be no advertising without the mass media. Even direct mail and discrete on-line media require mass networks of wires and post offices.

Advertising always rides in someone else's car. We call these cars media vehicles. Whenever we need a ride from the city to the shore, or from college to home, we leave when the driver wants to leave; we go where the driver wants to go; we pay for the gas and tolls; we listen to the driver's preferences in music and follow the driver's etiquette about smoking. Advertisers have a similar relationship with media vehicles and their editors, publishers, producers, or owners. Advertisers ride in the media; they have to get along to go along.

The media are essential to advertising. It is the decision to invest in media time and space that makes a manufacturer or marketer an advertiser.[7] It is precisely when a steel fabricator, car maker, frozen food marketer, bank, or law firm buys space in a print vehicle, or time in a broadcast vehicle, that they become advertisers. If they do not buy their way into exposure through the media, they are not advertisers.

STARTING POINT

What follows from the recognition and acceptance that advertising is always riding in and dependent on media vehicles? The point of view of this text is not so much that the recognition underlines the importance of media planning, but rather that it indicates how media planning must and can best be done. It identifies the starting point for advertiser thinking about media.

Some advertisers, investors, and critics emphasize how important advertising is to the media. They point out that the consumer contribution to a magazine's business barely covers 50 percent of the cost of producing and marketing magazines. Advertising makes up the difference. Broadcast stations and networks are one hundred percent dependent on advertising dollars. These and similar facts make critics wary of potential influence brokering and some investors insistent that communication products serve the marketing communications needs of segments of the advertising community before they venture their capital. We should not be surprised, therefore, that some advertisers and agencies become arrogant and look upon the media simply as "facilitating institutions," there to serve their needs.

Arrogance has no place in media planning. Regardless of the economics, consumers are drawn first to communication products, not advertising. If communication products serve a consumer need or interest, they not only create an audience, but also create a market. That is the formula for a communication product becoming a media vehicle. As every editor, programmer, reader, viewer, and listener knows, creating an audience comes first. The key for the media planner is to understand how this audience—and, therefore, this market—was created and is kept alive. In this context, humility is the path to insight.

ART AND SCIENCE

There is a scientific side to media planning, and many of the above observations may sound like "so much poetry" to dollar-focused, bottom-line-driven marketing managers and businesspeople. Many media planning practitioners will confess an interest in how vehicle audiences are created and kept alive, but assert, at the same time, that this kind of knowledge has very little to do with how they do things.

What many media practitioners do in the regular course of their work is whatever they believe will make their business and marketing clients comfortable. What makes clients comfortable—the argument goes—are numbers and apparently scientific logic. In practice, therefore, media planning often becomes a process of number crunching and the efficient purchase of the media vehicles that the numbers apparently dictate.

Media planning draws on the "scientific" disciplines of sociology, anthropology, psychology, economics, and mathematics. Media planning involves the analysis of extensive product purchase and usage data, elaborate information on media types and individual media vehicles, and surprisingly precise research on all aspects of consumer behavior. Complicated computer programs have been designed in an attempt to control the information overload, and to manage the process of spending so much money in so many ways. The field of media planning is data rich. Nobody spends the kind of money advertisers spend on media without a plethora of data.

Nevertheless, it cannot be proven that any particular media plan is unquestionably the best plan. A media plan begins as a working hypothesis and concludes as a convincing judgment. Media planning begins with an imaginative invention of what might be true and practical. In that sense, it begins as a theory that we invent, test, criticize, modify, and codify until it ends up, as nearly as we can make it, both a reflection and a tool of real life.

What we lack at every step of the operation is verification. Media planning is future oriented. Its verification is in the effectiveness of next month's or next year's marketing communications. The proof, as far as it ever exists, comes from our use of the plan. As in much else in human life, we eventually sign off on a belief in the hope that it accurately reflects reality. The goal of a media planner is economic vitality, which emerges from social vitality, which emerges from persuasion. In that kind of human equation, there is never "scientific" certitude. Media planning is an artistic act of informed judgment. The question, therefore, is how to use the numbers, interpret the data, and see through the statistics.

WHY USE MEDIA?

The key fact is that people buy media; people do not buy advertising. Consequently, media planning can be defined as the conscious and conscientious placement of a secondary object of attention and perception within a primary object of attention and perception. There are three reasons for this use of media:

1. The simplest reason is to distribute an advertising message efficiently and, consequently, to develop awareness among prospects.
2. Another reason is to develop a sense of need by asserting a market match between the product or service and the prospects gathered together by the media vehicle.

3. The most difficult reason to comprehend is to energize demand through the establishment of a synergism between the product or service and the reasons that people are
communicating in and through the particular media vehicle.

CREATING AWARENESS

We have often been told that advertising is selling in a different form, a substitute of
media for face-to-face selling. If we begin with the assumption that the face-to-face
salesman's technique is rooted in personality and pressure, the shift to advertising
during the Industrial Revolution—with its emphasis on style and repetition—is readily understood as a substitute.

Media planning developed during the second half of the nineteenth century simply as the organization of media buying. Using newspapers and magazines was a more
efficient way of creating buyer awareness than sending salesmen door to door. "All-
you-can-afford" budgets could produce the repetition of the seller's message, which
substituted for the salesman's pressure tactics. Packaged goods advertisers, who
demand little more than efficient tonnage (in other words, the maximum number of
impressions), and per inquiry direct response advertisers are examples of this century-
old strategy in action today. Efficient media purchasing can create awareness, and many
advertisers continue to demand little else.

MATCHING PRODUCTS AND PROSPECTS

By the 1950s, it had become clear that consumers were not just isolated, though homo-
geneous, individuals who were simply more easily reached through mass media than
door-to-door. Rather, mass audiences were composed of social groups, each with different needs and wants, depending on the age, gender, income, education, and geographical location of the different consumer groups. More importantly, researchers
had developed the tools for identifying these groups. Consequently, demographics
became the key to both marketing and media planning.

Once it became possible to identify the demographics of media and vehicle audiences, and once the marketing community reached the consensus that all consumers
were not equal prospects for all products, targeting was born. Media planning became
a matching game of efficiently aligning advertisers' media schedules with their demographically defined prospects.

Not many years later, the idea that buying is a result of cognition and learning
became commonly accepted. Four hundred years earlier, a pedagogical text had argued
that "repetition is the essence of learning." The new discovery was that there seemed
to be an ideal number of repetitions for an advertising message. The planning idea was
to reach the maximum number of prospects this defined number of times. As soon as
researchers were able to develop models of vehicle usage that estimated how often
prospects saw a particular advertisement in a schedule, the necessary executional tool

was available. (Frequency distribution and effective reach will be discussed at length in chapter 8.)

By placing advertising in media vehicles used primarily by certain demographic groups, the planner can assist the advertiser in developing a consumer need. When combined with copy and art that are designed specifically for the same target prospects, the best media efforts support the message that a specific product is manufactured exclusively for consumers in a given peer demographic group with unique needs.

When this planning strategy is combined with the careful measurement of the ways in which a particular demographic group gets information, media can be used with an efficiency unknown to door-to-door salesmen. Thus, as media planning developed between the 1950s and 1970s, advertising became less a substitute for face-to-face communications, and more intrinsically dependent on media to develop efficiently the consumer's perception of need necessary to the marketing system.

ENERGIZING DEMAND

Magazines, newspapers, and radio and television broadcasts may be media vehicles in an advertiser's perception. To their buyers and users, however, these communication products are cultural vehicles.

> Mass communications is the process through which the information base of a culture is created, distributed, and shared. . . . Mass communication institutions play indispensable roles through the packaging, distributing, popularizing, validating, and commercializing of the cultural information base.[8]

Media products are the essential tools that people use in working out their culture.

Culture represents the point of view and values of a society, the mind-set with which its members approach other people and the world. Culture combines a social grouping's underlying assumptions and norms into a way of organizing experience. Culture is the coherent way in which a group of people approach birth, death, and all the existential situations between.

Culture is the motivator of marketing. It determines our wants and needs, how we make decisions, and what meaning we attach to things.[9] The organization and structure of an individual consumer's drives and satisfactions—into which a marketer wishes to insert the specific needs and wants that sell products—is definitively determined by culture.[10] Culture is the foundation of buying behavior, and marketing is a system for transferring cultural meanings to consumer products.[11] For the purposes of media planning, we must recognize that mass culture is created by, and happens in, mass communications.

The making, negotiating, unmaking, and remaking of culture is embedded in communicative practice.

> Communication and culture reciprocally influence each other. The culture from which individuals come affects the way they communicate, and the way individuals communicate can change the culture they share.[12]

Culture is the result of society communicating at every level. As John Dewey expressed it: "Society not only continues to exist by transmission, by communication, but it may fairly be said to exist in transmission, in communication."[13] What we are and what we do, therefore, are born in and gain their meaning through our communications.

The constant development of new products, coupled with the growth of disposable income, has produced intensive competition and multiple choice in the marketplace. Simultaneously, extensive mobility and fragmented communications have created multiple and distinct lifestyles, which produce selective attention and selective perception, which, in turn, are multiple and distinct markets.[14]

A nontextbook definition of advertising might be that advertising is a communication that tells you who or what, when, where, and why to buy or believe. Most often, the givens in this dynamic are the "who" or "what," the "when" and the "where." The main issue for advertising, whether one is the seller or the buyer, is "Why?" Distinct groups have distinct motivations. In turn, these motivations are derived from their culture, which is made and unmade through communications. Thus, media choices are the first way consumers answer the question "Why?"

Consumers are what they eat, in media terms. What a prospect knows is a result of what the prospect reads, sees, and hears. What a prospect does is a result of what the prospect knows. People buy and consume because of who they are, and work out who they are in communications. Consequently, that is precisely the time and place where marketers must be when they have something to sell and a need to create the demand for their product.

This understanding of the process is supported by a Yankelovich Partners study released in 1993 (Exhibit 1.3). It concluded that the media that people consume, especially the magazines they read, may more accurately forecast their consumer behavior than demographic data can. "People have a psycho-centric world view that is supported and reinforced by the media," the Yankelovich spokesman explained. "When people freely select media, their choices are consonant with how they define themselves."

What marketers have learned is that buying is the result of a very free choice, that buying is a result of cognition and learning, and that the consumer's will may be free, but that consumers always act on what their own intelligence presents to them as good. Marketers have also discovered that cognition and learning are a product of motivation. Motivation drives learning, and learning drives choice. Motivation is a product of lifestyle; it is personal and social. For consumers, buying is a personal act in a social environment. Throughout the process, however, it is communications which create the conditions of choice.

Advertisers must use media, because media make up the environment in which demand is negotiated. This is a much more fundamental understanding than the perception of media as merely an efficient substitute for the door-to-door salesman. Media choices are the first articulation of consumer demand and the necessary condition for the transferring of cultural meaning to consumer products.

EXHIBIT 1.3 JUDGING CONSUMERS BY THEIR MEDIA CONSUMPTION

A new research survey suggests that what people read, particularly which magazines they choose, can accurately predict their behavior as shoppers and consumers. The survey divides readers into five categories, or media communes.

	"Home Engineers"	"Real Guys"	"Ethnic Pewneps*"	"Information Grazers"	"Armchair Adventurers"
Typical magazines read	Family Circle Good House-keeping Woman's Day	Guns & Ammo Popular Mechanics Mechanix Illustrated	Ebony Essence Jet	People Time Bon Appétit	Reader's Digest Modern Maturity Travel & Leisure
Primary Sex	Female	Male	Both	Male	Both
Income†	$33,000	$39,000	$26,000	$44,000	$35,000
Politics	Mixed	Mixed	Democrats	Democrats	Republicans
Favorite television programs	*Oprah* *60 Minutes* *Donahue*	*Cheers* *America's Most Wanted* *N.F.L. Live*	*Arsenio Hall* *Oprah* *Fresh Prince of Bel Air*	*L.A. Law* *Roseanne* *A Current Affair*	*Matlock* *60 Minutes* *Wheel of Fortune*
Most frequently used products	Eye shadow Face powder Foundation, makeup	Disposable diapers Bottled water Contact lens products	Nail polish Contact lens products Instant coffee	Disposable diapers Powdered drink mixes Frozen desserts	Antacids Decaffeinated coffee Instant coffee

*Shorthand for "people who need people."   †Average annual household income
Source: Yankelovich Partners Inc.

NEED FOR MEDIA IMAGINATION

The data bank available to marketers and advertisers suggests that it is possible to identify all—or effectively all—of the forces that have an impact on our personal decisions in a contemporary social environment. What we require imagination for is a felt understanding of the organic dynamism of the process and the omnipresent role of media as the field of its being.

No sophisticated contemporary marketer fails to analyze the various aspects of consumer and buyer behavior before developing or positioning a product to satisfy a particular group's needs and expectations. No sophisticated advertiser fails to study and determine what values and perceptions excite these particular consumers before crafting a commercial message and its appeals. Equally, no sophisticated media planner is unaware of the media that these same buyers consume. As we will see, "It is in the book," and "You can look it up."

The problem is that every message is a new message, and success or failure in advertising is dependent on the subtle calibration of the effects of new messages in new marketing environments. Today's consumers do not have either commanding internal disciplines, or sharply detailed images of themselves and society. Insecure and full of doubts, they rely on their contemporaries and the mass media for advice, but their contemporaries are also looking to the mass media. Everyone is looking to everyone else, who is looking to the mass media, which are looking at everyone. In this context, mass media become the vehicles of social and cultural influence. The media become the organ of expectation, guidance, and approval.

It is not all one way, or course. Our peers decide which information, ideas, or styles that appear in the media they share, will be accepted. The media do not repeat those that are not accepted, while the accepted information, ideas, and styles are recycled to contiguous groups until they reach their limit. The mass media are not dictatorial, but in a fundamentally opinionated world, the media are the engine and context of fleeting behavioral norms.

Advertising, by its nature, is an attempt to persuade and promote change. Media planning is an act of creating an environment for change. Through an understanding of how and why individuals and groups approach media vehicles and how they react to the ever-changing messages of these media vehicles, a media planner can synchronize the delivery of specific advertising messages to maximize their effectiveness.

How can this be accomplished? The media planner must:

1. Imagine the profiles and the communications situation of the prospects.
2. Imagine what communications dynamic helped the prospects become who they are.
3. Imagine what communications dynamic, evolving out of the prospects' current communications situation, will facilitate the specific new consumer judgments required by the marketing plan.

The distinction we are making is between writing or reading a novel and writing or reading a sociology text. The realization that we are all fundamentally affected by our family life, and the ability to group families by size, income, education, or ethnicity, combined with the recognition that the individuals in these different groups act in similar ways and use similar media, does not provide the same kind of commanding insight as does a good novel about one of these families. The difference is not only in becoming "up close and personal," and feeling the inner dynamics through the art of fiction. The difference is also in becoming capable of predicting how this family and its individual members will react to new situations and events. As novelists tell us, they reach a point when the characters "talk back" to them.

It is not fundamentally difficult to mesh the social science data utilized by marketers with available media research data. It is easy because many of the dynamics that create product markets have already acted to create media markets. This is reflected in the ancient maxim that "Media follow people and advertisers follow media" (Figure 1.1).

In today's sophisticated world, no media plan produced with reasonable attention to a brand's marketing imperatives, and to the media source material, can be radically

FIGURE 1.1

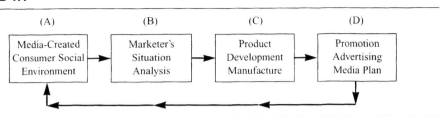

(A) Consumers negotiate their sociocultural values in and through the media. (B) Marketers analyze the consumer sociocultural environment to identify wants and needs. (C) Marketers develop products and services to satisfy the wants and needs they have identified. (D) The advertiser promotes these products or services through the very media that facilitated the emergence of the consumers' wants and needs.

wrong, whether its worth is measured by efficiency or by effectiveness. Media planning, however, is future oriented and projects a dynamic exchange. The string of data upon which the planner depends is also a series of estimates on top of estimates. For both reasons, media planning that entirely relies on static descriptions of past events must be wrong to some degree. Furthermore, it is impossible to model perfectly the impact of advertising impressions made in one environment, at one price, versus impressions made in another environment at another price.

A sophisticated media planner would be a fool to overlook historical research and effects modeling based on testing. An advertiser, however, cannot have one hundred percent confidence in a plan exclusively based on these resources, and a media planner should not become a slave to them. We rely on the planner's creative imagination to compensate for the limitations of historical data.

COGNITIVE IMAGINATION

Media planning judgments are generally divided between quantitative and qualitative considerations. Quantitative criteria are perceived as objective, and include such measures as the delivery of variously described targets, cost, and geographic distribution. Qualitative criteria are perceived as subjective, and include estimates of audience involvement, editorial environment, and perceived authority. When we speak of the imagination, however, either we are limiting it exclusively to quantitative or qualitative considerations, or we are applying it to both.

Quantitative criteria are those that result from numerical data and statistical description. Miles, for example, can quantify distance. This numerical expression can be useful in projecting time of travel, or the amount of fuel required. Mileage, however, does not tell us anything about the landscape through which we might be traveling, so we might add a phrase such as "through the mountains." The mountains can also be measured and described in various objective ways. No matter how far we proceed along this path of objectification, however, we are always describing, or linking a chain of measured observations, without experience.

Theodore Levitt, one of the seminar thinkers of modern marketing, explained the problem this way:

> The difference between data and information is that while data are crudely aggregated collections of raw facts, information represents the selective organization and *imaginative interpretation of those facts*. This requires knowing, in some sort of direct and systematic way, the world with which one presumes to deal. It requires *getting inside the lives and work of the people* one is trying to understand. Crudely aggregated collections of data merely represent what's been serially recorded about discrete events or categories. Information represents the imposition of order, categories, and ideas on the collected data. To do this merely by means of increasingly elaborate methods of statistical and mathematical refinement and calculation, whatever their merits, loses the *throbbing pulse of the reality the data sought to capture*. [Emphasis added.][17]

The objective world of quantitative logic is a world of signs and symbols that are useful, but empty. They neither capture, describe, nor communicate "what it is like when." That is the job of the storyteller, the job of the imagination. We have to learn to see through the numbers to the experiences the numbers summarize, much as Helen Keller had to learn to connect words with experience.

Helen Keller's teacher, Anne Sullivan, had always tapped out "w-a-t-e-r" onto the blind and deaf Helen's hand, but it was only when her teacher placed Helen's hand into water gushing from a well pump, and simultaneously tapped out the word, that Helen could see through the letters to the experience. She wrote:

> I stood still, my whole attention fixed upon the motions of her fingers. Suddenly I felt a misty consciousness as of something forgotten—a thrill of returning thought; and somehow the mystery of language was revealed to me. I knew then that "w-a-t-e-r" meant that wonderful cool something that was flowing over my hand. That living word awakened my soul, gave it light, hope, joy, set it free![18]

When we look at numbers—the signs and symbols of quantification—we should yearn for such an awakening.

We can rightly ask if Helen Keller's experience of water was any less objective than the formula H_2O. Was her imaginative memory of the experience so subjective as to be untrustworthy as a description of universal experience? Is Shakespeare's *Romeo and Juliet* an objective response to the question: "What is it like to be a teenager in love?" Or is *Romeo and Juliet* to be dismissed as appallingly imaginative, subjective, and qualitative when confronted with a statistically sound, quantitative survey of teenagers' attitudes toward romance?

What prevents most of us from seeing particularized, multimotivated consumer vitality through the numbers of media and marketing research is too many years of disparagement of the imagination, and too few years of practice in how to use it. We have been led to believe that human beings are of two minds: the intellect and the imagination. The intellect, we are told, provides us with the trustworthy disciplines of abstract and logical thought. Imagination is the untrustworthy world of fantasy and art.

"The human organism, that body which has the gift of thought," Elizabeth Sewell has written of the presumed dichotomy between intellect and imagination, "does not have a choice of two kinds of thinking. It has only one, in which the organism as a whole is engaged all along the line. There has been no progression in history from one type of thought to another. We are merely learning to use what we have been given, which is all of a piece."[19] It is as if numbers have the capacity to tell us where to look without telling us what is going on before our eyes. Not knowing where to look, on the other hand, results in a wandering imagination. The mind uses both skills—abstract analysis and insightful imagination—in the process of cognition. In effect, our brains are mindless until they can display images internally and manipulate those images in the process called thought.[20]

Levitt argues that "to decide correctly what's to be done and how to do it requires having good data about customers, competitors, and markets. Even more, it requires the imaginative conversion of these data into meaningful and usable information. The best way is to know your prospects in a way that is more fundamental and compelling than what's usually yielded by the purely metrical methods so common in market research today."[21]

The first effort of the cognitive imagination is not to make things up, but rather to assert that our thought can develop something that resembles an objective correlative of the world outside ourselves and through which we can experience communal life. This goal of objective correlation, which drives both the arts and sciences, is the opposite of rampant subjectivity, carelessness, opinion, fancy, and convenience.

The second effort of the cognitive imagination is what Einstein called "the combinatory play of images." It is a process of identifying, isolating, sifting, weighing, and combining images; of consciously constructing clusters of images; rejecting and recombining until we become aware of experience, meaning, and the approximation of objective reality. This moment of recognition—the moment when the image, or combination of images, provides an experience that is itself the very recognition of experience—is the substance of verification. Such images are replicable and retrievable, and hold up under the tests of time and the experiences of others.

Most of us might hear a poet talking of the imaginative process when an author writes: "It begins as a story about a Possible World—a story which we invent and criticize and modify as we go along, so that it ends up being, as nearly as we can make it, a story about real life." The author, however, is the Noble Prize–winning biologist, Sir Peter Medawar, writing about the process of scientific thought and discovery.[22] He is describing the same process that Einstein described as the "combinatory play of images," and suggesting the same kind of verification that Aristotle called "recognition." We often forget that $E = MC^2$ is, after all, an invitation to think and experience, and that the formula was verified in recognition long before it could be observed in engineered experiments.

The work of the cognitive imagination is a process of candor and practice. It applies to the process of seeing through the numbers, and it applies to the process of recognizing media vehicles as persons in dialogue. It can be, and should be, operative throughout the whole media planning enterprise because it is our only entree to consumers as people and to media vehicles as communicators communicating.

Even if we accept this far too brief exposition of how all minds work at their creative best, we will need help in knowing how and when to apply it. Throughout this text, we will continually identify moments of imaginative effort and reflection as we pursue the process of "thinking through" media planning. Sewell describes this process as "a way of using mind and body to build up dynamic structures (never fixed or abstract patterns) by which the human organism sets itself in relation to the universe and allows each side to interpret the other."[23]

The cognitive imagination works the same way in every trade or discipline, and the method can be learned on the stage, or in the laboratory, or on a walk, or in a studio. We will only recognize the value of such opportunities, however, in their exercise; and their exercise is up to us.

COMMUNICATIONS JUDO

Success in advertising depends on the use of the dynamic of society communicating in and through the media. Imagination is necessary for an understanding of the details and rhythms of this dynamic. "No amount of modern marketing science or heavy analysis will work," Levitt has observed, "without the protean powers of the marketing imagination and high spirits."[24]

Media planning—when functioning as an exercise of the marketing or cognitive imagination—could be described as "communications judo." Judo is an art that uses an opponent's momentum, his weight and strength, against him. Media planning—scientifically and artfully—uses the means and momentum of society communicating for the exploitive purpose of marketing products, services, and ideas. It is an imaginative task.

SUMMARY

*Media planners are the investment counselors and faithful stewards of the expenditures that make an advertiser an advertiser.

*Advertising functions through the mass media.

*Media serve the function of society communicating.

*Media produce cultures and lifestyles, which are markets.

*Consumers identify themselves by the media they use.

*Media planning utilizes the dynamic of cultural production though communications to synchronize the advertiser's message with defining communications consumptions.

*The only true access to the dynamic of society communicating is through the cognitive imagination.

QUESTIONS

1. Why can it be said that until advertising appears in the media it is not advertising?
2. Explain what is meant by the description of media planners as advertising investment counselors.
3. Discuss how the creation of audiences is, in fact, the creation of markets.
4. In view of all the available data, why does media planning fall short of "scientific" certitude?
5. What are three reasons for an advertiser's use of media?
6. Explain the role of media as a necessary condition for creating awareness and motivation.
7. What is the relationship between culture, marketing, and communications media?
8. Why does media planning require imagination and judgment?

EXERCISE

Familiarize yourself with the following print vehicles and then briefly describe an individual who is a regular reader of each indicated combination.

A.	Barron's	G.	Money
B.	Forbes	H.	Time
C.	Fortune	I.	Newsweek
D.	Business Week	J.	U.S. News
E.	Wall Street Journal	K.	Sports Illustrated
F.	Inc.	L.	New York Times

Describe a regular reader of each of the following combinations:

1. A–D–E–J   2.   C–E–F–K
3. B–E–G–H   4.   L–K–F–I

Do you agree with the statement that "You are what you eat in media terms"?

ASSIGNMENT

List on a piece of paper the three magazines your mother (or a significant other) buys and/or reads regularly. List also his/her three favorite television programs. This is a blind test. Do not put your name, or any other name, on the paper.

Randomly trade these lists with other students. The receiving student should then describe the person indicated on the list with the media they use. Let the class decide whether the description fits the media evidence. Then, you decide whether they have described your nominee accurately and, if not, why.

NOTES TO CHAPTER 1

1. William Wells, John Burnett, and Sandra Moriarty, *Advertising: Principles and Practice* (Englewood Cliffs, N.J.: Prentice Hall, 1989), pp. 23–24.

2. Courtland L. Bovée and William F. Arens, *Contemporary Advertising* (Homewood, Ill.: Richard D. Irwin, 1992), p. 18.

3. Frank Rowsome, Jr., *They Laughed When I Sat Down* (New York: McGraw Hill, 1959), p. 43.

4. "How Advertising and Advertising Agencies Started and Grew in the U.S: A Brief History," *Advertising Age*, December 7, 1964, p. 2.

5. Wells, Burnett, and Moriarty, p. 25.

6. "Rethinking Media, Burnett Style," *Advertising Age*, July 25, 1994, p. 54.

7. David A. Aaker and John G. Myers, *Advertising Management* (Englewood Cliffs, N.J.: Prentice Hall, 1987), p. 1.

8. Todd Hunt and Brent D. Ruben, *Mass Communications: Producers and Consumers* (New York: HarperCollins, 1993), p. 10.

9. James F. Engel, Roger D. Blackwell, and Paul W. Miniard, *Consumer Behavior* (Hinsdale, Ill.: Dryden, 1990), pp. 59–63.

10. Karl Mannheim, *Ideology and Utopia* (New York: Harcourt, Brace, 1936), p. 2. Grant McCracken, "Advertising: Meaning or Information?" in Melanie Wallendorf and Paul Anderson, eds., *Advances in Consumer Research*, vol. 14 (Provo, Utah: Association for Consumer Research, 1987), pp. 121–124.

11. William B. Gudykunst, Stella Ting-Toomey, and Elizabeth Chua, *Culture and Interpersonal Communication* (Newbury Park, Calif.: SAGE Publications, 1988), p. 1.

12. Edward T. Hall, *The Silent Language* (Garden City, N.Y.: Anchor Books, 1959). Melvin L. De Fleur, *Theories of Mass Communication* (David McKay, 1966), p. 90.

13. John Dewey, *Democracy and Education* (New York: Macmillan, 1916), p. 5.

14. Engel, Blackwell, and Miniard, pp. 342–353.

15. Theodore Levitt, *The Marketing Imagination* (New York: Free Press, 1986), p. 138.

16. Helen Keller, *The Story of My Life* (New York: Doubleday, Page and Company, 1908), p. 24.

17. Elizabeth Sewell, *The Orphic Voice: Poetry and Natural History* (New Haven, Conn.: Yale University Press, 1960), p. 19.

18. Antonio Damasio, *Descartes' Error* (New York: Grossett/Putnam, 1994).

19. Levitt, pp. 137–138.

20. Peter Medawar, *Pluto's Republic*.

21. Sewell, p. 19. See also: Konstantin Stanislavski, *Creating a Role* (New York: Theatre Arts Books, 1961), p. 8.

22. Levitt, p. xxv.

2

Marketing and Media Planning

Media planning is an extension of marketing. The media planner must understand the **"5Ps"**: **product**, **price**, **place**, **promotion**, and **playback**, which determine the product's market existence. Media planning is an execution and requires an understanding of the factors that make up the marketing strategy. An efficient media plan follows the logic of the product's marketing plan. The media planner must be able to imagine the added values and intended exchange of the marketing system in order to produce a creative and effective media plan.

MARKETING

Marketing is both a concept and a management system. The concept is a philosophical understanding of how a business enterprise and an economy should function. As a management system, marketing represents both a conjunction of tools and a series of decisions. Generally, the tools are information, and the decisions are informed judgments.

    Marketing can be defined as "the process of planning and executing the conception, pricing, promotion and distribution of ideas, goods, and services to create exchanges that satisfy individual and organization objectives."[1] The operative phrase in this definition is "to create exchanges."

    A contemporary American might conclude that this definition of marketing differs very little from the capitalistic idea of supply and demand, from the American concept of free markets, and from the simple necessity of surviving in both circumstances.

This concept of American business has, in fact, so permeated professional life as the received wisdom that it is difficult to imagine a time when this wasn't true, or what the alternatives might be.

From the Industrial Revolution to World War II, however, American business was production and sales oriented. The idea was that consumers would buy any fairly priced, well-made product. The object of business was to engineer and manufacture more products more efficiently. During this period, manufacturing dictated product designs, and production costs dictated price.

The salesman's job in this environment was simply to sell the products as they were made. When production capacity exceeded demand, or when recession or depression reduced demand, the sales department increased in importance. A premium would be put on the hard sell. The salesman, however, was still charged with selling whatever was made. Production and engineering dominated business, and companies defined themselves in terms of their products.

The post war economy changed all this. American industry began an about-face; it focused primarily on discovering customer needs and producing products to fit those needs. This reversed the process of manufacturing products and then finding, or creating, customers to buy them. From this experience, marketing began to emerge as a concept, in other words, as an understanding and determinant of business.

It was in this context that Theodore Levitt was able to distinguish between a company being in the railroad business from its being in the transportation business.[2] The former is involved with a product, but the latter is concerned with a consumer need that the company can dedicate itself to serving with multiple and changing products. The new **marketing concept** proposed that a business existed first to fulfill a consumer's wants and needs, and second to make a profit from the products it manufactured.

This marketing concept of business represented a sea change for most companies and industries. Business firms began to perceive themselves as marketers, and used marketing as their method of finding, satisfying, and retaining customers. They focused on the exchange between buyer and seller in the marketplace, and concluded that if you wanted to guarantee a profitable exchange, you first had to discover what the consumer needed or wanted.

By the 1970s, Peter Drucker gave voice to a nearly universal belief when he wrote that "a business is not defined by the company's name, statues, or articles of incorporation"—nor, we might add, by its product line. "It is defined," Drucker continued, "by the want the customer satisfies when he buys a product or service. To satisfy the customer is the mission and purpose of every business."[3]

In many ways people working in an advertising agency or department may feel like premarketing salespeople, rather than marketers. After all, the product and all its related attributes already have been defined. In effect, they are given the product and are told to sell it. Advertising may be perceived as a function of marketing, but as a practical matter most of the defining decisions have been made before the advertising team gets up to bat. For the media planner, this most often includes the message and the advertisement itself. If you are just an intermediary, or the equivalent of a 1920s salesman, what relevance does marketing have to your function? Why care about marketing?

The simple answers are: first, in order to know what is expected of you, and, second, in order to do your job well.

To whatever extent a company is governed by the marketing concept, it correspondingly uses a **marketing management system**, which is an integrated program for directing and controlling the marketing process. To perform these functions, managers must make decisions based on consciously developed information.

Every marketing-oriented company has its own set of criteria for information gathering and decision making. Advertising decisions—especially the major financial investment decisions involved in media planning—are part of this systematic process. A media planner, therefore, must know and understand the system in order to be effective.

Any management system is made up of objectives, plans, and the evaluation of their eventual success or failure. Media planning is not only organized and evaluated in the same terms by definition, but it is also concerned with the expectations of the client company. The media planner must understand these established rules or customs, as well as the larger context of company objectives and plans, in order to develop effective outcomes. Marketing know-how is necessary for an understanding of the elements of a marketing management system, as well as for doing the media planning within it. Thus, an understanding of marketing is necessary for both the internal operational efficiency and the external effectiveness of media planning.

MARKETING AND MEDIA PLANNING

The most popular understanding of the basic elements of marketing was developed by Jerome McCarthy, and is known as the "4Ps."[4] They are product, place, price, and promotion. Many people have long known that the final step, which closes the loop from defining customer needs and wants through product development and sales, is the information received back from the marketplace. Consumer feedback restarts the process. To accommodate this element in the system we can propose the "5Ps of Marketing" (Exhibit 2.1).

EXHIBIT 2.1 THE 5Ps OF MARKETING

Product—includes product design, development, branding, and packaging.
Place—includes all the channels of distribution utilized between the manufacturer and the buyer.
Price—includes both the price at which the product or service is offered, and the levels of profitability expected.
Promotion—includes personal selling, promotions, public relations, and advertising.
Playback—includes sales, competitive success, consumer attitudes, and usage.

At its roots, marketing is a creative, and not simply an operational, act. Its purpose is to create exchanges, and the purpose of creating exchanges is to grow and maintain demand for a company's productive resources.

All of the 5Ps are based on the goal of creating such exchanges. The exchange is a satisfaction of a want. We concluded in chapter 1 that the development of our wants is rooted in communications. Media are the next to last point of the market exchange, as well as the foundation of the consumer's perception of the product. To manage this process productively and effectively, the media planner must understand the premises and logic that led to this moment of potential consumer decision (Figure 2.1).

VALUE ADDED

Each of the basic elements of marketing represents a judgment about the consumer's perception of the value added at each step. Theodore Levitt explains that "if marketing is seminally about anything, it is about achieving customer-getting distinction."

> To attract a customer, you are asking him to do something different from what he would have done in the absence of the programs you direct at him. He has to change his mind and his actions. The customer must shift his behavior in the direction advocated by the seller. Hence the seller must distinguish himself and his offering from those of others so that people will want, or at least prefer, to do business with him. The search for meaningful distinction is a central part of the marketing effort.[5]

The **product** is fundamentally the result of a production process that transforms a raw material into a more desirable utility, for example, not only metals into tools, but also chemicals into detergents. **Value added** is the term used to describe the qualities that make the product desirable. Marketing research defines the features and benefits that must be designed into the product. Other added values include the packaging, which adds convenience, safety, attractiveness, and a design message. **Branding**, the identification of a particular company's product, adds personality to the product and is the foundation of perceived quality and consumer loyalty.

Place represents the added value of providing customers with the product where and when they want it. This implies both geographical and shopping convenience.

Price is keyed to the consumer's perception of cost and value, as well as to the producer's profit objectives. An excellent recent example of contrasting pricing strategies was General Mills's decision in May 1994 to reduce prices on Cheerios, Wheaties, and other key brands by an average of 11 percent. At the same time, rival Kellogg was raising its general prices by an average of 2.6 percent, and that of Corn Flakes by 7 percent, counting on the consumers' perception of value to support the increases.

Promotion is first of all news about the product, its utility, cost, and availability. Promotion, however, also is often the basis for an addition of emotional and psychological values that accompany the exchange, and the reinforcement of these satisfactions after the exchange. **Playback** is an added value, for it is information that will benefit the consumer in future exchanges if the system is followed.

If a media planner carefully follows the linear logic of the marketing decisions embodied in each of the 5Ps, the resulting media plan should have an almost sleek

FIGURE 2.1 THE MARKETING SYSTEM

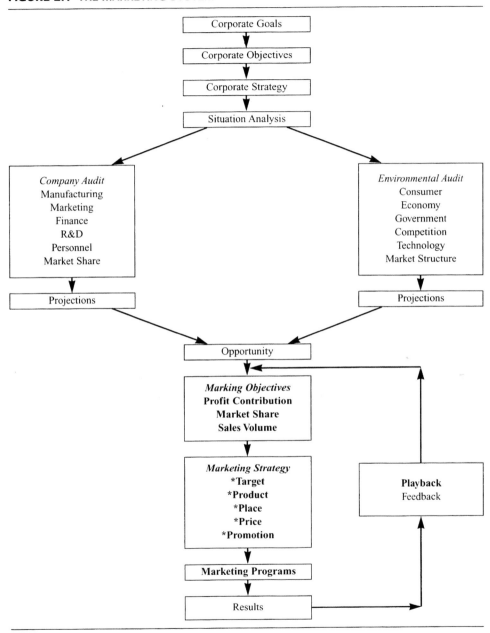

operational efficiency. Creative effectiveness, however, results only from the planner's ability to imagine the exchange before it happens, as well as the values added at each step of the marketing process to stimulate and close that exchange. Before a planner can creatively select the media and combination of vehicles most synergistic as the conditions of the exchange, the planner must have in mind an image of the intended exchange, of the consumer and business wants that the exchange will satisfy, and the communications source of those wants.

The first **payout** of the media planner's marketing sophistication is in the planner's ability to follow the linear logic of the marketing plan through to an efficient media solution (Figure 2.2). The second payout is in the planner's ability to imagine an exchange based on the felt perception of the added values intended to stimulate the exchange. The result of this imaginative effort is the addition of electric effectiveness to apparently efficient plans. Media planning, viewed this way, is marketing; it adds to the system. Media planning is an integral part of the marketing system that both reflects and extends other decisions made within the system. Media planning also adds to the system through its own decisions and insights.

In chapter 5, we will analyze each specific marketing issue relevant to the media planning process. While uncovering the basic concepts of marketing communications in this chapter, however, we are also identifying prisms of the marketing imagination. The first is the imagination of the exchange. A second emerges from an analysis of the role of advertising in the marketing system.

MEASURING SUCCESS

Advertising is a controlled communication; it is also very expensive. When anything is both controlled and expensive, you naturally want to know, as precisely as you can, what you get for each dollar you spend. Consequently, it is not unnatural for a marketer to want to know what every dollar spent on advertising returns in sales dollars. It is also natural, therefore, for a marketer to think of advertising in terms of sales goals and to set specific sales objectives as the objectives of advertising.

Unfortunately, no one has been able to determine regularly the specific sales impact of advertising. It may be true that the coupling of model building and experiments can go a long way toward solving the perennial problem of advertising accountability, but most companies simply lack the expertise and financial resources necessary to do it. As a practical matter, the measurement and accountability of advertising, in terms of sales effects, is impossible. What is possible is the measurement and accountability of advertising in its own terms.

It is certainly fair to say that the role of advertising is to generate sales and repeat purchases. That is also the role played by all the other elements within the marketing system. More to the point is the question of what advertising must accomplish so that the system will generate sales and repeat purchases. As a communication, advertising has the role of making customers aware of the product and to add to its perceived value.[6]

DAGMAR

To a great extent the terms of this debate were established by Russell Colley in his now classic work *Defining Advertising Goals for Measured Advertising Results* published

FIGURE 2.2 MEDIA PLANNING EXTENDS AND EXECUTES MARKETING

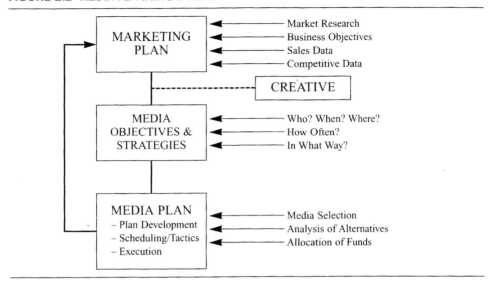

by the Association of National Advertisers.[7] The two key points of Colley's thesis, which has come to be known as the DAGMAR approach, are:

1. An advertising goal should be a specific communication task rather than a marketing task.

2. The advertising goal should be measurable in terms of a defined audience, a starting point, and a fixed period of time.

In general, Colley argued, advertising should be evaluated only by what advertising, by itself, can reasonably hope to accomplish.

Since advertising is a communication, it can reasonably hope only to accomplish communication tasks, which generally can be described as producing awareness and attitude change. The assumption is that certain levels of awareness and certain attitudes are the foundation of a sale, or lead to a sale. The issue is whether awareness and attitudes, which advertising can influence, are enough to cause the closing of a sale.

The marketing system, when it is working well, has determined what reasonably specific awareness levels are necessary, or what kinds of attitudes and perceptions must be changed—from what and to what—among specific customer groupings. Often the media planner is called upon to contribute to these judgments. In any case, this is the specific information a media planner must formulate, or must be provided with, in order to imagine the communications dynamic required by the marketplace. When planning communications, the planner needs a specific communications goal.

PERSUASION MODELS

Colley's DAGMAR system belongs to the **communicative effects** school of advertising. These scholars base their theories on a model of persuasive communications, variously called Response Models, Hierarchy of Effects Models, or Readiness to Buy Models. They are valuable not only for identifying the communications problem that advertising must solve, but also in providing a structure through which a planner can imagine the competitive communications dynamic.

Exhibit 2.2 is a graphic presentation of these models. Each model identifies three distinct and progressive levels. For the media planner, each of these levels suggests a different level of media activity and a different combination of media types and vehicles.

The strategic issues and tactical responses suggested by these models will be the subject of future chapters. The thing to recognize, in the present context, is that the various communications models can help the planner frame an imaginative picture of the communications tasks facing a marketer. Without such an imaginative picture, the media planner cannot be an active participant in the process.

To complete the imaginative picture, the planner must be aware of the specific history and positioning of competitive brands. Exhibit 2.3 presents a simple four-case variation that can be elaborated by adding brands and their various situations. This example might represent a comparatively new product category and the situation of the first, second, and third brands entering the marketplace. To be concrete, it might represent the situation at one time after ibuprofen was approved for over-the-counter sale, followed by the introduction of Advil, Nuprin, and Medeprin, in that order. Specific percentage levels for awareness, trial, and loyalty can be added to complete the grid.

These models suggest that marketing, after all, is a form of communication based first, on the diffusion and adoption of the idea inherent in a product category, and second, on the diffusion and adoption of the ideas inherent in competitive brands within the category. The idea inherent in the category or brand is what Drucker described as "the want the consumer satisfies when he buys a product or service." Adoption represents the exchange that brings the want and its satisfaction together and makes them concrete. This concrete and satisfying exchange is the goal of marketing. Different marketing communications strategies are required, depending on both the category's and the brand's perceived position within this **diffusion and adoption continuum**, that is, how well the category and the specific brands are known, and the degree of consumer acceptance and loyalty they are each experiencing.

PRODUCT LIFE CYCLE

A similar understanding is at the foundation of the concept of a **product life cycle**. As illustrated in Figure 2.3, experience teaches that most products eventually pass through four stages of life. Some product lines and brands, such as Jell-O or Kleenex, seem to be immortal—to sell forever—and others, such as Campbell Soups, are kept vigor-

EXHIBIT 2.2 RESPONSE MODELS

Stage	AIDA**	DAGMAR**	Effects**	Adoption**	Processing**	Consumer
COGNITIVE	Attention	Awareness Comprehension	Awareness Knowledge	Awareness	Presentation Attention Comprehension	What do consumers know about brand or category?
AFFECTIVE	Interest Desire	Conviction	Liking Preference Conviction	Interest Evaluation	Yielding (attitude change) Retention (of new attitude)	Are consumers neutral, negative, or positive?
BEHAVIORAL	Action	Action	Purchase	Trial Adoption	Behavior	Do they buy the brand, reject the category, buy others, or repurchase?

**E.K. Strong, *The Psychology of Selling* (New York: McGraw-Hill, 1925). **Russell H. Colley, *Defining Advertising Goals for Measured Advertising Results* (New York: Association of National Advertisers, 1961). **Robert J. Lavidge and Gary A. Steiner, "A Model for Predictive Measurements of Advertising Effectiveness," *Journal of Marketing,* October 1961, pp. 59–62. **Everett M. Rogers, *Diffusion of Innovations* (New York: Free Press, 1962). **William J. McGuire, "An Information Processing Model of Advertising Effectiveness," in Aaker and Myers, *Advertising Management* (Englewood Cliffs, N.J.: Prentice Hall, 1975), p. 261.

EXHIBIT 2.3 RESPONSE VARIATIONS

Stage	Product Category	Our Brand X	Their Brand Y	Their Brand Z
Unaware	No	No	No	Yes
Aware	Yes	Yes	Yes	No
Interested & Yielding	Yes	Yes	Yes	No
Preference & Conviction	Yes	Yes	No	No
Purchase Trial	Yes	Yes	No	No
Brand Loyalty	No	No	No	No

ously alive with line extensions, or new variations. In general, however, most products are in one stage or another of their life cycle. The optimum situation for a marketer is the maturity phase, when, with widespread product acceptance and large volume, the brand becomes a cash generator instead of a cash drain.[8]

Combined with diffusion and adoption theories, the product life cycle model not only suggests different roles and objectives for advertising, but also different communications strategies for media planning. Frequently, the first brand in a category, for example, must absorb the task of developing primary demand by informing

FIGURE 2.3 PRODUCT LIFE CYCLE

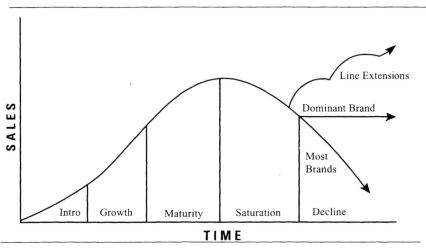

and educating customers about the product category. "Unaware is unacceptable," that is, it is necessary to make consumers aware of the brand's existence, its applications and benefits. The media planner must be most conscious, in this situation, of the role of opinion leaders and interpersonal diffusion networks when developing plans to generate the right kind of awareness among the right kind of people.

One of the disadvantages of success in the diffusion and adoption of ideas, of course, is that everyone gets the idea. Among the first to do this are competitive marketers, who quickly develop products to satisfy this newly identified consumer want. In this situation, the brand's advertising must constantly repeat its assertions while developing symbolic associations that distinguish it from competitive alternatives in the eyes of consumers. Unfortunately, this situation is full of the noise of competitive claims and activities. The planning consequence in this situation is that while the media planner is generating efficient repetition with one hand, the planner must be refining a convincing match, with the other hand, between media exposure environments and each subgroup's opinion leaders who, after all, are the agents of change. They are the core of brand loyalty, repetitive sales, and competitive market share.

Consumers learn from more than one source and in more than one context. The media planner must be able to imagine this process and its dynamics in order to select the right target sources of influence and the most effective environments for a brand in an ever-changing competitive situation. The various diffusion, adoption, and decision models, applied to a product life cycle model, enable the planner to imagine what communications task must be accomplished with whom. Basically, the models help us visualize what communications have, are, will, and must occur. Minimally, these models should reinforce the planner's understanding that he or she is trying to stimulate a cultural perception that occurs only in and through communications media. The models are prisms for the imagination.

MEDIA AND VEHICLE EFFECTS

One of the key questions at the juncture of communications and marketing is whether a prospect exposure in one medium or vehicle has more impact than another exposure. It should be obvious, at one level, that different media and different media vehicles perform different functions in society. Consequently, they must have differing impacts. Each medium and vehicle differs in its authority among different consumer groups. Each generates a different kind and level of interest, and each is perceived as more or less important.

In our later discussion of media considerations (chapters 9, 10 and 12), we will examine media effects in greater detail and suggest how they may be measured, estimated, and imagined. It is only necessary for the present discussion to recognize that such differences probably exist. If they do, they raise the amount of specific information a media planner needs in order to imagine a prospect's communications situation, the attitudes and beliefs they have, and what communication dynamics got them that way. In the long run, only this imagined picture will enable the planner to recommend securely the communications environments in which advertising can affect consumer decisions.

MEDIA TOOLS

Media planning is a craft with a vocabulary that translates its insights into tools. The key terms for translating the response models into actionable plans are **reach, average frequency, motivational frequency level**, and **effective reach**. When these tools are properly utilized, they emerge out of media strategies that reflect the marketing and response models, interpreted and applied in specific brand circumstances.

We will discuss these terms and elaborate on their applications more fully in chapter 9. In concluding the present discussion of marketing communications, however, it is useful to have a modest grasp of these terms of the craft.

Reach is an estimate of the number of different people who are exposed to one or more vehicles in a media schedule. It is a measurement of unduplicated audience and is usually expressed as a percent of the target population base.

Average Frequency is the number of times the average member of the audience is reached by the media schedule.

Motivational Frequency Level is the minimum number of exposures—normally within a four-week period—considered necessary to motivate the average prospect in the target audience in order to accomplish a specific advertising objective. Some call this "effective frequency."

Effective Reach is the number, or percentage, of the target prospects reached by the media schedule at an established motivational frequency level. Effective reach is based on the assumption that all frequency levels are not of equal importance.

The purpose of media planning is to maximize effective reach in the right environments at a given budget. Insuring that the marketer's message reaches a sufficient number of the most promising prospects on the right number of occasions over an appropriate period of time is the craft of media planning. It is an intellectual task. Understanding the communication that occurs when prospects become audiences, and selecting the most meaningful media and most significant vehicles for transferring cultural values to the marketer's product, is the art of media planning. It is an imaginative task.

The purpose of this chapter has been to analyze and understand why media planning is marketing, and what role it plays in the marketing system. It has also been our purpose to grow in our appreciation of media planning as an imaginative act. Media planning deals with learning and behavior. The models of persuasion and marketing are most useful when they are used as prisms through which the planner can imagine the dynamics of society communicating.

SUMMARY

*Media planners must understand marketing in order to know what is expected of them and in order to do their job well.

*The purpose of marketing is to create exchanges that satisfy consumer wants.

*A media planner must have an image of the intended exchange, of the wants the exchange satisfies, and the communications source of those wants.

*Advertising should be evaluated by the awareness levels and attitude changes that advertising, as a communication, can reasonably hope to accomplish.

*The role of media planning is to determine the environmental foundation for advertising messages and the penultimate condition of consumer decisions and market exchanges.

*Various response models provide a prism through which to view competitive communications circumstances and to develop marketing communications strategies.

*The purpose of media planning tools is to translate marketing and communication insights into effective strategies and executions.

QUESTIONS

1. What distinguishes the shift from a production economy to a market economy?
2. Why must a media planner understand a client's marketing system?
3. Explain how both marketing and media planning involve the planner's imagining an exchange before it happens.
4. In what way does media planning add to the marketing system?
5. Should advertising be held accountable in terms of sales goals, or in terms of communications objectives? Explain.
6. How should a media planner use the hierarchy of effects, or response models, of advertising?
7. What is the impact of "product life cycle" on media planning?
8. What is meant by "media and vehicle effects"?
9. What are the executional terms that translate response models into practical plans?

EXERCISE

Recall the brand name and influential circumstances of the last pair of sneakers or athletic shoes you purchased. On a piece of paper, write down one or two sentences explaining why you purchased that particular brand.

On a separate piece of paper, make notes about how and where you learned about the brand you chose and about its benefits. If possible, identify the specific advertising and its location; any discussions you had about the product and its category; whether anyone was particularly influential in your choice.

1. Share and discuss these reflections and recollections with others in the class.
2. After the class selects one example as the best reflection of their experiences, create a model of the diffusion, adoption, decision process involved in effecting the marketing exchange.

ASSIGNMENT

Sketch out how you would plan a strategy for communicating with yourself—not the advertising itself or its message content—on behalf of a brand competitive to the one you most recently purchased. This strategy might facilitate your decision to switch to this competitive brand the next time you make a purchase.

NOTES TO CHAPTER 2

1. "AMA Board Approves New Marketing Definition," *The Marketing News*, March 1, 1985, p. 1.
2. Theodore Levitt, "Marketing Myopia," *Harvard Business Review* 38, July–August 1960, pp. 45–56.
3. Peter Drucker, *Management: Tasks, Responsibilities, Practice* (New York: Harper & Row, 1973), p. 79.
4. E. Jerome McCarthy and William D. Perreault, Jr., *Basic Marketing*, 9th ed. (Homewood, Ill.: Irwin, 1987).
5. Theodore Levitt, *The Marketing Imagination* (New York: Free Press, 1986), p. 128.
6. For further discussion, see: P. Kotler, *Marketing Management: Analysis, Planning and Control*, 5th ed. (Englewood Cliffs, N.J.: Prentice Hall, 1984).
7. Russell H. Colley, *Defining Advertising Goals for Measured Advertising Results* (New York: Association of National Advertisers, 1961).
8. Theodore Levitt, "Exploit the Product Life Cycle," *Harvard Business Review*, November–December 1965, pp. 81–94. For a condensed discussion of the marketing strategy implications of the Product Life Cycle, see: Dereck F. Abell, "Competitive Market Strategies: Some Generalizations and Hypotheses," Marketing Science Institute Working Papers; Report no. 75–107 (Cambridge, Mass.: Marketing Science Institute, 1975).

3

Foundation Skills

OVERVIEW

The process of media planning utilizes a great many numbers. The manipulation and interpretation of these numbers requires minimal mathematical skills. This first "skill chapter" introduces the basic terms and calculations that underlie the interpretation of data. These include averages, percentages, and indexing. Examples and exercises in the calculations are provided.

MEDIA MATH

Most American citizens do not need a presidential task force or an authoritative commission to tell them that most of us are uncomfortable with mathematics. Many people simply freeze and stare with glazed eyes when they are confronted with a page of numbers. Others remember nothing but painful past struggles with math homework and never want to revisit those days again. It is unfortunate for those people that media planning is steeped in numbers.

Media planners have often been described as number crunchers and the myth has developed that media planning is nothing but number crunching. Fortunately, this is not true. It is true that media planners have always used adding machines and calculators. In the days before computers, huge mechanical calculators would be lined up on desk after desk in a large room. Now computers are on most desks, and computers do most of the numerical work. The image persists, however, that media planners are number crunchers and that media planning is numerology, the study of the occult significance of numbers.

What is often overlooked, misunderstood, or simply unknown, however, is that most of the mathematics involved in media planning—whether computer assisted or not—is very simple arithmetic. Arithmetic may be the science of numbers, but it is important for beginning media planners to remember that arithmetic is neither geometry, nor trigonometry, nor algebra, nor calculus.

Yes, there are statistics involved in media planning. Statistics deal with the collection, analysis, interpretation, and presentation of masses of numerical data. There are masses of numerical data in media planning. Fortunately, however, the sophisticated knowledge of statistics is generally located in the research department. It is valuable for a media planner to know both statistics and research methods, but a media planner who is supported by a research department or a research supplier needs to know little more than basic grammar school arithmetic to do the planning job itself.

Research in communications and consumer communicative behavior is critical to media planning as a discipline. Computer programs and the models they are built upon are essential tools of media planning. Media planning, however, is a job function as well as an intellectual discipline. As a job function, media planning is focused on developing marketing communications strategies. The planner's task is to use the results of research and the tools of computer programs. It is not the planner's job to create either.

The media director of a large advertising agency should be schooled in statistics, communications research, modeling, and computer programming. Correspondingly, a student of media planning should seek opportunities to learn these disciplines. As a practical matter, however, that knowledge is not necessary to perform the media planning function, nor is it necessary for a client to know these things in order to evaluate a media plan. It is necessary, however, to be able to think and talk in numbers, and that implies a certain ability in and comfort level with, basic arithmetic.

For our purposes, we will call these basic skills Media Math. At each point in the process of media planning, when these skills are required and can be applied, we will pause to define and describe them. We will also provide exercises that will help you acquire the skill and apply it easily. The more sophisticated the skill involved, the more important is an understanding of the principle involved, rather than an understanding of the complicated calculations. The more complicated the calculations, the more probable it is that they will be performed by a computer. In order to control the process and manage the data to a meaningful conclusion, however, you have to know the principle. A machine cannot do your thinking for you. Media planning is imaginative thinking; you cannot think unless you are relaxed. The exercises in the Media Math sections of this book are designed primarily to help you relax so that you can think clearly.

AVERAGES

An **average** is a numerical measure that is typical or representative of a group of quantities. To find the average, divide their sum by the number of quantities. The sum of a group of quantities divided by their number is also called the **mean**. For example, the average of 2, 4, 6, 8, and 10 is 6.

$$\frac{2 + 4 + 6 + 8 + 10}{5} = \frac{30}{5} = 6$$

(or)

$$
\begin{array}{r}
2 \\
4 \\
6 \\
8 \\
+\ 10 \\
\hline
30 \div 5 = 6
\end{array}
$$

EXAMPLES

1. Sparrow Industries has been advertising for the past seven years. In the first year, it spent $3,100,000. Its spending has grown modestly each year since then, and it is now spending at a rate of $5 million annually. What has been Sparrow Industries's average annual advertising expenditure?

Year	Expenditure
1985	$3,100,000
1986	3,565,000
1987	3,743,400
1988	4,200,000
1989	4,315,400
1990	4,380,000
1991	5,000,000
Total	$28,303,800
	÷ 7
	$4,043,400

Sparrow Industries has spent $28,303,800 in total over the seven years. The total divided by 7 is the average. Therefore, $28,303,800 ÷ 7 = $4,043,400. Sparrow Industries's average annual advertising expenditure has been $4,043,400.

2. The average cost of a prime time television commercial varies by quarter. What was the average cost of a prime time 30-second commercial in 1990?

1990	Cost
1st Qtr.	$119,600
2nd Qtr.	136,300
3rd Qtr.	100,000
4th Qtr.	139,000
Total	$495,006 ÷ 4 = $123,900

The sum of the quarterly costs of a 30-second commercial in 1990 is $495,600. The total divided by 4 is the average. Therefore, $495,600 ÷ 4 = $123,900. *The average cost of a prime time 30-second commercial in 1990 was $123,900.*

Comments

An average can be very useful when you are trying to represent the general significance of a set of numbers. It helps in summarizing a tendency or a trend. An average is an approximation and is useful only when an approximate level of detail would be sufficient to the analysis being performed. Averages are frequently used as part of more complicated analyses.

Averages are not only subject to interpretations, but they also can be misleading. If you are an employer, for example, and two entry level college graduates are applying for a job, and each has a 2.8 grade point average, does that mean that the two applicants are equally bright and diligent? Not necessarily. One student may have received an A in each of three courses and barely passed a fourth course. The other student might have consistently received high Cs and low Bs. One of these students is obviously brighter. A false impression is created by the extremely low grade in one course. The other student, however, gives evidence of consistent diligence, and the GPA is more representative of this student's talent.

Another difficulty is that many people use "average," "mean," and "median" as synonyms. An average is the arithmetic mean. Median signifies something else.

Median identifies the point in a series of numbers at which there are as many instances above it as there are below it. It represents the midpoint. The average of 1, 3, 6, 7, and 8, for example, is 5. The median number in this series, however, is 6.

The difference between average (mean) and median could be significant, for instance, in the identification of typical household income. The Census Bureau usually reports median family income as, for example, $28,500. Many people assume that this signifies that the average family income is $28,500, when what it really signifies is that half of all families earn all kinds of amounts above that, and another half earn all kinds of amounts below that. The median is not affected by extreme values at either end, or by radical variation on either side. That is both the advantage and disadvantage of using the median as a tool of interpretation. Most importantly, a media planner should be on the alert both when presenting and when analyzing numbers that median and average (mean) are not the same.

EXERCISES

1. The sales figures for Sparrow Industries have been increasing for the past seven years, since they began advertising in 1985. What have been their average annual sales? What has been their average annual sales increase?

	Sales	Increase
1985	$100,000,000	
1986	118,002,000	18,002,000
1987	124,830,000	6,828,000
1988	135,000,000	10,170,000
1989	143,843,000	8,843,000
1990	146,000,000	2,157,000
1991	160,000,000	14,000,000

Average annual sales =   _____.

Average annual sales increase = _____.

Note: Results should be rounded off to the smallest part represented in the problem or question.

2. An employment agency surveyed fifteen advertising agencies of different sizes to gain a perspective on the salaries of media supervisors. What was the median salary of the supervisors?

Supervisor	Salary
A	$42,600
B	18,400
C	33,100
D	37,200
E	25,900
F	40,500
G	35,700
H	40,000
I	38,400
J	32,700
K	29,300
L	41,600
M	24,900
N	36,800
O	53,500

Their median income is _____.

PERCENTAGES

A **percentage** is part of a whole expressed in hundredths. Percentage is used in arithmetic to denote that a whole quantity divided into 100 equal parts in the standard of measure. Percent means hundredths and is indicated by a percentage sign (%). It may also be expressed as a decimal. Thus, $2\% = .02 = 2/100$; $75\% = .75 = 75/100$. Percentages may be added, subtracted, multiplied, or divided just as other ordinary numbers are treated.

To change a percent to a fraction, divide the percent quantity by 100 and reduce to its lowest terms. Thus $40\% = 40/100 = 2/5$.

To change a percent to a decimal, drop the percent sign (%) and place a decimal point two places to the left. Thus, 5% = .05; 55% = .55; 5.5% = .055

To change a decimal to a percent , move the decimal point two places to the right and add a percent sign (%). Thus, .025 = 2.5%; .25 = 25%; .255 = 25.5%; 2.55 = 255%.

To find the percent of a number, change the percent to a decimal and then multiply that decimal times the number. Thus, to determine 14% of $3,000, first change 14% to .14 and then multiply $3,000 × .14 = $420.

To find what percent one number is of another, divide the percentage by the base. Thus, to answer "150 is what percent of 300?" divide 150 by 300, or 150 ÷ 300 = 50%. To answer what percent 50 is of 75: 50 ÷ 75 = 66%.

To find a number when the percent of that number is known, divide the rate by the percentage. Thus, to answer "255 is 25% of what amount?" divide 225 by 25%, or 225 ÷.25 = 900. To answer 100 is 85% of what amount: 100 ÷ 85 is 117.65.

EXAMPLES

1. There are 174,900,000 adults in the United States. *Business Week* has 4,920,000 adult readers. What percent of U.S. adults are readers of *Business Week?*

    4,920,000 ÷ 174,900,000 = 2.813%

    Approximately 2.8% of U.S. adults are *Business Week* readers.

2. *Business Week* has 4,920,000 adult readers. 45.1% of them graduated from college. How many *Business Week* readers graduated from college?

    4,920,000 × .451 = 2,219,000 (rounded off)

    Approximately 2,219,000 readers of *Business Week* are college graduates.

3. 17.4% of *Bride's* readers, or 543,706 readers, graduated from college. How many readers of *Bride's* are there?

    542,706 ÷ .174 = 3,119,000

    There are approximately 3,119,000 readers of *Bride's*.

Comments

Percentages are normally rounded off to one decimal point. When dealing with money, however, rounding off to two decimal points is more often appropriate. When there is doubt, the percentage should be rounded off to the lowest or smallest dimension included in the question or problem. In general, the level of preciseness required by the circumstances dictates the style of the numerical expressions.

When dealing with media research data, both the base and the percentage frequently have been rounded off. Consequently, the reconciliation of percentages usually won't total 100 percent.

The arithmetic involved in determining percentages is the kind of arithmetic required in the media planning process. The math principle involved is $A \times B = C$. In any such equation, a knowledge of any two (of the three) terms gives you the ability to determine the third by changing the order of the equation. Thus $A \times ? = C$ becomes $A \div C = B$ and $? \times B = C$ becomes $C \div B = A$.

EXERCISES

1. If there are 90,860,000 television homes in the United States, and if Home Improvement was viewed by 27.5% of those homes last night, how many homes were in Home Improvement's audience last night?

   Answer: _____.

2. Sparrow Industries had $160,000,000 in sales last year. What is each quarter's percent of sales?

Quarter	Sales	Percent
1st Qtr.	$44,800,000	?
2nd Qtr.	30,400,000	?
3rd Qtr.	25,600,000	?
4th Qtr.	59,200,000	?

3. Sparrow Industries's competitor had $49,830,000 in sales in the 4th quarter. This represented 39% of its total sales. What were the total sales for the year?

   Answer: _____.

INDEXING

An **index** is a ratio in the form of a percentage expressed as a whole number. It is a percentage of a selected base number without the percentage sign. An index is used to show a proportional relationship between several amounts.

To index several numbers, first select the **base**, the quantity to which all others will be compared. Usually, the base either is one of the numbers in the group, or it is the average of the numbers in the group. Second, divide all the other numbers by the base. An index is expressed as a whole number. Therefore, move the decimal point of the base two places to the left before dividing. In the final indexing, the base will have an index of 100. If 20 is the base, then 22 will index as 110. Thus,

$$22 \div 20 \times 100 = 110 \ [\text{(or) } 22 \div .2 = 110]$$

EXAMPLES

1. Develop an index of Sparrow Industries's sales growth in the past seven years.

Year	Sales	Index
1985	$100,000,000	100 (Base)
1986	118,002,000	118
1987	124,830,000	125
1988	135,000,000	135
1989	143,843,000	144
1990	146,000,000	146
1991	160,000,000	160

Sparrow Industries's sales grew by 60% since 1985.

2. To compare any year's performance, develop an index of Sparrow Industries's sales based on average annual sales for the seven years.

Year	Sales	Index
1985	$100,000,000	75
1986	118,002,000	89
1987	124,830,000	94
1988	135,000,000	102
1989	143,843,000	109
1990	146,000,000	110
1991	160,000,000	121

Average Sales = $132,525,000   100 (Base)

Although they continued to grow, Sparrow Industries's sales were starkly below the growth trend in 1990.

Comments

Indexing is one of the most extensively utilized tools of analysis and expression in both marketing and media planning. It enables the user to present multidigit numbers in a meaningful way. Indexing facilitates comparison and contrast. When properly used and understood, indexing also describes a dynamic. Indexes identify a particular energy. Indexing also enables managers to align their efforts with one another.

The selection of the base is often routine, for instance, such as average monthly sales, or the average audience of a television program, or sales performance compared to a sales area's population. Frequently, however, the most important decision in developing an index involves determining the base.

If the devil could quote statistics, one of his methods would be to select a misleading base for indexing. Changing the base year, for example, could make the inflation rate, or our picture of the current situation, look a lot better or worse than it is. The proper, fair, and reasonable selection of the base, then, is the most important aspect of indexing. Selecting the base is the judgment call that creates the foundation of meaning.

EXERCISES

1. Determine the Sparrow Industries's quarterly sales index in 1991. Use average quarterly sales as the base.

Quarter	Sales	Index
1st Qtr.	$44,800,000	_____
2nd Qtr.	30,400,000	_____
3rd Qtr.	25,600,000	_____
4th Qtr.	59,200,000	_____

2a. Develop an index comparing quarterly advertising expenditures with quarterly sales results for Sparrow Industries.

% Sales	% Advertising	Index
28	25	_____
19	22	_____
16	20	_____
37	33	_____

2b. What significance might this indexing have? What other information would you want before making a decision?

3. Index the afternoon audience of each television station in Los Angeles. Each station's average quarter-hour audience is listed.

Station	Audience	Index
A	640,000	_____
B	160,000	_____
C	80,000	_____
D	400,000	_____
E	160,000	_____
F	80,000	_____
G	320,000	_____
H	240,000	_____
I	160,000	_____

ANSWERS TO CHAPTER 3: EXERCISES

Pages 35–36

    1a. $132,525,000

    1b. $10,000,000

    2. $36,800

Pages 37–38

    1. $24,986,500

    2.   28%; 19%; 16%; 37%.

    3. $127,769,230

Pages 39–40

    1.   112; 76; 64; 148.

    2a.   89; 116; 125; 89.

    2b.   The significance lies in the planner's ability to align quarterly advertising expenditures with quarterly sales results. Before aligning the efforts, however, the planner would want to review similar indexing for previous years. There might have been a decision to increase advertising in weaker sales periods and/or evidence that after a point in good sales periods, increased advertising expenditures do not have an impact on sales results.

    3.   258; 65; 32; 161; 65; 32; 129; 97; 65.

        (Base = 9-station average audience)

4

Information Resources:
Markets and Targets

OVERVIEW

Media planning is both data hungry and data rich. This chapter introduces the basic resources that are used in the marketing background analysis that leads to the definition of the plan's media objectives and strategies. The basic questions are: Who is selling what, where? Who is buying and using the product or service? Who is communicating, where and how much are they advertising? The research resources for answering these questions are identified and explained with examples and exercises.

DATA RICH

More than one researcher has been heard to remark: "If people only knew how much we know about them." Most people would be shocked to learn just how much this is. Once they got over their shock, however, it would be productive if they accepted the "factness" of the data. A good example of how people react to data on their behavior can be found any week in *TV Guide*. Each week the Nielsen television ratings, as well as the top video rentals, are reported. It does no good to complain about the survey methods involved, because they are far more accurate than psyche-protective doubters are ever willing to accept. The data is real, it reports real behavior, and it applies to ourselves as well as to our fellow citizens. The question should be: "What does the data tell us about ourselves?"

Advertising and marketing are data rich. Numerous types of research are constantly being conducted across the full range of the American economy and opinion.

Every possible method, from focus groups to large statistical surveys, is used to conduct research on consumers, industries, media, and products. The information is available and valid, because there are always enough people who are willing to tell researchers anything and everything, if the questions are asked correctly.

The net result is that media planners discover that they have both too much and too little data to work with. The information comes from syndicated sources, from published reports by journalists and stock analysts, from client and agency research, and from the media. The sheer amount of the data can be daunting. For example, one page of a Nielsen television report contains 2,272 numbers. One page of a Simmons Market Research report contains 1,190 numbers. The media planner must look at many such pages from multiple sources when analyzing, planning, buying, and accounting in the process of spending millions of dollars. So it should be; no advertiser would want someone to spend its money blindly. The volume of the available data can be overwhelming, but if the data is available, the media planner has to use it and must know how to use it.

The planner also has the task of determining whether or not the research data is valid, reliable, useful, and projectable. This is the point at which everyone wishes that there were more numbers that could further verify the data. There are three distinct tasks involved:

1. Determining whether any individual package of data is reliable within acceptable parameters.

2. Being careful not to construct a house of cards by building one survey on top of another until the final result no longer reflects reality.

3. Protecting against inundation to the point that you lose any sense of consumer and media interactions.

The media planner's ultimate job is to see consumers and communications through the numbers, and not to become a victim of the numbers.

The good news is that sufficient data is almost always available. The better news, perhaps, is that it is all understandable with a rudimentary knowledge of arithmetic (See chapter 3). It is possible to apply elaborate formulas, modeling, and regression analysis to the data, but these are seldom the task of the media planner. In any case, the first task is to understand the basic source materials.

THE BASIC QUESTIONS

The production of a media plan comes in three parts, representing three distinct activities. The critical path in approaching and understanding the research resources begins with recognizing the current phase of the planning process. There are major distinctions between analysis and execution, between buying and accountability, between understanding and strategy, and all of the other steps in the planning process. It is critical to take one step at a time and always to know where you are.

The information relevant to the first phase of the media planning process concerns markets and targets. The key questions are:

1. Who is selling what, where, when?

2. Who is buying/using the products?

3. Who is communicating and how much?

For a market situation analysis, you need to know sales volume, brand shares, and any geographical or seasonal variations. You need to know the character and habits of consumers who are buying and using competitive products and brands. You need to know who is advertising at what budget levels, with what results, using which media and strategies. This is the information that everyone would want to know before devising strategies for the spending of millions of dollars of their own—and especially someone else's—money. To go much beyond these questions at the beginning of the planning process, however, can be both confusing and risky.

Prudent Procedures

Before reaching for the first syndicated research report you wish to consult, it is always wise to keep several guidelines in mind:

Always start with a question.   The sources are often very much like phone books. Novelists have been known to flip randomly through the pages of a phone book to find names for the characters in their stories. This is a kind of free-association. Most of us, however, find it much more useful to start looking for a specific name, which we generally know how to spell, and to follow this with a question about a phone number and/or address. This is a useful approach to syndicated research.

Check out the territory.   Every syndicated research report includes directions on how to use it. Furthermore, almost every page of data in these reports contains all of the reference terms necessary for interpreting the data on the page. The simple message is: Read the instructions before reading the data. It is in the interests of every research firm that publishes data to make access to its data as easy as possible. Firms do alter the format of their data from time to time, however. Therefore, always review the clues on the data page or in the introduction before plunging into the data itself.

Don't be fooled.   Most research reports are based on samples of various sizes, use different information-gathering methodologies, and employ different statistical standards. Consequently, you must be cautious in comparing data from different sources or in building data from one source on top of data from another source. This often increases the margin of error geometrically. Finally, the existence of any margin of error should be a warning that the data are estimates and not fact statements.

No certain guide.   It is always comfortable to believe that a supervisor, some other operational manager, a teacher, or a trainer can tell you exactly what to look for—no more and no less—in a page of data, and exactly how it is to be used, but they cannot.

An analogy might be made to computer chess: Most computer chess programs probably could beat most of us, but no computer program has yet been able to beat a chess champion. We have yet to be able to match the brain's ability to sift combinations and possibilities, or to leap to insights. Similarly, it is possible to identify the most common uses and interpretations of research data, but it is impossible to exhaust the possibilities.

Know when to stop. Swimming in research can be like living in a dream world. It is important to remember that both advertising and media planning are practical arts, which must at some point stop analyzing, searching for certitude, or reaching for creativity. Furthermore, it is important to remember the limits of our own abilities and the abilities of those with whom we are working. Therefore, stop when you have done what you know how to do, and stop when the work has to get out. A lot of good goes undone, or is done too late, because someone was uncomfortable with imperfection or ambiguity.

Insight versus presentation. When you are trying to understand a market or its consumers, it is reasonable to look at every piece and kind of data you can get your hands on. When you are presenting your insights, however, it is important to use only the data that is generally acceptable, or is recognized as acceptable, in your community of interest. The purpose of presentations is to develop consensus and united action. Neither is served by the use of data that creates more questions than answers.

Simple versus superficial. The goal of analysis is simple and supportable insight. The analogy might be the classical simplicity of an ancient Greek temple. The planner should be suspicious of any point that takes too many numbers or calculations to articulate or explain. While avoiding the baroque, however, the planner also must avoid superficiality. Too often planners are too quick, too anxious, and too irresponsible in their analysis and presentation of numbers.

Don't believe your own poetry. Leaps of imagination or tentative hypotheses are often both creative and useful in data analysis. The problem is that this kind of mythological thinking can take on the substance of fact. Consequently, it is important not to fool yourself into using certain imaginatively developed numbers in future formulations. You should be creative, but you must control the use of creative products.

These guidelines are the fruit of experience. There is no substitute for experience in developing a comfort level with all the data available to media planners. The final advice before plunging into the research resources, therefore, is: Do not be afraid of experience or of making mistakes.

MARKET ANALYSIS

The basic questions are: Who is selling what, and where? The questions imply both national and annual information, as well as geographically and chronologically specific information. Once a category (or direct and indirect competition) has been defined, the key questions are:

1. How large is the market for products or services in this category?
2. Is the market static, growing, or declining?
3. What share(s) does each company's sales represent?
4. Are there any geographical or seasonal variations in these sales and shares?

Almost every business covered by the general business and financial press (for example, *Business Week, The New York Times*), almost every industry through its trade press (for instance, *Progressive Grocer, Advertising Age*), and nearly every company, through its own intelligence gathering, provides information on annual sales and shares. Whatever the source, the media planner should have this kind of generalized and generally available information when beginning the planning process.

Clients may also subscribe to the A. C. Nielson Food and Drug Indices, or other reports based on supermarket scanner data. If so, the client may also be willing to share this information, which could be essential to sophisticated media planning. The data can tell you, for example, not only how much American consumers spent on ready-to-eat cereals in the past year, but also how much they spent in the previous several weeks. Furthermore, this data is broken down by each competitive brand for each television market. Thus, it reports on both General Mills's Cheerios and Kellogg's Corn Flakes sales by week and by year in Buffalo, Philadelphia, Miami, and all other markets. These reports, therefore, can inform marketers not only of the success of promotional efforts, but also of pricing strategies (as described in chapter 2).

This kind of data eventually can help the planner follow either an investment strategy, a uniform conformity strategy, or a defensive strategy in allocating advertising dollars. Formulas that enable the media planner to determine markets of opportunity, as well as to allocate advertising efforts to local markets in relation to sales, are described in chapter 6.

At the earliest stages of market analysis, however, the sales data is most important to an understanding of the dynamics of the market, its growth or decline, the competitive standing of its players, its good times and bad times of year, and its better or worse geographic areas. Read with imagination, sales data can also tell you about consumers and their living habits.

CONSUMER ACTIVITY

When you deal with data that can serve more than one purpose, it is often helpful to recall that it is possible to be both logical and creative. This is also true of disciplined patience and efficient executions, as well as effectiveness and efficiency.

The major syndicated resources used by media planners, for example, can inform the planner about the demographics and psychographics of product users, and how they use the brands, as well as the demographics, consuming characteristics, and exposure patterns of media vehicle audiences. Thus, the same data sources can be used:

1. for the purposes of understanding markets and consumers,
2. for selecting target prospects, and
3. for the selection and purchase of individual media vehicles.

Each of these uses, however, represents quite different steps in the planning process.

Both human nature and the pressures of business life encourage the temptation to collapse these three distinct steps into one act. This is especially true when the data sources—the same book in your hand, so to speak—can serve all three purposes. Therefore, it is best to begin the process with some philosophic caution. Too often the rush to execution in media planning produces ineffective plans. There is no contradiction between effectiveness and efficiency, but you need patient discipline in order to take one step at a time in the planning process. Therefore, we will identify and explain the use of the consumer research data as it is relevant to each step of the planning process.

The first task of media planning is to understand the marketplace, and that requires an understanding of consumers: who they are and how they consume. This requires data and imagination. Both can be adulterated by rushing past the task at hand, and executional anxiety can blind us to an insightful understanding of the market. Therefore, in this chapter we will examine the use of syndicated sources for consumer insights. In subsequent chapters we will examine many of the same resources to develop targeting strategies (chapter 8) and to select vehicles in plan execution (chapter 12).

The Sources

The basic question is: Who is buying/using the products? The two most widely used syndicated research resources for answering this question are published by Simmons Market Research Bureau (called SMRB, or Simmons) and Mediamark Research Inc. (MRI). First, we will explain how to read and interpret each of these research products, and second, we will explain how they can be best applied to an understanding of consumers as part of a market situation analysis.

Simmons Market Research Bureau reports the results of an annual probability survey of nineteen thousand adults and households. Their report—Study of Media and Markets—covers forty-three volumes and provides data on product usage (Exhibit 4.1), publication audiences, and multimedia audiences. The product volumes are most important to an understanding of consumers in the marketplace. These volumes provide data on more than eight hundred product categories, on the brands comprising each category, and on consumer usage patterns. The demographic information of this data include age, education, employment, marital status,. race, census/marketing regions, income, and the number of persons per household.

Mediamark (Exhibit 4.2) parallels the information found in Simmons in both product and media volumes. The data is derived from a survey of twenty thousand

EXHIBIT 4.1 SIMMONS MARKET RESEARCH

0043 P 15

[1] ▶ REGULAR COLA DRINKS (CARBONATED, NOT DIET): ALL USERS, USERS IN LAST 7 DAYS AND KINDS ◀ [2]   (ADULTS)

0043 P 15

	TOTAL U.S. '000	ALL USERS A '000	B DOWN	C ACROSS %	D INDX	HEAVY USERS EIGHT OR MORE A '000	B DOWN	C ACROSS %	D INDX	BOTTLED A '000	B DOWN	C ACROSS %	D INDX	CANNED A '000	B DOWN	C ACROSS %	D INDX
TOTAL ADULTS	187747	116443	100.0	62.0	100	40781	100.0	21.7	100	67416	100.0	35.9	100	83598	100.0	44.5	100
MALES	90070	60171	51.7	66.8	108	22123	54.2	24.6	113	34737	51.5	38.6	107	43353	51.9	48.1	108
FEMALES	97676	56272	48.3	57.6	93	18657	45.8	19.1	88	32679	48.5	33.5	93	40245	48.1	41.2	93
PRINCIPAL SHOPPERS	115901	69226	59.5	59.7	96	23395	57.4	20.2	93	39402	58.4	34.0	95	49071	58.7	42.3	95
18 - 24	23951	18155	15.6	75.8	122	8512	20.9	35.5	164	11911	17.7	49.7	138	14019	16.8	58.5	131
25 - 34	41492	29727	25.5	71.6	116	11919	29.2	28.7	132	17962	26.6	43.3	121	21883	26.2	52.7	118
35 - 44	40678	26728	23.0	65.7	106	9554	23.4	23.5	108	16428	24.4	40.4	112	18996	22.7	46.7	105
45 - 54	29045	17131				5731	14.1	19.7	91	8981	13.3	30.9	86	12518	15.0	43.1	97
55 - 64	21263	11058				2371	5.8	11.1	51	5428	8.1	25.5	71	7514	9.0	35.3	79
65 OR OLDER	31318	13645				2694	6.6	8.6	40	6706	9.9	21.4	60	8668	10.4	27.7	62
18 - 34	65443	47882				20431	50.1	31.2	144	29872	44.3	45.6	127	35902	42.9	54.9	123
18 - 49	122143	84416				33517	82.2	27.4	126	51286	76.1	42.0	117	62349	74.6	51.0	115
25 - 54	111215	73586				27204	66.7	24.5	113	43371	64.3	39.0	109	53397	63.9	48.0	108
35 - 49	56701	36535				13086	32.1	23.1	106	21414	31.8	37.8	105	26447	31.6	46.6	105
50 OR OLDER	65603	32027	27.5	48.8	79	7264	17.8	11.1	51	16130	23.9	24.6	68	21249	25.4	32.4	73
GRADUATED COLLEGE	37353	20997	18.0	56.2	91	5164	12.7	13.8	64	11761	17.4	31.5	88	16319	19.5	43.7	98
ATTENDED COLLEGE	39301	24312	20.9	61.9	100	8947	21.9	22.8	105	13863	20.6	35.3	98	18121	21.7	46.1	104
GRADUATED HIGH SCHOOL	73139	47354	40.7	64.7	104	17169	42.1	23.5	108	27770	41.2	38.0	106	33414	40.0	45.7	103
DID NOT GRADUATE HIGH SCHOOL	37954	23781	20.4	62.7	101	9501	23.3	25.0	115	14022	20.8	36.9	103	15745	18.8	41.5	93
EMPLOYED MALES	62041	43938	37.7	70.8	114	16694	40.9	26.9	124	25568	37.9	41.2	115	32343	38.7	52.1	117
EMPLOYED FEMALES	53100	32042	27.5	60.3	97	10400	25.5	19.6	90	18635	27.6	35.1	98	23781	28.4	44.8	101
EMPLOYED FULL-TIME	99735	65910	56.6	66.1	107	23879	58.6	23.9	110	38595	57.2	38.7	108	48109	57.5	48.2	108
EMPLOYED PART-TIME	15406	10070	8.6	65.4	105	3215	7.9	20.9	96	5608	8.3	36.4	101	8014	9.6	52.0	117
NOT EMPLOYED	72606	40463	34.7	55.7	90	13687	33.6	18.9	87	23214	34.4	32.0	89	27475	32.9	37.8	85

(1) Designates the market. (2) Identifies the usage time frame. (3) Identifies the primary demographic category. (4) Estimate of people in the primary demographic category. Forms the base for all percentages across—reading left to right. (5) Number of people in the primary demographic category who are active in the market. (6) What percentage of the primary demographic category they represent. (7) Identifies the total and the number of those active in the marketplace for any demographic subgroup. (8) Identifies the percent that a demographic subgroup represents of all those who are active in the marketplace. (9) Identifies what percent the marketplace actives represent of their total demographic peers. (10) Indexes the proportion of marketplace actives in a demographic subgroup to the typical proportion of actives in the primary demographic category. (11) Breaks out the demographics for various levels of usage, following a consistent format.

Source: Simmons Market Research Bureau, 1994

adults and covers more than 450 products. The fundamental difference between MRI and SMRB is in one aspect of their research techniques. MRI's technique, **recent reading**, relies on the use of "flash" cards containing magazine logos, which the respondents sort into those they have read recently and those they have not. The results then become the basis of subsequent questioning. Simmons's technique, **through the book**, utilizes stripped-down or skeleton copies of magazines as the basis of its research. There has been great debate over these competing techniques, but both are now generally accepted by the research community. They do, however, produce different specific results. Consequently, either one source is agreed upon by the product's agency and client, or the data from both sources is averaged in one way or another.

Both MRI and Simmons enable the planner to identify:

*Total number of users of a brand category

*Users by volume of usage of the category

*Number of users by brand

EXHIBIT 4.2 MEDIAMARK RESEARCH

40   LOW CALORIE DOMESTIC BEER

GLASSES/LAST 7 DAYS

BASE: ADULTS	TOTAL U.S. '000	ALL A '000	B %DOWN	C %ACROSS	D INDEX	HEAVY MORE THAN 5 A '000	B %DOWN	C %ACROSS	D INDEX	MEDIUM 2-5 A '000	B %DOWN	C %ACROSS	D INDEX	LIGHT LESS THAN 2 A '000	B %DOWN	C %ACROSS	D INDEX
All Adults	187756	41172	100.0	21.9	100	11522	100.0	6.1	100	13162	100.0	7.0	100	16488	100.0	8.8	100
Men	89686	23703	57.6	26.4	121	7825	67.9	8.7	142	7309	55.5	8.1	116	8569	52.0	9.6	109
Women	98070	17469	42.4	17.8	81	3697	32.1	3.8	61	5853	44.5	6.0	85	7919	48.0	8.1	92
Household Heads	112300	25617	62.2	22.8	104	7829	67.9	7.0	114	7871	59.8	7.0	100	9918	60.2	8.8	101
Homemakers	113548	22468	54.6	19.8	90	5937	51.5	5.2	85	7258	55.1	6.4	91	9273	56.2	8.2	93
Graduated College	36908	10379				2405	20.9	6.5	106	3059	23.2	8.3	118	4916	29.8	13.3	152
Attended College	45320	11640				3597	31.2	7.9	129	3906	29.7	8.6	123	4138	25.1	9.1	104
Graduated High School	66703	13691				3980	34.5	6.0	97	4467	33.9	6.7	96	5243	31.8	7.9	90
Did not Graduate High School	38825	5461				1539	13.4	4.0	65	1731	13.2	4.5	64	2191	13.3	5.6	64
18-24	24565	6556				2500	21.7	10.2	166	2015	15.3	8.2	117	2041	12.4	8.3	95
25-34	43511	12671				3612	31.3	8.3	135	3801	26.9	8.7	125	5259	31.9	12.1	138
35-44	40062	10391				2783	24.2	6.9	113	3213	24.4	8.0	114	4395	26.7	11.0	125
45-54	26903	5138	12.5	19.1	87	1338	11.6	5.0	81	1802	13.7	6.7	96	1998	12.1	7.4	85
55-64	21657	3425	8.3	15.8	72	689	6.0	3.2	52	1264	9.6	5.8	83	1472	8.9	6.8	77
65 or over	31057	2989	7.3		44	599	5.2	1.9	31	1067	8.1	3.4	49	1324	8.0	4.3	49
18-34	68076	19228	46.7	28.2	129	6112	53.0	9.0	146	5816	44.2	8.5	122	7299	44.3	10.7	122
18-49	122914	32732	79.5	26.6	121	9806	85.1	8.0	130	10160	77.2	8.3	118	12766	77.4	10.4	118
25-54	110477	28200	68.5	25.5	116	7734	67.1	7.0	114	8816	67.0	8.0	114	11651	70.7	10.5	120
Employed Full Time	101651	27425	66.6	27.0	123	7713	66.9	7.6	124	8893	67.6	8.7	125	10819	65.6	10.6	121
Part-time	16140	3753	9.1	23.3	106	1030	8.9	6.4	104	1165	8.9	7.2	103	1558	9.4	9.7	110
Sole Wage Earner	32213	7678	18.6	23.8	109	2431	21.1	7.5	123	2360	17.9	7.3	105	2886	17.5	9.0	102
Not Employed	69965	9994	24.3	14.3	65	2779	24.1	4.0	65	3104	23.6	4.4	63	4111	24.9	5.9	67
Professional	17019	4525	11.0	26.6	121	1078	9.4	6.3	103	1241	9.4	7.3	104	2206	13.4	13.0	148
Executive/Admin./Managerial	15493	4604	11.2	29.7	136	1078	9.4	7.0	113	1569	11.9	10.1	144	1956	11.9	12.6	144
Clerical/Sales/Technical	36098	9167	22.3	25.4	116	2375	20.6	6.6	107	3155	24.0	8.7	125	3637	22.1	10.1	115
Precision/Crafts/Repair	13369	3543	8.6	26.5	121	1102	9.6	8.2	134	1160	8.8	8.7	124	1283	7.8	9.6	109
Other Employed	35813	9339	22.7	26.1	119	3109	27.0	8.7	141	2934	22.3	8.2	117	3296	20.0	9.2	105
H/D Income $75,000 or More	24947	7047	17.1	28.2	129	1827	15.9	7.3	119	2241	17.0	9.0	128	2980	18.1	11.9	136
$60,000 - 74,999	17096	4761	11.6	27.8	127	1127	9.8	6.6	107	1652	12.6	9.7	138	1984	12.0	11.6	132
$50,000 - 59,999	17758	4750	11.5	26.7	122	1037	9.0	5.8	95	1510	11.5	8.5	121	2202	13.4	12.4	141
$40,000 - 49,999	22389	5862	14.2	26.2	119	1686	14.6	7.5	123	1913	14.5	8.5	122	2263	13.7	10.1	115
$30,000 - 39,999	26782	5706	13.9	21.3	97	1371	11.9	5.1	83	2008	15.3	7.5	107	2328	14.1	8.7	99
$20,000 - 29,999	29687	5553	13.5	18.7	85	1617	14.0	5.4	89	1911	14.5	6.4	92	2025	12.3	6.8	78
$10,000 - 19,999	29468	4679	11.4	15.9	72	1744	15.1	5.9	96	1083	8.2	3.7	52	1853	11.2	6.3	72
Less than $10,000	19628	2813	6.8	14.3	65	1113	9.7	5.7	92	845	6.4	4.3	61	855	5.2	4.4	50
Census Region: North East	39636	8391	20.4	21.2	97	1685	14.6	4.3	69	2750	20.9	6.9	99	3956	24.0	10.0	114
North Central	44632	12275	29.8	27.5	125	3684	32.0	8.3	135	3595	27.3	8.1	115	4996	30.3	11.2	127
South	64330	12412	30.1	19.3	88	4287	37.2	6.7	109	3928	29.8	6.1	87	4197	25.5	6.5	74
West	39158	8095	19.7	20.7	94	1865	16.2	4.8	78	2891	22.0	7.4	105	3338	20.2	8.5	97
Marketing Reg.: New England	10397	2742	6.7	26.4	120	435	3.8	4.2	68	1038	7.9	10.0	142	1269	7.7	12.2	139
Middle Atlantic	33199	6440	15.6	19.4	88	1563	13.6	4.7	77	1838	14.0	5.5	79	3039	18.4	9.2	104
East Central	25537	6056	14.7	23.7	108	1846	16.0	7.2	118	1593	12.1	6.2	89	2616	15.9	10.2	117
West Central	28708	8508	20.7	29.6	135	2447	21.2	8.5	139	2808	21.3	9.8	140	3252	19.7	11.3	129
South East	35150	6226	15.1	17.7	81	2071	18.0	5.9	96	2187	16.6	6.2	89	1969	11.9	5.6	64
South West	20457	4638	11.3	22.7	103	1704	14.8	8.3	136	1365	10.4	6.7	95	1569	9.5	7.7	87
Pacific	34307	6563	15.9	19.1	87	1454	12.6	4.2	69	2335	17.7	6.8	97	2773	16.8	8.1	92

(1) Designates the market. (2) Identifies the usage time frame. (3) Identifies the primary demographic category. (4) Estimate of people in the primary demographic category. Forms the base for all percentages across—reading left to right. (5) Number of people in the primary demographic category who are active in the market. (6) What percentage of the primary demographic category they represent. (7) Identifies the total and the number of those active in the marketplace for any demographic subgroup. (8) Identifies the percent that a demographic subgroup represents of all those who are active in the marketplace. (9) Identifies what percent the marketplace actives represent of their total demographic peers. (10) Indexes the proportion of marketplace actives in a demographic subgroup to the typical proportion of actives in the primary demographic category. (11) Breaks out the demographics for various levels of usage, following a consistent format.

Source: Mediamark Research Inc., Spring 1994.

  *Share of total users by brand

  *Share of total volume by brand

  *Demographics of category and brand users, including age, education, income, region, and so on

  *Media usage patterns of each group of users

This combined data provides the media planner with a reasonably thorough picture of any market from a consumer perspective.

Using MRI and Simmons

The first task is to identify the overall dimensions and dynamics of the market. The Product Summary volumes of both MRI and Simmons provide a snapshot of the market and can be used in conjunction with Nielsen, and other market-by-market sales data. For example, MRI's Summary Table on the Baking Chip market (Exhibit 4.3) tells us that female homemakers are the primary users of baking chips and that 41 percent of them have used baking chips in the last six months. They definitely prefer semisweet chocolate in their baking, and Nestlé is the predominant brand. The Volume/Users Index indicates reasonably consistent habit patterns, although you can see some skew between Baker's premium brand and generally less expensive store brand users. Most striking is the fact that only 5.1 percent of consumers account for a huge 44.4 percent of volume. Put another way, less than 30 percent of the users account for almost 75 percent of the volume.

Most media planners have market size and brand share information from other sources. If they do not, MRI and Simmons can be used for these purposes. What these sources mainly provide, however, is a sense of the consumer dynamics of the market-place, that is, of the behavior that creates the sales figures you already know. In the instance of Baking Chips, the new insights would include the rather consistent habit patterns of competing brand users and the extraordinary importance of heavy users.

A valid question, at this point, is whether product summary data from either Simmons or MRI can be an adequate substitute for sales data from industry sources, Nielsen and others. The answer is no. Data extrapolated from user interviews can be inaccurate or misleading in relation to information about actual sales and brand volume. What the product summary does provide is a snapshot of user perceptions and behavior. It offers the possibility of a first insight into a consumer understanding of the marketplace.

The second task is to identify the demographic characteristics of significant consumer groups. The key questions are: quantity and quality, size and energy, and number and vitality. The key figures, therefore, are the numerical size of each demographic group and its index.

An analysis of MRI or Simmons (Exhibit 4.4) would tell the planner (#1) that 85 percent of female homemakers have used breakfast cereal in the last seven days. By looking at both gross numbers in each demographic category, and by looking at their corresponding index, the planner might conclude that the core of the market (62.2 percent) is represented (#2) by 25- to 54-year-olds. They also represent (#3) the highest and most energetic group of heavy users. The more educated people are (#4), the more likely they also are to be heavy users. Not surprisingly (#5), they are married parents. They tend to live in (#6) suburban counties in (#7) the South and Midwest. They are generally of (#8) middle income and (#9) own their home.

Not everyone who lives in the Midwest is a Midwesterner, nor is everyone who lives in New York City a cosmopolitan big-city slicker. The portrait of the prototypical female breakfast cereal user, however, is the classic suburban housewife of American folklore. Suddenly, the planner has an image of the person standing in front

EXHIBIT 4.3 BAKING CHIPS

BASE: FEMALE HOMEMAKERS (86,474,000)	ALL '000	ALL %	UNWGT	SHARE OF USERS	SHARE OF VOLUME	VOLUME/ USERS INDEX	MALE HOMEMAKERS (27,074,000) '000	%	UNWGT
Total Used in Last 6 Months	35142	40.6	3692				4474	16.5	546
Types:									
Butterscotch	4949	5.7	478						
Peanut Butter	4641	5.4	443						
German Sweet Chocolate	903	1.0	89						
Milk Chocolate	8733	10.1	870						
Mint Chocolate	1030	1.2	118						
Semi-Sweet Chocolate	27072	31.3	2850						
Kinds:									
Mini	3660	4.2	400						
Regular	26236	30.3	2716						
Brands:									
Baker's Big Chips	1034	1.2	95	2.1	2.6	124			
Baker's Regular Chips	4609	5.3	428	9.5	11.1	117			
Hershey	7217	8.3	726	14.9	9.8	66			
M & M's Baking Chocolate Candies	1352	1.6	123	2.8	3.0	107			
Mrs. Fields	231	.3	32	.5	.1	20			
Nestle' Toll House	23577	27.3	2531	48.6	50.9	105			
Reese's	2777	3.2	271	5.7	4.1	72			
Store's Own Brand	4929	5.7	519	10.2	10.0	98			
Other	2765	3.2	311	5.7	8.3	146			
Bags/Last 30 Days									
L None	12620	14.6	1383						
L 1	11776	13.6	1235						
M 2	6362	7.4	661						
H 3	2066	2.4	188						
H 4	1171	1.4	108						
H 5	415	.5	35						
H 6	327	.4	44						
H 7	79	.1	5						
H 8	146	.2	11						
H 9 or more	181	.2	22						
L Total	24396	28.2	2618	69.4	26.7				
M Total	6362	7.4	661	18.1	28.9				
H Total	4384	5.1	413	12.5	44.4				

Source: Mediamark Research Inc., Spring 1994.

of the cereal display in the supermarket and making the choices that will be reflected in Nielsen sales numbers.

But how does this woman see herself? If we apply the conclusions of our previous conceptual analysis (chapter 1), we will want to know more about her culture. This sense of self, supported by a lifestyle and reflected in **psychographics**, can be found in a person's communications habits. The product volumes of both MRI and Simmons tell us about precisely that (Exhibit 4.5).

The purpose here is not to select media vehicles, but to enhance our understanding of consumers in the marketplace. The method would be to identify this consumer's three favorite magazines, and then to identify the picture these magazines create together. In this instance, the three magazines chosen on the basis of their gross number of users/readers might be *Better Homes and Gardens*, *Family Circle*, *Good Housekeeping*, and *Reader's Digest*. If we look for the magazines with high index numbers for heavy users, we note such books as *Colonial Homes*, *Field and Stream*, *1001 Homes Ideas*, and *Parents*.

What this combination of magazines tells the planner is that the consumer sees herself as a solid—almost stolid—suburban American homemaker with a practical, self-reliant, self-improving frame of mind. She doesn't perceive these virtues as either old-fashioned or square; rather she sees herself as actively alive and engaged. This self-image is further confirmed by her special interest in adult contemporary radio when the children are at school, and by her favorite television programs.

EXHIBIT 4.4 SMRB DRY CEREAL MARKET

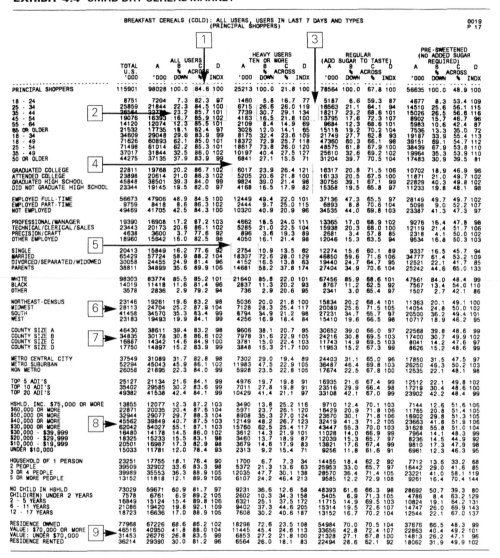

Source: Simmons Market Research Bureau, 1994

The planner might conclude from all of this that:

1. The power block of consumers in the cereal market are better-educated, married women with children, aged 25 to 54, living in the suburbs;

2. The motives energizing this consumer segment are shared by most buyers and users; and

EXHIBIT 4.5 BREAKFAST CEREALS (COLD)

		ALL				INDIVIDUAL PORTIONS/LAST 7 DAYS: HEAVY MORE THAN 8				MEDIUM 4 - 8				LIGHT LESS THAN 4			
BASE: FEMALE HOMEMAKERS	TOTAL U.S. '000	A '000	B % DOWN	C % ACROSS	D INDEX	A '000	B % DOWN	C % ACROSS	D INDEX	A '000	B % DOWN	C % ACROSS	D INDEX	A '000	B % DOWN	C % ACROSS	D INDEX
All Female Homemakers	86474	77418	100.0	89.5	100	21921	100.0	25.3	100	25871	100.0	29.9	100	29626	100.0	34.3	100
American Baby	3553	3417	4.4	96.2	107	1135	5.2	31.9	126	1171	4.5	33.0	110	1111	3.8	31.3	91
American Health	2482	2211	2.9	89.1	100	738	3.4	29.7	117	743	2.9	29.9	100	730	2.5	29.4	86
American Hunter	*453	*453	.6	-	-	*231	1.1	-	-	*95	.4	-	-	*128	.4	-	-
American Legion	1386	1255	1.6	90.5	101	*192	.9	13.9	55	*592	2.3	42.7	143	*471	1.6	34.0	99
American Rifleman	677	645	.8	95.3	106	*271	1.2	40.0	158	*198	.8	29.2	98	*177	.6	26.1	76
American Way	396	379	.5	95.7	107	*58	.3	14.6	58	*191	.7	48.2	161	*130	.4	32.8	96
American Way/SW Spirit (Gr)	703	635	.8	90.3	101	*102	.5	14.5	57	*291	1.1	41.4	138	*242	.8	34.4	100
Architectural Digest	2546	2298	3.0	90.3	101	495	2.3	19.4	77	834	3.2	32.8	109	969	3.3	38.1	111
Atlantic	432	359	.5	83.1	93	*111	.5	25.7	101	*168	.6	38.9	130	*80	.3	18.5	54
Audubon	778	659	.9	84.7	95	*197	.9	25.3	100	*166	.6	21.3	71	*295	1.0	37.9	111
Automobile	*396	*364	.5	-	-	*140	.6	-	-	*83	.3	-	-	*141	.5	-	-
Baby Talk	2267	2119	2.7	93.5	104	654	3.0	28.8	114	708	2.7	31.2	104	757	2.6	33.4	97
Barron's	*380	*342	.4	-	-	*95	.4	-	-	*91	.4	-	-	*156	.5	-	-
Bassmaster	*546	*487	.6	-	-	*232	1.1	-	-	*116	.4	-	-	*139	.5	-	-
Better Homes & Gardens	24697	22401	28.9	90.7	101	7029	32.1	28.5	112	7383	28.5	29.9	100	7989	27.0	32.3	94
BHG/LHJ Combo (Gr)	40421	36828	47.6	91.1	102	11437	52.2	28.3	112	12014	46.4	29.7	99	13377	45.2	33.1	97
Black Enterprise	1037	992	1.3	95.7	107	*316	1.4	30.5	120	*404	1.6	39.0	130	*272	.9	26.2	77
Bon Appetit	3633	3171	4.1	87.3	97	896	4.1	24.7	97	1154	4.5	31.8	106	1121	3.8	30.9	90
Bridal Guide	2055	1959	2.5	95.3	106	*442	2.0	21.5	85	687	2.7	33.4	112	830	2.8	40.4	118
Bride's	2144	2014	2.6	93.9	105	*650	3.0	30.3	120	614	2.4	28.6	96	750	2.5	35.0	102
Business Week	1633	1454	1.9	89.0	99	*292	1.3	17.9	71	541	2.1	33.1	111	622	2.1	38.1	111
Byte	*500	*484	.6	-	-	*143	.7	-	-	*156	.6	-	-	*185	.6	-	-
Cable Guide/Total TV (Gr)	6049	5542	7.2	91.6	102	1491	6.8	24.6	97	1916	7.4	31.7	106	2135	7.2	35.3	103
Car and Driver	534	502	.6	94.0	105	*240	1.1	44.9	177	*116	.4	21.7	73	*145	.5	27.2	79
Car Craft	*315	*289	.4	-	-	*73	.3	-	-	*140	.5	-	-	*76	.3	-	-
Colonial Homes	1877	1720	2.2	91.6	102	547	2.5	29.1	115	548	2.1	29.2	98	624	2.1	33.2	97
Compute	*380	*380	.5	-	-	*107	.5	-	-	*102	.4	-	-	*171	.6	-	-
Conde Nast Select (Gr)	38775	34362	44.4	88.6	99	9299	42.4	24.0	95	11857	45.8	30.6	102	13204	44.6	34.1	99
Conde Nast Traveler	1347	1148	1.5	85.2	95	*242	1.1	18.0	71	*404	1.6	30.0	100	502	1.7	37.3	109
Consumers Digest	2888	2733	3.5	94.6	106	738	3.4	25.6	101	910	3.5	31.5	105	1086	3.7	37.6	110
Cooking Light	3269	2935	3.8	89.8	100	826	3.8	25.3	100	992	3.8	30.3	101	1117	3.8	34.2	100
Cosmopolitan	10366	9220	11.9	88.9	99	2217	10.1	21.4	84	3272	12.6	31.6	106	3731	12.6	36.0	105
Country America	2090	1957	2.5	93.6	105	674	3.1	32.2	127	662	2.6	31.7	106	622	2.1	29.8	87
Country Home	6058	5575	7.2	92.0	103	1883	8.6	31.1	123	1709	6.6	28.2	94	1982	6.7	32.7	95
Country Living	8983	8342	10.8	92.9	104	2693	12.3	30.0	118	2814	10.9	31.3	105	2835	9.6	31.6	92
Country Music	3419	3090	4.0	90.4	101	923	4.2	27.0	106	900	3.5	26.3	88	1267	4.3	37.1	108
Delta's SKY Magazine	549	478	.6	87.1	97	*81	.4	14.8	58	*173	.7	31.5	105	*224	.8	40.8	119
Discover	2057	1818	2.3	88.4	99	724	3.3	35.2	139	479	1.9	23.3	78	616	2.1	29.9	87
Disney Channel Magazine	5349	5035	6.5	94.1	105	1740	7.9	32.5	128	1580	6.1	29.5	99	1715	5.8	32.1	94
Easyriders	*385	*382	.5	-	-	*139	.6	-	-	*139	.5	-	-	*104	.4	-	-
Eating Well	1470	1244	1.6	84.6	95	*370	1.7	25.2	99	375	1.4	25.5	85	498	1.7	33.9	99
Ebony	5249	4584	5.9	87.3	98	1535	7.0	29.2	115	1517	5.9	28.9	97	1531	5.2	29.2	85
Elle	2469	2062	2.7	83.5	93	561	2.6	22.7	90	658	2.5	26.7	89	843	2.8	34.1	100
Endless Vacation	773	702	.9	90.8	101	*241	1.1	31.2	123	*159	.6	20.6	69	*302	1.0	39.1	114
Entertainment Weekly	2882	2669	3.4	92.6	103	762	3.5	26.4	104	978	3.8	33.9	113	930	3.1	32.3	94
Entrepreneur	1069	994	1.3	93.0	104	*309	1.4	28.9	114	*321	1.2	30.0	100	*364	1.2	34.1	99
Esquire	981	902	1.2	91.9	103	*287	1.3	29.3	115	*305	1.2	31.1	104	*310	1.0	31.6	92
Essence	3327	2981	3.9	89.6	100	893	4.1	26.8	106	1025	4.0	30.8	103	1063	3.6	32.0	93
Family Circle	21931	20133	26.0	91.8	103	6491	29.6	29.6	117	6349	24.5	28.9	97	7294	24.6	33.3	97
Family Circle/McCall's (Gr)	36651	33493	43.3	91.4	102	10641	48.5	29.0	115	10877	42.0	29.7	99	11976	40.4	32.7	95
Family Handyman	1138	1085	1.4	95.3	106	*398	1.8	35.0	138	*378	1.5	33.2	111	*309	1.0	27.2	79
Field & Stream	2660	2526	3.3	95.0	106	1034	4.7	38.9	153	837	3.2	31.5	105	655	2.2	24.6	72
Field & Strm/Outdr Life (Gr)	3983	3773	4.9	94.7	106	1564	7.1	39.3	155	1236	4.8	31.0	104	973	3.3	24.4	71
First For Women	4183	3922	5.1	93.8	105	1144	5.2	27.3	108	1320	5.1	31.6	105	1458	4.9	34.9	102
Flower & Garden	3146	2913	3.8	92.6	103	756	3.4	24.0	95	933	3.6	29.7	99	1224	4.1	38.9	114
Flower & Grdn/Workbench (Gr)	4291	4039	5.2	94.1	105	1099	5.0	25.6	101	1330	5.1	31.0	104	1609	5.4	37.5	109
Food & Wine	1943	1780	2.3	91.6	102	*492	2.2	25.3	100	546	2.1	28.1	94	742	2.5	38.2	111
Forbes	1180	1056	1.4	89.5	100	*205	.9	17.4	69	450	1.7	38.1	127	401	1.4	34.0	99
Fortune	1438	1287	1.7	89.5	100	*234	1.1	16.3	64	*449	1.7	31.2	104	605	2.0	42.1	123
4 Wheel & Off Road	*378	*342	.4	-	-	*138	.6	-	-	*32	.1	-	-	*172	.6	-	-
Four Wheeler	*242	*239	.3	-	-	*105	.5	-	-	*41	.2	-	-	*92	.3	-	-
FW/Financial World	*187	*159	.2	-	-	*28	.1	-	-	*84	.3	-	-	*47	.2	-	-
Glamour	7833	7075	9.1	90.3	101	1963	9.0	25.1	99	2384	9.2	30.4	102	2728	9.2	34.8	102
Golf Digest	1031	995	1.3	96.5	108	*278	1.3	27.0	106	*385	1.5	37.3	125	*332	1.1	32.2	94
Golf Digest/Tennis (Gr)	1508	1420	1.8	94.2	105	*398	1.8	26.4	104	503	1.9	33.4	111	518	1.7	34.4	100
Golf Magazine	961	824	1.1	85.7	96	*298	1.4	31.0	122	*249	1.0	25.9	87	*277	.9	28.8	84
Good Housekeeping	22169	20424	26.4	92.1	103	6287	28.7	28.4	112	6576	25.4	29.7	99	7562	25.5	34.1	100
Gourmet	2761	2411	3.1	87.3	98	552	2.5	20.0	79	924	3.6	33.5	112	935	3.2	33.9	99
GQ (Gentlemen's Quarterly)	1424	1321	1.7	92.8	104	*333	1.5	23.4	92	*496	1.9	34.8	116	493	1.7	34.6	101
Guns & Ammo	*528	*506	.7	-	-	*175	.8	-	-	*185	.7	-	-	*146	.5	-	-
Hachette Magazine Ntwk (Gr)	31060	28389	36.7	91.4	102	9032	41.2	29.1	115	9112	35.2	29.3	98	10245	34.6	33.0	96
Hachette Men's Package (Gr)	3574	3314	4.3	92.7	104	1215	5.5	34.0	134	1019	3.9	28.5	95	1079	3.6	30.2	88
Harper's Bazaar	2450	2171	2.8	88.6	99	*524	2.4	21.4	84	606	2.3	24.7	83	1041	3.5	42.5	124
Health	2693	2349	3.0	87.2	97	*593	2.7	22.0	87	783	3.0	29.1	97	973	3.3	36.1	105
Hearst Combo Power (Gr)	32872	30322	39.2	92.2	103	9930	45.3	30.2	119	9747	37.7	29.7	99	10646	35.9	32.4	95
Hearst Homes (Gr)	19359	17770	23.0	91.8	103	5395	24.6	27.9	110	6012	23.2	31.1	104	6361	21.5	32.9	96
Home	2737	2533	3.3	92.5	103	767	3.5	28.0	111	818	3.2	29.9	100	949	3.2	34.7	101
Home Mechanix	*410	*355	.5	-	-	*104	.5	-	-	*159	.6	-	-	*92	.3	-	-
Hot Rod	604	*551	.7	91.2	102	*195	.9	32.3	127	*164	.6	27.2	91	*191	.6	31.6	92
House Beautiful	5644	5131	6.6	90.9	102	1403	6.4	24.9	98	1766	6.8	31.3	105	1962	6.6	34.8	101
Hunting	*490	*458	.6	-	-	*177	.8	-	-	*201	.8	-	-	*80	.3	-	-
Inc.	872	823	1.1	94.4	105	*207	.9	23.7	94	*194	.7	22.2	74	*421	1.4	48.3	141
Inside Sports	*560	*491	.6	-	-	*142	.6	-	-	*163	.6	-	-	*186	.6	-	-
Jet	3688	3347	4.3	90.8	101	1137	5.2	30.8	122	1168	4.5	31.7	106	1042	3.5	28.3	82
Kiplinger's Personal Finance	1104	1000	1.3	90.6	101	*362	1.7	32.8	129	*288	1.1	26.1	87	*350	1.2	31.7	93
Ladies' Home Journal	15724	14427	18.6	91.8	102	4408	20.1	28.0	111	4631	17.9	29.5	98	5388	18.2	34.3	100
Life	8062	7339	9.5	91.0	102	2514	11.5	31.2	123	2496	9.6	31.0	103	2330	7.9	28.9	84
Mademoiselle	3792	3356	4.3	88.5	99	919	4.2	24.2	96	1187	4.6	31.3	105	1249	4.2	32.9	96
Martha Stewart Living	1613	1466	1.9	90.9	102	411	1.9	25.5	101	623	2.4	38.6	129	431	1.5	26.7	78
McCall's	14720	13360	17.3	90.8	101	4150	18.9	28.2	111	4528	17.5	30.8	103	4682	15.8	31.8	93
Men's Fitness	*246	*244	.3	-	-	*108	.5	-	-	*33	.1	-	-	*103	.3	-	-
Men's Health	*517	*504	.7	-	-	*166	.8	-	-	*176	.7	-	-	*162	.5	-	-
Metropolitan Home	1778	1551	2.0	87.2	97	414	1.9	23.3	92	560	2.2	31.5	105	577	1.9	32.5	95
Metro-Puck Comics Network	21492	19501	25.2	90.7	101	5671	25.9	26.4	104	6500	25.1	30.2	101	7330	24.7	34.1	100
Midwest Living	1600	1559	2.0	97.4	109	*540	2.5	33.8	133	523	2.0	32.7	109	496	1.7	31.0	90
Mirabella	1872	1634	2.1	87.3	97	*440	2.0	23.5	93	471	1.8	25.2	84	723	2.4	38.6	113
Modern Bride	2757	2482	3.2	90.0	101	705	3.2	25.6	101	862	3.3	31.3	105	915	3.1	33.2	97

EXHIBIT 4.5 BREAKFAST CEREALS (COLD) CONT.

		ALL				INDIVIDUAL PORTIONS/LAST 7 DAYS: HEAVY MORE THAN 8				MEDIUM 4 - 8				LIGHT LESS THAN 4			
BASE: FEMALE HOMEMAKERS	TOTAL U.S. '000	A '000	B % DOWN	C % ACROSS	D INDEX	A '000	B % DOWN	C % ACROSS	D INDEX	A '000	B % DOWN	C % ACROSS	D INDEX	A '000	B % DOWN	C % ACROSS	D INDEX
All Female Homemakers	86474	77418	100.0	89.5	100	21921	100.0	25.3	100	25871	100.0	29.9	100	29626	100.0	34.3	100
Money	3925	3448	4.5	87.8	98	1004	4.6	25.6	101	1184	4.6	30.2	101	1259	4.2	32.1	94
Motor Trend	*389	*328	.4	-	-	*146	.7	-	-	*115	.4	-	-	*66	.2	-	-
Muscle & Fitness	1346	1198	1.5	89.0	99	*360	1.6	26.7	106	*305	1.2	22.7	76	533	1.8	39.6	116
National Enquirer	11258	10318	13.3	91.7	102	2726	12.4	24.2	96	3600	13.9	32.0	107	3992	13.5	35.5	104
National Geographic	13284	12160	15.7	91.5	102	4262	19.4	32.1	127	3849	14.9	29.0	97	4048	13.7	30.5	89
National Geographic Traveler	1654	1461	1.9	88.3	99	*390	1.8	23.6	93	518	2.0	31.3	105	553	1.9	33.4	98
Natural History	718	558	.7	77.7	87	*155	.7	21.6	85	*173	.7	24.1	81	*229	.8	31.9	93
Newsweek	8677	8011	10.3	92.3	103	2054	9.4	23.7	93	2855	11.0	32.9	110	3103	10.5	35.8	104
New Woman	2942	2614	3.4	88.9	99	666	3.0	22.6	89	838	3.2	28.5	95	1109	3.7	37.7	110
New York Magazine	833	647	.8	77.7	87	*53	.2	6.4	25	*196	.8	23.5	79	397	1.3	47.7	139
New York Times (Daily)	1068	872	1.1	81.6	91	*159	.7	14.9	59	*292	1.1	27.3	91	421	1.4	39.4	115
New York Times Magazine	1903	1620	2.1	85.1	95	387	1.8	20.3	80	422	1.6	22.2	74	812	2.7	42.7	125
The New Yorker	1609	1383	1.8	86.0	96	*242	1.1	15.0	59	444	1.7	27.6	92	696	2.3	43.3	126
North American Fisherman	*528	*528	.7	-	-	*224	1.0	-	-	*102	.4	-	-	*202	.7	-	-
North American Hunter	*406	*390	.5	-	-	*149	.7	-	-	*122	.5	-	-	*119	.4	-	-
Omni	1152	973	1.3	84.5	94	*239	1.1	20.7	82	*302	1.2	26.2	88	433	1.5	37.6	110
Organic Gardening	1956	1723	2.2	88.1	98	519	2.4	26.5	105	639	2.5	32.7	109	*565	1.9	28.9	84
Outdoor Life	1323	1247	1.6	94.3	105	*530	2.4	40.1	158	*399	1.5	30.2	101	*318	1.1	24.0	70
Outside	477	451	.6	94.5	106	*164	.7	34.4	136	*178	.7	37.3	125	*109	.4	22.9	67
Parade	36608	33151	42.8	90.6	101	9780	44.6	26.7	105	11312	43.7	30.9	103	12059	40.7	32.9	96
Parenting	4168	3844	5.0	92.2	103	1326	6.0	31.8	125	1181	4.6	28.3	95	1337	4.5	32.1	94
Parents' Magazine	8415	8039	10.4	95.5	107	2885	13.2	34.3	135	2591	10.0	30.8	103	2563	8.7	30.5	89
PC Computing	1313	1254	1.6	95.5	107	*300	1.4	22.8	90	*351	1.4	26.7	89	603	2.0	45.9	134
PC Magazine	1586	1478	1.9	93.2	104	*384	1.8	24.2	96	408	1.6	25.7	86	685	2.3	43.2	126
PC World	1574	1468	1.9	93.3	104	*453	2.1	28.8	114	*371	1.4	23.6	79	645	2.2	41.0	120
Penthouse	519	*439	.6	84.6	94	*161	.7	31.0	122	*128	.5	24.7	82	*150	.5	28.9	84
Penton Executive Netwk (Gr)	3374	3217	4.2	95.3	107	940	4.3	27.9	110	1096	4.2	32.5	109	1184	4.0	35.1	102
People	19918	17698	22.9	88.9	99	5201	23.7	26.1	103	5944	23.0	29.8	100	6552	22.1	32.9	96
Petersen Magazine Netwk (Gr)	5068	4721	6.1	93.2	104	1667	7.6	32.9	130	1538	5.9	30.3	101	1515	5.1	29.9	87
Playboy	1647	1519	2.0	92.2	103	*481	2.2	29.2	115	*470	1.8	28.5	95	567	1.9	34.4	100
Popular Hot Rodding	*218	*218	.3	-	-	*104	.5	-	-	*47	.2	-	-	*67	.2	-	-
Popular Mechanics	1318	1164	1.5	88.3	99	*472	2.2	35.8	141	*402	1.6	30.5	102	*290	1.0	22.0	64
Popular Science	1089	978	1.3	89.8	100	*357	1.6	32.8	129	*310	1.2	28.5	95	*311	1.0	28.6	83
Premiere	699	649	.8	92.8	104	*240	1.1	34.3	135	*142	.5	20.3	68	*266	.9	38.1	111
Prevention	7302	6503	8.4	89.1	99	2110	9.6	28.9	114	2372	9.2	32.5	109	2020	6.8	27.7	81
Reader's Digest	27007	24327	31.4	90.1	101	7243	33.0	26.8	106	8298	32.1	30.7	103	8785	29.7	32.5	95
Redbook	10703	9898	12.8	92.5	103	3643	16.6	34.0	134	3171	12.3	29.6	99	3084	10.4	28.8	84
Road & Track	*402	*394	.5	-	-	*203	.9	-	-	*113	.4	-	-	*78	.3	-	-
Rodale Active Network (Gr)	1763	1544	2.0	87.6	98	*348	1.6	19.7	78	643	2.5	36.5	122	554	1.9	31.4	92
Rolling Stone	2483	2144	2.8	86.3	96	*410	1.9	16.5	65	824	3.2	33.2	111	909	3.1	36.6	107
Runner's World	656	540	.7	82.3	92	*113	.5	17.2	68	*197	.8	30.0	100	*230	.8	35.1	102
Sassy	1166	1088	1.4	93.3	104	*299	1.4	25.6	101	*393	1.5	33.7	113	*396	1.3	34.0	99
Saturday Evening Post	2352	2201	2.8	93.6	105	634	2.9	27.0	106	726	2.8	30.9	103	840	2.8	35.7	104
Scientific American	629	557	.7	88.6	99	*268	1.2	42.6	168	*156	.6	24.8	83	*133	.4	21.1	62
Self	3238	2843	3.7	87.8	98	634	2.9	19.6	77	1008	3.9	31.1	104	1201	4.1	37.1	108
Sesame Street Magazine	4570	4301	5.6	94.1	105	1675	7.6	36.7	145	1387	5.4	30.4	101	1239	4.2	27.1	79
Seventeen	4020	3721	4.8	92.6	103	1161	5.3	28.9	114	1030	4.0	25.6	86	1531	5.2	38.1	111
Shape	1936	1668	2.2	86.2	96	457	2.1	23.6	93	468	1.8	24.2	81	743	2.5	38.4	112
Ski	591	493	.6	83.4	93	*146	.7	24.7	97	*190	.7	32.1	107	*158	.5	26.7	78
Skiing	547	460	.6	84.1	94	*137	.6	25.0	99	*174	.7	31.8	106	*149	.5	27.2	80
Ski/Skiing (Gr)	1138	953	1.2	83.7	94	*283	1.3	24.9	98	364	1.4	32.0	107	*307	1.0	27.0	79
Smithsonian	3883	3391	4.4	87.3	98	1044	4.8	26.9	106	1146	4.4	29.5	99	1201	4.1	30.9	90
Soap Opera Digest	6077	5652	7.3	93.0	104	1381	6.3	22.7	90	2127	8.2	35.0	117	2144	7.2	35.3	103
Soap Opera Weekly	4185	3891	5.0	93.0	104	1219	5.6	29.1	115	1246	4.8	29.8	100	1426	4.8	34.1	99
Southern Living	8677	7955	10.3	91.7	102	2352	10.7	27.1	107	2785	10.8	32.1	107	2818	9.5	32.5	95
Southern Outdoors	*591	*520	.7	-	-	*242	1.1	-	-	*140	.5	-	-	*139	.5	-	-
Spin	*409	*385	.5	-	-	*114	.5	-	-	*118	.5	-	-	*154	.5	-	-
Sport	546	*495	.6	90.7	101	*112	.5	20.5	81	*214	.8	39.2	131	*170	.6	31.1	91
The Sporting News	*368	*354	.5	-	-	*60	.3	-	-	*118	.5	-	-	*176	.6	-	-
Sports Afield	*678	*663	.9	-	-	*332	1.5	-	-	*149	.6	-	-	*182	.6	-	-
Sports Illustrated	4717	4319	5.6	91.6	102	1407	6.4	29.8	118	1422	5.5	30.1	101	1489	5.0	31.6	92
Star	6037	5444	7.0	90.2	101	1374	6.3	22.8	90	1839	7.1	30.5	102	2231	7.5	37.0	108
Success	*543	*514	.7	-	-	*129	.6	-	-	*129	.5	-	-	*257	.9	-	-
Sunday Mag/Net	15009	13127	17.0	87.5	98	3820	17.4	25.5	100	4391	17.0	29.3	98	4916	16.6	32.8	96
Sunset	3346	3085	4.0	92.2	103	929	4.2	27.8	110	1227	4.7	36.7	123	928	3.1	27.7	81
Teen	1968	1894	2.4	96.2	107	640	2.9	32.5	128	713	2.8	36.2	121	541	1.8	27.5	80
Tennis	477	425	.5	89.1	100	*120	.5	25.2	99	*118	.5	24.7	83	*186	.6	39.0	114
Texas Monthly	1158	1029	1.3	88.9	99	*238	1.1	20.6	81	*431	1.7	37.2	124	*360	1.2	31.1	91
Time	10082	9057	11.7	89.8	100	2871	13.1	28.5	112	2893	11.2	28.7	96	3293	11.1	32.7	95
Times Mirror Mag. Netwk (Gr)	8193	7481	9.7	91.3	102	2748	12.5	33.5	132	2544	9.8	31.1	104	2191	7.4	26.7	78
Town & Country	2220	1967	2.5	88.6	99	480	2.2	21.6	85	628	2.4	28.3	95	859	2.9	38.7	113
Traditional Home	1632	1500	1.9	91.9	103	*431	2.0	26.4	104	407	1.6	24.9	83	662	2.2	40.6	118
Travel/Holiday	842	752	1.0	89.3	100	*142	.6	16.9	67	*315	1.2	37.4	125	*294	1.0	34.9	102
Travel & Leisure	2182	1941	2.5	89.0	99	*434	2.0	19.9	78	582	2.2	26.7	89	925	3.1	42.4	124
True Story	3335	3043	3.9	91.2	102	*751	3.4	22.5	89	1086	4.2	32.6	109	1206	4.1	36.2	106
TV Guide	22218	19881	25.7	89.5	100	5868	26.8	26.4	104	6691	25.9	30.1	101	7323	24.7	33.0	96
USAir	905	777	1.0	85.9	96	*149	.7	16.5	65	*322	1.2	35.6	119	*305	1.0	33.7	98
U.S. News & World Report	4332	4033	5.2	93.1	104	1253	5.7	28.9	114	1076	4.2	24.8	83	1704	5.8	39.3	115
Us	2645	2458	3.2	92.9	104	642	2.9	24.3	96	793	3.1	30.0	100	1023	3.5	38.7	113
USA Today	1483	1374	1.8	92.7	103	*447	2.0	30.1	119	*487	1.9	32.8	110	440	1.5	29.7	87
USA Today Baseball Weekly	*151	*144	.2	-	-	*49	.2	-	-	*55	.2	-	-	*40	.1	-	-
USA Weekend	16404	14866	19.2	90.6	101	4388	20.0	26.7	106	5021	19.4	30.6	102	5457	18.4	33.3	97
Vanity Fair	3080	2543	3.3	82.6	92	706	3.2	22.9	90	861	3.3	28.0	93	975	3.3	31.7	92
VFW Magazine	1032	952	1.2	92.2	103	*191	.9	18.5	73	*410	1.6	39.7	133	*351	1.2	34.0	99
Victoria	2855	2577	3.3	90.3	101	752	3.4	26.3	104	884	3.4	31.0	103	940	3.2	32.9	96
Vogue	6977	6182	8.0	88.6	99	1909	8.7	27.4	108	1991	7.7	28.5	95	2281	7.7	32.7	95
Walking Magazine	1221	1040	1.3	85.2	95	*236	1.1	19.3	76	*407	1.6	33.3	111	*397	1.3	32.5	95
Wall Street Journal	1335	1221	1.6	91.5	102	*272	1.2	20.4	80	*401	1.5	30.0	100	547	1.8	41.0	120
Weight Watchers	3702	3333	4.3	90.0	101	1038	4.7	28.0	111	1260	4.9	34.0	114	1035	3.5	28.0	82
Woman's Day	20502	18929	24.5	92.3	103	6075	27.7	29.6	117	6057	23.4	29.5	99	6797	22.9	33.2	97
Woman's World	4959	4528	5.8	91.3	102	1536	7.0	31.0	122	1312	5.1	26.5	88	1680	5.7	33.9	99
Workbasket	2120	1846	2.4	87.1	97	*537	2.4	25.3	100	*528	2.0	24.9	83	781	2.6	36.8	108
Workbench	1145	1126	1.5	98.3	110	*343	1.6	30.0	118	*397	1.5	34.7	116	*385	1.3	33.6	98
Working Mother	2553	2394	3.1	93.8	105	860	3.9	33.7	133	737	2.8	28.9	96	797	2.7	31.2	91
Working Woman	2823	2419	3.1	85.7	96	825	3.8	29.2	115	872	3.4	30.9	103	722	2.4	25.6	75
WWF Magazine	*593	*521	.7	-	-	*56	.3	-	-	*201	.8	-	-	*264	.9	-	-
Yankee	1434	1267	1.6	88.4	99	*534	2.4	37.2	147	370	1.4	25.8	86	363	1.2	25.3	74
YM	1281	1245	1.6	97.2	109	*341	1.6	26.6	105	*388	1.5	30.3	101	*515	1.7	40.2	117

Source: Simmons Market Research Bureau, 1994

3. These consumers see themselves as sharing those cultural values most often described as Middle American, or Norman Rockwell's America, regardless of where they live. They also see themselves as self-reliant people who get things done.

BRANDS AND CONSUMERS

At this point in the imaginative analytic process, the planner has come to understand the character and style of the consumer energy that drives the marketplace. The planner is also capable of describing the prototypical consumer in both demographic and psychographic terms. What is missing is information on consumers of individual brands and consumption. Both Simmons and MRI provide information (Exhibits 4.6 and 4.7) which enables the planner to examine the relationship between product users and brand users, and between users of our brand and users of other brands in the category.

Even a quick examination of the numbers would reveal that Miller Lite drinkers are in many ways prototypical of the general market (Exhibit 4.7) but that the weakness in their market is among younger and more frequent users. Bud Light, on the other hand, exhibits a strong loyalty among this segment. Through an examination of this kind of data, especially when it is supported by client-sponsored attitude and usage studies, the planner can describe the interaction between product usage and brand usage. Ideally, the planner would be able to describe the demographics and psychographics of:

1. Those who use your brand only—**sole users**;
2. Those who mostly use your brand but also use other brands—**primary users**;
3. Those who only occasionally use your brand—**secondary users**;
4. Those who use the product but not your brand—**nonusers**.

Even when the planner lacks sufficient information to answer all of these questions definitively, the syndicated information generally available can elaborate on the dimensions of the consumer market. A study of the information in both Simmons and MRI can inform the planner about:

*What percentage of the population uses the product.

*What percentage uses your brand.

*How these percentages compare to competing brands.

*The demographic profile of the category and competing brands.

*The importance of heavy, medium, and light users.

*The relative importance of these categories to your brand's performance.

It takes imagination to combine these numbers into a profile of living consumers. If the planner also follows the disciplines of media imagination and seeks insights from these same consumers' media habits, the planner can contribute a psychographic profile to demographic dimensions of the market.

EXHIBIT 4.6 SMRB LIGHT DOMESTIC BEER CATEGORY

0149
P 14

REGULAR DOMESTIC BEER (IN CANS OR BOTTLES): ALL USERS AND KINDS (ADULTS)

0149
P 14

	TOTAL U.S. '000	ALL USERS				TOP THIRD USERS SEVEN OR MORE IN LAST 7 DAYS				KINDS: BOTTLED				CANNED			
		A '000	B DOWN	C % ACROSS	D INDX	A '000	B DOWN	C % ACROSS	D INDX	A '000	B DOWN	C % ACROSS	D INDX	A '000	B DOWN	C % ACROSS	D INDX
TOTAL ADULTS	187747	50632	100.0	27.0	100	12809	100.0	6.8	100	28995	100.0	15.4	100	33046	100.0	17.6	100
MALES	90070	33199	65.6	36.9	137	9546	74.5	10.6	155	18392	63.4	20.4	132	22473	68.0	25.0	142
FEMALES	97676	17433	34.4	17.8	86	3263	25.5	3.3	49	10604	36.6	10.9	70	10573	32.0	10.8	61
PRINCIPAL SHOPPERS	115901	26884	53.1	23.2	86	6502	50.8	5.6	82	15141	52.2	13.1	85	17057	51.6	14.7	84
18 - 24	23951	8525	16.8	35.8	132	2143	16.7	8.9	131	6065	20.9	25.3	164	5538	16.8	23.1	131
25 - 34	41492	14579	28.8	35.1	130	4176	32.6	10.1	148	9209	31.8	22.2	144	9232	27.9	22.2	126
35 - 44	40678	11830	23.4	29.1	108	2904	22.7	7.1	105	6986	24.1	17.2	111	7820	23.7	19.2	109
45 - 54	29045	6933	13.7	23.9	89	1684	13.1	5.8	85	3437	11.9	11.8	77	4447	13.5	15.3	87
55 - 64	21263	4045	8.0	19.0	71	917	7.2	4.3	63	1701	5.9	8.0	52	2773	8.4	13.0	74
65 OR OLDER	31318	4721	9.3	15.1	56	986	7.7	3.1	46	1598	5.5	5.1	33	3237	9.8	10.3	59
18 - 34	65443	23104	45.6	35.3	131	6319	49.3	9.7	142	15274	52.7	23.3	151	14769	44.7	22.6	128
18 - 49	122143	39121	77.3	32.0	119	10230	79.9	8.4	123	24304	83.8	19.9	129	25220	76.3	20.6	117
25 - 54	111215	33341	65.8	30.0	111	8764	68.4	7.9	115	19632	67.7	17.7	114	21498	65.1	19.3	110
35 - 49	56701	16017	31.6	28.2	105	3910	30.5	6.9	101	9030	31.1	15.9	103	10451	31.6	18.4	105
50 OR OLDER	65603	11511	22.7	17.5	65	2580	20.1	3.9	58	4692	16.2	7.2	46	7826	23.7	11.9	68
GRADUATED COLLEGE	37353	11434	22.6	30.6	114	1637	12.8	4.4	64	7406	25.5	19.8	128	7256	22.0	19.4	110
ATTENDED COLLEGE	39301	10985	21.7	28.0	104	2384	18.6	6.1	89	6784	23.4	17.3	112	7321	22.2	18.6	106
GRADUATED HIGH SCHOOL	73139	19755	39.0	27.0	100	6024	47.0	8.2	121	10392	35.8	14.2	92	12839	38.9	17.6	100
DID NOT GRADUATE HIGH SCHOOL	37954	8458	16.7	22.3	83	2765	21.6	7.3	107	4414	15.2	11.6	75	5630	17.0	14.8	84

Source: Simmons Market Research Bureau, 1994

EXHIBIT 4.7 SMRB LIGHT DOMESTIC BEER BRANDS

0143
P 14

LIGHT/LOW CALORIE DOMESTIC BEER (IN CANS OR BOTTLES): BRANDS (ADULTS)

0143
P 14

	TOTAL U.S. '000	BUD LIGHT				COORS LIGHT				MILLER GENUINE DRAFT LIGHT				MILLER LITE			
		A '000	B DOWN	C % ACROSS	D INDX	A '000	B DOWN	C % ACROSS	D INDX	A '000	B DOWN	C % ACROSS	D INDX	A '000	B DOWN	C % ACROSS	D INDX
TOTAL ADULTS	187747	17934	100.0	9.6	100	11155	100.0	5.9	100	6750	100.0	3.6	100	10656	100.0	5.7	100
MALES	90070	9390	52.4	10.4	109	6315	56.6	7.0	118	4015	59.5	4.5	124	5482	51.4	6.1	107
FEMALES	97676	8544	47.6	8.7	92	4840	43.4	5.0	83	2735	40.5	2.8	78	5174	48.6	5.3	93
PRINCIPAL SHOPPERS	115901	9933	55.4	8.6	90	5971	53.5	5.2	87	3669	54.4	3.2	88	6131	57.5	5.3	93
18 - 24	23951	3415	19.0	14.3	149	2493	22.3	10.4	175	1200	17.8	5.0	139	1974	18.5	8.2	145
25 - 34	41492	5228	29.2	12.6	132	3209	28.8	7.7	130	2280	33.8	5.5	153	2999	28.1	7.2	127
35 - 44	40678	4156	23.2	10.2	107	2248	20.2	5.5	93	1392	20.6	3.4	95	2870	26.9	7.1	124
45 - 54	29045	2472	13.8	8.5	89	1759	15.8	6.1	102	911	13.5	3.1	87	1522	14.3	5.2	92
55 - 64	21263	1390	7.8	6.5	68	686	6.1	3.2	54	485	7.2	2.3	63	683	6.4	3.2	57
65 OR OLDER	31318	1272	7.1	4.1	43	760	6.8	2.4	41	482	7.1	1.5	43	609	5.7	1.9	34
18 - 34	65443	8643	48.2	13.2	138	5702	51.1	8.7	147	3480	51.6	5.3	148	4972	46.7	7.6	134
18 - 49	122143	14030	78.2	11.5	120	8976	80.5	7.3	124	5441	80.6	4.5	124	8610	80.8	7.0	124
25 - 54	111215	11856	66.1	10.7	112	7216	64.7	6.5	109	4584	67.9	4.1	115	7391	69.4	6.6	117
35 - 49	56701	5387	30.0	9.5	99	3274	29.3	5.8	97	1961	29.1	3.5	96	3638	34.1	6.4	113
50 OR OLDER	65603	3904	21.8	6.0	62	2180	19.5	3.3	56	1309	19.4	2.0	55	2046	19.2	3.1	55
GRADUATED COLLEGE	37353	4025	22.4	10.8	113	3080	27.6	8.2	139	1625	24.1	4.4	121	3132	29.4	8.4	148
ATTENDED COLLEGE	39301	3800	21.2	9.7	101	2827	25.3	7.2	121	1525	22.6	3.9	108	2810	26.4	7.1	126
GRADUATED HIGH SCHOOL	73139	7438	41.5	10.2	106	4269	38.3	5.8	98	2526	37.4	3.5	96	3651	34.3	5.0	88
DID NOT GRADUATE HIGH SCHOOL	37954	2672	14.9	7.0	74	981	8.8	2.6	43	1074	15.9	2.8	79	1063	10.0	2.8	49

Source: Simmons Market Research Bureau, 1994

SELF TEST

1. Study the category and brand data on the analgesic market in either SMRB or MRI.

2. Draw a profile of the characteristic consumer based on the demographic characteristics of consumers, and their psychographics derived from their predominant media habits.

3. How are heavy users distinguished both demographically and psychographically?

4. What are the key demographic and psychographic distinctions between acetaminophen (Tylenol) and ibuprofen (Advil, Nuprin) users?

SIMMONS' CREDIBILITY, SURVIVAL AT STAKE

Simmons Market Research Bureau's stunning decision to abandon its trademark magazine readership methodology, coming in the midst of a controversy over the accuracy of its data, puts its credibility and survival squarely on the line.

"Any business decision as radical as this, there is a risk," concedes Tim Bowles, chief executive of MRB Group, the London-based parent of Simmons.

The controversy was spawned by a leaked committee report of the Magazine Publishers of America. Simmons' initial reaction was to attack the MPA, claiming its data was sound. But two weeks ago the company told clients it is abandoning the way it has conducted research for 30 years and adopting a method similar to rival Mediamark Research Inc. Simmons is dropping "through-the-book" methodology, which consists of displaying stripped-down magazines to interviewees, and adopting the "recent reading" procedure employed by MRI.

Simmons also told its clients in recent weeks that president and chief executive officer Ellen Cohen was being replaced by Rebecca McPheters of Gruner & Jahr. The company says Cohen actually resigned last November, but that Bowles had convinced her to stay on until last week.

The methodology switch has generated considerable anger at the beleaguered Simmons, even from supporters who gave the MPA report little credence when it became public.

"We are extremely disappointed Simmons has retrenched the through-the-book technology without sitting down with their clients, like us and other agencies, and detailing the problems they have been having," says Steven Farella, executive vice president of media services at Jordan, McGrath, Case & Taylor.

"As far as we are concerned, this move is a risk," adds Farella. "We are not sure their recent-reading technique is going to work." Farella's comments are significant because JMC&T, one of few agencies that is a Simmons-only shop, initially assailed the MPA when its report was leaked to Inside Media.

Some of Simmons' magazine clients are troubled as well. "I'm disappointed," says Jane Friedenthal, director of corporate advertising research at Time Inc., Simmons' biggest magazine client. "It looks like a move of expediency. I understand that times have changed, but unfortunately, recent reading isn't the only solution."

Simmons claims that it was working on the change before the MPA report was publicized, and that the two are unrelated, but not everyone buys this. "Now I am convinced something is screwed up," says one ad agency research executive. "I think the MPA thing precipitated this. I'm more suspicious than ever."

Bowles insists that the MPA study "had absolutely nothing to do [with dropping through-the-book] whatsoever. We started planning this two years ago. We started the pilot work in the spring of this year. We could not have designed and got that into the field as any kind of response to the MPA."

Some agency researchers who attended briefings on the new Simmons plan in recent weeks question Bowles' assertion. "They call this huge meeting to announce to the industry that they are changing methodologies, and they have absolutely no answers to any questions," says one exasperated agency executive. "They have done no testing. They had no data to show us."

The sea change at Simmons comes just before a scheduled Sept. 23 meeting with the American Association of Advertising Agencies to address questions raised by the MPA report. What remains to be seen is whether the Four A's will press Simmons to explain the issues raised by the MPA.

Simmons will now offer clients two surveys instead of one, which has contained both magazine readership and product-usage data. The magazine readership analysis portion of the new service, called the Survey of American Readership (SAR), will provide readership and demographic information derived from a trimmed-down, 25-minute interview.

Previous Simmons interviews took at least an hour. As the company now admits, those sessions were too long and were fraught with the potential for error. "We believe many of the problems of interviewer and respondent burden are removed, increasing our chances to getting at some key reader groups," says Bowles.

The product and media portion of the new survey is called the New Survey of Media and Markets. It will be calculated from a separate sample conducted by telephone, followed by a mail questionnaire. Instead of releasing data once a year, Simmons will publish numbers for both surveys on a quarterly basis, with the first release scheduled for May 1995. In addition, through a mathematical formula that is similar to what is done in the U.K., Simmons will fuse the two sample bases, SAR and SMM, so that clients can link product and magazine information.

Because it hasn't tested the new services fully, Simmons runs the risk of pushing its strongest supporters into the MRI camp.

"If people stayed with Simmons because of through-the-book, and now they have to switch to the thing they don't like, why would they switch to the *untested* thing they don't like?" asks Joanne Burke, senior vice president and worldwide media research director at Foote Cone Belding.

"The danger [for Simmons] is having to go out and sell a new service to every one of its clients," says one agency executive. "Even though you are differentiating the service from your competitor, it is essentially the same service."

Bowles disagrees, saying the two-survey approach has the potential to offer more than MRI. He adds that the surveys will be "extremely aggressively" priced.

Some executives wonder why Simmons didn't examine newer methods of magazine research, perhaps electronic, to move a step ahead of its competitors and position itself for the future. "They claim that have been doing this for two years, and the best they can come up with is recent reading?" says one executive. "I am just really fed up. They clearly put no thought into this." Bowles notes that the majority of the world uses recent reading and that Simmons wants to expand globally.

Not all reaction is negative. Says Taylor Gray, advertising research services director for Reader's Digest, "I'm excited. It's the first time there will be a pure readership study."

Some magazine research directors are waiting to see how ad agency research executives respond to the Simmons plan before they move. "What we do on the publishing side depends on what happens on the agency side," says Gray. "It's important they sell this in to the agencies. Then we will follow."

Simmons has its work cut out with agencies because it recently sold its 1994 data, which won't be compatible with the new surveys. This is a big problem for agencies that rely exclusively on Simmons.

"I told them I want a refund," says one irate ad agency executive. "They have sold me data that is now, by their own admission, obsolete."

As if all this weren't enough, from a computer standpoint, Simmons clients must grapple with how to gather and prepare the new data. Two key questions are how recent-reading data can be put in the same software format as through-the-book, and if it is in a different format, how the data will be accessed.

Source: *Inside Media*, September 21, 1994.

COMMUNICATIONS

Advertising through the media connects buyers and sellers. To understand any market thoroughly, a planner must understand who is communicating. Not only do we need to know the levels of media competition arrayed against our brand, but we also want to know what media strategies seem to be working, what advertising patterns (and, therefore, what assumptions) specific competitors are following, and where consumers discover the information they want in their buying decisions.

Investigative reporters often recommend that you "follow the money." It should come as no surprise, therefore, in an industry that spends billions of dollars each year and is composed of aggressive competitors on both the buying and selling sides of media, that many reporting services have evolved to follow the money. Consequently, there are several syndicated research sources for analyzing competitive activity available to the media planner.

Basically, there are two kinds of sources: The first reports advertising activity across media. This data enables the planner to describe the overall competitive communications environment of a market, and to analyze the general media strategies of specific competitors. The second group of reports provides data on specific vehicle purchases by advertisers in each medium for each of twelve months. Since both types of reports have been available for many years, it is also possible to track media strategies and tactics with marketplace changes from year to year.

The good news is that this kind of competitive data is readily available and that it is easy to read. There is little subtlety and no math involved in the reporting. The bad news is that you can't believe everything you read. Not every dollar is reported, and the dollars that are reported do not reflect the often large negotiated discounts enjoyed by major advertisers. Finally, misreads and typos can happen when the data entry person is confronted by a multiproduct or multibrand ad. Nevertheless, the data available is enormously useful both for understanding market activity and for tracking competitive activity.

Information Resources

The primary source of general media activity is the **Arbitron/BAR/LNA Multimedia Service**, which reports expenditures across ten media by most national advertisers. It is available in three volumes. One volume describes individual company expenditures and the brands within each company. A second volume provides an alphabetical listing of brands, their parent company, product category, expenditures, and media used. The third, and frequently most useful, volume lists media investments by category, by company within the category, and by brand (Exhibit 4.8). This volume provides an overview of activities in a product category. The category, however, can be rather broadly defined, for example: Coffee, Tea, Cocoa, and Derivatives. The first task is to identify the specific competitive framework, for instance, Instant Decaffeinated Coffee, and second, to extrapolate the information in order to create the narrower competitive picture the planner usually needs.

The resulting competitive picture is frequently all that is required in many media planning circumstances. Nevertheless, such an overview leaves out a great deal of information. For example, an overview does not tell you which magazines were purchased; it does not tell you which television programs, in what dayparts, in which markets, were purchased; it does not provide monthly, quarterly, or seasonal investments. In short, the overview leaves out much strategic and most tactical detail. This information is available from other sources.

LNA-PIB (Publishers Information Bureau) reports magazine expenditures on a monthly basis for companies, brands, and product classes. It can tell you, for example, the magazines in which Nestlé's Tasters Choice Instant Coffee advertised during the month of June, what size the advertisements were, and whether or not they were in full color.

Media Records reports advertising expenditures in newspapers in most major markets. It summarizes category investments, top 10 and top 50 brand expenditures in each category, and any brand spending more than $15,000. The data is reported on a monthly, quarterly, and year-to-date basis.

Broadcast Advertisers Report provides data on network television, radio, and cable. It reports dollar volume by parent company and brand, as well as the time of day, network, and program purchased. A. C. Nielsen's Brand Cumulative Audience supplements this information with tactical outcomes data. Barcume reports on spot television activity in seventy-five markets. The Radio Expenditure Report records spot radio advertising activity.

The net result of the availability of these and other reporting services is that a planner can identify annual expenditures for all competitors and analyze the strategies

EXHIBIT 4.8 LNA/MEDIAWATCH MULTI-MEDIA SERVICE

CLASS/BRAND $

January - September 1994

QUARTERLY AND YEAR-TO-DATE ADVERTISING DOLLARS (000)

CLASS/COMPANY/BRAND	CLASS CODE		10 MEDIA TOTAL	MAGAZINES	SUNDAY MAGAZINES	NEWSPAPERS	OUTDOOR	NETWORK TELEVISION	SPOT TELEVISION	SYNDICATED TELEVISION	CABLE TV NETWORKS	NETWORK RADIO	NATIONAL SPOT RADIO
F171 COFFEE, TEA, COCOA & DERIVATIVES --							*CONTINUED*						
NESTLE SA (CONTINUED)													
NESTLE QUIK	F171	Q1	2,498.9					1,108.2	248.5	710.4	431.8	--	--
		Q2	3,606.0					1,332.5	215.8	976.9	480.8	--	--
		Q3	2,415.0	131.7				1,235.9	58.3	601.8	387.3	--	--
		94 YTD	8,519.9	131.7				4,276.6	522.6	2,289.1	1,299.9	--	--
		93 YTD	2,372.5					842.1	107.0	1,002.3	421.1	--	--
TASTERS CHOICE INSTANT COFFEES	F171	Q1	8,899.6					6,584.0	96.6	1,566.7	652.3	--	--
		Q2	4,481.7					3,529.0	54.3	337.6	314.2	--	--
		Q3	2,803.3	246.6				2,641.6	4		156.8	--	--
		94 YTD	16,184.6	246.6				12,754.6	155.8	1,904.3	1,123.3	--	--
		93 YTD	9,651.0					8,915.3	4.0		731.7	--	--
TASTERS CHOICE INSTANT COFFEES-VIGNETTE	F171-8	94 YTD	10.5						10.5			--	--
		93 YTD	10.5						10.5			--	--
COMPANY TOTAL		Q1	22,640.5	246.6		115.0	68.3	15,500.3	602.4	4,598.0	1,939.8	--	133.9
		Q2	26,067.6	131.7			4.1	19,857.0	397.1	3,157.3	2,207.4	--	589.6
		Q3	7,853.6	378.3		115.0	72.4	5,436.2	158.6	601.8	816.0	--	723.5
		94 YTD	56,561.1	225.2		115.0		40,793.5	1,158.1	8,357.1	4,963.2	--	
		93 YTD	28,171.0					17,855.3	5,535.1	2,757.0	1,798.4	--	
PARADISE TROPICAL TEA													
PARADISE TROPICAL TEA	F171	Q2	23.9			23.9						--	--
		Q3	9.5			9.5						--	--
		94 YTD	33.4			33.4						--	--
PHILIP MORRIS COS INC													
BROTHERS GOURMET COFFEES DECAF COFFEE	F171	Q2	1.6				1.6					--	--
		Q3	27.1			27.1						--	--
		94 YTD	28.7			27.1	1.6					--	--
CRYSTAL LIGHT FRUIT TEA DRINK MIX	F171	Q3	425.4					60.8	364.6			--	--
		94 YTD	425.4					60.8	364.6			--	--
		93 YTD	12.3						12.3			--	--
GENERAL FOODS INTL INSTANT COFFEE	F171	Q1	7,104.4	833.1				3,400.9	65.0	2,315.3	489.7	--	--
		Q2	4,973.4	1,980.5				3,542.1	96.7	2,796.4	757.4	--	--
		Q3	7,659.4	1,079.3				3,135.2	114.2	2,614.4	516.3	--	--
		94 YTD	23,736.9	3,892.9				10,078.2	275.9	7,726.5	1,763.4	--	--
		93 YTD	15,453.2	6,343.1				5,092.9	246.8	3,332.5	437.9	--	--
GENERAL FOODS INTL REG & SGR FEE COFFEES	F171	Q1	3,620.8					1,753.1	59.8	1,508.7	299.2	--	--
		Q2	0.5						0.5			--	--
		Q3	29.4						16.3		12.8	--	--
		94 YTD	3,650.4					1,753.1	76.6	1,508.7	312.0	--	--
		93 YTD	3,716.2					1,828.4	75.1	1,577.9	234.8	--	--
GENERAL FOODS INTL SUGAR FREE INST COFF	F171	Q1	789.9	789.9								--	--
		Q2	789.9	789.9								--	--
		94 YTD	892.2	888.4			3.8					--	--
MAXWELL HOUSE CAPPIO ICED CAPPUCCINO	F171	Q1	94.8			54.5				40.5		--	--
		Q2	1,371.9			39.5			1,312.1	20.3		--	--
		Q3	1,561.4						1,552.6	8.8		--	--
		94 YTD	3,028.1			93.8			2,864.7	69.6		--	--
		93 YTD	13,099.4	703.5		61.7		6,245.9	295.8	5,341.2	451.3	--	--
MAXWELL HOUSE CAPPUCCINO	F171	Q1	4,474.3					2,534.8	82.3	1,651.1	206.1	--	--
		Q2	1,860.5					1,354.9	20.8	369.5	115.3	--	--
		Q3	3,382.9					2,460.5	39.6	637.7	245.1	--	--
		94 YTD	9,717.7					6,350.2	142.7	2,658.3	566.5	--	--
		93 YTD	8,938.7					6,679.8	193.1	1,567.4	498.4	--	--

----- CONTINUED -----

they imply. The planner can compare competitive expenditures on a market-by-market basis, or month-to-month basis, or both. The planner can analyze executional strategies by examining the magazines, newspapers, and television programs that a competitor purchases. In short, a planner can know as much about any and all competitors' media activities as the planner needs or wants to know. Most important in the earliest stages of media planning, however, is the determination from expenditure data of how competitors view the market, their target audience, and their own positioning. After all, media actions often speak louder than copy words.

Category Spending

Competition is not always easy to define, but the client marketing strategy usually has identified the competitive frame to be used in advertising activities. On this assumption, the planner then investigates and reports the general media activity of these competitors.

The first task is to identify total category spending. Using such data in Exhibit 4.9, a planner would conclude that the disposable diaper category accounted for $126 million of advertising spending in 1994. The planner should then calculate expenditures in the previous five years in order to identify whether the category spending has increased, remained steady, or decreased. This should be articulated in a chart aligning the expenditures with their percentage change. Only those percentage growths that vary from inflation's are of particular significance.

Share of Voice

The second task is to identify and explicate each brand's media expenditures as a percentage of category spending. This is called **Share of Voice (SOV)**, and it is calculated by dividing the total category spending into each particular brand's advertising expenditures. It is also called the advertising share (Exhibit 4.10).

Generally, these brand dollars and SOV are articulated in a chart that also correlates the data with each brand's corresponding **Share of Market (SOM)**. This chart would quantify whether a brand's SOV is relatively greater or less than its SOM. Some research indicates that a brand's share of voice should always exceed its share of market. Without such a relationship, the argument goes, a brand will cease to grow, or may even face decline. Other research argues that market share follows advertising share.

It is often true that brands that have long enjoyed the number one position in their category also enjoy greater leverage in their advertising. Therefore, these brands will invariably show a greater share of market vis-à-vis their share of voice. Whatever the case, it is impossible to make competitive strategic decisions without a clear understanding of how advertising share (SOV) and market share (SOM) are functioning in a particular brand's category.

Media Mix

The third task is to identify and analyze the **Media Mix** employed by category competition. This entails the identification of the way each competitor has invested its

FIGURE 4.9 LNA/MEDIAWATCH MULTI-MEDIA SERVICE—DIAPERS

-CLASS/BRAND $

January - December 1994

QUARTERLY AND YEAR-TO-DATE ADVERTISING DOLLARS (000)

CLASS/COMPANY/BRAND	CLASS CODE		10 MEDIA TOTAL	MAGAZINES	SUNDAY MAGAZINES	NEWSPAPERS	OUTDOOR	NETWORK TELEVISION	SPOT TELEVISION	SYNDICATED TELEVISION	CABLE TV NETWORKS	NETWORK RADIO	NATIONAL SPOT RADIO
D127 DIAPERS-							*CONTINUED*						
JOHNSON & JOHNSON (CONTINUED) COMPANY TOTAL		Q1	2,362.7	101.5				1,953.9	8.3	155.3	245.2		
		Q2	2,493.5					2,041.1	6.4	122.1	222.1		
		Q3	1,350.7					839.6	198.0	113.7	179.4		
		94 YTD	8,492.2	101.5				6,499.5	323.5	305.9	870.4		
		93 YTD	5,443.5	804.1				3,754.4	106.8	260.1	518.1		
KIMBERLY-CLARK CORP													
DEPEND BLADDER CONTROL PRODUCTS	D127	Q1	2,543.8					1,878.6	282.3	44.4	71.3	311.6	
		Q2	1,464.4					1,008.0	393.0		63.1		
		Q3	989.5					575.0	43.6	208.7	45.3		
		94 YTD	5,825.9	153.6				4,156.8	784.0	253.1	220.4	311.6	
		93 YTD	5,831.3					3,393.7	1,304.0	83.9	106.6	789.5	
DEPEND EASY/FIT UNDERGARMENTS	D127	Q1	414.9	414.9									
		Q2	225.1	225.1									
		Q3	199.3	199.3									
		94 YTD	839.3	839.3									
		93 YTD	153.6	153.6									
DEPEND POISE FEMININE GUARD	D127	Q1	1,536.4	1,099.6				418.4	0.2		18.2		
		Q2	1,943.6	1,155.0				728.4	1.5		64.7		
		Q3	526.2	516.0				10.2			1.0		
		94 YTD	5,089.4	3,945.8				1,157.0	1.7		83.9		
		93 YTD	6,334.2	2,631.2		25.3		2,504.0	1,011.4	122.2	40.1		
KIMBERLY-CLARK CORP GP	D127-8	Q2	15.6										15.6
		Q3	9.3										9.3
		94 YTD	24.9										24.9
		93 YTD	18.9										18.9
KIMBERLY-CLARK CORP SPORTING EVENTS	D127-8	Q4	14.7										14.7
		94 YTD	14.7										14.7
KLEENEX HUGGIES DISPOSABLE DIAPERS	D127-4	Q1	39.2										39.2
		Q3	73.7	63.5			10.2						
		Q4	0.6					0.6					
		94 YTD	113.5	63.5			10.2		0.6				39.2
		93 YTD	14,117.4	123.6				12,982.8	322.5	69.2	619.3		
KLEENEX HUGGIES PULL-UPS DISP TRAIN PANT	D127-4	Q1	3,655.4	817.2				2,655.1	51.3	131.8	232.1		
		Q2	9,215.1	1,214.6				6,818.5	84.0	98.0	98.8		
		Q3	5,130.4	765.4				3,891.1	73.0	168.8	246.6		
		94 YTD	21,948.0	3,444.5				16,293.2	206.6	610.3	478.5	641.6	
		93 YTD	18,343.6	2,290.6				14,742.1	127.2	66.8	416.9	641.6	
KLEENEX HUGGIES PULL-UPS GOODNITES UNDER	D127-4	Q2	2,063.7	133.2				1,818.8	1.2	110.5			
		Q3	1,707.4	847.3				814.2	3.5	42.4			
		94 YTD	3,356.5	1,356.5				2,633.0	4.7				
		94 YTD	5,127.6							152.9			
KLEENEX HUGGIES SUPREME DISPSBLE DIAPERS	D127-4	Q1	665.6	96.6				374.9	194.1				
		Q2	1,899.7	366.8				1,258.4	274.5				
		Q3	1,428.3	363.8				657.3	407.2				
		94 YTD	3,645.4	587.2				2,467.7	490.5				
		93 YTD	7,639.0	1,514.4				4,758.3	1,366.3				
KLEENEX HUGGIES ULTRATRIM DISPOS DIAPERS	D127-4	Q1	6,558.1	761.0				5,729.6	67.5				
		Q2	5,699.0	742.9				4,911.5	44.5		66.6		
		Q3	7,735.7	650.4				6,523.5	490.0	5.2			
----- CONTINUED -----													

63

FIGURE 4.9 LNA/MEDIAWATCH MULTI-MEDIA SERVICE—DIAPERS

CLASS/BRAND $

January - December 1994

CLASS/COMPANY/BRAND		CLASS CODE	10 MEDIA TOTAL	MAGAZINES	SUNDAY MAGAZINES	NEWSPAPERS	OUTDOOR	NETWORK TELEVISION	SPOT TELEVISION	SYNDICATED TELEVISION	CABLE TV NETWORKS	NETWORK RADIO	NATIONAL SPOT RADIO
D126 DEODORANTS & ANTI-PERSPIRANTS							*CONTINUED*						
PROCTER & GAMBLE CO (CONTINUED)													
SURE SOLID DEODORANT	94 YTD	D126	15,172.6	- -	- -	- -	- -	8,009.8	1,975.7	2,548.2	2,808.9	- -	- -
	93 YTD		11,429.1	- -	- -	- -	- -	6,061.3	990.1	2,353.1	2,084.4	- -	- -
COMPANY TOTAL	Q1		14,715.5	949.0	- -	- -	- -	7,433.3	1,805.9	1,835.7	2,691.6	- -	- -
	Q2		17,861.9	1,532.4	- -	80.6	- -	9,467.9	1,886.1	1,746.1	2,792.7	156.0	44.8
	Q3		18,758.7	2,025.5	- -	- -	- -	9,552.6	1,996.9	1,613.6	3,461.6	58.5	17.2
	Q4		15,655.0	1,285.9	- -	80.0	- -	7,238.0	1,838.0	2,000.0	1,877.6	- -	1.0
	94 YTD		66,990.0	5,822.8	- -	- -	- -	33,692.1	7,526.9	7,195.5	11,612.7	- -	80.4
	93 YTD		53,409.3	6,567.6	- -	- -	- -	27,173.0	6,784.4	5,948.3	6,873.1	214.5	167.0
TOMS OF MAINE													
TOMS OF MAINE NATURAL DEODORANT & TOOTHPST	Q1	D126	158.6	- -	- -	158.6	- -	- -	- -	- -	- -	- -	- -
	Q2		2.4	- -	- -	2.4	- -	- -	- -	- -	- -	- -	- -
	Q3		2.4	- -	- -	2.4	- -	- -	- -	- -	- -	- -	- -
	Q4		2.0	- -	- -	- -	- -	- -	- -	- -	- -	- -	- -
	94 YTD		165.4	- -	- -	165.4	- -	- -	- -	- -	- -	- -	- -
UNILEVER PLC													
LADY POWER CLEAR ROLL-ON ANTI-PERSPIRANT	Q1	D126	1.2	- -	- -	- -	- -	- -	1.2	- -	- -	- -	- -
	94 YTD		5,859.1	1,173.7	- -	- -	- -	2,759.2	189.3	1,341.0	195.9	- -	- -
	93 YTD												
LADY POWER STICK ANTI-PERSPIRANT	Q1	D126	0.2	- -	- -	- -	- -	- -	0.2	- -	- -	- -	- -
	Q2		6.9	- -	- -	- -	- -	- -	6.9	- -	- -	- -	- -
	Q3		6.9	- -	- -	- -	- -	- -	6.7	- -	- -	- -	- -
	Q4		53.8	- -	- -	- -	- -	- -	53.8	- -	- -	- -	- -
POWER STICK ANTIPERSPRNT	Q1	D126	1.3	- -	- -	- -	- -	- -	1.3	- -	- -	- -	- -
	Q2		4.8	- -	- -	- -	- -	- -	4.8	- -	- -	- -	- -
	Q3		6.1	- -	- -	- -	- -	- -	6.1	- -	- -	- -	- -
COMPANY TOTAL	Q1		8,749.1	- -	- -	- -	- -	6,090.8	224.8	2,066.6	366.9	- -	- -
	Q2		2.7	- -	- -	- -	- -	- -	2.7	- -	- -	- -	- -
	Q3		11.5	- -	- -	- -	- -	- -	11.3	- -	- -	- -	- -
	Q4		14.2	- -	- -	- -	- -	- -	14.2	- -	- -	- -	- -
CLASS TOTAL	94 YTD		14,469.4	1,173.7	- -	- -	- -	8,850.0	475.3	3,407.6	562.8	- -	- -
	Q1		44,398.7	5,370.7	- -	158.6	3.8	25,781.8	3,138.1	4,360.2	5,540.9	156.0	8.6
	Q2		42,052.7	5,826.5	- -	83.0	- -	21,059.7	3,251.3	4,498.3	7,160.7	58.5	9.8
	Q3		49,726.3	8,593.9	- -	2.4	- -	23,421.6	3,899.8	5,565.1	8,224.0	- -	1.1
	Q4		32,264.0	5,206.5	- -	- -	- -	14,881.3	2,828.0	4,021.3	4,021.3	- -	- -
	94 YTD		168,441.9	25,200.6	- -	246.0	3.8	85,144.4	13,089.2	19,285.1	3,846.2	214.5	163.4
	93 YTD		188,287.6	23,076.7	- -	- -	- -	115,406.1	10,377.9	19,200.2	19,431.7	- -	187.0
D127 DIAPERS													
HANNAHCARE INTERNATIONAL INC													
DIGNITY PLUS ADULT UNDERGARMENT	Q1	D127	8.6	- -	- -	- -	- -	- -	115.5	- -	- -	- -	- -
	Q2		161.7	- -	- -	- -	- -	- -	79.4	- -	- -	- -	8.6
	Q3		80.5	36.4	- -	- -	- -	- -	65.8	- -	- -	- -	9.8
	94 YTD		316.6	36.4	- -	- -	- -	- -	260.7	- -	- -	- -	19.5
JOHNSON & JOHNSON													
SERENITY GUARD SUPER PLUS BLDR CTRL PROD	Q2	D127	101.5	101.5	- -	- -	- -	- -	- -	- -	- -	- -	- -
	93 YTD		116.7	116.7	- -	- -	- -	- -	- -	- -	- -	- -	- -
SERENITY SHIELD BLADDER CONTROL PRODUCTS	Q1	D127	2,362.7	- -	- -	- -	- -	1,953.9	8.3	135.3	245.2	- -	- -
	Q2		2,041.7	- -	- -	- -	- -	2,041.1	6.4	122.7	222.1	- -	- -
	Q3		1,350.7	- -	- -	- -	- -	859.6	198.0	113.7	179.4	- -	- -
	Q4		2,285.3	- -	- -	- -	- -	1,449.5	110.8	305.9	273.4	- -	- -
	94 YTD		8,390.7	687.4	- -	- -	- -	6,499.5	323.8	697.3	870.4	- -	- -
	93 YTD		5,326.8		- -	- -	- -	3,754.4	106.3	260.1	518.1	- -	- -
----- *CONTINUED* -----													

FIGURE 4.9 LNA/MEDIAWATCH MULTI-MEDIA SERVICE—DIAPERS

CLASS/BRAND $

LNA/MEDIAWATCH MULTI-MEDIA SERVICE
January - December 1994

QUARTERLY AND YEAR-TO-DATE ADVERTISING DOLLARS (000)

CLASS/COMPANY/BRAND	CLASS CODE		10-MEDIA TOTAL	MAGAZINES	SUNDAY MAGAZINES	NEWSPAPERS	OUTDOOR	NETWORK TELEVISION	SPOT TELEVISION	SYNDICATED TELEVISION	CABLE TV NETWORKS	NETWORK RADIO	NATIONAL SPOT RADIO
D127 DIAPERS (CONTINUED)							*CONTINUED*						
PROCTER & GAMBLE CO (CONTINUED)													
PAMPERS PHASES ULTRA DRY THINS DSPSBL DP	D127-4	Q4	5,720.9	941.0	--	--	--	2,054.9	1,694.6	1,595.2	376.9	--	--
		94 YTD	28,451.4	--	--	--	--	11,673.1	6,789.6	7,264.2	1,743.5	--	--
		93 YTD	9,630.4	--	--	--	--	5,246.4	2,067.8	1,548.2	768.0	--	--
PAMPERS TRAINERS DISPOSABLE PANTS	D127-4	Q1	1,360.7	743.3	--	--	--	1,540.3	1,267.4	1,564.8	610.0	--	--
		Q2	5,525.1	746.6	--	--	--	2,073.3	1,073.4	1,057.3	587.5	--	--
		Q3	5,688.8	615.8	--	--	--	1,627.4	1,334.9	1,368.1	523.2	--	--
		Q4	5,043.4	663.8	--	--	--	5,241.0	860.9	3,990.2	1,720.7	--	--
		94 YTD	17,588.0	2,699.5	--	--	--		4,536.6			--	--
		93 YTD	845.4	--	--	--	--		845.4			--	--
PAMPERS ULTRA DISPOSABLE DIAPERS	D127-4	Q1	286.5	286.5	--	--	--	--	--	--	--	--	--
		94 YTD	286.5	286.5	--	--	--	--	--	--	--	--	--
		93 YTD	537.5	537.5	--	--	--	--	--	--	--	--	--
COMPANY TOTAL		Q1	13,147.6	1,605.0	--	135.1	--	4,780.5	3,611.7	2,306.8	843.6	--	--
		Q2	25,657.8	5,327.2	1,040.6	--	--	9,324.9	2,779.0	4,936.4	2,114.0	--	--
		Q3	28,253.5	2,464.8	--	--	--	12,905.5	5,065.4	5,514.3	2,703.5	--	39.9
		Q4	22,221.9	1,842.2	675.4	--	--	8,445.7	3,967.0	4,988.3	2,263.4	--	39.9
		94 YTD	89,280.8	11,239.2	1,716.0	135.1	--	35,056.6	15,423.1	17,745.8	7,925.1	--	--
		93 YTD	36,687.9	4,432.8	--	--	--	16,015.4	5,689.5	6,874.6	3,675.6	--	--
UNIVERSAL CONVERTER													
BABY'S CHOICE & SUPER TODDLER DIAPERS	D127-4												
CUDDLES ULTRA DISPOSABLE DIAPERS	D127-4	Q1	5.4	--	--	5.4	--	--	--	--	--	--	--
		Q2	12.8	--	--	12.8	--	--	--	--	--	--	--
		Q3	12.4	--	--	12.4	--	--	--	--	--	--	--
		Q4	8.4	--	--	8.4	--	--	--	--	--	--	--
		94 YTD	39.0	--	--	39.0	--	--	--	--	--	--	--
COMPANY TOTAL		Q1	30.6	--	--	30.6	--	--	--	--	--	--	--
		Q2	12.8	--	--	12.4	--	--	--	--	--	--	--
		Q3	12.4	--	--	12.4	--	--	--	--	--	--	--
		Q4	8.4	--	--	8.4	--	--	--	--	--	--	--
		94 YTD	64.2	--	--	64.2	--	--	--	--	--	--	--
CLASS TOTAL		Q1	30,962.9	4,794.3	1,040.6	30.6	--	17,791.0	4,215.4	2,593.9	1,178.3	311.6	47.8
		Q2	49,858.0	9,302.7	--	147.9	10.2	27,909.7	3,699.9	5,267.3	2,464.5	--	25.4
		Q3	47,335.7	5,870.5	--	12.4	--	25,996.6	6,360.1	5,388.8	3,226.2	--	10.4
		Q4	40,818.7	6,171.2	675.4	8.4	10.2	19,382.4	6,383.5	7,325.5	3,795.2	641.6	54.6
		94 YTD	168,975.5	26,138.8	1,716.0	199.3	--	91,051.0	19,558.3	19,485.6	8,744.9	953.2	138.2
		93 YTD	98,729.5	14,606.7	--	25.3	--	61,104.3	8,603.1	7,715.4	5,866.3	789.5	18.9

Source: Competitive Media Reporting and Publishers Information Bureau, Inc. © 1995.

EXHIBIT 4.10 BRAND SPENDING/ SHARE OF VOICE

Brand	Spendings $	SOM%	SOV%
Huggies	**59,027,000**	**37.2**	**46.9**
Disposable	113,500	0.7	0.1
Pull-ups Train	21,948,000	13.8	17.6
Goodnites	5,127,600	2.9	4.0
Supreme	7,639,000	4.8	6.0
Ultratrim	241,999,400	14.9	19.2
LUVS	**16,445,000**	**14.7**	**13.1**
Disposable	11,175,400	10.0	8.8
Phases	3,692,900	3.2	3.0
Leakguard	1,576,700	1.4	1.3
Pampers	**50,219,000**	**29.2**	**40.1**
Disposable	2,916,800	1.7	2.4
Phases	1,262,800	0.7	1.0
Phases Ultra	28,451,400	16.5	22.6
Trainers	17,588,000	10.2	14.0
Total	**125,578,000**	**81.1**	**100.0**

money and a comparison with the general investment trends of the category. This is generally articulated in a detailed chart. Using the data from the research resources, each brand's spending is distributed across the reported ten media. These numbers are then translated into percentages (Exhibit 4.11).

It is reasonably easy to find the competitive data and to do the arithmetic necessary to articulate the information in usable form. The key issue is analysis. It is also fairly easy to identify from a useful chart whether one or more brands are acting differently than others and where your brand fits into the picture. It takes experience to know whether there might be a historical or corporation-specific reason for such differences. It takes imagination to determine what strategic thinking in a competitor's mind might have produced these differences. In any case it is important to be able to tell the competitive communications story of the marketplace before leaping to any planning decision.

SELF TEST

1. Research the competitive data available to you about the analgesic market.

2. Create three (3) charts articulating: Category and brand spending, Share of Voice, and Media Mix by brand.

SUMMARY

In this chapter we have identified the key research resources utilized in defining, measuring, and interpreting any market. The level of detail required is determined by the

EXHIBIT 4.11 BUDGET/MEDIA MIX

Brand	Spending $	Mags.	Sun. Mags.	Nwsp	OutDoor	NetTV	SpotTV	Synd.	CATV	NetRadio	SpotRadio
Huggies	**59,027,000**										
Disposable	113,500	56.0%	—	—	1%	—	—	—	—	—	35.0%
Pull-ups Train	21,948,000	15.7%	—	—	—	74.5%	1.8%	2.8%	2.2%	2.9	—
Goodnites	5,127,600	45.6%	—	—	—	51.3%	0.1%	3.0%	—	—	—
Supreme	7,639,000	19.8%	—	—	—	62.2%	17.8%	—	—	—	—
Ultratrim	241,999,400	11.2%	—	—	—	84.4%	3.9%	0.1%	0.3%	—	—
LUVS	**16,445,000**										
Disposable	11,175,400	0.7%	—	—	—	30.4%	13.1%	38.5%	17.0%	—	—
Phases	3,692,900	15.4%	—	—	—	33.4%	13.3%	19.4%	18.3%	—	—
Leakguard	1,576,700	89.4%	10.5%	—	—	—	—	—	—	—	—
Pampers	**50,219,000**										
Disposable	2,916,800	16.3%	—	2.7%	—	28.0%	9.7%	34.4%	5.5%	—	1.4%
Phases	1,262,800	87.5%	—	4.4%	—	—	7.3%	—	—	0.7%	—
Phases Ultra	28,451,400	3.4%	—	—	—	41.0%	23.8%	25.5%	6.1%	—	—
Trainers	17,588,000	11.9%	—	—	—	29.8%	25.8%	22.7%	9.7%	—	—

level of competition in the category, and by the customs, resources, and culture of both the client and the agency. It is possible, for example, to examine media mix variables on a monthly basis. However, this is not required as often as the temptations of the available data might suggest. The bottom line is that with access to the available resources, with familiarity with their formats and contents, and with a rudimentary knowledge of arithmetic, anyone is prepared to tackle the first elements of a Media Work Plan.

Part Two

Initial Planning Process

5

Media Work Plan:
Part I—Marketing Analysis

OVERVIEW

This chapter introduces the role and function of the Media Work Plan and how the process should be approached. Part I of the Media Work Plan describes the business situation that will have an impact upon media strategy development and establishes the foundations for the plan. The key inputs from the client, product group, or planner research are identified, and their use is explained.

WORK PLAN

The product of media planning is the **Media Plan**, which is the document that specifically identifies what media and vehicles will be purchased at what time, at what price, with what expected results. It includes such things as flowcharts, the names of specific magazines, reach and frequency estimates, and budgets. The Plan is what everybody wants to see, and it is also what novices are so anxious to learn how to do.

A media plan, however, is not the result of following instructions, but of analysis, thought, imagination, and judgment. Media planning is a process. Over the years, experienced people have learned "how to do it," to the extent that they know and can identify the necessary steps involved in the process. These steps are included in what can be described as the Media Work Plan.

IMAGINATIVE PROCESS

Most advertisers and agencies have a system for the orderly analysis of information and the logical presentation of recommendations. Like pilots who have checklists that they review before takeoff, marketers have checklists that they review before finalizing a marketing plan. The marketer's purpose, like the pilot's, is to be disciplined and comprehensive. The Media Work Plan performs these same functions for the media planner.

A disciplined and comprehensive checklist, however, never flew a plane. It is helpful to recall, in this context, the argument over manned space flight versus unmanned exploration. The astronauts argue that a machine cannot fly. There is such a thing as an automatic pilot, but that is not the same as flying. Similarly, the Media Work Plan can outline the process and get you to certain places, but following the outline and filling in the blanks is not the same as planning. It is critical, at the very beginning of the process, to appreciate that a Media Work Plan is primarily an outline for imaginative thinking before it is anything else.

Media planning relies on the social sciences and follows the logic of marketing systems. In applying the data and following the process, however, the planner quickly encounters the unpredictable volatility of human behavior and the very real, but fleeting and finally immeasurable, character of communications. Media planning is half science and half poetry, half craft and half art. The challenge, in the final analysis, is to bring discipline to imagination. The system is the Media Work Plan, but the imagination is the planner's.

THE WORK PLAN

The three sections in a Media Work Plan enable the planner to consciously and conscientiously develop practical executions, based on sound strategies, derived from a specific marketing analysis. The three parts are:

Part I	Marketing Background & Intentions
Part II	Strategic Objectives & Decisions
Part III	Executional Recommendations & Support

The Media Work Plan is an action-oriented product that includes all of the data, logical analysis, and "reasons why" for a specific set of executions. The Work Plan is a self-aware application of rhetoric, and it identifies the skills and techniques involved in distributing effective economic communications. The Work Plan represents a logical progression from situation analysis to accountable action.

Part I includes a description of the product, its market situation, and business proposition insofar as they relate to media strategy development. It identifies both the marketing objective and strategy, and the advertising message and style.

Part II identifies, articulates, and explains the appropriate media strategies at a specific budget level. It provides all of the data and reasoning required to support the strategic decisions that are being made as a result of the situation analysis articulated in Part I.

Part III articulates the executional plan and its characteristics. It demonstrates how the plan matches and fulfills the media objectives and strategies, and provides all of the necessary data in support of vehicle selections and budget applications.

The analysis and production of all these elements of the Media Work Plan can be both time consuming and exhausting. Thus, one does not have to be at the end of an eighteen-hour day to ask "Why?"

The first and foremost reason is that it works. Generations of advertising craftsmen have honed the process. They have come to a common understanding of what they need to know, and what they have to do. Secondly, the Media Work Plan is a consensus-maker. Advertising is a cooperative art, involving more officers than enlisted personnel. The business only works through shared understandings and mutual consent. Finally, as a system and as a record, the Media Work Plan provides for both management review and the flexible assignment of staff, for both quality control and the revolving door of promotions and hiring.

Pros and Cons

The form of the Media Work Plan presented here is, admittedly, the most elaborate. There is a growing movement for a new approach and new forms. One reason for this is the fax-happy speed of contemporary business. The pace of today's environment, the argument goes, does not allow for any leisurely processes. Others will argue that planning documents should not include and rehash what the product group and client already know—for example, the marketing background. Others are dissatisfied with the dull, linear thinking that they believe is induced by an elaborate and detailed system. The optimum word today is "creativity," and systematic logic is often perceived as the enemy of creativity.

There always were good reasons, however, for the more elaborate forms of the Media Work Plan. The first is that it does contain the whole process. It identifies all the necessary steps regardless of how the final results of the process are presented to others. This is especially important for a book that proposes to introduce and explain the process.

It is often helpful to think of the three parts of the Media Work Plan as three meetings. We all know that there will have to be a meeting in which the executional elements (Part III) of the Plan are presented and approved, but do we need two other meetings?

Do we need a meeting in which the client and agency agree on the identification of the business and marketing conditions that will direct the formation of the media strategy? Perceived as an intellectual process, the goal is to establish the foundation for developing strategically sound plans that directly address marketing and advertising conditions and objectives. Perceived as a business process, the goal is consensus. Media plans must work, and they must be sold.

It is imperative, in this context, that there be broad agreement on the facts, issues, and objectives that have an impact upon strategy. If the media planner has some unique marketing input, that must be resolved early. The imaginative media planner will have enough difficulty introducing and gaining acceptance for "surprises" in strategy and execution without at the same time taking on the added burden of proving a new set of marketing and advertising premises. Part I of the Media Work Plan would form an excellent outline for this meeting.

The meeting we have just imagined, however, may never occur. There may well be other procedures for insuring the media planner's recognition of the accepted marketing analysis, goals, and conditions, as well as for absorbing the planner's marketing and consumer insights. Nevertheless, the media planner should seek a level of specificity, precision, candor, and insight necessary for the imaginative and responsible task ahead. For their own sake, therefore, planners must accept and address the challenges of articulating the relevant marketing and advertising premises.

There are, perhaps, even more important reasons for imagining a meeting that follows the disciplines of Part II of the Media Work Plan, regardless of circumstances. First, the most important parts of a media plan are its strategies. Second, no one should be under the illusion that any aspect of advertising is poetry. It is rhetoric, which implies the necessity of matching practical execution to objectives and strategies; that is its art. Third, although it is true that no experienced and creative planner ever thinks entirely without some tentative examples in mind, it is impossible to build a strategy entirely out of the examples in an execution. Finally, practical experience universally teaches that disaster awaits the planner who does not achieve agreement on strategies before proceeding to executions, or who presents executions without the introduction of their strategic premises. Neither secrets nor presumptions lead to good agency-client relations, or to easy meetings about executional plans.

MEDIA WORK PLAN—PART I

An outline of the major analytical subheadings of Part I of the Media Work Plan is illustrated in Exhibit 5.1. The key to the application of this outline is that the planner should report, use, and write only that data and those insights that will be useful in planning media. It is not the purpose of Part I to rewrite or replicate the marketing plan. Rather, its purpose is to select and summarize the relevant points and issues.

Marketing communications are conducted by many kinds of companies and agencies. At one end of the spectrum, the media planner may be mostly left to his or her own devices in speculating on and developing a marketing background. At the other end of the spectrum are mammoth packaged goods companies served by mega agencies. The client, in these instances, has elaborate and detailed marketing plans, supported by proprietary research, while the agency has extensive systems and research resources of its own.

In general, the input sources for Part I are:

The client marketing department

The agency product group

Syndicated research

Proprietary research

Libraries (trade press, financial reporting, and so on)

EXHIBIT 5.1 MEDIA WORK PLAN: PART I

Advertising Period:

Market Description:

Product Description:

Product Positioning:

Competition:

Seasonality:

Geography:

Purchase Patterns:

Usage Patterns:

Pricing:

Distribution:

Trade/Consumer Promotion(s):

Testing History:

Marketing Objectives/Strategies

Creative:

•Message

•Tone

Whatever the situation, or whatever the source of information, the planner's job is to summarize and focus the marketing data in a manner useful to the development of effective media strategies.

In the process of struggling with the marketing data, the planner can accomplish two additional things:

1. Discover missing questions or data that come to light only when the basic marketing issues are addressed from the point of view of the distribution of communications messages.
2. Imagine the pattern in the kaleidoscope of communications that helped produce the current marketing situation.

What protects the media planner from a simply catechetical review of the marketing background is the understanding of marketing and communications discussed in chapters 1 and 2. The professional media planner brings these understandings to the process in the form of a unique belief system (Figure 5.1). The media planner believes that "everything is communications," and the prism of this belief system sheds a different light on the data. Furthermore, the planner's unique job is to create a pattern of communications. This demand helps the planner to perceive the pattern that does exist and forces the planner to demand information that will adequately support strategies to change the pattern.

ADVERTISING PERIOD

It might appear obvious that everyone who is involved in developing and placing a particular advertising campaign will be fully aware of the relevant time period. It might, therefore, be considered only a matter of form to note the advertising period at the beginning of the process.

Noting the advertising period, however, makes a concrete contribution to the thinking process. It serves to remind the planner and reader that the plan is a response to a particular time, place, and specific set of circumstances. The creativity of the plan is measured by its responsiveness to the quotidian conditions. Conditions have never been and never will be the same as they are for this particular advertising period.

The advertising period is normally a calendar year or a fiscal year. Conditions and/or marketing strategies may change in midcourse, and a six-month revision might be required under these circumstances.

The advertising period for a seasonal marketer might call for a seasonal plan. The plan for a new product introduction or a relaunch might well cover eighteen months to two years. A retail marketer might have a series of mini-plans contained within the framework of an annual advertising budget and effort. A bank, for example, might plan a series of promotions for different products such as deposit accounts, credit cards, auto loans, and so on, on an annual calender. Each of these promotions, however, might have different objectives and target markets and, therefore, different media plans. These

FIGURE 5.1 MEDIA BELIEF SYSTEM

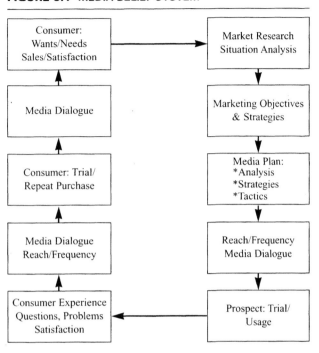

By controlling the time, place, and context of marketing communications, media planning directs consumer dialogue, perception, trial, and repeat purchase.

mini-plans might be entirely separate or subsumed in an annual plan. A purely promotional product, or a brand that is following a primarily promotional strategy, might have a separate media plan exclusively designed to support the short-term promotional effort. The advertising period in each of these cases should be appropriately limited.

MARKET DESCRIPTION

One of the recurring issues for anyone involved in an advertising campaign is how much of the market description, which has been elaborately set forth in the client's marketing documents, should be contained in supporting advertising documentations. Assuming that the agency is not, in effect, the client's marketing department, it is inappropriate for the agency to replicate, duplicate, or compete with the client's market analysis.

There are three reasons, however, that an agency should produce its own market description document. The first is that the agency should be able to demonstrate that it understands the client's business and problems. Second, advertising is not the same as marketing, and it requires its own vocabulary and insights. Third, an agency has many functional areas and its cooperative work requires a singular and retrievable focus. Consequently, the agency should possess a document that can be very helpful to the planner at this point, possibly eliminating the planner's need to replicate it.

Market Data

Assuming that we are only talking about planning, and assuming that an appropriate document exists within the agency, what in particular should a media planner focus on, whether or not the planner ends up writing it all out?

1. The definition of the product class or category that represents the brand's area of competition
2. The size of the market for this product class or category
3. Sales trends over the last five years, and sales projections, if they are available. This data should include not only the brand's sales and shares, but the sales and shares of all competitors in the category
4. The environmental conditions or competitive strategies that explain these market trends and shares
5. Expected new product introductions, or product improvements, whether by the brand or by its competitors
6. Any unusual events—past, present, or predictable—that affect the market: for example, court rulings, bad publicity, legislation, regulatory decisions, or inquiries

The result is a capsule description of a specific, dynamic market. It is the story of your brand.

Consumer Environment

This market background is not only the world in which your brand lives and competes, but it is also the world of products, services, and opportunities that surrounds the consumer. When people are under pressure to name a brand (as on a game show like *Family Feud*), they usually name the brand they use or the leading brand in the category. When they are asked to name several brands, the order of their responses often reflects, to a remarkable degree, the order of market share of each of the brands. The point is that consumers both perceive and create the world described in the market background for any product, and it is the planner's task to gain a sense of this market from the consumer's, as well as the client's, perspective.

Competitive Frame

The most important functional decision is the determination of the product class or category. Examples are the best way to introduce the tensions and difficulties of this decision.

*Does Sanka brand decaffeinated coffee compete against

    A.   All coffees

    B.   Only decaffeinated coffees

    C.   All hot beverages, or

    D.   All beverages, hot or cold?

*Do L.A. Gear sneakers compete against

    A.   All casual shoes

    B.   Specifically athletic shoes, or

    C.   Fashion footwear?

*Does Scope mouthwash compete against

    A.   All dental hygiene products

    B.   All mouthwashes, therapeutic and cosmetic, or

    C.   All cosmetic mouthwashes?

*Does Nuprin compete against

    A.   All analgesics

    B.   All nonaspirin analgesics, or

    C.   Only other ibuprofen products?

*Does our bank's credit card compete against

    A.   All other credit cards

    B.   All travel and entertainment credit cards

    C.   All bank credit cards, or

    D.   Only bank credit cards issued by local banks?

Both the client marketing department and the agency product group must answer these questions. They must describe the competitive frame and identify the product's direct and indirect competitors. This description is not only the foundation of marketing objectives, such as share, but also of the consumer dynamics you are trying to influence, such as usage occasions, and where and when purchase decisions are made.

**THE KEY ISSUES FOR AN INSIGHTFUL
MEDIA IMAGINATION OF THE MARKETPLACE ARE:**

1. **What is the added value(s) in the product class?**

2. **Are there any media that address these types of added values?**

3. **What is the order of magnitude of the competition?**

4. **Where in the product life cycle are the product and its category?**

It is while writing out, or simply following, the checklist of a market description that a media planner should start invigorating the media and marketing imagination, as discussed in chapters 1 and 2.

PRODUCT DESCRIPTION

These paragraphs in the Plan provide an actual description of the product as well as any relevant historical data, expected changes, improvements, line extensions, and so on.

The first point to be made is that it is remarkable how many advertising professionals cannot specifically describe the products they advertise. They may know what they are saying in their advertising, but without the aid of the brand name, they wouldn't be able to direct somebody to find it in a store. Put another way, could they themselves pick the brand out in a blind test?

If the planner cannot tell the difference between his or her brand and other brands in the category, how can the planner expect to know why the brand acts as it does in the marketplace? However obtained, an intimacy with the product is essential, and the ability to define the product is an excellent place to begin.

PRODUCT POSITIONING

What is the product or service's reason for being, and in what specific way should the product or service be perceived by consumers?

A product's position is the clarity with which consumers identify the product with a specific set of valuable attributes such as color and taste, classic and sporty, nutritious and satisfying, expensive and economical. Product positioning reflects the strengths you want the consumer to identify with the brand.

Most sophisticated marketers and agencies commonly articulate a product's position with perceptual mapping. An excellent example can be seen in the positioning of automobiles. General Motors, for example, has been known to place all of its nameplates on a geometric grid (Figure 5.2) that identifies how consumers currently perceive certain values as intrinsically associated with the cars. GM marketers then present a picture (Figure 5.3) of how they would like to have their automobiles perceived.

Oldsmobile was long perceived as a brand associated with family values: economical and reliable. GM foresaw the impact of the baby boom generation and its many yuppie children's values, so it attempted to reposition the Oldsmobile brand with style, sportiness, and other younger values. The result was the "It's not your father's Oldsmobile" campaign. Oldsmobile, however, could not shake off its traditional and deeply rooted consumer perceptions, and sales failed to meet projections. In subsequent campaigns GM decided to "reposition" Oldsmobile again as economical, reliable, family transportation.

Product positioning parallels product or benefit segmentations and can be derived from them. The difference is that positioning relates directly to consumer perceptions.

FIGURE 5.2 CURRENT PERCEPTIONS

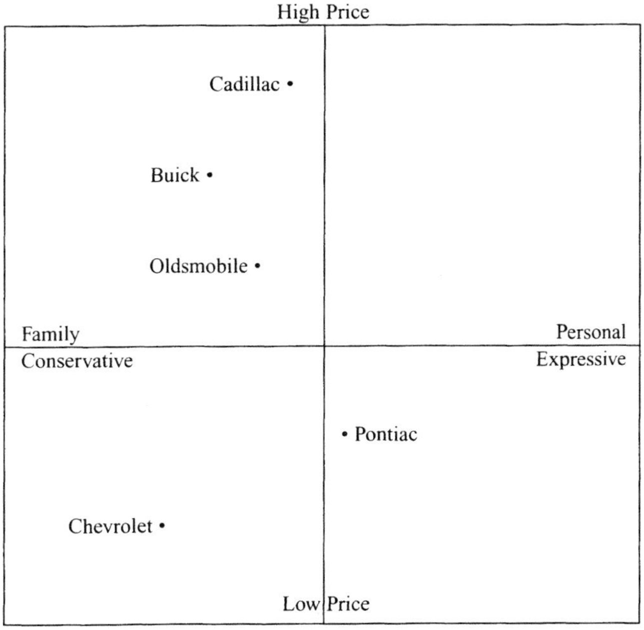

```
                              High Price
      ┌─────────────────────────┬─────────────────────────┐
      │                         │                         │
      │           Cadillac •    │                         │
      │                         │                         │
      │                         │                         │
      │         Buick •         │                         │
      │                         │                         │
      │                         │                         │
      │        Oldsmobile •     │                         │
      │                         │                         │
Family│                         │                Personal │
      ├─────────────────────────┼─────────────────────────┤
Conservative                    │                Expressive
      │                         │                         │
      │                         │ • Pontiac               │
      │                         │                         │
      │                         │                         │
      │       Chevrolet •       │                         │
      │                         │                         │
      │                         │                         │
      └─────────────────────────┴─────────────────────────┘
                              Low Price
```

FIGURE 5.3 PLANNED PERCEPTIONS

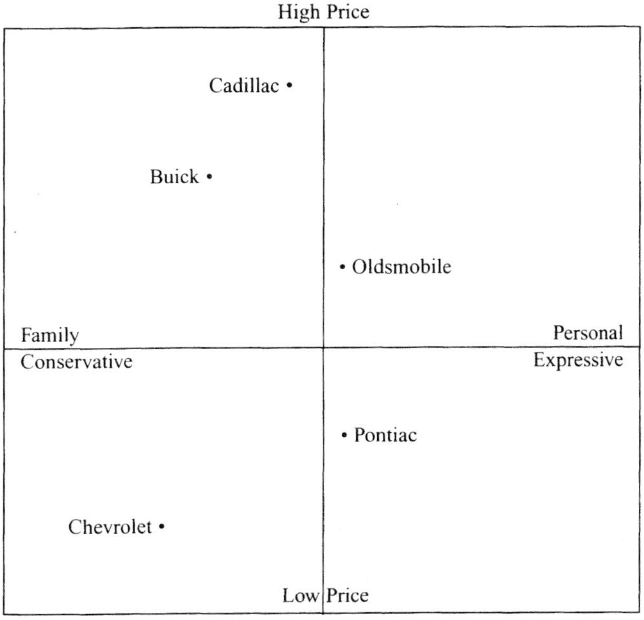

```
                              High Price
      ┌─────────────────────────┬─────────────────────────┐
      │                         │                         │
      │           Cadillac •    │                         │
      │                         │                         │
      │                         │                         │
      │         Buick •         │                         │
      │                         │                         │
      │                         │ • Oldsmobile            │
      │                         │                         │
Family│                         │                Personal │
      ├─────────────────────────┼─────────────────────────┤
Conservative                    │                Expressive
      │                         │                         │
      │                         │ • Pontiac               │
      │                         │                         │
      │                         │                         │
      │       Chevrolet •       │                         │
      │                         │                         │
      │                         │                         │
      └─────────────────────────┴─────────────────────────┘
                              Low Price
```

Product positioning is a discipline for matching the problem-solving benefits of a product with the consumer's understanding of his or her needs and desires. This is most useful to the marketing communications effort, because advertising's task is to create a value-laden image for a brand, and positioning is the foundation of the brand's desired image and perceived values.

Positioning focuses on perceived differentiations and develops the point of reference for consumers. This discipline is critical to the media planning because media types and vehicle selections are the fundamental conditions of consumer perceptions (see chapter 1). A product cannot be successfully positioned against consumer desires unless those desires have already been articulated in the communications the consumer seeks out and consumes (Figure 5.4).

THE KEY ACTIVITIES FOR AN INSIGHTFUL MEDIA IMAGINATION OF A BRAND'S PRODUCT POSITIONING ARE:

1. **Mentally visualize a product's current perceptual map.**
2. **Imagine which media patterns assisted consumers in coming to believe what they now believe about our brand and competitors.**
3. **Visualize the brand's desired perceptual map.**
4. **Simultaneously visualize a corresponding pattern of media and vehicles that could conceivably provide a substantive foundation for the desired consumer perception.**

This is not the moment for selecting specific media; that is Part III of the planning process. Nor is this the place to articulate the strategic gestalt of your plan to express and support the product's competitive positioning; that is Part II of the planning process. Since these two steps ultimately are the planner's responsibility, however, the planner must be able to articulate the product's positioning. Good media planners are always thinking in media terms.

COMPETITION

The definition of the category in which a brand competes and the identification of each competitor's sales and market share has already been executed, in the approach presented here. What is left for us to consider regarding competition is communications competition.

An essential part of a media planner's marketing thinking is an identification and evaluation of competitors' media efforts. The planner needs to know what each competitor's advertising expenditures are and how they are spent. The planner needs to determine competitive strategies from the media

FIGURE 5.4 POSITIONING BY MEDIA: PARALLELING GM AUTO POSITIONING

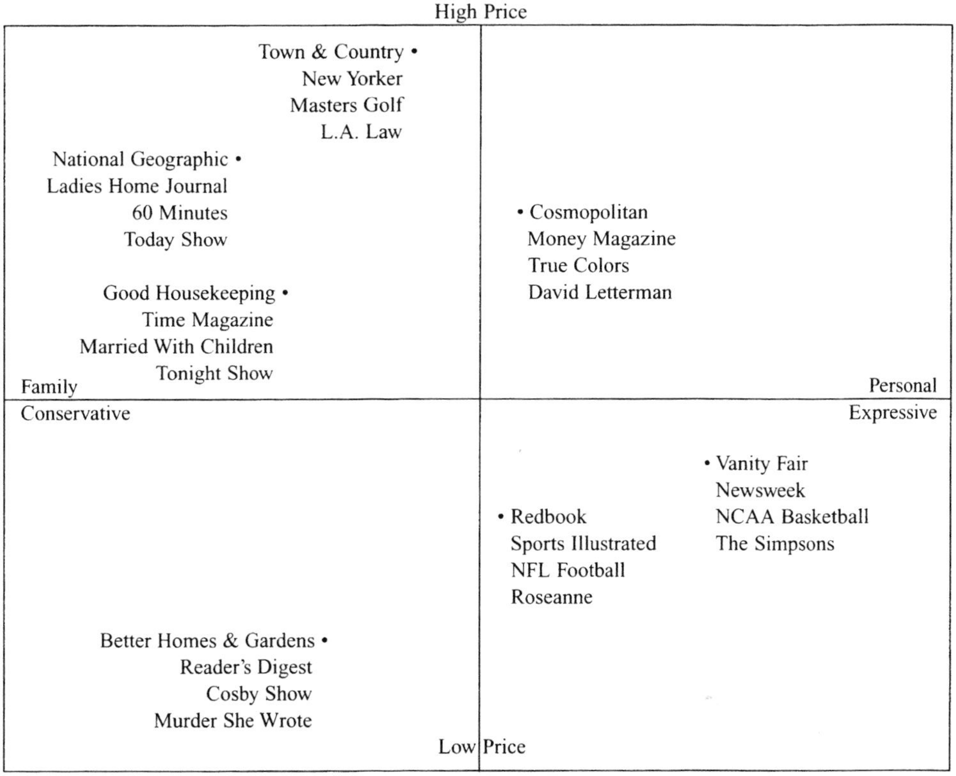

High Price

Town & Country • New Yorker Masters Golf L.A. Law	
National Geographic • Ladies Home Journal 60 Minutes Today Show	• Cosmopolitan Money Magazine True Colors David Letterman
Good Housekeeping • Time Magazine Married With Children Tonight Show	

Family   Personal

Conservative   Expressive

		• Vanity Fair Newsweek NCAA Basketball The Simpsons
	• Redbook Sports Illustrated NFL Football Roseanne	
Better Homes & Gardens • Reader's Digest Cosby Show Murder She Wrote		

Low | Price

types and vehicles that other brands are using, as well as when and where they are used. (The sources and articulation of this information are detailed in chapter 4.) Whatever the case, the media planner should articulate a judgment about competitive activities, as well as identifying them.

THE KEY ISSUES FOR AN INSIGHTFUL MEDIA IMAGINATION OF COMMUNICATIONS COMPETITION ARE:

1. **Is the category sensitive to changes in advertising weights? Why or why not?**

2. **Has any brand benefited from dramatic changes in media strategy?**

3. **Have any media been overlooked or disregarded, and are there good reasons for this?**

4. **Are the various strategies in tune with current market conditions and where each brand is in the product life cycle?**

SEASONALITY

It is easy to leap to strategic decisions when addressing seasonality, as well as subsequent issues such as geography. When following the process, however, the first question should always be "What is happening?" not "What should we do about it?"

The three basic questions are:

1. What are category sales by quarter, month, and so on, and to what degree do they vary?
2. What are our product's sales by the same calendar measures? Do they vary from category sales, and by what degree?
3. Are there any reasons for evident patterns, such as weather, tradition, price fluctuations, or holidays?

The key here is to recognize and understand the facts of your product's marketing life. You are looking for a pattern and the reasons for its development. Charts that index category sales, your product's sales, and your product's sales within the category at different times of the year are common tools of analysis and expression.

THE KEY ACTIVITIES FOR AN INSIGHTFUL MEDIA IMAGINATION OF SEASONAL SALES PATTERNS ARE:

1. **Imagine the actual conditions at the various times of the year when sales fluctuate.**
2. **Imagine the consumer's annual diary of attention, consideration, and motivation.**

GEOGRAPHY

To a media planner, geography represents product availability and variable sales by market. The first question is whether the brand is national, regional, local, or rolling-out in some pattern. The second question is whether, within this framework, sales vary by compass point, region, sales zones, or media markets, and whether the brand's sales parallel category sales.

The extent of the analysis and documentation under this heading varies a great deal. Many marketers have good reasons for being content with rather broad strokes, such as dividing the country into four or six equal parts and indexing sales to population. Others demand an extensive analysis of every media market. The methods used in these instances are a Category Development Index and a Brand Development Index. Both are described in chapter 6.

A question now arises: When should the planner present an extensive analysis? It is often sufficient to note, at this point in the planning process, whether there are quantifiable differences, and to reserve the more extensive media market-by-media market analysis for the point (in Part II) when the planner is forced to make choices in relationship to specific markets.

**THE KEY ACTIVITIES FOR A
MEDIA IMAGINATION OF GEOGRAPHY ARE:**

1. **Develop a sense of place and the consciousness of living there.**
2. **Imagine the influential media in each region, and experience their gestalts, which differ from significant place to significant place.**

PURCHASE PATTERNS

Consumer purchase patterns reflect competitive strength, consumer resistance, and the underlying dynamics of the category.

The basic formula, which we would all like to believe, argues that consumer recognition of a problem leads to inquiry, which leads to trial, which leads to satisfaction, which leads to repeat purchase. Several things are left out of this happy logic, however. First, buyers and users are not the same, and different people have varying influence in mercurial circumstances. Second, there are varying degrees of consumer involvement in different product categories. Finally, consumer inertia and the impact of competitive promotion must be considered.

Separating the issues, the planner needs to consider:

Brand Loyalty. Do customers regularly switch between brands, or are they reliable purchasers of one brand? Brand loyalty can be a characteristic of your own brand, but the issue relates more to the category. Different consumers can be loyal to different brands. What you are really measuring is the level of fickleness in the marketplace. In turn, this level will dictate the degree of difficulty that will be involved in increasing or maintaining market share.

Purchase Cycle. What is the average time lag between purchases? In this context, the greater the separation, the easier it will be for consumers to forget about brand claims and values. You also need to know the quantities bought on each purchase occasion. Do consumers purchase a lot or a little each time; do they stock up an inventory, or purchase the products just in time for use?

Urgency. Is the brand or category characterized by impulse buying, or by considered purchasing? In either case, you are analyzing a purchase decision sequence. The decision sequence generally is illustrated with a considered purchase product, such as a car. It is a good example, for it is easy to understand the steps in the drawn-out process. The same steps are experienced however, in impulse purchasing; but not necessarily in the same order. The parallel issue is: Where is the decision made? Is it made in the store, at home, or everywhere? A complete imaginative picture requires a sense of time, place, and process.

Influencers. The key fact is that buyers are not always users, and vice versa. You might ask a series of questions: "Who initiates the need question?" "Who is the opinion leader?" "Who is the decider?" "Who is the purchasing agent?" "Who is the final user?" The examples frequently used in this context are children's toys and adults' toys. Who is more important in a toy purchase: the demanding child or the purchasing parent? Who is more important in purchasing an automobile, a dishwasher, or a VCR: the husband or wife? Frequently, the real answer is not the one that we would prefer for our own image's sake, but marketing success goes to those who see the world candidly and securely.

**THE KEY ISSUES FOR AN INSIGHTFUL
MEDIA IMAGINATION OF PURCHASING ARE:**

1. **How much risk does the consumer experience?**
2. **What is the intensity of consumer involvement in the brand or category, and what is the reason for it?**
3. **Imagine the person who is making the purchase decision and how others may be influencing her.**
4. **Imagine the environment in which the purchase decision is made: (home, store, and so on).**

What the media planner is trying to understand at this point in the process is the very act of purchasing, and it takes imagination to enter the consumer's experience.

USAGE PATTERNS

To consume means to use up. Buying and consuming are two different acts, and there may be a significant time difference between purchase and usage. A marketer is not only interested in encouraging usage, which will presumably lead to repeat purchases. She or he is also interested in increasing the number of usage occasions that could lead to rapid expansion of the category. It is at this point that marketers focus on the differences between heavy and light users.

The key point is that use involves a different judgment and a different experience from those involved in purchasing. The planner needs to know the frequency of use and the time of day, week, month, or year when consumption takes place. The objective will be to reinforce the value associations of the brand at these times, as well as to encourage consumption at critical moments of usage decision.

**THE KEY ACTIVITIES FOR AN INSIGHTFUL
MEDIA IMAGINATION OF PRODUCT USAGE ARE:**

1. Imagine the experience of the product in the consumer's life.
2. Determine whether there is a major dichotomy between heavy and light users, or between users and nonusers, and imagine the lives of each group.

PRICING

In our economy, price is a measure of value, but value is a perception in the eye of the beholder. Price is a major determinant of demand, but it is also the foundation of profit. Pricing is a complex equation.

The key fact questions are:

1. What are industry sales at given price levels?
2. What is the brand's price relative to competition over time?
3. Are there any significant geographic differences in the brand's or competition's pricing?

This data need not be included in the Media Work Plan. Without this information, however, the planner would have to admit that he or she does not have a concrete understanding of the marketplace, or of the marketing objectives and strategies of the brand. Consequently, the planner must be familiar with the data regardless of where it is collected and codified.

The three basic choices facing a marketer are whether to price a product above, below, or at parity with the competition. The media planner should have an appreciation of the client's decision process in coming to one or the other of these conclusions.

Higher price objectives generally represent either a need to rapidly accumulate profits or an effort to substantiate a perception of high quality. The product may have patent protection and may therefore be difficult to copy. The product may be in its initial stages of the product life cycle, and there may be significant pressure to recover research and development costs. The product may have a short lifespan, which produces pressure for immediate cost recovery. The company may be focused on profits over sales, with a corresponding insistence on maintaining margins.

Lower price objectives generally represent either a need to expand the market or a need to resist competition. Lower prices can increase trial by bringing into the market new buyers who resist higher prices. The category might have extensive price elasticity where lower prices translate into greater profits through greater sales rather than through greater profit margins. It may be necessary to have lower prices to match competition, or to establish a lower price to keep out competitors who will have a difficult time matching your price because of their need to recover start-up costs.

Parity pricing, or matching your price to those of your competitors, is often a necessity, but it can also be a conscious strategy. This strategy works especially well if your company enjoys other advantages in distribution, service, or retailer relations. The strategy also works if your product has unique attributes in packaging or design for example, even though the basic product is little different from competition.

**THE KEY ISSUES FOR AN INSIGHTFUL
MEDIA IMAGINATION OF PRICING ARE:**

1. The degree of price sensitivity, or elasticity, in the category.
2. Consumer perception of price, and the degree to which price divides different classes of consumers.
3. The brand or company objectives that led to the pricing strategy.

DISTRIBUTION

The planner needs to know where or how the product or service is sold. Is it sold in grocery stores, drugstores, mass merchandisers, department stores, or boutiques? Is it sold through independent agents or through direct mail? The planner also needs to know how this method of distribution compares to competition and whether there are any advantages or disadvantages inherent in the method of distribution.

These distinctions can have a major impact on ultimate media strategies, particularly as they relate to retailer support. Equally important, however, is the added picture of consumers that emerges from an understanding of where they shop for products, especially for your product.

**THE KEY ACTIVITIES FOR A MEDIA
IMAGINATION OF THE EFFECTS OF DISTRIBUTION ARE:**

1. Recognize that shopping is a lifestyle and that different shopping patterns imply different values that are derived from different media experiences.
2. Imagine your consumer in his or her shopping environment.

TRADE/CONSUMER PROMOTIONS

Many planners find it difficult to resist recommending promotions. That, however, is not the purpose of a market background analysis and, most often, is not even the province of media planning.

What the planner needs to know is: Are any trade or consumer promotions planned for the product or service? What are they, and when will they run? These are simply questions of fact.

The ultimate issue will be coordination: Should advertising run in support of the promotion, or should it not run at the same time, so as not to confuse the consumer? Will the media planner be asked to purchase space for a coupon distribution or time for a sweepstakes promotion, both of which may be created by a different agency or by a client department? Since the issue is coordination, the need here is only for information on what and when.

THE KEY ISSUE CONFRONTING A MEDIA IMAGINATION IS THE NEED TO IMAGINE THE CONSUMER'S PERCEPTION OF THE IMPORTANCE OF PROMOTIONS IN THE PRODUCT CATEGORY.

TESTING HISTORY

Many of the most sophisticated clients are constantly testing something somewhere. Other clients have never run a media test. In either case, it is absurd for the planner to fly blind.

The planner needs to know about any media tests conducted in the last five years, and about their purposes and results. Generally, media tests relate either to spending levels or to different media mixes. A client may test higher than normal advertising weight levels, in order to determine their point of diminishing returns. A client also might test the substitution of radio for television, or the addition of magazines to a broadcast plan. In any of these instances, the planner needs to know what was done and what the results were before suggesting new strategies to the client.

The planner also needs to know about any tests, whether for media or copy, currently in progress. All of these tests must be protected, and the planner must be prepared to insure this protection.

THE KEY ISSUE CONFRONTING A MEDIA IMAGINATION IS THE NEED TO UNDERSTAND THE DYNAMICS OF THE MEDIA MIX OR SPENDING LEVEL THAT PRODUCED A SUCCESSFUL TEST.

MARKETING OBJECTIVE AND STRATEGY

Marketing is neither the corporation nor a division of a company. Rather it is a functional responsibility within an operating company and is subject to the restraints of corporate objectives and strategies. Consequently, many marketing executives set their objectives in terms of sales, market share, and profit contribution. These objectives as such, however, are often not as useful to the marketing communications effort as they might appear.

Marketing Objective

From a marketing communications point of view, sales, share, and profit contribution are goals. Useful marketing objectives should be those things that must be accomplished to reach these goals. The distinction between goals and objectives is consistently important to those with functional responsibilities. Objectives should be something that they are charged with accomplishing and that they accept as being in their power to control or influence directly.

The marketing function—especially those elements that directly relate to promotion—is concerned with altering human behavior. As such, marketing objectives should be articulated in terms of human behavior. Marketing objectives should define the modifications of human behavior that will result in the accomplishment of sales, share, and profit contribution goals. Life, however, is never textbook logical. The fact of life is that sales, share, and profit contribution goals are often set as the marketing objective, or are included in the marketing objective.

What must the media planner look for in marketing objectives? Regardless of how the marketing objectives are presented, the planner must make an effort to discover the behavior modification objectives of the marketing effort. The basic terms of market behavior modification are trial, usage, and repeat purchase levels. In order to achieve sales goals, for example, the marketer must induce trial among a certain percentage of the population, or must increase usage and repeat purchase. Each represents a choice for the marketer and, consequently, a valid objective. Share and profit contribution goals will be achieved in similar fashion. A focus on trial will produce an entirely different set of strategies and tactics than will a focus on increasing usage among existing customers. They may not be mutually exclusive objectives, but they are distinct from one another.

THE KEY ISSUE FOR A MEDIA IMAGINATION OF MARKETING OBJECTIVES IS A FELT UNDERSTANDING AND DYNAMIC PICTURE OF THE CONSUMER BEHAVIOR MODIFICATION REQUIRED.

Marketing Strategy

A marketing strategy identifies the **source generator** necessary to achieve the marketing objectives. (The source generator is often articulated as a target market. This is not the place, however, to articulate the target market in terms of demographics and psychographics.) The source generator should be described as primary or secondary users, non-users, heavy or light users.

The marketer must plan behavior modification by one or all of these source generator groups in order to be successful. Strategies may focus on increasing trial among nonusers, increasing usage among users, or promoting heavy use among light users. Put another way, where is the marketer looking for increased sales? What is the reservoir the marketer intends to draw upon for sales?

THE KEY ACTIVITIES FOR A MEDIA IMAGINATION OF MARKETING STRATEGY ARE:

1. **Visualizing the source generator.**
2. **Comprehending their degree of acquiescence/resistance to the required behavior modification.**

In the best of all possible worlds, the marketing objectives and strategies have emerged as a consensus, and have been articulated in these terms by the client and agency product group. If they have not, the media planner must make the decisions and subsequently must present them as the premises of the media objectives.

CREATIVE MESSAGE AND TONE

You wouldn't have to look very far in the advertising and marketing community to find people who believe that the sole purpose of media is to deliver the "creative." Even though the arrogance of so-called creatives is often misplaced, the marketer and media planner must recognize that the advertisement and its vehicle are equal and interdependent elements of marketing communications. Neither exists without the other.

The essential commercial elements are message and tone; these make up a campaign strategy that should guide and direct all the elements of the advertising effort over time.

The message content is often referred to as the "creative platform." The **message** identifies the basic promise we intend to communicate to the consumer. It also articulates the rationale, or argument of product claims, which supports the promise. The promise is the reward or benefit the consumer will enjoy in purchasing and using the product or service. It is directly derived from the positioning statement. The support for the promise includes all the reasons why the consumer should believe the promise.

The tone of the advertising message results not only from the copy style, but also from all the production elements in print or video that often communicate more than the words do. The **tone** of the advertising communicates a feeling that associates the brand's personality with the consumer's experience of need.

**THE KEY ACTIVITIES REQUIRED OF A MEDIA IMAGINATION
BY THE PROPOSED ADVERTISING MESSAGE AND TONE ARE:**

1. **Identifying, through an experimental matching process, the media
   vehicle that is most perfectly congruent with the message and tone.**
2. **Understanding how and why the specific dynamics of this "perfect
   match" work.**

In the most disciplined worlds of marketing communications, the message and
tone of the advertising are agreed upon before the copywriter and art director execute
their crafts. When this is the case, the media planner can have direct access to this
information and can use it as a guide to his or her own efforts. Unfortunately, this is
not always the case. When it is not, the planner can only hope for an opportunity to
see the advertising before spending any money on the time or space for its delivery.
The serious money is in media, and it is absurd for anyone to think that the advertising message and tone will work equally well in any and all media and vehicles.

REFLECTIONS

If the outline of Part I of the Media Work Plan (as presented here) proves anything, it
is that the system can support and absorb any level of superficiality or depth that is
required or appropriate.

In more complicated situations—especially in situations complicated by huge
budgets—Part I of the Work Plan provides a solid guide through elaborate data to subtle distinctions. Huge budgets do not necessarily translate into a great amount of time
for thought. The greater the time pressures, however, the greater the need for a work-
able outline and checklist. Furthermore, in huge budget situations, the work is often
parceled out among several planners at various levels. Without an understanding of the
outline of the larger picture, their work can be both unmotivated and unproductive.

The real problem in the use and application of Part I of the Media Work Plan
emerges in the vast middle ground of brands and budgets. In these circumstances,
impatience is complicated by the more difficult task of determining what levels of
depth and subtlety are relevant and meaningful.

The reason most often given for reviewing the marketing background is to insure
that media strategies and tactics are synchronous, in tune with marketing objectives
and strategies. Experience teaches us, however, that a review of the marketing environment does not necessarily lead to marketing compatible media strategies. Nor does
the market review always produce the ability to demonstrate the connections between

marketing and media planning. When this is the case, it is almost always the result of a failure of both logic and imagination.

Generally, the planner articulates his or her conclusions and insights through strategy selection. When proposing a strategy, the planner must defend, support, and sell the strategy, articulating and applying insights derived from the marketing review (see chapters 7 and 8). These insights are a result of applying imagination and discipline to an analysis of the communications causes of the marketing situation. They are a result of perceiving the pattern, of seeking and seeing through the numbers.

Strategy and top-line strategic solutions are never far from the minds of experienced media planners. Their problem is the risk of routine, of applying old strategies to new problems, or a fear of innovation and creativity. Nevertheless, their experience helps them to understand the relevance and direction of their marketing analysis. They do not feel like strangers in a foreign country when analyzing a market; nor do they doubt why they are there.

It also would be naive to believe that experienced planners' minds are blank and compartmentalized when they are working out a market analysis. Every fact and factor reminds them of previously successful solutions. As planners seek answers, they keep in mind the answers that have led to success (or failure) in the past. Experienced planners, however, also know that they must be cautious. They know that their initial reactions are raw thoughts that only suggest strategies.

As experienced planners consider each heading in Part I of the Media Work Plan, they cannot avoid a recognition of the possibilities. Each heading, standing alone, proposes a traditional set of responses. They know that everything is going to change when it comes time to develop a complete media strategy. At the same time, however, they know where it may be most fruitful to look for solutions, and they are beginning to gain a sense of where various demands on their efforts will have to accommodate one another. While articulating a market review or performing a situation analysis, however, experienced planners are preparing for strategy development. They do not leap to strategies.

SUMMARY

*Media planning is a process outlined in the Media Work Plan.

*The Media Work Plan is primarily an outline for imaginative thinking.

*The Media Work Plan has three parts: Market Analysis, Media Strategies, and Tactical Executions.

*Media planners must accept and address the challenges of articulating the relevant marketing and advertising premises.

*The planners' job is to summarize and focus the marketing data in a manner useful to the development of effective media strategies.

*Media planners can contribute distinctive market insights derived from their unique belief system, which is rooted in communications.

*All media plans are time specific.

*Understanding product positioning is critical, because desired consumer perceptions must coexist in consumer media.

*Competition is to be understood as media competition involving spending levels, strategic uses, and results.

*Media plans are responsive to seasonal and geographic sales fluctuations.

*Media planning is rooted in an understanding of consumer purchase and product usage patterns.

*Planners must understand client marketing objectives in terms of required consumer behavior modification.

*Marketing strategies should identify the source generator necessary to achieve the marketing objectives.

*The advertising message and tone are strategies that should guide and direct all the elements of the advertising effort over time.

*Media planners should be alert to the communications causes of the market environment.

QUESTIONS

1. What is the purpose of a Media Work Plan?
2. What are the three major parts of a Media Work Plan?
3. On what grounds can a media planner add marketing insights to a situation analysis?
4. Identify three examples in which a planner must exercise imagination to see through the numbers of a marketing review.
5. Why do experienced media planners resist leaping to strategy decisions while articulating a market analysis?
6. How must a media planner understand marketing objectives and strategies?
7. Why must a media planner be able to articulate the message and tone of the advertising?

ASSIGNMENT

Review the marketing, competitive, and consumer behavior data available to you on a case assigned in class or for a brand you are working on.

Develop Part I of a Media Work Plan for your case or brand. Compare your conclusions and insights with those of others working in your group. Is there any point at which you could have improved your imaginative insight into the consumers and communications driving the marketplace?

SAMPLE PLAN: MEDIA WORK PLAN—PART I

Budget Gourmet

Advertising Period: October 1993–September 1994

Market Description:

The frozen dinner and entree market became a $3.2 billion business in 1992, but the most recent six-month figures indicate an estimated decline of 5.7 percent compared to the same period last year. The market has been quite volatile and frequently experiences aggressive competitive pricing strategies.

The most significant brands are Stouffer's, Lean Cuisine, Weight Watchers, Healthy Choice, Banquet, Swanson, and Budget Gourmet. Con Agra's introduction of Healthy Choice in 1989 significantly altered the market and had a deleterious effect on Budget Gourmet. However, Budget Gourmet restored most of its share in 1992.

ESTIMATED BRAND SALES (MILLION) AND MARKET SHARES (%)

Brands	1990		1991		1992	
	Sales	Share	Sales	Share	Sales	Share
Total Market Sales	2000		2200		3200	
Stouffer's	390	19.50	332	15.09	454	14.19
Lean Cuisine	374	18.70	280	12.73	320	10.00
Budget Gourmet	**355**	**17.75**	**210**	**9.55**	**420**	**13.13**
Weight Watchers	336	16.80	279	12.68	310	9.69
Healthy Choice	250	12.50	328	14.91	426	13.31
Banquet	180	9.00	248	11.27	365	11.41
Swanson	160	8.00	220	10.00	373	11.66

BRAND MARKET SHARE TRENDS—1990–1992

Total Market Sales (000)		**2000**	**2200**	**+200**	**3200**	**+1000**
Brands	**Year**	**1990**	**1991**		**1992**	
		Share	**Share**	**+\−**	**Share**	**+\−**
Stouffer's		19.50	15.09	−4.41	14.19	−0.90
Lean Cuisine		18.70	12.73	−5.97	10.00	−2.73
Budget Gourmet		**17.75**	**9.55**	**−8.20**	**13.13**	**+3.58**
Weight Watchers		16.80	12.68	−4.12	9.69	−2.99
Healthy Choice		12.50	14.91	+2.41	13.31	−1.60
Banquet		9.00	11.27	+2.27	11.41	+0.13
Swanson		8.00	10.00	+2.00	11.66	+1.66

Stouffer's is the category leader, and although its share has declined, it retained its leadership in 1992's growing market. The second leading brand, Healthy Choice, grew consistently from the time of its introduction of a "health positioning" until last year, when its share declined.

Many brands are continually creating line extensions to stay abreast of the market. The combined attributes of single serving portions and health appears to be responsive to and accepted by the growing number of singles, two-worker families, and empty-nesters who are driving the market. We expect significant competitive introductions in the fourth quarter from Stouffer's, Healthy Choice Lunch Line, and Heinz Smart Ones.

Product Description:

Budget Gourmet is a line of twelve single-serving, microwavable, complete frozen dinners with uniform prices, cooking times, and oven temperatures. The entrees contain no preservatives, fillers, or additives. They are low-calorie, low-sodium, low cholesterol and low fat. The meals can be cooked in the blue and red packaging, on which all daily dietary information is displayed. The recipes are grouped as Italian (e.g., chicken marsala), Oriental (e.g., vegetable stir fry) and Meat and Potatoes (e.g., sirloin tips). The meals are prepared to provide a fresh, natural taste.

Product Positioning:

Budget Gourmet should be perceived as an extensive variety of low cost, convenient, delicious, healthy complete meals.

Competition:

Category spending totals $85,500,000, with the seven leading brands spending 86 percent of the total. By far the largest investors are the aggressive Healthy Choice (26 percent) and the defensive Stouffer's (22 percent). Budget Gourmet was a distant third (9.4 percent).

Brand	Spending $	SOM %	SOV %
Stouffer's	18,700,000	14.19	22.0
Healthy Choice	22,600,000	13.31	26.0
Budget Gourmet	**8,000,000**	**13.13**	**9.4**
Swanson	6,600,000	11.66	7.7
Banquet	5,000,000	11.41	5.8
Lean Cuisine	7,000,000	10.00	8.2
Weight Watchers	5,600,000	9.90	6.5
Others	12,000,000	14.40	14.0
	85,500,000	100%	100%

The market appears to be sensitive to advertising while experiencing considerable volatility. For example, Stouffer's lost considerable share in 1991, significantly increased its spending, and defended against continued erosion of share.

Healthy Choice had experienced continual growth and spent aggressively, but the effect was defensive for it lost share. On the lower side of Budget Gourmet, both Swanson and Banquet spent heavily vis-à-vis their shares and strengthened their positions in 1992. Budget Gourmet increased spending and significantly increased share.

As a general proposition, the competitors favor spot TV over network and continued to invest heavily in magazines.

Brand	Spending	Mags	Nwsp	NetTv	SpotTV	CATV	Radio
Stouffer's	18.7	51%	—	8%	40%	1%	—
Healthy Choice	22.6	17%	—	—	83%	—	—
Budget Gourmet	**8.0**	**31%**	—	—	**69%**	—	—
Swanson	6.6	50%	—	24%	26%	—	—
Banquet	5.0	48%	—	28%	24%	—	—
Lean Cuisine	7.0	23%	6%	66%	4%	1%	—
Weight Watchers	5.6	58%	42%	—	—	—	—

Seasonality:

Based on a monthly consumer sales analysis of frozen foods, peak sales occur in January–April and September–November (Nielsen National Scantrack). Frozen food sales decrease during the summer months.

Quarter 1	Quarter 2	Quarter 3	Quarter 4
41.8	14.5	8.8	34.9

It is significant, however, that sales decline from the end of November through December due to the holidays.

Month	Sales Index
January	109
February	110
March	108
April	101
May	99
June	92
July	86
August	90
September	100
October	108
November	102
December	94

Geography:

Usage is especially strong in the northeast and on the west coast, especially among heavy (+4/mo.) users.

Region	Total	Heavy	Medium	Light
Northeast	111	102	134	89
Midwest	102	94	101	121
South	87	90	82	88
West	109	125	93	106

Sales in the northeast and west tend to support the importance of cold weather usage in the category. The importance of the west coast, supported by the pattern of northeast usage, suggests the significance of lifestyle to category usage, which can also be observed in the importance of metropolitan and suburban living.

Region	Total	Heavy	Medium	Light
Metro/Ctr	103	107	105	92
Suburban	104	101	108	101
Non Metro	88	88	76	110

Purchase Patterns:

The decision to purchase in the category is planned as a regular element of the weekly shopping list, and purchases are often made before the home inventory is depleted. However, there is minimal brand loyalty, and many purchases are made in search of variety or price at the store display.

Budget Gourmet buyers track especially well with heavy users of the category. This is true even for light users of Budget Gourmet (Exhibit 5.1). The primary skew for Budget Gourmet is younger, more affluent, and better educated.

Interest in the category—especially in Budget Gourmet—is dictated more by lifestyle and life stage then by any single demographic characteristic.

Life Stage	% U.S. Pop.	% B.G. Volume	Index
Young Singles	21.2	26.3	124
Young Marrieds	4.0	4.4	112
Young Families	13.0	8.2	63
Mid. Age Single	6.9	8.9	130
Mid. Age Married/No Children	5.8	7.8	135
Mid. Age Married/Young Children	9.6	10.2	107
Mid. Age Married/Teen Children	4.9	7.3	149
Mature Singles	11.3	6.3	56
Empty-Nesters	20.8	12.7	61
Mature Married/Children	2.6	2.0	78

EXHIBIT 5.1 BUDGET GOURMET FROZEN ENTREES

Base: Adults

	% of U.S. Population		Category		Budget Gourmet		Heavy Category		HVY Category/ LT Budget Gourmet	
	%	Index	%	Index	%	Index	%	Index	%	Index
Men	47.69	100	46.79	98	43.58	91	46.5	98	40.92	86
Women	52.31	100	53.21	102	56.42	108	53.5	102	59.08	112
Age:										
18–24	14.1	100	15.24	108	14.53	103	13.98	99	14.59	103*
25–34	24.07	100	25.22	105	25.13	104	23.64	98	24.33	101
35–44	19.79	100	20.55	104	24.76	125	21.44	108	28.3	143
45–54	13.63	100	16.24	112	14.07	103	15.93	117	13.05	96
55–64	12.2	100	10.74	88	10.84	89	10.82	89	9.41	77
65+	16.23	100	13.01	80	10.68	66	14.19	97	10.28	63*
# of Kids in Households:										
1	16.95	100	18.39	108	19.64	116	18.16	107	19.63	115
2	14.92	100	16.59	104	14.45	97	14.22	95	14.32	96
3+	9.42	100	8.43	89	7.45	79	9.08	96	8.28	88*
Marital Status:										
Single	21.4	100	22.17	104	23.66	111	22.92	107	23.93	112
Married	60.6	100	59.83	99	56.43	93	57.75	95	54.27	90
Separated/Widowed/Divorced	18	100	18	100	19.91	111	19.33	107	21.8	121
Parents	34.31	100	35.04	102	34.23	100	33.77	98	33.95	99
HHI:										
$10,000–19,999	17.79	100	14.83	83	11.5	65	14.64	82	11.98	67
$20,000–29,999	17.18	100	17.89	104	17.65	103	18.52	108	18.12	106
$30,000–34,999	8.48	100	8.66	102	7.82	92	8.41	99	9.78	115
$35,000–39,999	7.57	100	7.77	103	8.13	107	7.7	102	7.81	103
$40,000–49,999	12.34	100	13.39	109	15.07	122	11.99	97	14.59	116
$50,000+	24.76	100	27.86	112	33.61	136	29.4	119	32.88	130

EXHIBIT 5.1 BUDGET GOURMET FROZEN ENTREES (CONT.)

	% of U.S. Population		Category		Budget Gourmet		Heavy Category		HVY Category/ LT Budget Gourmet	
	%	Index	%	Index	%	Index	%	Index	%	Index
Race:										
White	86.29	100	89.51	104	90.19	105	88.69	103	91.15	106
Black	11.2	100	8.61	77	7.68	69	9.55	85	7.84	70*
Other	2.51	100	1.87	75	2.13	95	1.75	70	1	40*
Education:										
Post-Graduate	7.78	100	8.72	112	12.05	155	9.5	122	13.32	171
Graduated College	18.17	100	20.9	115	26.62	147	21.42	118	25.23	139
Attended College	18.55	100	19.4	105	22.94	124	19.85	107	23.43	126
Graduated High School	39.26	100	39.68	101	36.24	92	37.43	95	37.78	96
Non-High School Graduate	24.02	100	20.02	83	14.19	59	21.31	89	13.52	56
Employment:										
Employed Full Time	54.68	100	58.04	106	64.68	118	59.28	108	64.85	119
Employed Part Time	8.95	100	9.66	109	10.14	115	8.79	99	10.21	115
Not Employed	36.47	100	32.29	89	25.18	69	31.94	88	24.9	68

*Predictions are relatively unstable. Use with caution.

Usage Patterns:

The product is used for quick, complete dinners on the go and for diet-conscious meals. Consumers who are time poor as a result of career or social commitments are the most likely users. They have little time for or interest in meal preparation, and meals are often perceived as interruptions of their active lifestyle and career interests. It is a life of get home, turn on the TV, turn on the microwave, turn on the shower, eat, get on with it.

Fifteen percent use these products solely as a dinner. Seventy percent as a primary dinner with other supplementary food.

Pricing:

Budget Gourmet is priced at less than $2.00 and is positioned as a lower-priced quality product. Heavy usage is important, and the price appeals to less affluent younger users and to two-career more affluent users. Affordability encourages heavier usage.

Distribution:

Distribution is national, and the product is sold in the crowded frozen food sections of super markets and grocery stores.

Promotions:

Unplanned.

Marketing Objective/Strategy:

Become the category leader with +14 percent share by generating trial and repeat purchases among heavy users.

Creative Message/Tone:

Budget Gourmet is an inexpensive, quick and easy, gourmet-style frozen entree that fits into your fast, complicated, diet-conscious lifestyle.

BUDGET GOURMET BACK TO THE FUTURE

FROZEN ENTREE MARKETER FINDS
VALUE NICHE IT LOST; SHOWS FIRST GAIN IN 5 YEARS

With a simple proposition of "great food at reasonable prices," the Budget Gourmet brand from a small California company flew up the sales charts in the 1980s.

Bought by Kraft General Foods, expectations were high, especially with the coming recession.

But blindsided by ConAgra's Healthy Choice line and mismanaged by KGF, Budget Gourmet lost sight of that basic brand identity.

Now Budget Gourmet is back.

The brand now is showing its first real share and sales gains in five years. And it is providing a textbook example of what happens when a marketer forgets what a brand is all about.

"When it started, Budget Gourmet had incredibly clear positioning, really one of the clearest positions of any consumer product," said Larry Benjamin, president of Kraft General Foods' All American Gourmet Co. Unit. "It was both budget and gourmet, distinctive taste and reasonable prices.

"The beauty . . . is that all we're doing today is going back to the beginning. We've recognized what the brand stands for—and around here, we're calling it back to the future," he said laughing.

Mr. Benjamin can afford to laugh now. Unit volume sales were up 40% for the 12 weeks ended Sept. 4 and 28.2% for the 52-week period, according to Nielsen Marketing Research data supplied by Kraft.

Those increases put Budget Gourmet ahead of Stouffer Foods' Lean Cuisine for the year, with a 14.8% share of the frozen entree market compared with Lean Cuisine's 14.5%.

For the quarter, Budget Gourmet claims to be the top entree brand, even ahead of Stouffer's red-box line (an 18.3% share of unit sales, to 16.7% for Stouffer's).

Those numbers are a source of special pride to Mr. Benjamin. In April 1992, two months after he became president, Budget Gourmet hit an all-time low share of 8.8%.

"All of us around here know that number," he said ruefully. "It was both our low-water mark and our rallying cry."

During the next six months, Mr. Benjamin led the drive to undo five years of mistakes.

After Kraft acquired All American Gourmet in 1987—calling it the cornerstone of a corporate expansion into frozen foods—both partners eagerly looked for growth opportunities.

Typical of Kraft's arrogance—it later repeated the same mistakes with the General Foods lines—management encouraged All American Gourmet to use the Kraft name for a new line of frozen entrees like macaroni & cheese.

Borrowing Budget Gourmet's signature packaging but sold at a premium price, the Kraft line had no identity of its own. Worse, it cannibalized Budget Gourmet sales.

"When [founder] Ernie Townsend was hands-on, he had a very clear vision of what his product was," a former ConAgra executive said. "But when Kraft got involved with the brand, it mostly ended up meddling."

Mr. Townsend moved to Kraft's suburban Chicago headquarters and left the company in 1988.

In August 1988, All American Gourmet began testing Eating Right, low-calorie entrees designed to compete with Stouffer's Lean Cuisine. But the arrival of ConAgra's Healthy Choice in early 1989 blew Eating Right out of the water, offering not only low calories but lower fat, cholesterol and salt.

Both the Kraft-brand line and Eating Right co-opted Budget Gourmet's package: the box designed to go straight from the freezer to the oven to the plate.

BUDGET GOURMET: BACK ON TRACK

Share of frozen entree market

Brand	52-week share	Change	12-week share	Change
Stouffer's	17.3%	−1.2	16.7%	−2.9
Budget Gourmet	14.8%	+1.4	18.3%	+3.1
Lean Cuisine	14.5%	+0.9	12.9%	+0.4
Weight Watchers	12.4%	+2.6	9.8%	−0.4

Source: Nielsen Marketing Research figures for unit sales ending Sept 4., 1993. Changes in market share are expressed in share points.

"Budget Gourmet had a lot going for it, and a real key was that package," the former ConAgra executive said. "Everyone, including Stouffer and ConAgra, missed out on that one, almost forever."

All American Gourmet also expanded the Budget Gourmet line in an attempt to offer something to everyone. In addition to the Kraft and Eating Right experiments, it tried out Budget Gourmet-branded dinners, low-cal entrees, "healthy" entrees, side dishes, a Hot Lunch line, "hearty" oversize dinners, even pizza.

Suddenly, Budget Gourmet sold products for as much as $2.69 inconsistent with its price image.

"Let's say the company got into areas they didn't know very well," Mr. Benjamin said.

When he started the brand's overhaul, he killed half the company's stock-keeping units. Gone were Kraft, Eating Right and many peripheral line extensions. In their stead came Special Selections, pasta-based dishes cheaper to make and sell—for Budget Gourmet-type prices like $1.39. Budget Gourmet Special Selections rolled out in early 1993.

Mr. Benjamin said though Budget Gourmet's overall dollar sales are flat this year—down 2.3% to $323 million, according to Information Resources Inc.— "we're doing that with half the products."

With distractions gone, All American Gourmet focused exclusively on the main Budget Gourmet brand. And the first step there was to cut prices.

In the early days, Budget Gourmet sought a price positioning between the freezer case's economy brands, Banquet and Swanson, and the premium entrees like Stouffer's. It was a great niche.

But after ConAgra's overnight success with Healthy Choice in 1989 and 1990, stunned competitors took after the new brand with price promotions and trade deals. ConAgra responded, and the subsequent price war made all frozen foods "reasonably priced." Budget Gourmet lost its point of difference.

Worse, it forgot all about "budget." With no one in the market making money but everyone anxious to eke out what they could, All American Gourmet raised its prices several times in the late 80s and early 90s.

"The pricing strategy really caused Budget Gourmet to lose identity," said a frozen food competitor. "Sure, the price problems were an industry event, but part of Budget's real problems were self-inflicted."

Last year, suggested retail prices for the Budget Gourmet Light & Healthy entrees were cut 14% to $1.89; the full-calorie entrees now sell for the same price, down from $1.99.

"We're back in the middle—just where we want to be—offering the best combination of price and taste," Mr. Benjamin said.

After pricing was in order, all American Gourmet re-evaluated its marketing.

"All the advertising done in the late '80s and early '90s was for the new stuff; there wasn't any support of the base Budget Gourmet business," Mr. Benjamin said.

With a target audience of 25-to-34-year-olds, and even some appeal to college students, Budget Gourmet last year hired a new agency, Young & Rubicam, New York, and created what Mr. Benjamin called " a perfect campaign" for the brand.

Using music adapted from a popular song and fast-paced graphics, the commercials positioned Budget Gourmet as "an interesting, hip lifestyle product," he said. "The ad is not for everybody; but our food is not for everybody."

Having used the TV commercials and print ads with limited spending for a year, All American Gourmet pledges to boost spending significantly for 1994—to the $24 million number bandied about when Y&R won the account last year.

Now, Mr. Benjamin feels good about Budget Gourmet's place in the supermarket.

"Value is here to stay; that's everywhere," he said. "And we're beautifully positioned to take advantage of that."

When he looks back, Mr. Benjamin doesn't blame the ownership changeover.

"I don't think the corporate acquisition really had a bearing," Mr. Benjamin said. "We just learned a simple lesson: What got Budget Gourmet off track was a loss of focus for what the brand stood for. It's great proof of the value of sticking to your knitting."

Source: *Advertising Age*, November 20, 1993.

6

Geographic Weighting: Skills and Resources

OVERVIEW

This chapter describes the concepts, skills, and resources utilized in determining geographic strengths, weaknesses, and opportunities. The media math involved in creating a Category Development Index and a Brand Development Index is explained and illustrated. The data sources of special importance to local or regional brands are identified, and their utility described.

SALES ARE LOCAL

Former Speaker of the House of Representatives Tip O'Neil was often quoted as saying that "all politics is local." Similarly, in the world of marketing goods and services "all sales are local."

Much of our effort throughout the previous chapters has been focused on imagining the individual consumer as well as his or her wants, needs, drives, satisfactions, and communication experiences. Markets are places where these individual consumers meet together with sellers of goods and services. One such meeting place is in media vehicles, another is a local store.

What stores and people have in common is geography—thus the old marketing aphorism that success is dependent on "location, location, location." The question faced by a merchant is: "Where should I locate a store?" The question faced by a sales organization is: "Where should I advertise?" The question faced by a sophisticated national marketer is: "Where should I invest extra advertising dollars?"

The method for answering all of these questions is much the same. What sets the questions apart, in most instances, is the level of information available to help in finding the answers. The recommended methods are the mathematics of dollars and sense. At the same time, however, we should recognize that a merchant studying store locations will probably be greatly influenced by visits to the potential sites. Similarly, media planners should use their imaginations to understand the meaning of the numbers and to search for the brand dynamics represented by local market sales indices.

THE BASIC IDEA

Imagine that you are the owner of a small chain of jewelry outlets, and you are going through the process of selecting the location for a new store in one of five counties currently served by your chain. What would you want to know in order to make a decision? You would probably want to know:

1. Absolute dollar sales by county
2. The relative strength of each county
3. The inclination of its consumers to spend money on jewelry
4. The inclination of consumers to be responsive to your retail strategy

Assume that the various Small Business Bureaus in each county report jewelry sales. To obtain a picture of each county's relative strength, their sales figures would be divided by the average for all five to create an index.

County	Sales	Index
Bergen	$2,040,000	73
Passaic	3,143,500	112
Hudson	5,320,300	190
Essex	1,674,000	60
Sussex	1,827,600	65

In such a small list of numbers, it is easy to identify the rankings of each market by sales. Developing an index, however, highlights each market's relative importance and is enormously helpful when you are studying a longer list of numbers.

How inclined is the population in each market to invest in jewelry? To discover this answer, you must create an index of each county's sales to its population. This is done by dividing each county's sales by its number of households, and then dividing these per household sales by the average for all five.

County	Households	HH Sales	Index
Bergen	7,472	273	76
Passaic	7,723	407	113
Hudson	13,641	390	108
Essex	5,400	310	86
Sussex	4,351	420	116

It is obvious in this instance that Hudson's relative importance decreased and that Sussex's increased dramatically. The relatively small population of Sussex is composed of vigorous jewelry buyers.

How strong is the recognition and vitality of your own stores? To find out, you must create a similar index of your own sales to the population.

County	Your Sales	HH Sales	Index
Bergen	18,360	2.46	30
Passaic	31,435	4.07	49
Hudson	159,609	11.70	141
Essex	11,718	2.17	26
Sussex	91,380	21.00	254

By now combining all three indices of market development, you have created a decision matrix, or a way of examining the answers to your original questions.

County	Absolute $ Potential	Relative $ Potential	Chain $ Results
Bergen	73	76	30
Passaic	112	113	49
Hudson	190	108	141
Essex	60	86	26
Sussex	65	116	254

By creating such a series of Market Development Indices, it is possible for you to discuss and decide on both investment and marketing issues.

If the question is only: "In which county should I invest in a new store?" the answer may be "Hudson" because of its above-average index on all factors. It would be hard to overlook Sussex, however, especially if its population is growing. In fact, you might decide to close the store in Essex and open new stores in both Hudson and Sussex.

If you were examining marketing performance, rather then investment strategies, your focus would fall first on Passaic. The county performs above average on all counts but your own. You might consider investing greater advertising in Passaic, firing the store manager, or both.

The purpose of this small hypothetical case is to highlight the common sense basis of local business judgments; to note the nature of the information you want; and to focus on the value of various Business Development Indices. The questions to be answered are:

1. What information is generally available?
2. How are these and similar questions addressed by national advertisers?

One useful reminder: national advertisers are often no more informed than are local merchants.

SURVEY OF BUYING POWER

Almost all advertisers and agencies can afford to buy the four volumes of *Sales & Marketing Management* magazine's Survey of Buying Power published by Market Statistics (Exhibit 6.1). The data is intended to be used for geographic market analysis and evaluation. It contains comparative information on states, counties, cities, metropolitan markets, and regions. The key data reports population, demographics, economic measures, and sales based on census data and projections.

The Survey has many applications, but it is most often used for choosing test markets or for determining appropriate local market advertising weights. These volumes do not report competitive brand sales data or competitive media investments. Sophisticated marketers may both require and possess this data and may wish to incorporate it through formulas of their own invention. The basic data, however, forms the foundation of many decisions.

The key factors in determining a market's potential are considered to be population, **Effective Buying Income** (**EBI**, the total income after taxes and social security contributions), and total retail sales. These three numbers can be added together for market comparisons. The Survey of Buying Power, however, provides its own **Buying Power Index (BPI)** based on a market's percentage of the United States for each category, followed by a weighting of each category and their addition. The suggested weights are: population = 50%, EBI = 30%, and sales = 20%. These weights represent "potential" and could be reversed if "actual" circumstances are judged more important.

When you approach the data in the Survey of Buying Power, everything depends on what you think is important and what question you are trying to answer. Your judgment will determine whether you use the general retail sales figures, for example, or one or more of the retail categories (for example, Food and Drug). Your judgment will determine whether you should examine specific demographic groups, and you may take into consideration other factors such as weather or transportation. Your judgment will also determine the weights to be assigned to each factor.

EXAMPLES

1. You represent a chain of fast-food outlets, located in three of New Mexico's major metropolitan areas. You have an advertising budget of $800,000. How would you allocate this budget to each area according to sales potential as suggested by the Survey of Buying Power? (See Exhibit 6.1.)

    The first step is to identify the relevant factors. You conclude that they are: Population, EBI, and Eating/Drinking Places. Second, select the appropriate data and arrange it in a table. Next, compute the sum of the factors for each metropolitan area and create a market value index (percent) for each area. Finally, apply these percentages to your budget for allocation to each market.

EXHIBIT 6.1 SALES MANAGEMENT SURVEY OF BUYING POWER

New Mexico

S&MM ESTIMATES: 1/1/94

POPULATION

METRO AREA County City	Total Population (Thousands)	% Of U.S.	Median Age Of Pop.	18-24 Years	25-34 Years	35-49 Years	50 & Over	Households (Thousands)
ALBUQUERQUE	647.6	.2495	32.7	9.	17.2	23.3	22.6	245.4
Bernalillo	522.9	.2015	33.0	9.7	17.3	23.5	23.0	203.6
• Albuquerque	416.5	.1605	33.3	10.1	17.5	23.5	23.5	167.9
Sandoval	73.9	.0285	31.0	7.0	17.6	22.5	20.4	24.8
Valencia	50.8	.0195	32.1	7.7	15.7	22.6	22.8	17.0
SUBURBAN TOTAL	231.1	.0890	31.4	7.7	16.8	22.9	21.1	77.5
LAS CRUCES	152.0	.0586	28.5	13.5	15.6	19.4	20.4	50.4
Dona Ana	152.0	.0586	28.5	13.5	15.6	19.4	20.4	50.4
• Las Cruces	68.4	.0264	31.0	13.3	16.1	19.5	24.1	26.0
SUBURBAN TOTAL	83.6	.0322	26.3	13.6	15.3	19.4	17.3	24.4
SANTA FE	126.2	.0486	35.7	7.5	14.9	27.9	23.7	49.0
Los Alamos	18.3	.0070	38.6	4.5	12.9	29.3	27.5	7.4
Santa Fe	107.9	.0416	35.3	8.0	15.2	27.6	23.1	41.6
• Santa Fe	60.3	.0232	36.9	8.7	14.6	27.3	26.3	24.7
SUBURBAN TOTAL	65.9	.0254	34.7	6.5	15.1	28.3	21.3	24.3

RETAIL SALES BY STORE GROUP

METRO AREA County City	Total Retail Sales ($000)	Food ($000)	Eating & Drinking Places ($000)	General Mdse. ($000)	Furniture/ Furnish. Appliance ($000)	Automotive ($000)	Drug ($000)
ALBUQUERQUE	5,675,287	977,052	645,881	697,563	372,475	1,402,843	164,566
Bernalillo	5,219,858	806,405	598,097	683,410	354,767	1,318,369	152,691
• Albuquerque	4,942,819	737,967	555,637	672,471	345,745	1,290,022	148,388
Sandoval	151,912	41,788	27,892	5,172	10,812	4,161	6,896
Valencia	303,517	128,859	19,892	8,981	6,896	80,313	5,179
SUBURBAN TOTAL	732,468	239,085	90,244	25,092	26,730	112,821	16,178
LAS CRUCES	825,329	163,285	93,164	136,647	38,641	170,460	12,016
Dona Ana	825,329	163,285	93,164	136,647	38,641	170,460	12,016
• Las Cruces	733,336	138,397	81,028	112,058	36,502	164,775	10,712
SUBURBAN TOTAL	91,993	24,888	12,136	24,589	2,139	5,685	1,304
SANTA FE	1,194,384	197,735	170,547	156,196	56,301	161,086	21,825
Los Alamos	94,935	46,541	9,276	1,730	414	1,291	2,244
Santa Fe	1,099,449	151,194	161,271	154,466	55,887	159,795	19,581
• Santa Fe	1,020,827	149,255	147,986	149,722	50,931	151,478	16,721
SUBURBAN TOTAL	173,557	48,480	22,561	6,474	5,370	9,608	5,104

S&MM ESTIMATES: 1/1/94

EFFECTIVE BUYING INCOME

METRO AREA County City	Total EBI ($000)	Median Hsld. EBI	% of Hslds. by EBI Group: (A) $10,000-$19,999 (B) $20,000-$34,999 (C) $35,000-$49,999 (D) $50,000 & Over				Buying Power Index
			A	B	C	D	
ALBUQUERQUE	9,741,592	32,744	17.1	24.5	19.4	27.1	.2486
Bernalillo	8,049,199	32,162	17.5	24.7	18.7	26.9	.2121
• Albuquerque	6,616,807	32,381	17.5	24.4	18.8	27.2	.1828
Sandoval	1,070,904	39,008	13.0	21.9	23.7	32.9	.0207
Valencia	621,489	30,213	18.6	25.0	20.7	21.9	.0158
SUBURBAN TOTAL	3,124,785	33,517	16.2	24.6	20.5	27.2	.0658
LAS CRUCES	1,596,348	25,298	22.4	25.0	16.7	17.8	.0427
Dona Ana	1,596,348	25,298	22.4	25.0	16.7	17.8	.0427
• Las Cruces	850,999	27,108	19.8	23.4	18.0	19.9	.0261
SUBURBAN TOTAL	745,349	23,781	25.1	26.9	15.2	15.6	.0166
SANTA FE	2,377,007	38,572	14.2	22.3	18.3	36.4	.0554
Los Alamos	480,416	63,191	6.3	11.2	14.8	64.8	.0085
Santa Fe	1,896,591	35,155	15.6	24.3	18.7	31.5	.0469
• Santa Fe	1,140,584	35,918	15.3	23.5	19.1	32.2	.0331
SUBURBAN TOTAL	1,236,423	41,739	13.1	21.1	17.3	40.8	.0223
OTHER COUNTIES							
Catron	22,385	19,840	25.9	33.4	9.6	6.6	.0006
Chaves	714,699	25,759	21.1	26.5	17.2	17.3	.0179
Roswell	574,668	25,990	20.4	26.6	16.7	18.1	.0152
Cibola	178,785	19,569	25.6	25.7	13.5	9.8	.0056
Colfax	156,975	26,145	22.9	25.9	18.1	16.9	.0045
Curry	500,986	24,860	23.5	28.9	16.4	16.3	.0152
De Baca	23,824	19,774	30.1	24.2	15.3	9.8	.0005

S&MM ESTIMATES: 1/1/94

EFFECTIVE BUYING INCOME

METRO AREA County City	Total EBI ($000)	Median Hsld. EBI	% of Hslds. by EBI Group: (A) $10,000-$19,999 (B) $20,000-$34,999 (C) $35,000-$49,999 (D) $50,000 & Over				Buying Power Index
			A	B	C	D	
Eddy	632,616	28,839	18.2	24.8	18.7	21.7	.0167
Grant	315,260	25,617	21.8	27.2	18.7	15.6	.0088
Guadalupe	29,543	15,082	28.5	22.8	10.9	4.3	.0011
Harding	11,249	22,315	26.0	31.0	12.2	13.0	.0002
Hidalgo	70,784	29,414	19.5	20.2	23.8	20.1	.0018
Lea	619,583	27,582	19.1	24.9	18.9	19.3	.0165
Lincoln	160,985	23,571	24.4	24.6	15.5	16.6	.0047
Luna	175,476	17,829	29.3	24.5	11.1	8.4	.0054
McKinley	514,092	21,621	19.9	22.8	14.8	15.3	.0183
Mora	32,860	16,051	27.7	22.4	7.1	10.2	.0008
Otero	655,287	28,554	19.5	30.9	18.3	19.4	.0162
Quay	101,944	20,045	24.4	25.5	14.1	10.4	.0032
Rio Arriba	307,900	20,796	25.6	24.7	14.6	12.3	.0088
Roosevelt	176,075	20,969	24.7	23.5	16.0	12.5	.0053
San Juan	910,411	25,178	19.5	23.7	18.1	17.3	.0295
San Miguel	252,741	21,822	23.3	25.8	14.5	13.3	.0073
Sierra	127,556	19,564	28.3	26.7	11.9	10.3	.0031
Socorro	166,871	24,329	20.7	21.5	16.1	19.1	.0040
Taos	243,404	19,136	26.5	25.2	11.7	11.0	.0079
Torrance	120,574	23,387	24.5	26.0	16.9	14.1	.0031
Union	45,194	19,621	28.4	20.5	14.6	13.9	.0010
TOTAL METRO COUNTIES	13,714,947	32,314	17.5	24.2	18.8	27.1	.3467
TOTAL STATE	20,983,006	28,677	19.3	24.8	17.8	22.5	.5547

Source: *Sales & Marketing Management*, August 30, 1994.

Market	Population (000)	EBI (000,000)	Eat/Drink (000,000)	Total (000,000)	Index %
	1	2	3		
Albuquerque	647.6	9,741.5	645.9	11,035.0	71.0
Las Cruces	152.0	1,596.3	93.1	1,841.4	12.0
Santa Fe	126.2	2,377.0	170.5	~~2,673.7~~	~~17.0~~
				15,550.1	100.0

	Allocation	
Albuquerque	71.0%	$568,000
Las Cruces	12.0%	96,000
Santa Fe	17.0%	136,000

These calculations/allocations assume that you do not possess actual sales data on your specific category and for your own outlets.

2. A variation and additional calculations occur when you are trying to compare one market to another on a national/regional basis, and/or when you are interested in a specific demographic.

Assume you are representing a chain of midpriced furniture stores. Your target customer is young adults (25–34 yrs.) with a household income of $20,000–$34,000. Furniture sales is the other variable. Create an index that will enable you to determine the importance of Albuquerque relative to other markets in the country.

A. All of the relevant categories are expressed as percentages in the data. These must be converted to whole numbers by multiplying the segment percentage by the total for the market. $\overset{4}{\frown}$

$$\text{Age } 25\text{–}34: \qquad 647.6 \times .172 = 111,387$$
$$\overset{5}{\frown}$$
$$\text{Income } \$20\text{–}34K: \qquad 245,400 \text{ HHs} \times .245 = 60,123$$
$$\overset{6}{\frown}$$
$$\text{Furniture Sales:} \qquad \$372,475,000$$

B. These numbers must be articulated as percentages of the total United States. The totals are listed elsewhere in each Survey report. The Albuquerque numbers must be divided by the relevant U.S. figures and multiplied by 100 to determine Albuquerque's percentage.

$$\text{Age:} \qquad \frac{111,387}{41,714,800} \times 100 = .267 \text{ \% U.S.}$$

$$\text{Income:} \qquad \frac{245,400}{21,513,600} \times 100 = 1.14\% \text{ U.S.}$$

$$\text{Furniture:} \qquad \frac{\$372,475}{\$114,345,139} \times 100 = 3.26\% \text{ U.S.}$$

C. You must now apply the weights that you have determined are relevant to your category and task in order to calculate the Buying Power Index.

$$(.267)(.5) + (1.14)(.3) + (3.26)(.2) = 1.13 \text{ BPI}$$

D. To complete this exercise, you would have to perform the same calculations on other U.S. markets to determine their BPI. The Albuquerque BPI would then be compared with the other markets through an indexing process to evaluate the relative strengths or to allocate advertising dollars.

EDITOR & PUBLISHER MARKET GUIDE

Editor & Publisher, the main trade magazine of the newspaper business, publishes an annual Market Guide (Exhibit 6.2), which contains a wide variety of unique information. It is often used in conjunction with the Survey of Buying Power.

One unique advantage of the Market Guide is that it reports on many of the smallest towns in America. It also lists the major businesses, shopping centers and the stores within them, supermarkets, and a wide variety of retail outlets. It estimates population and the number of automobiles. It identifies the banks and the most important local shopping days. In short, it tells you everything you could discover by studying the local newspaper, including the weather.

The Market Guide is often the only source of information on factors that one might wish to include in comparing various markets and their potential. It is also useful in selecting test markets and tracking retail sales.

CATEGORY AND BRAND DEVELOPMENT

Most sophisticated national advertisers possess very specific sales information on their brands and on the categories in which these brands compete (see chapter 4). When such information exists, it is almost always the primary database for allocating advertising budgets.

The issue facing the advertiser is a strategy decision. Some of the alternatives are:

1. A relatively small budget encourages the restriction of a campaign to local markets where the careful use of money can make a small brand look like a large brand.
2. A national brand with a sufficient budget may decide to spend a proportion of its budget in important local markets for either offensive or defensive reasons.
3. A regional brand with limited distribution can only benefit from local market advertising but must allocate its budget in some rational way.
4. A new brand is rolling out in widely dispersed markets and wishes to allocate its hypothetical national advertising budget in a manner that will reflect a future national campaign.

The fundamental decision-making tools in each of these instances are **the Brand Development Index** and **Category Development Index**. The arithmetic for each index is rather simple. The difficulty emerges when you are making the strategic decisions incorporated in the criteria of choice.

The assumption behind both a Brand Development Index (BDI) and Category Development Index (CDI) is that the sales for a brand or category should reflect the population, that is, sales should fluctuate in direct proportion to the population. Of course, this is never true. Both the BDI and CDI are means for measuring the deviation from this abstract norm.

EXHIBIT 6.2 **EDITOR AND PUBLISHER MARKET GUIDE**

Alaska   II-7

ALASKA SURVEYS

METROPOLITAN STATISTICAL AREAS

Anchorage - Anchorage Borough.

POPULATION ESTIMATES
(Thousands)

Age Group	1970	1980	1988
Under 5 Years	32	38	47
5-14 Years	71	70	87
15-24 Years	64	82	102
25-44 Years	88	146	182
45-64 Years	41	55	69
65 and Over	7	12	15
TOTAL	303	403	502

Based on U.S. Census

RETAIL SALES ESTIMATES
(Millions)

Kind of Business	1977 Census	1982 Census	1988 Est.
Bldg. Mat.-Hdwr.	150	340	638
General Mdse.	227	334	501
Food	427	632	918
Automobiles	241	430	791
Gasoline Stations	103	286	204
Apparel	69	127	184
Furniture	58	128	234
Eat-Drink Places	254	405	589
Drugs	80	136	201
TOTAL SALES	1,831	3,227	4,776

ANCHORAGE

1 - LOCATION: Anchorage County. E&P Map B-3 (MSA). Largest city in Alaska. Wholesale and retail distribution center for area extending 800 mi. W. Headquarters for Alaska's corporations, banks, communications, health facilities, petroleum industry, military establishment. Hub of rail, air and highway transportation. On main highway connecting W Alaska and U.S. via Canada. 550 mi. W of Juneau; 350 mi. S of Fairbanks; 1,450 mi. NW of Seattle.

2 - TRANSPORTATION: Railroads-Alaska. **Motor Freight Carriers**-23. **Freight Steamship Lines**-6. **Intercity Bus Lines**-Alaska-Yukon Motorcoaches, Kenai Peninsula Bus Lines, Anchorage Transit (People Mover). Mat-Valley Commuter. Greyline. **Airlines**-20 Intermediate stop of international flights. China Air, Flying Tigers; Air France. British Airways, Japan Airlines; KLM; Korean; Lufthansa; Sabena; Scandinavian Airways. Interior. Delta; Alaska; Northwest; Reeve Aleutian; Air Cal; TWA, Mark Air; United; Southcentral, Eastern, Hawaiian; Air Pac; ERA; Swiss Air. **Air Taxi** 60; **Helicopters** 14.

3 - POPULATION: Corp. City 80 Cen. 173,017, E&P 87 Est. 249,375. MSA/County 80 Cen. 173,017, E&P 87 Est. 249,375. NDM-ABC. (80) 225,877.

4 - HOUSEHOLDS: City 80 Cen. 60,042, E&P 87 Est. 89,974. MSA/County 80 Cen. 60,042, E&P 87 Est. 89,974. NDM-ABC. (80) 77,404.

5 - BANKS

	NUMBER	DEPOSITS
Savings & Loan	1	$40,839,000
Commercial	15	$3,977,227,000

6 - PASSENGER AUTOS: County 135,573.

7 - ELECTRIC METERS: Residence 85,558.

8 - GAS METERS: Residence 58,645.

9 - PRINCIPAL INDUSTRIES: Industry, No. of Wage Earners (Av. Wkly Wage N.A.)-Gov't 26,600, Whol. & Ret. Trade 29,000, Irons 4,250, Constr. 8,500, Mfg. 2,900, Petroleum, Servs. 27,200 Trans. Commun., Util. 9,700, Insurance, R.E., Finance 9,350, Mining 4,400.

10 - CLIMATE: Av. Temp. Jan. 13 degrees, July 57 degrees. An. rainfall 9 in.; av. an. snowfall 70 in.

11 - TAP WATER: Neutral, hard; fluoridated.

12 - RETAILING: Principal Shopping Centers-33 blocks on 4th, 5th and 6th Aves., 20 blocks on Northern Lights Blvd., 20 blocks on Dimond Blvd., 10 blocks Northway Drive.

Nearby Shopping Centers

Name (No. of stores)	Miles from Downtown	Principal Stores
Aurora Vlg.(12)	3	Carr's, Payless, Pay 'N Pak
Ionrface	6	Pay'N Save, Safeway
Country Village	4	Discount Fabrics
Dimond(160)	6	Safeway, Pay'N Save, Lamont's
Carr's Dimond	6	Carr's, Payless
Eastgate(11)	4	Carr's, Payless
Mountain View	2	Market Basket
Northern Lts.(15)	2	Safeway, Pay'N Save
Northway Mall(73)	NA	Safeway, Pay'N Save, Lamont's
Post Office Mall		Book Cache
Southcenter	5	
Spenard University	4	Lamont's, Pay'N Save
Univ. Ctr.(34)	NA	Safeway, Book Cache
Sears Mall(30)	3	Sears, Carr's, Payless
West Side City	8	
Eagle River(6)	15	Carr's, Payless

Principal Shopping Days-Thur., Fri., Sat., Sun. Stores Open Evenings-Mon. through Fri.

13 - RETAIL OUTLETS: Department Stores-Nordstrom, JC Penney, Sears, Lamont's 3, Sportswest 2. **Discount Stores**-Fred Myer 2; Price Savers; Cosco. **Variety Stores**-Woolworth, B&J. **Chain Drug Stores**-Pay'N Save 6; Payless 9; Rexall, Long's 2. **Chain Supermarkets**-Carr's 9; Safeway 6; Proctor's; Prairie Mkt. 2; Foodland 3. **Other Chain Stores**-Klopfensteins (men's), Zale's 3; Kinney Shoes 3, Pay 'N Pak, Jay Jacobs 2; McMahan's Furn.; Pacific Fabrics, Singer 2. Discount Fabrics, Leed's Shoes 2, Singer, Baskin-Robbins 4; Book Cache 13; Waldenbooks; Dalton Books, The Office Place; Computerland; Qwik Stop 28; 7-Eleven 7.

14 - NEWSPAPERS: DAILY NEWS (m) 54,712; (S) 67,971; Mar. 31, 1987 ABC. Local Contact for Advertising & Merchandising Data: Marge Campbell, Dir. of Mktg. & Research. DAILY NEWS, 1001 Northway Dr., PO Box 14-9001, Anchorage, AK 99514-9001; Tel. (907) 257-4200. National Representative: Cresmer, Woodward, O'Mara & Ormsbee. **TIMES** (e) 35,696; (S) 47,135; Mar. 31, 1987 ABC. Local Contact for Advertising and Merchandising Data: Arlene Sayers, Adv. Dir.; TIMES, 820 Fourth Ave., Anchorage, AK 99501; Tel. (907) 263-9000. National Representative: Branham/Newspaper Sales.

BDIs are an index of a brand's per capita sales in a given local market compared to the market's theoretical contribution. It compares the percentage of a brand's total national sales to the percentage of the national population base living in the same market.

$$BDI = \frac{\% \text{ Brand's Sales in Market}}{\% \text{ U.S. Population in Market}} \times 100$$

Therefore, if a brand's sales are distributed 50%, 30%, and 20% in three equalized regions of the country, the BDI calculation would be:

Region	% Volume	÷	% U.S.	=	BDI
A	50	÷	33.3	=	150
B	30	÷	33.3	=	90
C	20	÷	33.3	=	60

The CDI performs the same function for a product category. It compares the percentage of total national sales of the product category in a specific market with the percentage of the national population residing in that market.

$$CDI = \frac{\% \text{ Category Sales in Mkt.}}{\% \text{ U.S. Population in Mkt.}} \times 100$$

Thus, if:

$$\frac{\% \text{ Category Sales in Chicago}}{\% \text{ U.S. Population in Chicago}} = \frac{2.85}{1.70} \times 100 = 167 \text{ CDI}$$

Analysis

There are four possible combinations of CDIs and BDIs

1. High BDI and high CDI
2. Low BDI and high CDI
3. High BDI and low CDI
4. Low BDI and low CDI

Both BDIs and CDIs are important decision-making tools. One identifies the relative strengths and weaknesses of the brand, and the other the relative strengths and weaknesses of the category. High CDIs show market potential for any brand in a category. High BDIs identify the brand's profile in a market. They are frequently used together.

High BDI/High CDI An ideal market in which to act both offensively and defensively when allocating budgets.

Low BDI/High CDI The kind of market that gets your attention. There may be specific reasons (poor distribution, poor sales force, and so on) for the poor brand showing. All other things being equal, however, this market might suggest an offensive strategy.

High BDI/Low CDI This market might call for a defensive strategy, but it must be monitored for a declining sales trend.

Low BDI/Low CDI Generally, a no-win situation that might even suggest the withdrawal of advertising expenditures for use elsewhere or for other marketing purposes in the market.

These are basic strategic responses to only one set or one kind of information. Frequently, other criteria are included, such as the relative costs of media or general market conditions derived from other sources.

The most significant issue is the establishment of the criteria of choice once the data is assembled and parsed.

EXAMPLE

The criteria might read: BDI over 100 in markets representing at least 1% of total sales and a cost-per-thousand below $10. The data presentation might look like the following.

Market	% U.S.	% Volume	BDI	CPM
Baltimore	1.01	1.00	98	$8.57
Boston	2.28	3.92	172	9.98
Buffalo	.72	.87	121	7.61
Cleveland	1.64	2.01	125	5.97
Indianapolis	.92	.90	98	7.29
Milwaukee	.81	.74	91	6.57
New York	7.72	14.30	185	4.98
Orlando/Dade	.79	.90	114	13.62
Philadelphia	2.97	3.83	129	7.09
Pittsburgh	1.44	3.27	227	7.36
St. Louis	1.22	1.34	110	4.90
Washington, D.C.	1.75	1.59	91	5.90

In this example, Orlando would probably be the first market to be eliminated from consideration, followed by Milwaukee and Indianapolis. Buffalo, because of its low volume contribution, and Washington, D.C., because of its low BDI, represent slightly more difficult decisions. The most difficult decision is represented by Baltimore.

Whatever the case, or final decision, the purpose of BDIs, CDIs, and other indices of this type is to enable the marketer to make strategic decisions on some rational basis.

Part Three

Strategy Development

7

Media Work Plan: Part II—Objectives and Strategies

OVERVIEW

This chapter introduces and describes the second major step in the media planning process. Part II of the Media Work Plan identifies, articulates, explains, and supports the strategies that make the Plan cohesive. This is the point at which the fundamental decisions are made and the reasoning process made apparent.

STRATEGY

Strategic decisions are the most important part of the media planning process. It often comes as a surprise to those who love to see flowcharts, supported by budget and delivery summaries, that strategic thinking is not only the hardest, but the most significant part of media planning.

Strategic thinking is the necessary bridge between the marketing situation analysis and the media purchase proposals. Only a strategy consensus can persuasively argue for any particular set of executions, or one set of tactics versus another. Strategy decisions demand the full engagement of the mind and the imagination. They represent the moment when everyone must confront the fact that in the mercurial world of consumers and communications there cannot possibly be an absolutely perfect plan, except to the extent to which we give it consent.

There simply is no credible way to get from marketing conclusions to media executions except through strategic analysis and decision.

MEDIA WORK PLAN—PART II

Strategy decisions, which are rooted in the marketing situation, objectives, and strategies, constitute the second major step of the media planning process. An outline of the major strategic decision points of the planning process is contained in Part II of the Media Work Plan (Exhibit 7.1). The purpose of this section is to identify, articulate, and explain media strategies at a specific advertising budget while providing the data and reasoning upon which the strategic decisions have been based.

Media strategy determines who, when, where, and how often people will be communicated with, using various types of media. Strategy decisions are the point at which marketing meets cultural vehicles. They make up the rationale behind our actions and set the stage for creativity.

Part II of the Media Work Plan also identifies the media objective and budget. **Media objectives** are positive statements of what the media plan will achieve on a specific budget. Media strategies articulate how these media objectives will be accomplished.

MEDIA OBJECTIVES

It is always important for us to realize where we are in the chain of command and what kind of results we are responsible for in the "big picture." The basic discipline for understanding both the system and one's role within it is the ladder of objectives and strategies (Exhibit 7.2).

In what might be called the subsidiarity of objectives, the strategies of the higher corporate organ become the objectives of the lower. Following this principle of subsidiarity, marketing objectives are derived from corporate strategies, and advertising objectives are derived from marketing strategies. The intention throughout is that each department focus on what its specific tools can accomplish while every element of the corporation is working toward the same ends.

Setting Media Objectives

Media objectives are quantifiable statements of what the plan intends to accomplish. Objectives must be specific enough to provide guidance, realistically measurable, and sufficiently achievable to be practical within the available budget. The basic craft elements of media planning, which provide the foundation for measurable plan objectives, are reach, frequency, and continuity, qualified by their general geographic and/or prospect focus.

The key fact is that each of these factors costs money, and there is never enough money available to do everything a planner or marketer might wish. Therefore, reach, frequency, and continuity are constantly competing for a share of the budget. Media objectives provide direction for the resolution of this tension. In turn, these objectives establish the parameters for the strategic judgments yet to be made.

Economists would describe the budget competition between reach, frequency, and continuity as a **zero sum game**, which means that any addition to one element of the equation must be matched by a subtraction from another. This can be expressed geometrically as differently shaped triangles of the same area (Figure 7.1).

EXHIBIT 7.1 MEDIA WORK PLAN: SECTION II

Budget/Recommendation

Media Objective

Prospect Audience

    Basic Designation:

    Demographics:

    Psychographics:

Media Strategies

    Seasonality:

    Scheduling:

    Competition:

    Geography:

    Effective Reach/Frequency Goals:

    Creative Units:

Media Selection and Rationale

Proposed Testing

EXHIBIT 7.2 LADDER OF OBJECTIVES AND STRATEGIES

It is difficult for many media planners to distinguish goals, objectives, strategies, and tactics.

Goal is the end toward which any effort is directed. It establishes purposefulness and provides the ultimate reason that we are doing anything. A goal gives value and shapes the intrinsic merit of our actions. In corporate life, goals are usually the province of chief executive officers and boards of directors. They determine whether the reason for the corporation's existence and activities is continuity or growth, market share or return on investor equity, profits or social responsibility. Whatever its content, if a goal is accomplished, the members of corporate community will be entirely self-satisfied. They will believe that they have done good.

Objectives are positive statements of what must be accomplished to achieve the goal. An objective is a particular set of outcomes that any element of a corporation must accomplish in a specific period of time so that the corporation's goals will be realized. Objectives are tasks to be accomplished; they are set without any implication about how they will be accomplished.

Strategies represent the overriding plan of action that will guide someone's actions in the accomplishment of a particular objective or set of objectives. Strategies initiate action. They represent our best judgment about how to set about accomplishing our objectives. Strategy is the plan of attack and the discipline of command. A strategy may not accomplish its stated objective, but without a strategy all our actions eventually dissolve into chaos. Strategy is our defense against chance. Strategy enables us to evaluate various executions and creates the norms of our actions. Strategy alone enables us to have rational and imaginative flexibility in our choice of tactics.

Tactics are the specific activities that are chosen to implement strategy. Tactics are the details of any plan. Flowcharts of media activity and specific vehicle selections are tactics. Budget and delivery summaries are the arithmetic of tactics.

FIGURE 7.1 ZERO SUM TRIANGLES OF COMMUNICATION

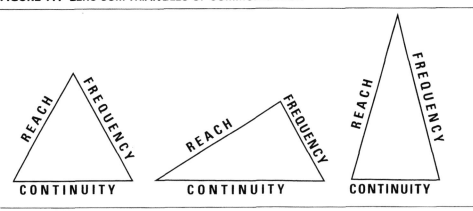

The variable importance of reach, frequency, and continuity is directly influenced by: a) the brand's position in the hierarchy of effects model; b) the brand's position in the product life cycle, and c) competitive circumstances.

Hierarchy of Effects and Media Objectives

We have emphasized the point of view that advertising should be evaluated only by what advertising itself can achieve. We focused, therefore, on the hierarchy of effects model as the most appropriate description of how the advertising/communications process works. This model is particularly relevant to translating marketing objectives and strategies into advertising media objectives. It enables the planner to set communications objectives precisely designed to carry out the marketing strategy.

The hierarchy of effects model suggests a logical consumer decision process from awareness to trial through various steps from attention to interest, preference, and action (Figure 2.1). When applied to market conditions, the model implies that competitive brands may be situated in various positions along the model's spectrum (Figure 2.2). The most obvious conclusion is that the media objective will change in direct relation to the brand's competitive position in the application of the hierarchy of effects model.

In the mercurial world of brands, consumers, and communications, however, it is demonstrably presumptuous to assume that consumers are always this rational. Consumption, like the rest of our lives, is often made up of nonlinear experiences. Consequently, there are three basic variations on the hierarchy of effects model that have a direct impact on the formulation of media objectives:

1. The hierarchy of effects model directly applies to **high involvement and clearly differentiated products** (for example, automobiles, computers, and foundation garments) (Figure 7.2).

FIGURE 7.2 HIGH INVOLVEMENT/HIGH DIFFERENTIATION

Cognitive ⟶ Affective ⟶ Behavioral

When this model applies to the product and marketing situation, prospect reach and advertising continuity form the basic parameters of the media objectives.

2. **Low involvement products**, however, are often purchased on the basis of top-of-mind awareness alone. This situation is brought about by perceived parity in frequently purchased product categories (for example, soaps, soups, mouthwash, and floor wax). Preferences may emerge, but only after multiple and effectively experimental uses (Figure 7.3).

FIGURE 7.3 LOW INVOLVEMENT/LOW DIFFERENTIATION

Cognitive ⟶ Behavioral ⟶ Affective

A brand's dependence on the leverage of top-of-mind awareness in this marketing environment generally requires a high frequency profile as the key media objective.

3. When **near parity** or modest differentiation is perceived to exist among **modest involvement products**, consumers are often especially affected by personal sources of information such as a relative, a presumably expert friend, or a friendly salesperson (for example, designer label clothing, hardware/tools, books, and computer programs). After the purchase is made, consumers tend to adopt a positive attitude—conforming their attitude to their behavior—while developing an awareness of the purchased brand's distinctive characteristics (Figure 7.4).

FIGURE 7.4 MODEST INVOLVEMENT/MODEST DIFFERENTIATION

Behavioral ──────▶ Affective ──────▶ Cognitive

In this marketing environment, advertising must narrowly target opinion leaders while providing positive reinforcement to those who have already purchased the brand. The situation requires extensive frequency against the opinion leaders and broad reach against the consumer universe as essential ingredients of the media objectives.

When setting media objectives, the planner must first determine which learning-decision process characterizes purchases in the category, and where competitive brands are situated in this dynamic. This judgment will be made on the basis of the planner's experience—through the cognitive imagination—of the consumer's purchase, usage, and decision behavior. The planner can then identify the best proportionate relationship between reach, frequency, and continuity for communicating effectively with the marketing target.

Product Life Cycle and Media Objectives

In our discussion of marketing, we noted that experience teaches us that most products eventually pass through four stages of life (Figure 2.5). Combined with diffusion and adoption theories, the stages of the product life cycle model suggest different communication objectives for media planning. Basic variations include:

Introduction The key effort is to initiate demand through news and education delivered to opinion leaders in a tight time frame. Rollout strategies often dictate limited geographic markets. Budgets are at an investment level. Reach is the primary concern.

Growth Media efforts are calibrated to expanding demand through an elaboration of targets and geographic markets. Budgets are still investment oriented. Reach remains most important, but frequency grows in importance as required for differentiation from emerging competition.

Maturity Product acceptance and competition produce wide markets and targets. Profits are emphasized, and budgets are calibrated to sales. Reach becomes more defined in terms of the brand's users as opposed to those who use competitive brands. Frequency becomes proportionately more important.

Decline Maintenance advertising task tends to favor fewer geographic markets and reach over frequency, with minimal budgets. Advertising probably comes in bursts.

The consideration of these potential objectives should be combined with the brand's and category's position in the learning-decision process. The prism of the product life cycle is especially helpful to the planner's cognitive imagining of the mechanics of the marketing system in action. Together, these models help the planner to visualize the communications that have, are, will, and must occur.

Competitive Circumstances

Three elements of the marketing situation analysis can be combined—for the purposes of setting media objectives—under the heading of Competitive Circumstances. The three are sales and share, product description, and share of voice. Each of these elements will reverberate throughout the strategy discussion and will often receive specific attention. As a group, however, they are relevant to setting the broad objectives for a plan, and no experienced media planner ignores their implications when setting objectives.

Sales and Share **High sales and shares** for your brand generally translate as an emphasis on a significant share of voice in all markets and among all consumers while the brand's existing franchise among its users is protected.

Low sales and shares for your brand generally lead to focusing on narrower market lists and narrower targets with bursts of advertising.

Product Description **Unique brand characteristics** generally imply narrower targets and relatively high budgets focused in media capable of communicating value. Time and place factors vary widely.

Parity brand positions generally translate as a need to be wherever and whenever the competition is, with an emphasis on frequency.

Share of Voice **Positive share** of voice generally translates as relatively high, broadly based budgets throughout the year.

Limited resources generally result in an attempt to maximize impact by concentrating budgets by time and markets so that budgets produce parity reach and frequencies when active against targets. Consideration must also be given to high profile media events (for example, unique TV entertainment specials) even when expensive.

The reality check introduced by an overall consideration of a brand's competitive circumstances tends to sharpen and limit the options considered under the previous models of communication and product growth. These competitive circumstances are usually reflected in the available budget.

Writing Media Objectives

From a consideration of the brand's position in the hierarchy of effects model relative to marketing objectives and strategies, from the recognition of the brand's position in the product life cycle, and with an acceptance of the competitive circumstances, a media planner can identify the key elements required of the media objectives. They include:

1. The relative importance of reach and/or frequency
2. Narrowness of focus of the target prospects as a source generator
3. Extent and character of the geographic distribution of messages
4. The degree of continuity required

Any budget-limited set of objectives is filled with tension. One purpose of media objectives is to bridge the gap between marketing strategies and media strategies. They represent a moment of candor and realism, as well as one requiring intelligence and skill. They also represent the first step in building consensus. For all these reasons, media objectives are difficult to write.

Although the variations are endless, five examples can illustrate the interdependence of media objectives and the marketing direction derived from the marketing objectives and strategies. (Exhibit 7.3)

The fundamental skill involved in writing media objectives is the ability to devise language that projects and, therefore, guides media strategies while obviously reflecting the marketing strategies and objectives. The insight required is derived from the various models of marketing and communication described above.

Writing media objectives is the first obvious point in the media planning process at which the cognitive imagination is clearly linked with technical skill. This is the point at which art meets craft. The two basic issues are:

1. Does the sudden introduction of craft demands enhance the imperatives of the cognitive imagination?
2. Is the felt experience of consumer behavior and communications dynamic lost as the demands of craftsmanship suddenly dominate the scene?

The answer is that we must incorporate both vitality and structure. If we reflect upon it, these are the two dominant issues in any critic's evaluation of a film, book, or play: great insights disfigured by inadequate execution, and marvelous executional skills undermined by the absence of insight. Either fails without the other.

One problem frequently encountered in the writing of media objectives is a blurring of the distinction between the role and function of the Media Plan and the role and function of the total advertising effort. The question is: Does the Media Plan directly connect to the marketing strategies and objectives, or is it filtered through the Advertising Plan? (Figure 7.5)

EXHIBIT 7.3

Marketing Direction	Media Objectives
1. Increase brand share to 50% by becoming the brand of choice among heavy users *(Growth stage of Low Involvement/ Low Differentiation product)*	Concentrate a high frequency of impressions against category's current heavy users with minimal sacrifices in continuity.
2. Increase brand sales by 2% through an increase in category consumption. *(Mature stage of High Involvement/ High Differentiation brand)*	Provide continuous reach against all prospects on a national basis while allocating added frequency to markets showing higher brand category opportunity.
3. Maintain brand's existing franchise by sustaining volume among current users. *(Decline stage of Low Involvement/ Low Differentiation Brand)*	Concentrate spending in line with seasonal category consumption patterns with focus on current brand users.
4. Introduce new brand to existing category and establish it as the dominant brand in the category with a 30% share of market. *(Growth stage of Low Involvement/ Low Differentiation Brand)*	Allocate a disproportionate percent of reach and frequency weight in the first 13 weeks of the introductory period to achieve rapid awareness and induce early trial.
5. Eliminate current inventory. *(Mature stage of Low Involvement/ Modest Differentiation Brand)*	Allocate spending in coordinated pattern coinciding with promotional activities in key sales areas.

FIGURE 7.5 ALTERNATIVE ADVERTISING MANAGEMENT PATTERNS

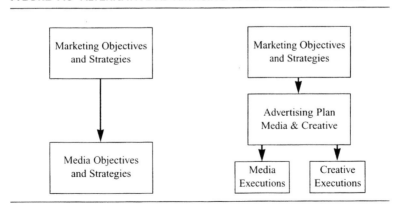

When an Advertising Plan exists and it is well executed, it generally includes the creative strategy and message along with the media objectives and strategies.

Whatever the case, the only way to encourage creativity in media planning is to focus on both the independent and the dependent aspects of the process. Focusing our attention on distinct media objectives, and differentiating media objectives from the full line of media strategies, force us to decide how we view media planning's contribution to the marketing process.

BUDGET/RECOMMENDATION

Identifying the working media budget at the beginning of the media strategy discussion is significant, because the utility, creativity, and practicality of any media plan must be measured against the available investment dollars.

When an advertising budget reaches the media planner, it is often just a fact of life. In some circumstances, however, either there is room for argument, or the client consciously and clearly requests the agency's input regarding budget levels. In both circumstances, the burden generally falls on account management, who review the traditional budget setting methods and make a recommendation. The typical methods are:

1. Category or industry tradition
2. Historical levels plus inflation
3. Percentage of sales or advertising-to-sales ratios
4. Competitive share-of-market/share-of-voice
5. Objective/task evaluation
6. Test markets and modeling

The media planner might be asked for input on any one of these approaches, but generally is not directly involved in the discussion or debate.

The media planner must be directly involved, however, in the objective/task method of budget development. This method begins with quantifiable communication objectives and then works backward to the cost of the advertising programs judged necessary to achieve these objectives. Since only the media planner possesses the unique skills needed for defining communication objectives, the media planner becomes the fulcrum of the effort.

The critical point in this effort is rooted in estimates of the reach and frequency required to achieve the stated objectives. (In chapter 9 we discuss the subject of setting reach and frequency goals.) In any case, the objective/task method of budget setting is an elaborate process and exists outside of the Media Plan. For the Plan, the budget would be a given.

There is one variation: Often the client (or the agency, on its own initiative) suggests that a plan at an alternative budget level be explored. In this instance, a brief paragraph of explanation of the difference the alternate plan is expected to make, and why this possibility is a prudent alternative, should be included to support the budget figure.

TARGET MARKET

If the client and agency are following the marketing system as taught in textbooks, the marketing strategy has identified the source generator for achieving the marketing objectives. The refinement of this direction and the selection/definition of the target market for media purposes requires strategic judgment for several reasons:

1. The marketing strategy only provides the most basic designation of the source generator.
2. The marketing strategy most often lacks any demographic specificity, and this is required for the guidance of media executions.
3. The nature of advertising may require a different or broader target definition than that found in marketing documents.
4. Whether or not target market demographics are provided, they do not always coincide or conform with the demographic categories reported by the research services. Such conformed data is necessary for accountable purchasing.
5. The media planner often has a distinctive contribution to make based on unique media data.

Each of these variables requires a judgment by the planner, who is required to go beyond the description and data provided by someone else. This is characteristic of strategic decisions. Targets sound like objects only when there is a bull's-eye. If there is a choice of various placements with equivalent scores, as in darts, however, then the specific choice is a strategic judgment.

Basic Designation

The basic prospect designation, as noted above, is often contained in the marketing strategy and is directly reflected in the media objectives statement. Both have already identified the broadest definition of the key prospect along the user/nonuser and/or brand loyalty axis. In the marketer's world view, one is either a buyer or nonbuyer of the category or brand, and either brand loyal or not. The only issues are intensity. Therefore, users can be described as heavy, medium, or light users. Brand loyalists can be described as sole, primary, or secondary users.

Demographics

Demographic measures define the primary prospect's or source generator's gender, age, marital status, income, family size, education, employment status, and where he/she is most likely to reside. This information is simultaneously compared to information about the total U.S. population in order to measure how realistic the parameters chosen are.

The key profiling numbers are population sizes and their index numbers, or quantity and quality. While making demographic decisions, the media planner will always be mindful of the contiguity of groups, since the greater their demographic proximity, the more likely it will be that the groups can be reached with the same media purchases.

Both effectiveness and efficiency norms can be applied to this demographically described prospect group. Effectiveness requires that the prospects identified and reached will actually purchase sufficient amounts of the brand to meet sales and marketing objectives. The largest consumer groups, however, may contain a great number of desultory consumers who are not very promising buyers. Efficiency measures suggest that smaller, more dynamic and energetic consumer groups represent a better pool of prospects. The target market, therefore, must be large enough, dynamic enough, and efficiently reachable.

Demographic definition is the result of a dialogue between population size and product usage dynamics. The planner can begin from either side of the equation (Figure 7.6). The planner can move from analyzing usage levels to measuring the relative size of the population base and back, or from demographic size parameters to usage dynamics and back to define the prospect profile.

FIGURE 7.6 TARGET MARKET PROFILING

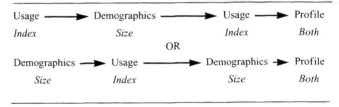

Each designator in this profile would be illustrated with all the appropriate data from the research source.

The planner also should be constantly aware of the direction of the media objective, which identified the relative importance of reach and frequency. The dictates of efficiency and limited budgets might, for example, dictate a narrower prospect (reach) definition in order to afford the necessary frequency.

A final check of the demographic profile is needed to confirm that the designated prospect group is large enough. This is done by applying the brand's normal share of market, or the expected conversion rate projected by research, to the prospect group. The result should approximate the sales volume required of the marketing effort.

Motivations

Demographic considerations may also begin the process of personalizing the consumer. Two different groups of demographic information are useful for constructing an imaginary dialogue. The first defines the prospect, and the second tells you how the prospect is most likely to think (Exhibit 7.4). The first step is always to define the

EXHIBIT 7.4 DIVISION OF DEMOGRAPHIC DATA

Prospect	Thought
Age	Education
Gender	Employment
Income	Family Size
Marital Status	Ownership
Geography	Geography

(Geography is listed twice, for it may suggest an "on the ground" focus for media efforts. For a national brand, it may indicate a set of attitudes.)

prospect and then to determine how the prospect thinks ("where they are coming from").

Every demographic cluster represents a social group, with substantive differences in their wants and needs (see chapter 1). Once the larger elements of the prospect profile are identified, however, subsequent demographic parameters can be a window into their thoughts and can provide a refined understanding of their attitudes. They can be a useful springboard for the cognitive imagination.

The more demographic data will be used to determine attitudes, the more important the index numbers become relative to quantitative measures. Whatever the circumstances and variations, however, demographic data is most useful when it is viewed in human, as well as numerical, terms. We should constantly recall Theodore Levitt's encouragement of the "imaginative conversion of data" as the best way to know your prospects in a fundamental and compelling way.

Lifestyles and Psychographics

Lifestyles and psychographics can be distinguished in a technical and abstract way, but they tend to be used interchangeably by nonresearch-oriented practitioners. Both, however, have been heavily influenced by the prospect's media habits. Their description, therefore, will become critical to designing strategies for reaching the prospect through the media. At the same time, the prospect's media selections can be utilized to help us comprehend the prospect's attitudes and beliefs.

Psychographics represent character traits rooted either in personality (funny/serious), or a social class that tends to share beliefs (liberal/conservative), or behavior patterns (passive/active sports interest). **Lifestyle** represents values, hopes, and expectations that unite individuals across social groups and that motivate their similar behavior. Psychographics are used to understand the motivations of demographically defined groups. Lifestyle research is used to define both consumers and the makeup of our society in a nondemographic manner. It is difficult, however, to avoid melding both into one concept.

Psychographics and lifestyle have already been considered by the most sophisticated marketers in both their market segmentation analysis and the positioning of their brands (see chapter 2). The process is the result of an effort to identify subgroups within demographic variables and the design of products and advertising appeals focused on the motives and interests of these subgroups. The analysis calls for clustering consumers according to common activities, interests, and opinions (AIOs), which can be quite different from demographic data (Exhibit 7.5).

To identify such subgroups and to develop compatible products and appeals, sophisticated marketers conduct extensive proprietary research. The media planner often has access to the conclusions of this research. The major agencies also conduct similar research to support their message selections and other creative efforts. The planner will have access to this research. Either or both of these instances are the natural place to begin developing a more detailed and vital description of prospects than is available through demographics alone.

VALS

The most commonly used syndicated research source for lifestyle segmentation, VALS (Values and Lifestyles), is produced by SRI International. VALS is an attempt to establish consumer segment classifications representing different decision making and behavior patterns that are reflected in product consumption tendencies.

The original VALS typography (Figure 7.7) clearly reflected the work of two prominent predecessors: David Riesman and Abraham Maslow. Riesman projected two types of personalities: **outer directed** people, who are heavily influenced by the opinions of others and their anxiety to fit in with the group, and **inner directed** people, who derive their values independently and live by their own standards. Maslow proposed that people are motivated by a **hierarchy of needs**, which they will seek to satisfy one after the other in rank order.

VALS 2, an evolution from these two concepts, suggests that there are eight types of consumers (Figure 7.8). Along a horizontal axis, consumers are classified by their basis for decision making: principle, status, or action. Along a vertical axis, consumers are identified by a hierarchy of their needs and the ability to satisfy these needs. Each group represents between 8 and 17 percent of the population, and the groups intersect in a way that demonstrates the ability to combine them into larger targets.

The generally perceived limitations in the kind of research utilized and the conclusions reached in these efforts focus on validity, availability, and compatibility.

Validity The research is based on very small samples, requires extremely subtle questioning, and is not demonstrably pertinent to the specific product category or to the motivations of its consumers.

Availability Both MRI and SMRB provide some psychographic data for their media audiences, and SMRB includes some lifestyle data, but even this limited data is not provided for television, radio, or newspaper audiences.

Compatibility Most of the available research has been developed without reference to media and does not reflect media preferences. Without a direct link to media habits, it is difficult to translate the data into media selections or vehicle purchases.

EXHIBIT 7.5 LIFESTYLE AND DEMOGRAPHICS

Activities	Interests	Opinions	Demographics
Work	Family	Themselves	Age
Hobbies	Home	Social Issues	Education
Social Events	Job	Politics	Income
Vacations	Community	Business	Occupation
Entertainment	Recreation	Economics	Family Size
Club Membership	Fashion	Education	Dwelling
Community	Food	Products	Geographic
Shopping	Media	Future	City Size
Sports	Achievements	Culture	Stage of Life Cycle

Source: Joseph T. Plummer, "Applications of Life Style Research to the Creation of Advertising Campaigns," in *Life Style and Psychographics*, ed. William Wells (Chicago, Ill.: American Marketing Association, 1974), p. 160.

FIGURE 7.7 VALUES AND LIFESTYLES (1) - SRI

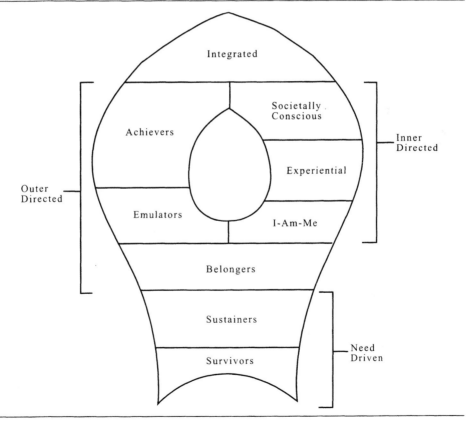

Source: Values and Lifestyles (VALS) Program SRI International, Menlo Park, CA.

FIGURE 7.8 VALUES AND LIFESTYLES (2) - SRI

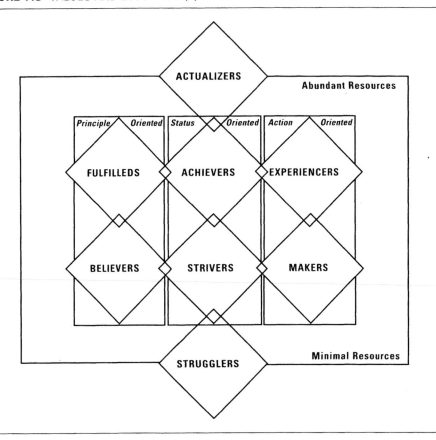

All of these critical limitations are real, but in fact they have not stopped anyone from using VALS categories as part of target audience descriptions. If the VALS categories are imaginatively understood, they can be cognitively significant.

Media Planning Uses and Inputs

Lifestyle and psychographic data are focused on consumer motivations, which are the key to the exchange that creates markets (see chapter 2). Just as media planners should imagine this exchange, they can also imagine the media that gave rise to its motivations. Media planners can trigger the "combinatory play of images" (see chapter 1) by applying consumer psychographic and lifestyle descriptions to media types and vehicles and using them to define the motivations of consumers. The "recognition" of a match will indicate an "objective correlative" and have cognitive value.

When pursuing this line of thought, it is useful to recall the exercise (or experiment) recommended at the end of chapter 1. The only conclusion you can derive from the success of this kind of experiment is that media planners might have the unique disciplines needed for making a positive contribution to consumer lifestyle descriptions.

This is how you apply the process: Both SMRB and MRI report overall media habits for each demographic, indicating heavy or light television viewing, radio listening, magazine readership, and so on.

1. Identify the two or three media that index especially high.
2. Select three vehicles from each of the two most favored media types. The vehicles selected, which may never show up in the actual plan, should provide the greatest coverage of the target market, and/or the composition of their readership indexes should be especially high.
3. These six vehicles provide two opportunities to triangulate your target market's attitudes and interests: for example, *Rolling Stone*, *People*, *GQ*, plus *Fraser*, *Seinfeld*, and *Northern Exposure*.
4. Describe the personality and lifestyle of the person so identified on the basis of what you know of the media vehicles the person consumes most heavily or passionately.

The result of this process will provide both a lifestyle description and a description that is extensively compatible with media execution. Furthermore, this description will be as broadly accurate as that derived from any other source. The triangulation is data based; the accuracy of the description depends on the communications expertise of the media planner.

For example, the following lifestyle and psychographic descriptors were once provided by CBS:

Ask tough questions.	Remember: Rock 'n' roll is therapy.
Look beneath the surface.	
Take chances.	Don't date men with pinky rings.
Trust your instincts.	
Wear black to the office.	Risk failure.
Fight gravity.	Avoid bow ties.
Don't answer to "honey."	Go against the grain.
Be vocal.	Buck trends.
Act silly occasionally.	Make waves.
Radiate intelligence.	Rock the boat.
Demand equality.	Puncture the pompous.
Tell 'em to get their own coffee.	Get even.
View panty hose as optional June–August.	When in doubt, wear heels.
	Hold out.
Wear leather to big meetings.	Always accept cashmere.

This list ran opposite a full-page photo of Candice Bergen in her role as Murphy Brown. Experiments have shown that students have no difficulty in identifying the television program and character suggested by the list. Correspondingly, noticing that a group of consumers are especially heavy viewers of *Murphy Brown* should enable the media planner to describe the consumers' motivations and lifestyle in substantive and useful ways.

Writing the Profile

In the final analysis, the psychographic/lifestyle description of the target market should:

1. Identify and elaborate on the appropriate VALS categories.
2. Incorporate whatever descriptions are provided by agency and/or client research.
3. Be synthesized with the description that the planner derived from the triangulation of the prospect's most significant media consumption habits.

The result of these three combined efforts should provide the planner with a significantly vital understanding of the person behind the demographic numbers.

GEOGRAPHY

Geography is one of the key connection points between marketing and media. The easy situations are represented by a local marketer with only one store in one county, and by a national advertiser whose sales parallel population density in every town and region in the country. However, a media planner will rarely confront a case this straightforward.

If a product is distributed in more than one market, it is likely that sales performance will differ by market. Even a casual observer would expect that these differences haven't escaped the consciousness of the relevant marketing executives and that they have considered these differences in constructing their marketing strategy. However, this too is not always the case, and it may become the task of the media planner to focus on the distinctions.

The reason that the media planner must care about geographical sales patterns—and in some instances may be the first to care—is that the planner must devise the best allocation of expensive media investments. Media is always expensive, and geographic markets hardly ever have equal value. The strategic question is where to advertise.

The variables in establishing a geographic strategy are:

1. Distribution patterns
2. Brand sales vis-à-vis category sales
3. Demographics

   4. Competition and efficiency
   5. Compensation
   6. Promotions

Each of these variables can represent the only norm required, or they can be applied as a group. The possible general decisions are to advertise nationally (or to the widest distribution) only; to mix national and local advertising; and to employ only local media. The specific decisions become the allocation of spending to national versus local media, and the selection of the individual local markets identified with their share of media investments.

Distribution

Some products are national, some are regional, some are local, and some have uneven distribution patterns. These alternative circumstances dictate the outside parameters of any geographic target. It is useless to advertise in a place where a product is not available. Generally, media investments follow distribution. The fact is, however, that because of history or distinct consumer preferences, a brand may be virtually invisible in certain markets where it is distributed.

The planner's task is to express market parameters in compatible media terms. It is counterproductive to define markets in a manner in which they cannot be purchased or efficiently reached by media. Marketers may use census boundaries, standard metropolitan statistical areas, cities and counties, broadcast signal areas, or sales zones. Newspapers and magazines have now adopted the broadcast market parameters, and most major agencies have computer systems for translating other parameters (for instance, sales zones) into ADIs or DMAs.

Brand Sales and Category Sales

No marketer could overlook distinctive differences in sales performance by market. Generally speaking, each market should represent a share of sales proportionate to its share of the total population of the distribution areas, but this is seldom the case. Wide disparities exist. Most marketers have taken cognizance of these facts and, consequently, may provide specific direction to the media planner. The planner's task, then, is not to pick the strategy or markets, but simply to express the arithmetic of allocation. In other circumstances, the media planner must recommend the market selection as well.

The methods generally used in market appraisals are a Brand Development Index and a Category Development Index (see chapter 6). It is possible, however, for a market to show very high BDIs and CDIs without making a significant contribution to sales. The reverse is also possible. Therefore, market appraisals also include the identification of the market's percentage contribution to sales. Finally, media may be more or less expensive on a market by market basis. Consequently, market appraisals also report the cost per thousand (CPM) for the primary medium to be utilized (TV, for instance) or an aggregated cost expressed as high, average, or low.

Demographics

Demographics can be a key determinant of a geographic strategy. Age and ethnicity are the key determinants, simply because retirees tend to flock to the same warm weather states, and ethnic groups tend to congregate in specific cities or regions. In fact, however, demographics generally only introduce a variation on sales and distribution. If a brand is of special interest to, or has a special interest in, one of these demographically defined groups, sales and distribution should reflect this interest.

Competition and Efficiency

Competition and efficiency represent a more intricate set of choices. Both have proactive and reactive elements.

A **proactive competitive stance** is rooted in a market development strategy. A key variation would be the strategy of a less affluent brand to focus only on a limited number of markets where they can afford to spend on an even basis with more affluent competitors. A **reactive competitive stance** would be based on intelligence about competitive activities. It may be known, for example, that a competitor plans to introduce a new product in certain markets, or to run a unique promotion. In these cases it might be useful to allocate certain investment to blunt or negate these efforts.

A **proactive efficiency strategy** is generally limited to major advertisers who buy extensive media at discount prices. It is possible for the brands of such companies to focus on an extensive list of markets with national impact. This skewing of the normal national/local parameters is made possible by the efficiencies enjoyed from corporate purchasing power. A **reactive efficiency strategy** is similar to the proactive competitive strategy of less affluent brands. It is possible for a brand to bundle its local dollars to negotiate lower prices in a limited number of markets. Such a strategy can become too subtle and complicated, but there are occasions when it represents a prudent option.

Compensation

Compensation is fundamentally a variation on a national strategy. Network television programming does not deliver audiences in a homogenous way; programs perform better in some markets than in others. For instance, for network broadcasts of championship games in baseball, football, and basketball, the markets represented by the teams involved have much higher ratings than other markets. In fact, some important markets may show very little interest. Sophisticated marketers who use extensive network schedules can become very sensitive to market variations in network delivery. In these instances they purchase local media to create a parity of impressions across all markets.

Promotions

Almost all promotions are local in one form or another, and they frequently require or invite advertising support. The reverse proposition is that advertising should not compete with, and possibly contradict, local promotional efforts. In either instance, whether one is adding or subtracting local weight, a geographic strategy is at work and should be reflected in the Media Plan.

Writing the Strategy

It is part of American folklore that all politics are local. In many ways the same can be said of marketing and media. More and more often our complex society is forcing marketers to "think local," and distinctive local media continue to emerge. Consequently, geography is becoming an increasingly important part of media strategy considerations.

In stating geographic strategies, we must remind ourselves that strategies must be specific, they must be explained, and they must be supported. This means that markets must be named, and their numbers must be displayed. A full treatment of the markets and numbers may be reserved for an appendix to the Media Plan, but they must be available. Without specificity, a strategy is just an idea. Without numbers, it is difficult to be persuasive.

SEASONALITY

The prototypical strategy statement regarding seasonality is that "advertising expenditures will be aligned with quarterly (or monthly) sales patterns." In short, not only should advertisers spend more heavily in higher sales months, but they also should reduce or cease advertising in poor sales months.

Whatever the case, the strategy requires the ability to list brand and category sales by month as a percentage of total sales. These numbers can then be applied to the allocation of the media budget, but they must be adjusted.

Media, especially broadcast media, do not cost the same in every quarter. For example, daytime television costs are 30 percent higher in the fourth quarter than in the third quarter, while the cost for commercials in weekend children's programming triples. A straight allocation of the media budget by monthly sales percentages would result, at various times, in both underdelivery and overdelivery. Adjusting allocations by sales and by the cost of advertising is an essential part of media strategy.

There are occasions when advertising should precede heavy sales periods, or when advertising should follow seasonal usage patterns rather than seasonal sales patterns. These strategies are not prototypical, however, and their relevance should be examined in the market situation analysis. Imagining the consumer's annual diary of attention, consideration, and motivation is especially productive in these considerations.

COMPETITION

A competitive media spending analysis is contained in Part I of the Media Plan as presented here. As a result the planner should know how much competitors are spending,

what media they are using, where and when they are advertising, and their probable
reach and frequency goals.

The strategic question is: What should we do given what we know about the
competition's media activities? Are there any actions we should take in recognition of
competitive activity? The three key areas are:

1. Spending levels
2. Media usage
3. Product introductions or promotions

Spending Levels

Many people seem to believe in outspending the competition, or, at least, spending as
much as the competition does. Unless your brand is number one or number two in the
marketplace, however, neither overspending nor equal spending is a viable alternative.
For the number one brand it is often deemed prudent to insure that the share of voice
is one and a half times the share of market. A number two brand might try to pursue
a similar strategy.

The key to competitive strategies, however, does not lie in raising budgets, but
rather in considering other strategic possibilities from a competitive point of view.
Generally, these involve scheduling, geography, and media types.

Media Use

Competitors may have successfully experimented with unusual media selections or
with advertising in a counterseasonal manner. If this is so, you should never be too
smart to learn. It is possible that competition is being creative rather than foolish. If
the actions appear prudent and/or creative, it is often wise to mimic them if the budget allows.

Promotions and Introductions

The natural instinct is to attempt to use advertising weight to blunt competitive promotions or new product introductions. This requires heavier than normal investments
at the same time and in the same places that these competitive activities are taking
place. It is generally not a good idea, however, for any other than leading brands to
attempt this line of aggressive defense. Other brands might consider a slight increase
in investment after the competitive promotion, or product introduction, has run its
course.

Many planners express strategies in competitive terms, but this language is often
more show than tell. For most brands, there should be sound marketing communications reasons for market selections, timing strategies, and so on, which are rooted in
the brand and its consumer dynamics. Competition can often be a distraction and lead
to counterproductive strategies.

SUMMARY

*Strategic decisions are the most important part of the media planning process.

*Only strategy consensus can persuasively argue for any particular set of executions.

*Clear thought requires a clear understanding of the distinctions between goals, objectives, strategies, and tactics.

*Marketing strategies are the foundation of media objectives.

*Media objectives should be phrased in media terms that bridge the gap between marketing and media strategies.

*Media objectives will change in direct relation to the brand's position in the product life cycle and its competitive position in the application of the hierarchy of effects model.

*Objectives are quantifiable statements of what the plan intends to accomplish.

*Objectives should be specific and achievable.

*Media planners become directly involved in the objective/task method of budget setting.

*The basic designation of the target market is derived from the source generator identified in the marketing strategy

*Target markets must be detailed in media-compatible terms.

*Both effectiveness and efficiency norms apply to the explication of the target market.

*Strategic decisions reflected in the target profile will become normative in the selection of media types and vehicles.

*Lifestyle and psychographic descriptions are significant in imagining the marketplace exchange and the media that support consumer motivations.

*Media planners have unique disciplines appropriate to making a positive contribution to consumer lifestyle descriptions.

*Geography represents the strategic decision about where to advertise.

*The percentage allocation of budgets is the specific strategic decision required after geographic considerations.

*Seasonal spending patterns normally are aligned with monthly sales patterns, adjusted for variable media costs.

*Strictly competitive moves should be carefully considered and affordable in the context of a brand's other strategies and objectives.

QUESTIONS

1. What are the differences between goals, objectives, strategies, and tactics?
2. What is the function of Part II of the Media Work Plan?

3. Why are objectives and strategies considered the most important part of a Media Work Plan?

4. What is the relationship of the product life cycle and the hierarchy of effects models to the setting of media objectives?

5. What are the characteristics of a well-articulated media objective?

6. What are the tensions between reach, frequency, and budget that must be resolved in the media objective?

7. What role do media planners play in budget setting?

8. From what source is the basic target audience designation derived?

9. What are the characteristics of a well-articulated demographic profile?

10. Why are lifestyle and psychographic descriptions important?

11. Do media planners have any independent contribution to make to lifestyle and psychographic descriptions?

12. What are the key variables in strategic decisions about where to advertise?

13. Why must percentage budget allocations by quarter be adjusted beyond sales percentages?

14. Is it always a wise idea to attempt to directly blunt competitive activities?

ASSIGNMENT

Develop the elements of Part II of the Media Work Plan discussed in this chapter for the product or case for which you developed a marketing analysis in Part I.

SAMPLE PLAN: MEDIA WORK PLAN—PART II

BUDGET GOURMET

Budget: $20,000,000

Media Objectives:

Concentrate impressions against Budget Gourmet users, both nationally and in high sales potential markets. Emphasize reach during fourth quarter launch, to build awareness, and frequency thereafter, to generate usage. Deliver messages in a consistent environment most relevant to prospects.

Prospect Audience

Basic Designation Budget Gourmet users and category heavy users.

Demographics Interest in and need for frozen entrees is dictated more by life stage and lifestyle than by any single demographic. Four life stage segments are recommended for targeting, based on strong Budget Gourmet volume contribution.

Target	Age	%US	%Cat.	Index	%BG	Index
Young Singles	18–34	21.2	23.4	110	26.3	124
Young Marrieds	18–34	4.0	3.6	91	4.4	112
Middle Age Singles	35–49	6.9	7.6	110	8.9	130
Mid. Age Marrieds/No Children	35–49	5.8	6.7	115	7.8	135
Totals		**37.9**	**41.3**	**109**	**47.4**	**125**

Psychographics These prospects are extremely self-focused self-marketers and mostly achievers or emulators. They are highly independent. Most are affluent, but all are free spending in categories that support or articulate their lifestyle. They tend to be physically and socially active, with interests in sports, movies, concerts, eating out, entertaining, and travel. They all perceive themselves as time poor, pressed by busy work and social schedules.

Seasonality

Advertising will concentrate in the heavy consumption months of September–November and January–April. December sales are below average, but support will be continued through the month to preclude the effects of impending competitive introductions. A hiatus is recommended for June, July, and August, when consumption falls below 90% of average. Fourth quarter will be given 50% greater support to establish awareness.

	1st Qtr.	2nd Qtr.	3rd Qtr.	4th Qtr.
% GRPs	30%	5%	20%	45%

Third quarter allocation represents September relaunch.

Scheduling

Advertising will be flighted through the months of activity in conjunction with print activity, which will maintain continuity. Schedules will reflect importance of Light & Healthy launch to the February–April diet season. Consideration will be given to key promotion periods, which are yet to be determined.

Competition

Key competitors advertise in traditional TV and magazines and are heavy users of spot. Local activity is recommended for defensive, as well as offensive, reasons. Nontraditional vehicles, keyed to the target's unique interests, represent significant opportunities underutilized by competitive brands.

Geography

An approximate 60%/40% split between national and local activity is recommended. Due to the increased budget, the national effort will be sufficient to reestablish and maintain brand awareness across the country. Markets with high concentrations of target life stage groups, representing over 50% of volume, are recommended for additional support to promote heavy brand usage.

Market	%U.S.	%BG Vol.	%Cat. Vol.	18–34 Index	35–49 Index
Los Angeles/San Diego	6.4	14.3	14.1	132	142
San Francisco/Sacramento	3.9	6.9	8.6	123	149
New York	7.6	6.6	5.3	123	131
Boston/Hartford/Providence	3.9	5.5	7.5	133	133
Baltimore/Washington	2.9	5.2	7.0	131	135
Chicago	3.4	4.7	4.5	133	137
Miami/Fort Lauderdale	1.4	4.5	4.3	107	124
Dallas	1.9	3.3	1.8	137	144
Philadelphia	2.9	3.2	4.1	130	128
Detroit	1.9	2.4	2.8	138	135
Totals	36.3	56.5	57.9	—	—

Incremental

Five key volume markets are recommended for aggressive incremental support to combat competitive inroads. Los Angeles, San Diego, San Francisco, New York, and Boston are recommended for this defensive activity.

Effective Reach/Frequency Goals

Multibrand research indicates that 60%–70% awareness levels are required for a new brand to achieve 15%–20% trial. Motivational frequency analysis (Exhibit 1) suggests a 3.5+ frequency. The recommended effective reach goal, therefore, is 70/3.5+.

Media Selection and Rationale

Overview All four life stage targets are especially interested in music, entertainment, fashion, sports, and fitness (Figure 1). They tend to be heavy magazine readers and radio listeners. They are light TV viewers (Figure 2), but they skew toward heavy viewership of dayparts (e.g., late night) and programming (e.g., music and comedy), which conform with their lifestyles. They are particularly heavy viewers of cable television, a medium they made happen.

Strategy Television and magazines are proposed as the primary marketing media. Vehicle selection will be based primarily on life stage compatibility with an emphasis on entertainment themes and particular interests of the prospect lifestyles.

Television is recommended for its ability to build rapid and impactful reach with lifestyle flexibility. Both broadcast and cable networks have national applicability. Late news and prime access are the focus of local market efforts because of their efficiency. Cable television prime, late night, and news programming will characterize all flights. Music, sports, and entertainment networks that reflect the prospect lifestyle interests will be emphasized, along with news networks that provide additional reach and daypart coverage. Prime broadcast will be used during the fourth quarter for the creation of quick awareness and to initiate the relaunch. Late night will replace prime in subsequent flights, for it is more affordable and more frequency oriented. Spot television will feature prime access and late news, since they provide both extensive coverage of the target and relative efficiency.

Magazines are heavily utilized by the lifestyle-conscious prospects and will provide three quarters of continuity in support of flighted television. Magazines will also extend reach among light viewing prospects. Magazines will represent approximately one third of the national budget. Music, entertainment, health, fitness, sports, food, and other focused interest editorial will dictate title selection.

EXHIBIT 1 MOTIVATIONAL FREQUENCY ANALYSIS

Marketing Factors	Rationale	Frequency
Established vs. New Brand	Brand is relaunching	High = 4+
Market Share	Brand has been growing in last 12 months and has returned to # 3 share position.	Mid. = 3+
Brand Dominance	Brand is not 1950s Yankees but more Boston Red Sox.	Mid. = 3+
Brand Loyalty	Prospects lack any serious brand loyalties, but will form habits for short periods of time.	Mid. = 3+
Purchase Cycle	Heavy user target exhibits weekly purchase pattern.	High = 4+
Usage Pattern	70% use for quick dinner on frequent basis.	Mid. = 3+
Competition	Market is volatile; exhibits annual change; leaders spend equally.	High = 5+
Pricing	Brand enjoys price advantage that is intrinsic to its positioning.	Low = 2+

Campaign Factors		
New/Continued Campaign	New campaign featuring new packaging and line extension.	High = 5+
Message Complexity	Simple message: price and taste.	Low = 2+
Expression Uniqueness	Campaign tests at average recall.	Mid. = 3+
Image/Product Sell	Combined image/product sell because of lifestyle/life stage significance	High = 4+

Media Factors		
Vehicle Clutter	Daypart selections are in high clutter time periods. Print placement is unique.	High = 4+
Editorial	TV environments are carefully target style specific, which generates higher attention in low-attention medium. Print is lifestyle specific and generates attention.	Mid. = 3+
Vehicle Involvement	Target is deeply involved in print dialogue.	Low = 2+
Media Mix	TV and print combination is very productive.	Low = 2+
	Spot TV is diffuse, cluttered, competitive.	High = 4+

Motivational Frequency weights higher and should be established at 3.5+ level.

Proposed Testing

If budgets allow, radio should be tested as part of the media mix in selected local markets.

FIGURE 1 BUDGET GOURMET—SPECIAL INTEREST ANALYSIS

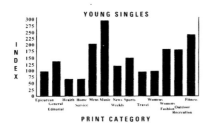

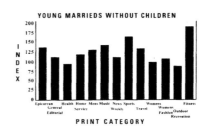

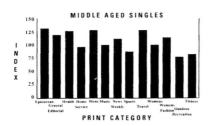

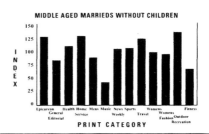

FIGURE 2 BUDGET GOURMET—MEDIA USAGE ANALYSIS

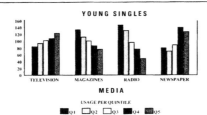

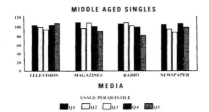

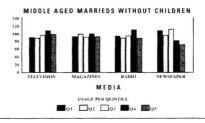

8

Media Work Plan:
Part II—Scheduling
Reach and Frequency

OVERVIEW

Scheduling reach and frequency represents key strategic decisions, for this is the point where learning theory meets marketing resources. Scheduling alternatives are identified and described. Reach, frequency, motivational frequency, and effective reach are defined, and a decision matrix is explained and demonstrated.

LEARNING AND CHOICE

The essential function of media planning is to establish advertiser presence during the consumer's process of consideration and choice. Media make up the environment in which demand is negotiated (see chapter 1). They are coincident with learning and choice. Therefore, it is the media planner's job to make the delivery of advertising synchronous with the consumer's processes of attention and perception, learning and motivation. **Scheduling** is the planned coincidence of advertising presence and consumer consideration. **Reach and Frequency** are the planned parallels of consumer learning and motivation.

It is hard to escape the ideal that advertising should recur and operate at precisely the times when consumers ask themselves questions like "What should I prepare for dinner?"; "How will I get this bathroom really clean?"; "What will I wear to the wedding?"; "What kind of car should I drive and where can I see it?" It is next to impossible, however, to afford such a coincidence and coexistence of advertising with every consumer at every moment of attention and consideration. The art of media planning is to understand the coincidence of media and choice. The craft of media planning is to get the most out of a specific advertising budget through the efficient scheduling of reach and frequency.

SCHEDULING

The basics of budgeting tell us that we never want to spend more than is necessary nor less than is sufficient. The budget in most media planning situations, however, not only is an established given, but is also already allocated by seasonal quarter. What the media planner must do is to work toward insuring that these monies are spent efficiently and effectively. Scheduling incorporates both of these goals.

The basic challenge in scheduling advertising is to work around budget constraints in such a way as to insure that the impressions produced fulfill the original purposes of the advertising. The key is timing; the issues are how often and to what degree advertising can be inserted in the consumer's processes of purchase consideration, decision, and usage.

Purchase and Usage

Purchase and usage patterns vary widely and are frequently unknown in any concrete, data-based way. Imagination and judgment may be the only guides available. Whatever the case, a description of both purchase and usage patterns should be contained in Part I of the Media Work Plan. The task at hand is to utilize this information in the most efficient and effective way possible.

The information has provided the answers to several key questions. The planner should be aware of the degree of fickleness and/or brand loyalty in the marketplace, the average time lag between purchases, and where on the spectrum between impulse and considered purchase the product operates. The planner should also know the time, place, and frequency of usage occasions and whether the person whose value judgments are most influential on these usage occasions is the purchaser or someone else.

The premise is that the more familiar the planner is with a product's purchase and usage patterns, the more able the planner will be to produce effective and efficient advertising schedules. Reality is never that simple; it is full of confusion and contradiction. For example, should you emphasize the purchase pattern or the usage pattern for a brand of tea? Five percent of consumers purchase tea on an average weekday, but 22 percent have used tea on the same day and in a different time frame than their purchase activity.

Furthermore, tea may be one of more than half of the grocery store items that are purchased on the spur of the moment. The consumers' rule of thumb in such circumstances is to buy one of the brands that they already consider acceptable. If your brand is any other than the dominant brand in such a category, repeated advertising close to the moment of purchase decision significantly affects your brand's chances of being selected.

What would you recommend? Advertise in the evening when tea is being consumed by both purchaser and influencers? Or advertise earlier in the day, coincident with purchasing? The answer is both, but it is frequently impossible to afford both. Furthermore, it is difficult to afford either one all of the relevant time.

Continuity and Flighting

Both products purchased on a regular basis and products with long consideration patterns benefit from a constant advertising presence. **Continuity** describes advertising that runs at a constant level throughout a selling period. The assumption is that the advertising level is sufficient. But as a concept, continuity begs the question of sufficiency and sufficiency for what advertising objective? The fact is, however, that few advertisers can afford anything other than a low level of advertising on a continuous basis and this low level may not be persuasive enough to achieve the advertising objective.

One variation on continuity, **pulsing**, builds higher levels of advertising on top of lower continuous levels of advertising. Pulsing can be utilized to respond to heavier selling periods, or to energize sales in correspondence with other advertising objectives. As a variation of continuity, however, pulsing only aggravates the demands of affordability.

Affordability is generally addressed by **flighting**, a scheduling pattern that alternates periods of advertising activity with periods of no advertising at all. One application of flighting is to leverage peak demand periods efficiently. In another application, flighting performs the same functions as pulsing for brands that cannot afford continuity.

FIGURE 8.1 ALTERNATIVE SCHEDULING PATTERNS

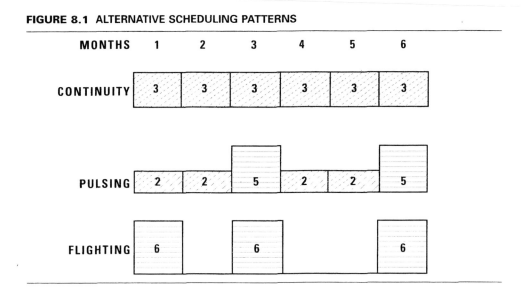

Flighting, continuity, and pulsing all raise the question of sufficiency. The issue unique to flighting is how long the advertiser can afford to be a nonadvertiser. The keys are the consumers' ability to forget and the speed with which advertising can regain its effectiveness. Sporadic advertising can seem never to be absent only if it catches consumers before they have forgotten the earlier advertising message. This stroboscopic affect can be very efficient, but it runs the risk of leaving the consumer in darkness too long.

Three issues become readily apparent in any discussion of scheduling:

1. Scheduling requires that the planner discern sufficient levels of reach and frequency.
2. Scheduling involves all of the implications of "when," including time of day and week, as well as month and year.
3. Scheduling involves more than one medium, and it can follow multiple patterns.

The first question addresses sufficiency; therefore, we will first move to the evaluation of reach and frequency before completing our discussion of scheduling. We will return to scheduling after we have discussed the various media and their role in the plan.

REACH AND FREQUENCY

Reach and frequency are the core concepts and practical tools necessary for the management of the marketing communication process. **Reach** is a measure of how many different people or households in a target audience are exposed to a brand's advertising messages during a specific period of time. **Frequency** is an estimate of how many times a specific segment of the target audience is exposed to the advertising message.

Reach is significant because it represents the outside parameters of a brand's sales potential resulting from current advertising. If market research suggests, for example, that 20 percent of prospects exposed to advertising will become purchasers, it will make a great deal of difference if the advertising reaches 500,000 or a million prospects, 50 percent or 100 percent of the target audience.

Frequency is significant because the effect of advertising on an individual consumer's learning and motivational processes is directly related to the number of the consumer's exposures to the advertising message. In this sense, repetition is the essence of persuasion. In order even to contemplate translating reach into sales, a marketer must understand the relationship of the cognitive, affective, and connotative dimensions of advertising to the number of exposures to the advertising message.

The key question is: How many prospects must be reached how many times in a specific time period, in order to achieve the brand's marketing objectives?

The problem is that budget constraints intrinsically limit one or more of these elements: reach, frequency, and time (see chapter 7). The function of media strategy is to make a judgment about how these elements should be balanced. The media objective, derived from the marketing situation and the role of advertising, provides some guidance, but it leaves two questions unexamined: the percentage to be reached, and the frequency level. Since an advertiser always wants to reach as many prospects as possible, frequency levels become the critical issue.

Advertising Frequency

"How many times do I have to tell you?" is one of the clichés of frustrated parenthood. It also happens to be one of the basic questions confronted by the advertising process. It is the driving force behind budgets and is a fundamental concern of media planning.

Although it wouldn't be prudent politics under the circumstances, all children could tell their parents that the number of times they have to be told depends on a lot of things. It depends on the child, or—in advertising terms—the target audience. It depends on the issue, or the extent of the behavior modification required. It depends on the parent, or the effectiveness of his or her communication. Occasionally, children can fairly answer, "I didn't hear you," which means that you haven't reached them or made an impression.

Advertising is part of life, and it is a simple fact of life that it is often difficult to be heard. We often have to be heard more than once if we hope to have a positive influence on someone's behavior. At the beginning of what can become a complex statistical discussion, therefore, it is wise to recall that a planner's greatest strength may be the ability to identify with and understand the receiving prospect. Imagination is the key to an understanding of the dynamics of persuasion.

We have taken the position that it is the decision to invest in media that makes an advertiser an advertiser. It is also generally accepted that to advertise effectively, you have to communicate frequently. Any cost pressure on budgets, however, puts pressure on frequency. Therefore, a critical path issue has become the determination of the relationship between consumer exposure frequency and consumer sales. Put in direct terms, the questions become:

1. How many times must individual consumers be exposed to my advertising message for it to have a discernible or practical effect on their attitudes and behavior?
2. In what time frame or repeated time frames must these exposures occur?

Effective Frequency

In 1979 the Association of National Advertisers published a monograph titled *Effective Frequency: The Relationship Between Frequency and Advertising Effectiveness* by Michael Naples of Lever Brothers. The purpose of this volume was to survey all the known research on the subject and to make it available in one place. Its message was that "much is already known," and some of its conclusions were:

1. One exposure of an advertisement to a target consumer group (within a purchase cycle) has little or no effect.
2. Because one exposure is usually ineffective, the main thrust of media planning should be on emphasizing frequency rather than reach.
3. Most of the research studies suggested that two exposures within a purchase cycle are an effective threshold level.
4. Three exposures within a purchase cycle, however, are felt to be optimal.
5. After three exposures within a purchasing cycle, advertising becomes more effective as frequency is increased, but at a decreasing rate.

The general conclusion of Naples's survey of the research is that the importance and effectiveness of frequency can be expressed as an S-shaped response curve. It clearly argues that the first exposure to an advertising message has zero impact. A positive response begins with the second exposure, and the response accelerates with the number of exposures. Eventually, a point is reached at which continuing exposures decline in impact, until they have little or no value at all.

There have been many criticisms of this S-shaped model of advertising response. Starting with a zero response, for example, denies the residual effectiveness of previous advertising and the consumer's relationship with the brand. Similarly, it is difficult to dismiss entirely the possibility (especially in the context of residual effectiveness) that one exposure has some effect on consumer awareness and action. It is also argued that there is a difference between diminishing returns and negative returns. The advertiser may not get as much for added exposures at high frequency levels, but the increased exposures never actually work against positive consumer behavior.

The alternative model of the effects of advertising, therefore, would suggest a convex response curve. This model suggests that each exposure has a positive effect on consumers, that each additional exposure has an increasing effect, and that after some point continued exposures have less and less effect.

If we are using the models to describe the general effect of advertising, the convex response curve is probably most representative. It can be especially useful in determining where on the curve significant responses begin to occur, how much probably must be spent to achieve projected sales levels, and the optimum profit contribution level (the return for each additional dollar invested).

If, on the other hand, we are seeking a practical guide for the purposes of investing this year's established budget at specific times during this year, the S-shaped response curve may prove to be a more useful model. The planning issue is **allocation**, which implies making judgments and being accountable for sufficient advertising effectiveness in limited time frames. Complex calculations of the appropriate balance between reach and frequency for a specific burst of advertising on a limited budget must result in a practical decision about how much is enough, rather than about the abstract statistical formulas often used in budget setting.[1]

Whatever the case, there is universal agreement that frequent consumer exposures bring positive results.

Audience Duplication

The question is: How do you determine the frequency in a schedule? The best place to begin is with a commonsense picture of what might be going on. Imagine three episodes of a popular television program, and picture its regular viewers. You may consider yourself a regular viewer, but for one reason or another—homework, a social commitment, visiting a friend in the hospital, and so on—you may miss an episode or two. Another regular viewer may not miss any of the three. A picture of the audiences for these three episodes (Figure 8.3) would show that some people saw all three episodes, some two, and some only one. There are seven possible combinations.

FIGURE 8.2 ADVERTISING RESPONSE CURVES

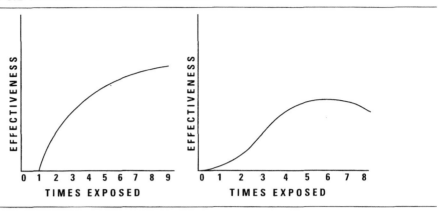

FIGURE 8.3 AUDIENCE DUPLICATION/ACCUMULATION

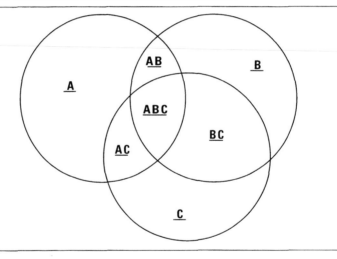

In this example, **reach** is the sum of the people who viewed the program. This number doesn't change, whether they saw the program one, two, or three times. **Frequency**, on the other hand, reflects the number of times someone saw the program. If you wanted to know how many times the typical person viewed the program, you would calculate the **average frequency**. If you wanted to know the total number of times the program was viewed you would multiply the average frequency by the reach. This would be called a **gross audience**, because it would include duplication.

The next step in imagining what is going on as audiences consume media is to create an example using real-looking numbers. In this instance, imagine three magazines with over a million in circulation each (Figure 8.4). Using commonsense, we know that some consumers read only one of these magazines, but others read as many as two or three. There are seven combinations.

FIGURE 8.4 AUDIENCE DUPLICATION OF 3 MAGAZINES

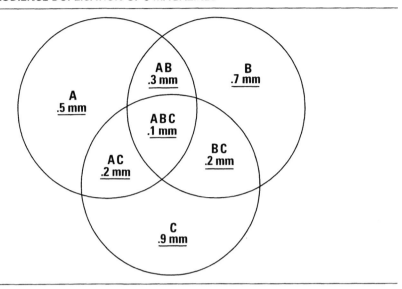

In this example, the unduplicated reach for one advertising insertion in each of the three magazines would be 2.9 million and not 3.8 million, which would be the gross readership. When determining reach, we are trying to identify the number of separate persons exposed one or more times. In our first example (Figure 8.3), we observe the accumulation of an audience for one program or vehicle. In our second example (Figure 8.4), we observe how audiences may accumulate and duplicate across or between vehicles.

One of the interesting things about broadcast television is the rather consistent way in which programs of all types in all dayparts accumulate their audiences and produce reach and frequency (Figures 8.5–8.8). The reach levels of primetime schedules of one week, four weeks, or thirteen weeks are similar across the board. Variations are minor and lead us to believe that similar GRP levels will produce the same prospect reach regardless of whether compacted into one week or extended over a month or a quarter. Daytime network schedules accumulate reach much more slowly and some real differences can be seen in how audiences accumulate across extended periods of time. Four week flights will generate higher reach.

What should be reasonably obvious by this juncture is that a communication vehicle's audience both changes and remains the same over time. Thus, whenever an advertiser enters the relationship between a vehicle and its audience by purchasing time for a commercial insertion, the advertiser enjoys a certain predictability in terms of the number of people who might be exposed to the advertisements, and the frequency of exposure.

The way to express this process in mathematical terms is also reasonably obvious. The number of impressions is the result of the number of people exposed mulitiplied by the average number of times they are exposed. Since advertisers find it more

FIGURE 8.5 TYPICAL REACH CURVE

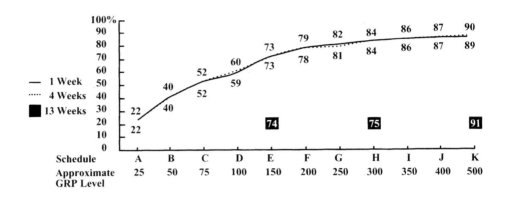

Source: Nielsen Media Research. *Television Audience 1994*. Reprinted by permission.

FIGURE 8.6 REACH CURVES OF TWO TELEVISION PROGRAMS

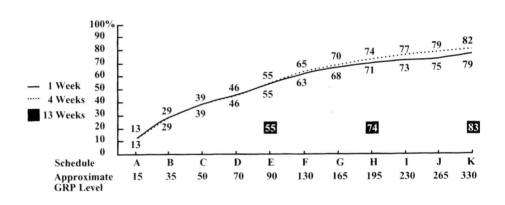

Source: Nielsen Media Research. *Television Audience 1994*. Reprinted by permission.

interesting and useful to express things in terms of the percentage of their target audience, this simple formula utilizes percentages. Therefore, the total number of impressions and the individual audience reached are normally expressed as percentages.

Gross Rating Points (GRPs) are a measure of the total exposures produced by an advertising schedule, expressed as a percentage of the total population. Reach is also expressed as a percentage. The formula for measuring the basic dynamic of media usage is:

FIGURE 8.7 NET REACH MULTIPLE PROGRAMS 26 WEEKS

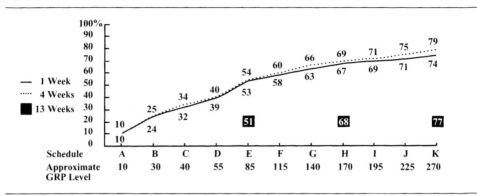

Source: Nielsen Media Research. *Television Audience 1994*. Reprinted by permission.

FIGURE 8.8 NET REACH CURVES AT DIFFERENT WEIGHT LEVELS

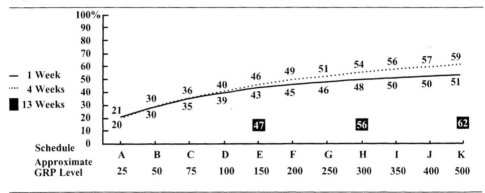

Source: Nielsen Media Research. *Television Audience 1994*. Reprinted by permission.

Gross Rating Points = Reach × Frequency
Reach = Gross Rating Points ÷ Frequency
Frequency = Gross Rating Points ÷ Reach

It must be obvious (as easy as it may be to understand the concept) that reality demands that we have, as a starting point, some practical measure of the duplication of audiences. Furthermore, if frequency is so precisely related to consumer awareness, motivation, and action, it is also important for the planner to know the **exposure distribution**, the number of times a certain percentage of the target market might see the advertisement. The key questions, then, are:

1. How do we determine the duplication?
2. What is the distribution beyond the average?

Both duplication and exposure distributions are estimates; they are not known facts, but statistical probabilities accepted as facts. Services such as SMRB measure audiences duplicated between magazine pairs (for example, *Good Housekeeping* and *Family Circle,* or *Time* and *Newsweek*). SMRB's numbers, however, are themselves audience estimates based on sample data. These sample-based estimates become even less realistic when more than two vehicles are involved, and/or when vehicles of two or more media types are involved, such as magazines and television. Simply put, no one knows for certain what the actual distribution is.

A variety of methods for solving this problem have been developed over the years. For example, one could use the Inclusion/Exclusion formula of Boolean Algebra. The Inclusion/Exclusion Principle states that the probability of exposure to Magazine A or Magazine B or Magazine C is "equal to the sum of the probabilities of exposure to each of them minus the three pair-wise duplication probabilities, plus the probability of triplication." This is clearly not the kind of thing media planners want to spend their time figuring out.

One set of estimating formulas is based on no particular theory but is claimed to reflect the known reach for particular schedules (and can, therefore, serve as a projection tool). One of the first was developed in 1961 by J. M. Agostini, and was both criticized and refined by H. J. Claycamp and C. W. McClelland in 1968. Another such formula in wide use was developed by P. Hofmans in 1966. Tests of his formula and other formulas show an error rate close to 3 percent (2.8 to 2.82). This level of error rate is often considered "close enough" considering both the complexity of the problem and the exigencies of execution.[2]

Other estimating formulas are built out of hypotheses about duplication and accumulation. Those who use these stochastic models argue that the actual audience dynamics are chance happenings subject to the processes of probability. Such statistical methods have been applied to other areas of life, and mathematicians have studied the issues for a long time. Thus, media researchers express a certain comfort level with the results of these methods. Such formulas have been developed by G. P. Hyett in 1958, by E. J. Sainsbury in 1963, by R. Metheringham in 1964, and by S. M. Kwerel in 1969. These methods work best when applied to one media type (for example, prime time television), but always have the advantage of providing a positive identification of the frequency distribution. The error rates for these formulas, however, varies widely (from 12.69 to 2 percent).

Most major agencies have developed their own formulas and have packed them into mainframe computers. Smaller agencies buy such services from research and computer suppliers.[3] In general, they combine the methods reported above, often with the addition of simulation models. The prototypical output of these models and formulas is a frequency distribution (Exhibit 8.1). Note how misleading the average frequency of 3.1 would be in evaluating the schedule.

As a practical matter, the two important things for a media planner to know at this point are: the importance of frequency in affecting consumer behavior through advertising, and that computer programs are available for estimating the practical information required. The typical program will provide information on the total

EXHIBIT 8.1 FOUR-WEEK PRIME TIME TV FREQUENCY DISTRIBUTION

(240 GRPs—Adults 18+)

Exposures	Percent	Rating Pts.
0	23.3	0
1	22.2	22.2
2	17.3	34.6
3	12.5	37.5
4	8.0	34.3
5	5.8	29.0
6	3.8	22.7
7	2.5	17.4
8	1.7	13.5
9	1.2	10.7
10	0.8	8.0
11	0.5	5.4
12	0.4	4.7
	76.6	240.0

[240 GRPs ÷ 76.6 Reach = 3.1 Avg. Frequency]

impressions, gross rating points, reach, average frequency, and frequency distribution, and an estimate of impressions by each frequency level.

It is useful always to be aware, however, that the numbers spewed out by the computer are radical estimates (estimates built upon estimates), and that one program's estimates will be different from another's. It is important to be aware of this, in order to liberate the imagination while maintaining a focus on the responsibilities of judgment. The numbers are a tool, not a solution.

MOTIVATIONAL FREQUENCY

Motivational frequency is the minimum number of exposures, within a purchase cycle, considered necessary to motivate the average prospect in the target audience to accomplish an advertising objective. In most of the literature, motivational frequency is most often called effective frequency. "Motivational frequency" is a better description of the phenomenon, and it avoids redundancy and confusion with "effective reach." **Effective reach** is the percentage or number of target prospects exposed to the media schedule at an established motivational frequency level.

Motivational frequency and effective reach are based on the assumption that all frequency levels are not of equal importance. In our discussion of frequency, we noted that there is some debate about:

1. The value of the first advertising exposure, or, any exposure below the established motivational frequency level.

2. The value of incremental exposures beyond the established motivational frequency level—or, how high is up.

Each of these issues in debate, however, is based on, and then is measured against, the initial estimate of the generally required exposure level, or of the necessary minimum for most prospects. In the practical order required by allocation judgments, therefore, planners generally are following the S-curve model. Consequently, the key question is: How do I arrive at a conclusion about the motivational frequency level?

The normal starting point for selecting a motivational frequency level is the rather extensive theoretical literature. In general, this reflects one version or another of the hierarchy of effects model of advertising (see chapter 2). Reviewing these models would suggest that it takes either three, four, or five prospect communications to bring about consumer action. When synthesized, the models propose a logical progression from cognitive to affective to behavioral experiences. These various considerations have led many planners to live by the "rule of three," meaning that they make the assumption that the base for motivational frequency is three exposures.

In chapter 7, however, we came to terms with the recognition that consumers do not always function in this quite logical manner. They also do not act in the same way in all product categories. Consumers can act on experience, imitation, or belief, or they can act on impulse or after long consideration periods. In each instance we would have to rework the theoretical framework to suggest different prospect/product situations and different consumer starting points.

These situations and starting points, in turn, suggest different motivational frequency levels, from one to several more than three. As a practical matter, however, few media decision makers are comfortable enough with these theoretical discussions to use them as bases for judgment. Furthermore, the literature reviewed by Naples for the ANA reinforces the "rule of three." The cases supporting this view are limited, but to some extent they are all that is available.

The obvious solution is to use various research techniques to estimate the pattern of effects your advertising has had on your brand's advertising objectives. These could include:

Brand personality or image research

Attitude and usage research

Tracking studies

In-market tests and experiments

Regression analysis of share of market vis-à-vis share of voice, relative price, and so on.

These and other research efforts can suggest how dependent certain market results are on advertising exposures in short-term and long-term circumstances. The practical problem is that few advertisers are equipped to conduct, analyze, and apply the results of this kind of research, either once or over time. The desired data, therefore, is generally unavailable.

We also may know more than we think we know. For example, we know that the nature of our product, the product category, and competition all have significant effects on our communication task. We know that poor, average, or outstanding advertising can make a difference. We know that different media pose different challenges. All of these issues have been researched, and their conclusions are publicly available. When we combine what we know with theoretical constructs and brand experience, we may have sufficient knowledge to make practical—and well-founded—decisions.

Establishing Motivational Frequency

Over a period of more than fifteen years, Young & Rubicam evolved a system for deciding on motivational frequency levels. At a workshop of the Advertising Research Foundation in 1982, Joseph W. Ostrow, then the worldwide Media Director of Y&R, went public with this frequency setting system. The genius of the system (Exhibit 8.2) is, first, that it is a system—both a checklist of relevant factors and a structure on which to base judgments. Second, it is rooted both in validated research and in experience with thousands of brands. The more one knows, the more vital the system becomes. In short, it is a practical tool for a practical job.

The way to use the Motivational Frequency Grid to set frequency goals is first to recognize the number and character of the factors to be included. The three basic factor categories are Marketing, Campaign, and Media. Each factor requires a judgment about whether the actual brand circumstances demand normal frequency, or higher/lower than normal frequency, for advertising effectiveness. The second step involves making further judgments.

The Motivational Frequency Decision Grid presented here is a variation of that developed by Young & Rubicam. The initial issue it raises is: "What is the middle?" It is useful to know whether one factor or another suggests higher or lower frequency, but higher or lower than what?

We have already discussed the advantages and disadvantages of the "rule of three," which is frequently used as a practical midpoint. The hierarchy of effects model, however, might as easily argue for a frequency of five as for three. The solution is to select the middle in two ways:

1. Identify which variation of the hierarchy of effects model is functional in your product category. Then, estimate the frequency needed to achieve your advertising objectives against the first step identified in the application of the model. Is the first step cognitive or behavioral?
2. Review competitive expenditures and estimate the prototypical frequency achieved by brands in the category.

Each of the these analyses will provide a frequency estimate, which then becomes the midpoint between low and high in the application for the decision grid.

Process and Judgment

Exposures do the work of advertising, and they cost money. Consequently, estimating the required frequency of exposures is at the core of advertising budgets. Some

EXHIBIT 8.2 MOTIVATIONAL FREQUENCY DECISION GRID

(Decide)	Low	To	High
Marketing Factors			
Established vs. New Brand	*Established* High Awareness Positioning Known		*New* Must Build Awareness Establish Selling Message Preempt Competition
Market Share	*Major* High Market Share Good Distribution Advertising History		*Minor* Small Market Share Build Distribution New to Most
Brand Dominance	*Present* Awareness High Positive Acceptance Category Franchise		*Absent* Increase Awareness Enhance Credibility Increase Share
Brand Loyalty	*Strong* Positive Repeat Purchase Alert Top-of-mind		*Weak* Erratic Repeat Purchase Low Top-of-mind
Purchase Cycle	*Long* Tends to Considered Purchase Leverage Reach		*Short* Lower Interest Category Shopping List Reminder Combat Brand Switching
Usage Pattern	*Infrequent* Selective Occasions Continuous Presence		*Frequent* Deplete Pantry Develop Preference
Competition	*Weak* Minimal Clutter Lack Outside Pressure Advertising Sensitive		*Strong* Consumer Confusion Heavy Category Advertising Minimal Brand Differentiation
Campaign Factors			
New/Continued Campaign	*Continued* Comprehension Established Reminder Effort Wear Out Risks		*New* Generate Rapid Awareness Insure Recall Exploit Freshness
Message Complexity	*Simple* Quick Comprehension		*Detailed* Absorb Argument
Expression Uniqueness	*Unique* Stands Out in Category Facile Recall Gains Word of Mouth		*Average* Easily Confused Less Intrusive Low Attentiveness
Image/Product Sell	*Image* Minimal Complexity Long-Term Goals		*Product* Parity Competition Retail Impact

EXHIBIT 8.2 MOTIVATIONAL FREQUENCY DECISION GRID (CONT.)

Media Factor		
Vehicle Clutter	*Minimal* High Attention	*Extensive* Low Attention
Editorial	*Compatible* Insulates Opportunity to See Rub-off Credibility	*Unrelated* Easy Pass By Unleveraged
Vehicle Involvement	*Intense* Focused Target Marriage of Interests	*Casual* Egalitarian Target Eclectic Attention
Media Mix (Each Media Type)	*Multiple* In Consumer Sync.	*Singular* Compensates Randomness
(Combined Types)	*Few* Presumed Effectiveness	*Many* Addition of Minimums
Television	Gross Cost Intrusive Sight-Sound-Motion	Clutter Low Attention Transitory
CATV	Vertical Interest	Broadcast Clone
Magazines	Long Issue Life Editorial Compatibility Target Focus	Considered Purchases Complex Messages Slow Build
Newspapers	Promotion Linkage Gross Costs	Retail Traffic Clutter

** Note: The Grid helps the planner decide on higher or lower frequency demands based on the determining factors of the brand's marketing and communications situation. The subheadings under each category are suggestive details derived from either research or experience.

marketers continue to view advertising as an expense, while others perceive it as an investment. An investment outlook is preferred but, in either case, arguments are bound to emerge. The basic reason is that not enough about the effects of advertising is sufficiently measurable or predictable to provide certainty about costs or investment. There is no formula.

Planners often feel insecure about the absence of formulas and certitude at this point. When they do, they should recall that businesspeople hardly ever enjoy a level of certitude when making investments. Investment is always a game of guess and risk. Should we spend many millions of dollars on new computers given the rapid pace of technology that might make our investment obsolete the day we make it? Should we invest in remodeling an automobile line, when it could become an Edsel? Why should the planning of advertising investments be any different?

Setting frequency levels is not done by using a formula; it is a process. We share experience and research of all kinds, but we lack method and certitude. What we can provide is an orderly pattern of dialogue and judgments that will lead to a credible decision.

Persuasive Articulation

The Motivational Frequency Grid is a fallible instrument when it is used in isolation to establish advertising budgets. It has enormous value, however, as an operational tool for bringing thoroughness and logic to a judgmental process. Within the boundaries of an established budget, the Motivational Frequency Grid appears far less arbitrary and its natural margin of error is far less threatening to those who fear risk. It produces reasonable results when it is used for reasonable allocation.

When developing the grid for a specific brand in a concrete situation, the planner should:

1. Recognize that the overall effort, as well as the effort at any given point, should be aimed at making reasonable judgments.
2. Operate from the point of view of those consumers who will be exposed to the advertising, and whose behavior is the object of change.
3. Evaluate the end product according to its persuasiveness, that is, by the experience of recognition and intuitive satisfaction it produces.

When the task is to make a decision about effectiveness in a data-limited environment, only reasonable judgment is practical. When the task is persuasion, only recognizable articulations that add up to an apparently realistic story will carry the discussion. Either one is an imaginative task based on experience. In practical terms, this means constructing a grid (Exhibit 8.3) in which every line is a defensible judgment.

Not every possible line of the generic grid presented earlier need be utilized. Some may not be especially appropriate or revealing for the brand or its situation. Furthermore, the generic grid presented here is not intended to be all-inclusive. In a given situation, for example, a planner might wish to reflect on the implications of pricing on frequency, or wearout and the size of the commercial pool on frequency considerations, or the attentiveness levels of the various media. The key is to tell a relevant and credible story.

Making the Choice

A basic issue is how to conclude the process. Some believe that the only way to draw a conclusion is to average all of the individual frequency judgments. Others believe that the pluses and minuses of highs and lows can be given a numerical value of +/− 0.1 or 0.2, depending on how radical the departure from the norm might be. This system allows the planner to draw a conclusion through addition and subtraction.

As a system, the addition/subtraction method allows the novice to come to a practical conclusion, but it also implies a higher degree of accuracy in weighting than might be viable for an admittedly soft series of estimations. More relevant might be the quite relative and variable weighting of the factors open to an imaginative effort at finding the pattern. If the planner rightly begins by imagining the exposures and a consumer

EXHIBIT 8.3 MOTIVATIONAL FREQUENCY GRID: PACKAGED GOOD

Marketing Factors	Rationale	Frequency
Established vs. New Brand	Brand has a long consumer history.	Low = 2+
Market Share	Brand enjoys a major share of market . among most user segments	Low = 2+
Brand Dominance	Perceived as market leader.	Low = 2+
Brand Loyalty	Once high; new consumers are more inclined to switching on price.	Mid = 3+
Purchase Cycle	Heavy users exhibit rapid turnover; others tend to hold in pantry.	High = 4+
Usage Pattern	Twice/week declines rapidly to once/month. Must maintain/increase.	High = 4+
Competition	Modest direct competition but heavy secondary competition	Mid = 3+
Pricing	Large advantage against secondary competition. Parity against primary competition.	Mid = 3+

Campaign Factors		
New/Continued Campaign	New campaign emphasizing multiple uses, targeted to less than heavy users.	High = 4+
Message Complexity	Simple messages but extraordinary for uninitiated lighter users.	Mid = 3+
Expression Uniqueness	Refreshing style (art direction) but familiar vocabulary and platform.	Mid = 3+
Image/Product Sell	Need for retail promotional impact to drive lighter users and empty inventory.	High = 4+

Media Factors		
Vehicle Clutter	Heavy reliance on television in high clutter dayparts.	High = 4+
Editorial	Corporate leverage in print vehicles will insure excellent adjacencies.	Low = 2+
Media Mix	Combining TV and print is very productive.	Mid = 3+

Conclusion: An analysis of all the relevant marketing, communications, and media factors suggests a motivational frequency level between 3+ and 4+. In the context of a new campaign targeted to lighter users, a frequency level of 4+ for the introductory period, and a frequency level of 3+ against target prospects on a typical four-week basis for the remainder of the fiscal year would appear most appropriate.

template, then the best conclusion will be a recognition of the pattern necessary for practical consumer persuasion.

Today's corporate culture glories in statistical decision theories. At the core of these theories is the weighting of alternative probabilities. When dealing with the mercurial world of consumers and communications, however, we simply lack the hard evidence necessary to build a model that even resembles an actuarial table. Therefore, the planner is often dealing with subjective probabilities. Nowhere is this clearer than in the judgments required to speculate, and finally draw a conclusion, about a brand's frequency strategy. After all else is said and done, this act of imagination and informed judgment is what a planner is paid to do.

EFFECTIVE REACH GOALS

After determining a motivational frequency level, the planner must decide on the minimum number of prospects that must be reached at this frequency level. When the planner is dealing only with average frequency, it is fairly easy to achieve reach levels of 70 to 80 percent (and not to be satisfied with reach levels below 60 percent) while maintaining a respectable-looking average frequency. The recognition of frequency distribution and the concept of motivational frequency, however, put enormous pressure on reach. In practice, therefore, achieving an appropriate balance is a difficult problem for strategic scheduling.

Before a planner can debate and resolve the issues raised by effective reach, however, an effective reach goal must be established. The place to begin setting such a goal is with the premise of success implicit in setting motivational frequency.

The premise of the whole frequency consideration process is that frequency works. On the premise that the right frequency of exposure will produce a successful consumer behavior outcome, therefore, the planner should ask: How many prospects do I have to reach to meet the brand's sales objectives? How many consumers, acting the way we hope to persuade them to act, are necessary to produce the results we require? The answer, in most instances, will be remarkably lower than you might expect.

A dramatic example might be the Baking Chip market described in chapter 4 (Exhibit 4.3). In this case, only 41 percent of female homemakers accounted for 100 percent of sales. If you were targeting users, your reach goal would not exceed 41 percent. Furthermore, only 5.7 percent of female homemakers and 13.9 percent of users are heavy users, and they account for almost 47 percent of sales. This means that a shift in loyalty among less than 3 percent for the demographic group, or 7 percent of users (50 percent of heavy users), has the potential for increasing a brand's share by 25 percent or more, depending on the brand's existing share. Baking Chips represent a radical example, but the market dynamics could argue for a very low effective reach goal.

So precise an argument however, requires an enormous level of confidence in all the research numbers involved and in the ability of media vehicles to deliver the desired target precisely. Since all of the research numbers accumulate a large margin of error, since media vehicles are not as focused as laser beams, and since all of the estimates involved in the motivational frequency decision are so soft, it is reasonable to increase the effective reach goals that an absolutely strict interpretation of the data and premises would suggest. The rule of thumb for setting an effective reach goal is to double the minimum number of buyers necessary for marketing success as a percentage of the target population.

To some extent, the media planner can have it both ways when it comes time for execution. The experienced media planner would know how a frequency distribution works (see Exhibit 8.1). Setting an effective reach goal of 25 percent at a motivational frequency level of 4+, or 40 percent at 3+, could easily produce a reach of 75 to 80 percent, with an average frequency of 3. (Reach tables and tactical alternatives can be found in chapter 10.) Small changes in average frequency and different media mixes can have a significant impact on frequency distribution. It often happens, therefore, that by following the planning disciplines for effective reach—the most demanding expression of media accountability—the planner actually can satisfy the highest expectations of overall target reach and average frequency.

PRACTICAL SCHEDULING

There is little doubt that, at almost any budget level, motivational frequency and effective reach calculations almost force advertising schedules to utilize a flighting pattern. Given the number of people who must be reached and the frequency deemed necessary to persuade them, it is almost always time, or continuity that is sacrificed.

The goal of scheduling, however, is to schedule the right amount of reach and frequency at the right time. It is difficult to accept that the right time will always be determined according to a schedule created by budget limitations, which are so highly leveraged by effective reach. After all, for most products consumers are in the market all the time.

Faced with such commonsense questions, media planners are led to defend flighting with references to the "learning and forgetting curve," or to stroboscopic effects that create a virtual reality of continuous presence. What enables them to propound such theories with such panache, however, is their fundamental belief in motivational frequency.

Arguments for Reach and Continuity

The arguments for making continuity a paramount consideration were introduced in our discussion of convex vs. S-curve theories of advertising. Those who favor a convex model argue that some sales result from the first advertising exposure, and that more significant sales result from only two exposures than are suggested by an S-curve model. It should not be surprising, therefore, that there is continuing research confirming a convex model.

Recent evidence adds a critical time dimension to the convex model. The proposed discovery is that the convex model works especially well when the consumer has been exposed to the advertising once within the twenty-four hours prior to a purchasing occasion, or twice within seven days of purchasing. The conclusion is:

1. Since people are buying almost every day, and
2. Since consumers respond to recently exposed advertising at low frequency levels,
3. The presence afforded by continuity is critical.
4. Therefore, reach is more critical than frequency.

The strategy proposition resulting from this argument is that the average weekly reach of the target is the most important scheduling parameter (Exhibit 8.4).

Faced with limited budgets, however, a planner has to make two other arguments to support this strategy. First is an argument based on a communication effects model of advertising: After a consumer is aware of a brand (cognitive) and has formed a positive attitude toward the brand (affective), all other communications must be action-oriented (behavioral). Put another way, after the consumer passes through the first two stages of this psychological process, each subsequent exposure is the equivalent of a third exposure.

The strategy proposition, resulting from this interpretation of the communication effects model of advertising effectiveness, argues that after the introduction of a new campaign that carries the consumer through the first two stages, a weekly frequency greater than two is wasteful. Strict logic would argue that a weekly frequency greater than one is wasteful. The leap to two is based on the recognition that the data is far too imprecise and, therefore, a frequency of two is necessary to insure exposure.

The second, commonsense, argument against effective reach is that it leads to flighting and that it defies common sense to argue that customers are only in the marketplace and making purchases during these bursts of advertising weight. Where, then, does the argument for reach with continuity lead? This strategy invariably leads to high-reach mass media or to prime time television and prime access spot. After all, mass merchandisers always provide lower relative costs and can be perceived as more cost effective.

It defies common sense, however, to pursue a strategy that inevitably leads to prime time television. It denies the value of all other communication media (for example, radio and magazines) and all other media vehicles. Furthermore, if continuous reach translates into broadcasting, it reduces media simply to a delivery system and denies the character and function of communications in society. It also denies the recognizable relationships of media to culture and of culture to consumer motivation. Something must be wrong with such a strategy.

Preserving Motivational Frequency

Passionate believers in any specific policy often argue for practical common sense while accusing their opponents of abstract orthodoxy. When you do not believe sufficiently in audience reports and frequency distributions to accept an average frequency

EXHIBIT 8.4 ADVERTISERS QUESTION EFFECTIVE FREQUENCY

NEW RESEARCH MODEL MAY REDUCE MEDIA COSTS

Some major advertisers are pointing to a new system of analysis, debunking the 20-year-old media theorem called "effective frequency," as a potential means of cutting their media costs.

Back in November, the Advertising Research Foundation devoted a whole day to "effective frequency," which started the current ruckus among advertising agency researchers concerning media planning. Effective frequency, traditionally, is equated to mean that a message needs to be delivered at least three times in a given week for it to be effective.

Now, new thinking principally from a book to be published by Professor John Philip Jones of Syracuse University, titled, "When Ads Work: New Proof of How Advertising Triggers Sales," counters all this. Jones' premise is that just one message is enough to be efficient.

"This has turned media planning on its head," says Erwin Ephron, partner at media consultancy, Ephron, Papzian & Ephron. "Although the fallout hasn't gotten everywhere yet."

Some major advertisers are already planning to cut dollars out of media plans, according to a number of executives. Advertising agency research executives, however, are trying to pull in the reins on the potential for misunderstanding these new surveys.

"We are afraid advertisers might take this too far," says Joanne Burke, senior vice president, worldwide media research director at Foote, Cone & Belding. "It's really about how to communicate."

Using Nielsen Media Research's single source data, which links product sales with the number of TV advertising messages, Jones concluded that just one exposure is sufficient to produce a sales response because advertising works when people are ready to purchase.

To consultant Ephron, the key pieces in the book are: 1) Advertising works in the short term or it doesn't work at all. 2) Consumers are not potatoes—they screen messages that are relevant to them. 3) Finally, near the time of the purchase one exposure has a far greater impact than additional exposures.

"You don't want to reach people often over short period of time, not because you won't get more response, but because it isn't a good use of the money," says Ephron. He says you'd be better off placing media dollars to reach new people in another time period. Thus, reach, not frequency, becomes the important factor.

What does that mean for advertisers? The new surveys could mean less flighting and fewer gross rating points in a particular period. It also means an increasing continuity among GRPs throughout the year.

Ephron views it this way: "If you tell a kid three times at 11 a.m., 'Remember to wash your hands before dinner,' then you are using frequency to teach. But if you tell him once, right before dinner, this will have a greater impact."

But FCB's Burke doesn't know if it's quite that simple. What would happen, she says, "if you didn't know *when* the kid was eating dinner?"

Source: *Inside Media* November 2, 1994.

---

of one, it is hard to insist that others are so orthodox as to believe both in a liner application of the communication effects model and in an estimated frequency of three.

The argument for motivational frequency has several parts: First, to the extent that it argues for the importance of frequency as such, motivational frequency supports the belief that advertising messages are at least as complex as nursery rhymes. Second, motivational frequency does not argue for isolated frequency (for example, commercials for the same brand in the same TV program), but for frequency over time.

Motivational frequency is realistic. It recognizes that consumers may act on the basis of one well-timed exposure but also recognizes that that well-timed exposure may belong to a competitor's brand. Consumers are constantly receiving thousands of messages, and high frequency involves an effort at being the latest to be heard.

Finally, motivational frequency does not automatically accept a linear application of the communication effects model. Rather it argues that the model may work frontward or backward, based on the situation of the consumer, the brand category, and the brand in a continuum of motivation and action.

If motivational frequency is based on the "rule of three," then it is equally valid to argue for a "rule of two." If motivational frequency is a more complex notion, however, then it gets us closer to our goal—making the delivery of advertising coincident with the consumer's processes of motivation and choice. It also gets us closer to the difficult strategic decisions required by the marketplace than does any other existing theory.

Choosing a Strategy

The fundamental issue is a practical allocation, and a final judgment will be based on an interior dialogue. This dialogue can be posed as a series of questions and answers. The sequence begins with the broadest set of marketing communication questions:

1. Does the product demand continuity because of the character of its purchase and usage cycles?
2. Do the marketing and advertising objectives demand continuity?
3. What general levels of four-week reach and frequency will the allocated budget buy?

The answer to the first two questions will determine whether or not continuity should be established as an intrinsic goal. The answer to the third question will inform the planner if the budget allows for a reasonable number of exposures on a continuing basis.

The next set of questions should help the planner to refine the shape of the continuity levels required, or to begin the creation of a schedule in which continuity is not an absolute. These questions are:

1. Is there any particular skew to the seasonal sales of the product?
2. Is there any need to respond to expected competitive activity at a particular time?
3. Are there any specific promotional activities or other marketing efforts that will demand special support at predictable times?

The answers to these questions will inform the planner a) if there is a need (or special opportunities) for pulsing in a continuous advertising strategy; b) when this pulsing should occur; and c) if flights in a flighting strategy must occur at any specific time. If continuity is both called for and affordable, and if the planner can identify when pulsing must or should occur, the basic scheduling strategy decisions are complete.

The mental dialogue continues, however, if continuity is not called for, or is not consistently affordable. If the product does not call for continuity, the planner will most likely recommend flighting synchronous with seasonality. If continuity is called for, the planner will recommend flighting as a solution to affordability. (The same issues will emerge if the advertising is to be flighted synchronous with seasonality but requires continuity during the selling seasons, and affordability remains a problem.)

The goal under all circumstances is both efficiency and effectiveness. The planner's effort is to close any gap between the two. In this context, the planner must look forward to the next strategic judgment—media selection—and to possible media buying outcomes. For example, is it possible to address the need for continuity with one medium and the need for high seasonal frequencies with another?

The imperatives of media selection and purchase, however, may make any form of continuity or complex flighting unaffordable. If continuity is unaffordable under these circumstances, flighting is the solution. If complex flighting is unaffordable, an alternative flighting pattern must be discovered. The problem with both is that there will be times when the brand will not be advertising.

Hiatus—when and how long an advertiser will be a nonadvertiser—becomes the final issue for a planner deciding on a scheduling strategy. Hiatus raises two questions:

1. What is the minimal amount of time that advertising must be exposed in order for it to be effective?

2. What is the maximum amount of time that advertising can go unexposed without significant deleterious effects on the brand?

The first fact is that advertising needs time to work: time to build an audience and time to speak with it. Reach and frequency require presence.

The second fact is that advertising has residual effects and need not be present still to be working. Competitive circumstances have a lot to do with this. For example, you may be representing a dominant brand, or a classic brand with a long history, or be in a category in which all other brands are flighting, or enjoy extensive brand loyalty among heavy users. Considering these and other circumstances, the planner must decide how long the brand can be out of sight before it is also out of mind.

The strategic decision when dealing with flighting, therefore, concerns the number of days or weeks to be in and the number of days or weeks to be out. Both should be clearly stated, and the pattern should be articulated. The assumption, when a schedule is recommended, is that the articulated guidelines for reach, frequency, motivational frequency, and effective reach can be achieved in the periods when the advertising is actively exposed.

Resolution

Both marketing objectives and marketing resources make the scheduling of reach and frequency difficult. Strategy is the hard part of media planning, and requires informed experience, sensitivity, flexibility, and confidence. You can not persuade others if you cannot persuade yourself. You cannot persuade yourself without an imaginative understanding of the needs and circumstances, or without the development of a compatible solution. Like an artist working on a canvas and looking at the dynamic subject on the other side of the canvas, the planner should not stop until each side is a reflection of the other. The result will be that the strategy works. This means that the solution passes every test. It also means that the planner will be able to persuade others in an area that lacks statistical certitude and in which belief in judgment is the only viable option.

SUMMARY

* Scheduling is the planned coincidence of advertising presence and consumer consideration.
* Reach and frequency are the planned parallels of consumer learning and motivation.
* The art of media planning is to understand the coincidence of media and choice.
* The craft of media planning is to get the most out of a specific advertising budget through the efficient scheduling of reach and frequency.
* The more familiar the planner is with a product's purchase and usage patterns, the more able the planner will be to produce effective and efficient schedules.
* Continuity describes advertising that runs at a constant level. Pulsing builds higher levels of advertising on top of lower continuous levels. Flighting is a scheduling pattern that alternates periods of advertising activity with periods of no advertising at all.
* Scheduling requires the discernment of the levels of reach and frequency that will be sufficient.
* Reach is significant because is represents the outside parameters of a brand's sales potential directly resulting from an advertising schedule.
* Frequency is significant because the effect of advertising on the consumer's learning and motivational processes is directly related to the number of exposures to the advertising.
* Gross Rating Points (GRP) are a measure of the total exposures produced by an advertising schedule, expressed as a percentage of the total population. They are the product of the number of people exposed and the average number of times they are exposed.
* Statistical formulas and computer systems are available for the estimation of frequency distribution, but they are only estimates.
* Motivational frequency is the minimum number of exposures, within a purchase cycle, considered necessary to motivate the average prospect in the target audience to accomplish an advertising objective.
* Planners can develop a decision process, based on a wide range of research data and experience, to determine the probable motivational frequency requirements of the brand and its circumstances. The overall effort is to make reasonable judgments.

* The rule of thumb for setting an effective reach goal is to double the minimum number of buyers necessary for marketing success as a percentage of the target population.
* One of the purposes of scheduling is to resolve the tension between motivational frequency and affordability.

QUESTIONS

1. What are the functions of scheduling in an advertising media plan?
2. What are reach, frequency, motivational frequency, and effective reach?
3. What is the importance of a brand's purchase and usage cycle to media planning?
4. What are pulsing and flighting as scheduling techniques?
5. What is the variable importance of frequency under differing brand conditions?
6. What is meant by "frequency distribution"?
7. How does a planner determine the motivational frequency level for a brand?
8. Why is it important for a planner to evaluate, by its persuasiveness, the articulated process followed in setting motivational frequency?
9. What is the rule of thumb for setting an effective reach goal, and why is it a practical solution?
10. What are the arguments against using effective reach as part of a scheduling strategy?
11. Why is hiatus a critical path issue?

ASSIGNMENT

Develop a motivational frequency grid and schedule recommendation for the brand or case you are working on.

NOTES FOR CHAPTER 8

1. Simon Broadbent, *The Advertiser's Handbook for Budget Determinations* (Lexington, MA: D.C. Heath & Co., 1988), pp. 90–93. This is a generally sensible text on various advertising models, their implications and implementation.
2. J. D. Leckenby, and Kuen H. Ju, "Advances in Media Decision Models," *Current Issues and Research in Advertising* 12, 2 (1989), pp. 311–357.
3. B. Guggenheim, "Advertising Media Planning and Evaluation," *Current Issues and Research in Advertising,* 7, 2 (1984), pp. 119–131. Also, Peter B. Turk and Helen Katz, "Making Headlines: An Overview of Key Happenings in Media Planning, Buying and Research from 1985–1991," *Current Issues and Research in Advertising* 14, 2 (1992), pp. 19–34.

9

Media Work Plan: Part II—Alternative Media Selection

OVERVIEW

The selection of the right medium, or the most creative combination of media, to carry the advertising message is at the core of media planning as a strategic discipline. The effort requires an understanding of media at the foundations of society and culture, and how the various media function in people's lives. This chapter describes each medium and details the strategic choices available to the media planner.

UNDERSTANDING MEDIA

Out-of-office management seminars often feature a session designed for "mind expansion," or a speaker who tries to stimulate the competitive juices by outlining the shape of threatening new technologies. Over cocktails after just such a session, the publisher of a prominent New England newspaper was being hazed about threats from new on-line services. He calmly said that he wasn't worried about the future of newspapers. "What's the first thing you do when you wake up in the morning?" he asked. "You read about the game you were at the night before." He was a baseball fan and a newspaper fan. He was certain neither would disappear from American society.

The question for media planners is not whether this publisher was correct about the future, but whether he was right about the present. In an anecdotal way, he was describing a fundamental relationship between consumers and newspapers. That fundamental relationship is what advertisers require to sell their products. Advertisers are not only dependent on media to carry their messages; they are dependent on how the media work for the success of their messages.

The essence of media planning as a strategic advertising discipline is rooted in the media themselves. We can identify a great many characteristics of the various media with the help of the social sciences, and we can enumerate their audiences in reams of statistical data, but neither the data nor the theories provide an imaginative and athletic penetration of the experience of reading or watching, of looking or listening. Data alone cannot provide entree to the dynamic dialogue between producer, editor, writer, artist, and performer, on the one hand, and the audience that chose them and pays them with time, attention, and dollars on the other. Media planning is about more than numbers.

RECALLING THE FOUNDATIONS

In the earliest chapters of this text we discussed the media meaning at the foundations of advertising. We suggested that advertising's dependence on mass media identifies the appropriate starting point for advertiser thinking about media planning. This dependence also proposes the framework for how media planning can best be done.

The purpose of marketing is to effect an exchange that satisfies a consumer want. The purpose of advertising is to facilitate this exchange by affecting the consumer's perception of value. Advertising does this by stimulating the transfer of cultural meaning to particular products, services, and ideas. Culture, however, is the product of society communicating, and communications media create the conditions of choice. Consumers are the market, and media are the marketplace. In today's society, media are the inescapable environment in which demand can be negotiated.

At the root of media planning as a strategic discipline, therefore, is the recognition that media choices are the first way consumers answer the question "Why?" This is true because people work out who they are in communications. Consequently, these communications take place precisely where and when marketers not only want to be, but also must be, when they have something to sell and a need to create demand.

Communication media set the conditions for choice. The function of media planning, from this point of view, is to determine the penultimate condition of the marketing exchange and the substrate of the advertising message. **Media strategy** consists of designing the plan through which the marketer will utilize the means and momentum of society communicating to borrow value and effect a sale.

IMAGINATION AND MANAGEMENT

Nothing sucks out the vitality, or smothers the effectiveness, of media planning as much as the perception of the media as nothing more than facilitating institutions and efficient vehicles. These perceptions reduce media planning to media buying, and then judge the buying only by standards of cost and efficiency. Advertising actually is an investment, however, and media strategies and executions should be evaluated in terms of their effectiveness, as well as in terms of their efficiency. Efficiency can be discovered through cost-of-performance numbers, but potential effectiveness will only be discovered through imagination.

In order to understand their product and its consumers, media planners must imagine the marketing exchange, and they also must imagine the media that gave rise to its motivations. The media planner must imagine the prospects' communications situation: the prospects' attitudes and beliefs and the communication dynamics that produced these beliefs. This is an artistic act of informed judgment and a three-step imaginative process:

1. Imagine the prospects' profile and their communications situation.

2. Imagine the communications dynamic that helped the prospects become who they are.

3. Imagine the communications dynamic, evolving out the prospects' current communication situation, that will facilitate the specific new consumer motivations and judgments required by the marketing plan.

Consumers learn from more than one source and in more than one context. The media planner must be able to imagine this process and its dynamics. This imaginative effort is necessary if one expects to select securely the right sources of influence and the most effective environments for a brand in an ever-changing competitive world. Only in this way can the planner see through the numbers to the art of delivering advertising in a fashion synchronous and coincident with the consumers' processes of attention and perception, learning and choice.

STRATEGY IMPACT

Imagine a media representative on a sales call. The salesperson has made a clear case that the vehicle's audience and the marketer's target prospects are identical in every respect. The salesperson has pointed out the dynamic features of the vehicle and has clearly proven that it enjoys many competitive efficiencies. The salesperson walks out without a sale; what happened?

The facts of life are that if an advertiser or agency has not already bought into the medium of which the salesperson's vehicle is an example, there never will be a sale. The buyer simply hasn't been listening, because the medium is not on strategy. Strategy either opens or closes the door for vehicle sales; it makes the critical difference.

This is the lesson that can be learned from Del Monte's dramatic shift from television to magazine advertising (Exhibit 9.1). Concerned with the possible impact of rising broadcast costs on continuity, Del Monte changed its media strategy. In 1987, Del Monte brands spent more than two thirds of their budgets on television. They flipped their magazine and broadcast budgets in 1988, and their plans were 90 percent print in 1990.

During this time, Del Monte brands doubled the performance average in their categories. While industry sales were growing at an annual rate of 5 percent, Del

EXHIBIT 9.1 DEL MONTE SPENDING PATTERNS

	Magazines (000)	Television (000)	Total (000)
1987	$8,723.0	$20,504.5	$30,142.9
1988	14,206.5	8,094.1	26,627.3
1989	22,349.1	2,362.9	25,502.4
1990	23,304.1	959.8	25,893.4

Author estimates based on competitive and media reports

Monte brands were growing at 10 percent. Del Monte concluded that since they had a strong brand name presence in a number of different product categories, they didn't need the instant awareness and brand name recognition provided by television as much as they needed the continuity they could achieve on their budgets through magazines.

The point here is not to encourage the use of magazines over television. Rather, the point is that the shift was a strategic decision. As such, it would have been first articulated and supported in the section of the Media Work Plan we are discussing. If the decision continues to prove correct, it also suggests two further points: First, an imaginative understanding of the consumers' communication matrix probably would have uncovered the reality years earlier. Second, the proof of seriousness is the investment of resources, and the investment of sufficient resources to prove the point.

MEDIA CONSIDERATIONS

Each of the many media performs different cultural functions in American society. This is true because each of these communication types is experienced and used by consumers in a specific way. Effective media planning requires imaginative access to this personal and social dynamic.

At the same time, years of collective experience in the use of media for marketing purposes have produced a common understanding of the advantages and disadvantages of each medium as a carrier of advertising. Experience has also produced guidance systems for the uses and applications of each medium.

An understanding of how a medium works (social role) and why it works that way (technology and creative talent) tells the planner what the medium is. What the medium's creators do and how well they do it make up the medium's existential expression. This phenomenal expression determines how the medium can and is experienced and used by consumers. This experience and use produces motivations, lifestyles, and culture.

Each medium creates a distinct advertising possibility in terms of reach and frequency, efficiency and awareness. The way a medium is used and experienced determines its effectiveness in achieving advertising objectives relating to motivation and behavior. An understanding of how and why a medium works, combined with an understanding of how it is experienced and used, establishes a basis for both creativity and sound strategic judgments.

As a practical matter, the initial identification of media on the way to their strategic consideration involves:

1. An understanding of the components or functional characteristics of each medium

2. An understanding of each medium from their makers' point of view; what they are doing when they do their job

3. An understanding of each medium's cultural role; how people use the medium in their lives

4. An understanding of the advantages and disadvantages of each medium, based on advertiser experience

5. An understanding of various past successful uses and applications of each medium in solving marketing problems

These five media considerations represent the basic knowledge necessary for setting the process of strategic thought in motion.

In the following pages, we will address each of these considerations for each of the major media available to the media planner. Our purpose is to inform in such a way as to trigger imaginative thought. Consumer attention, consumer thought, and media communications are all behavior. Only imagination can encounter and manage behavior. Consequently, when we think about media, we should think imaginatively.

TELEVISION

Television programs come and go, but television, it seems, is always with us. In a typical family household, the television set is on nearly sixty hours a week, and single persons spend as many hours per week in television viewing as they do at their jobs. New technologies only increase television viewing, while extending the margins of its possibilities and expanding the parameters of its programming. If there is any such thing as the national mood, the national imagination, the national outlook and intention, it is informed, shaped, and reflected in the arena of television.

Technology

When David Sarnoff introduced television at the New York World's Fair in 1939, he called it "radio's world of tomorrow," for it would add "radio sight to sound." Television has turned out to be a greater social force than radio, but Sarnoff's engineering mind understood the similarity in their root technologies: electricity and airwaves.

Television is instantaneous and simultaneous because it is electronic, and it is democratic, egalitarian, and pervasive because it is broadcast electronics. Television shared these facts with radio in 1939, but the addition of "radio sight" was more than a visual aid to audio. Television is more broadly mimetic; because it communicates the look, the sound, the weight, and the motion of physical life, it provides an almost direct imitation of reality, whether it presents us with actual or with simulated experiences. Television presents behavior as behavior. For this reason, it is readily internalized, capable of becoming part of our experience without the filter of self-reflection and without the need for the abstract identification and organization of experience.

Television does not require a "detour through the describing word," as Rudolph Arnheim noticed at its very beginning. Whatever television broadcasts, everyone can experience directly the same exposure to behavior at the same time that a real or simulated activity is occurring. Television is a community experience.

Perceived Advantages

Television is considered the optimal vehicle for brands with broad prospect and geographic targets, the need for high reach, and the creative availability of audio/visual presentation or demonstration. In general, the perceived advantages of television are derived from its technical characteristics.

Mass Coverage Television is capable of reaching a large segment of a brand's target audience very quickly.

Efficiency The relative cost of reaching a wide audience or covering broad demographic groups (for example, men, women, or children) compares favorably to other media.

Flexibility Television offers virtually unlimited selectivity of time of year, month, week, and day, combined with a choice of national or local expressions. Thus, reach can be calibrated to consumer purchase and usage considerations, or it can be timed to correspond to promotional activities.

Impact Television provides sight, sound, motion, intrusiveness, and demonstration ability, which can be combined with humor, spectacle, or drama. The medium can capture human situations from children, husbands, or wives asking for things at home to in-store shopping while weighting them with emotion.

Influence Television is persuasive, but it is also dominant. Therefore, the medium helps to insert or maintain a brand's presence in the social mainstream.

Perceived Disadvantages

Some of the disadvantages of television as an advertising medium are rooted in its technology, while others are rooted in its economic practice.

Cost Television presents a high out-of-pocket cost, both for commercial production and the initial purchase of one commercial exposure. The repeat purchase of time to achieve the levels of reach and frequency required for changing attitudes and perceptions rapidly multiplies these costs to the point of eliminating the medium from consideration for many advertisers.

Transient Television exposures are a moment in time; they are as short lived as the length of the advertisement. There is no passalong, and the only way to repeat exposure is to repeat the purchase of time.

Clutter The actual number of advertisements and promotional messages grouped together in a commercial block diminishes differentiation and lowers consumer attention. The viewer perception of overcommercialization resulting from the forced interruption of programming has a negative impact on consumer attitudes; often the viewer does unmeasurable amounts of zapping to avoid commercial exposure.

Inflexibility To gain efficiency, many advertisers negotiate the purchase of time up front and many months in advance of use. A frequent result is that it can be difficult to be responsive to changing market and business requirements.

Limited Selectivity Television advertising is sold and purchased on a GRP basis, with the seller trying to control inventory and the buyer trying to maximize efficiency. This structure limits the ability of even the largest advertisers to exercise the degree of program selectivity they might otherwise wish. Smaller advertisers have an even greater difficulty in purchasing the time slots and programming environments they seek.

For those advertisers who can afford television, the medium provides the sense of assurance that prospects have been reached through a medium that generates high awareness and recall during consciously scheduled commercial activity.

Creative Intentions

Television programming is generally identified as either news or entertainment. The spectrum of entertainment programming stretches from game shows, daytime serials, and cartoons to situation comedies, action adventure series, mysteries, and dramas. The only thing they have in common is the desire to entertain, a desire shared by Shakespeare, Mozart, standup comics, and vaudevillians. As entertainers, television producers and performers share three perspectives:

1. No entertainers wish to fail. They wish to gather and maintain a happy audience. They all want to generate a full house in the largest venue they can.

2. Entertainers of every variety are aware that their act, their form of entertainment, satisfies distinct needs and appeals to distinct psychologies.

3. All entertainers know that both initial and continued success depends on the ability to accurately depict and reflect their community's changing interests. They are radi-

cally dependent on their own observations, and their success is dependent on their finger-in-the-wind sensibilities.

Everyone connected with a situation comedy, to use one example, wants to produce an *I Love Lucy*, *M.A.S.H.*, *All in the Family*, *Cheers*, *Roseanne*, or *Murphy Brown*, which both defined and became an integral part of their times. The same can be said of other program types, from the *The Untouchables* to *Charley's Angels*, *Columbo*, and *LA Law*, and from *Milton Berle* to *Laugh-In* to *Jeopardy*.

Television journalists, from network anchors to local sportscasters, are trying to bring us the outlines and essence of events we do, or might, care about. They are constantly confronted with the problems of selectivity and depth. They must consider, however, the defining facts of events, as well as their relevance and significance. Their goal is to earn viewer trust, and the viewer has an infinite variety of ways to test the television journalist's trustworthiness constantly. In fact, successful television journalists grow to be perceived as among the most trustworthy citizens of their communities.

Television journalists and entertainers of all types are trying to capture and reflect reality. In the process, they create experience. Within the extraordinary abundance of television, there is an extraordinary abundance of experiences that attract different audiences.

Fundamental to an understanding of the audience's experience is the ability to understand what the creator of that experience was about at the time of creation, as well as how these creators go about constructing the experience. This is the surest way to understand what attracts an audience and what the audience is experiencing when the advertiser presents it with commercials. Recognizing the character of the experience shared by creator and audience is important, because advertisers are seeking a synergy of motivations when they use a media vehicle or attempt to transfer cultural values to a brand.

Social Function

The basic social functions of communications as articulated by many sociologists of communications include:

1. Surveillance of the environment, reporting on dangers and opportunities to the individual and the community

2. Correlation of the components of society in arriving at a response to these reports

3. Transmission of the culture, or social inheritance, to new members of the community

4. Entertainment of the people for their own enhancement and enjoyment of life

As the basic mass medium of our times, television performs all of these social functions. This is true whether or not television, as we know it, performs these functions well.

A mistake often made is the assumption that television news and documentaries perform the surveillance and correlation functions and that other programming entertains the population while transmitting traditional culture and/or creating a popular culture. In fact, the selection and treatment of events by television journalists affects our cultural perceptions, and many people find entertainment in the discussion of public issues. Similarly, the articulation of social concerns such as AIDS, or civil rights, or welfare reform in entertainment programming is often a source of information and the engine of consensus for many in the audience.

Television is the central nervous system of our society. It creates experience for everyone and reflects most people's experience.

Television creates awareness because people use it to gain awareness.

Television influences perception because people use it in an experiential way.

Television is efficient because so many people utilize it for entertainment and information.

Television influences the style of consumer behavior because its programs cannot be successful without reflecting the mood of the times.

Advertising Applications

Television programming and its use as an advertising vehicle is generally defined by dayparts. The driving force behind the programming schedule is made up of the demographic characteristics and concentrations of the available and viewing audience (Figures 9.1 and 9.2). Correspondingly, the effectiveness and efficiency of each daypart's programming as an advertising vehicle depends on the characteristics of the brand's target prospects and communication strategies.

Prime time is characterized by the high-profile programming broadcast in the evening between 8 P.M. and 11 P.M. weekdays, or 7 P.M. to 11 P.M. Sundays EST. Prime time is generally perceived as a reach vehicle that produces high attention and recall scores. It is expensive, costing as much as $1.5 million to reach 75 percent of adult consumers. For most advertisers, therefore, prime time is not perceived as a frequency vehicle.

Daytime is characterized by the weekday programming of game shows, serial dramas, talk shows, and reruns aired between 9 A.M. and 4 P.M. EST. At the most extravagant purchase levels, daytime advertising is only able to reach 65 percent of the adult population, and it builds this reach very slowly. Therefore, daytime is generally perceived as an efficient vehicle for generating frequency against concentrated elements of the female consumer base. There is greater clutter and, for all but the serial dramas, lower attention levels in daytime.

Early daytime is characterized by the morning news and talk programs, aired between 7 A.M. and 9 A.M. EST. These programs have become increasingly popular and

FIGURE 9.1a HOUSEHOLD TELEVISION VIEWING: ANNUALLY BY DAYPARTS

Hours:Minutes—Distribution of Viewing per TV Household per Week

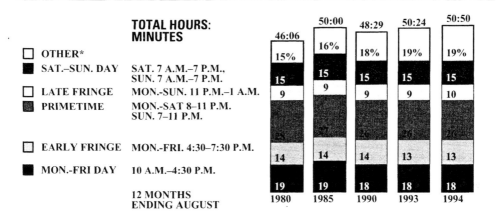

Note: Data for 1980–85 based on NTI Audimeter sample

*Includes Mon.–Fri. 1–10 A.M., Sat.–Sun. 1–7 A.M. and Mon.–Sat. 7:30–8 P.M.

Source: Nielsen Media Research. *Television Audience 1994.* Reprinted by permission.

FIGURE 9.1b HOUSEHOLD TELEVISION VIEWING: QUARTERLY BY DAYPARTS

Hours:Minutes—Distribution of Viewing per TV Household per Week

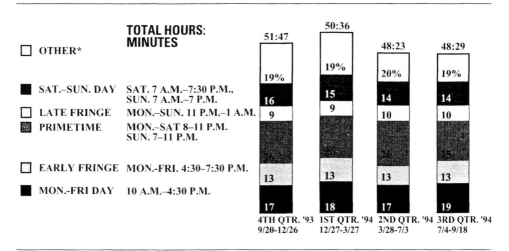

*Includes Mon.–Fri. 1–10 A.M., Sat.–Sun. 1–7 A.M. and Mon.–Sat. 7:30–8 P.M.

Source: Nielsen Media Research. *Television Audience 1994.* Reprinted by permission.

FIGURE 9.2a PERSONS VIEWING—ANNUAL TREND

Average Hours:Minutes of Viewing per Week

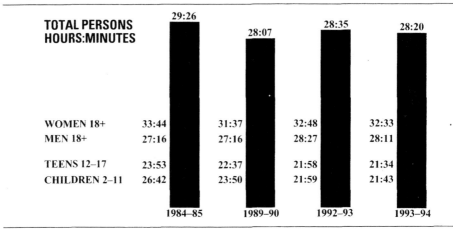

TOTAL PERSONS HOURS:MINUTES	29:26	28:07	28:35	28:20
WOMEN 18+	33:44	31:37	32:48	32:33
MEN 18+	27:16	27:16	28:27	28:11
TEENS 12–17	23:53	22:37	21:58	21:34
CHILDREN 2–11	26:42	23:50	21:59	21:43
	1984–85	1989–90	1992–93	1993–94

Note: Data prior to 1982–88 based on NTI Audimeter/Diary.

1984–85 data based on average of Nov., Feb., May, and July each year.
1989–90 data based on Sept.–Aug. each year.
1992–94 data based on broadcast seasons—mid-September to mid-September each year.

Source: Nielsen Media Research. *Television Audience 1994.* Reprinted by permission.

FIGURE 9.2b HOUSEHOLD VIEWING

Average Hours:Minutes of Viewing per Week

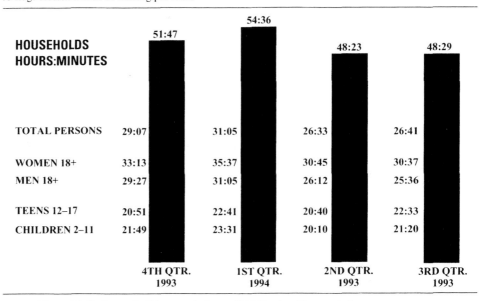

HOUSEHOLDS HOURS:MINUTES	51:47	54:36	48:23	48:29
TOTAL PERSONS	29:07	31:05	26:33	26:41
WOMEN 18+	33:13	35:37	30:45	30:37
MEN 18+	29:27	31:05	26:12	25:36
TEENS 12–17	20:51	22:41	20:40	22:33
CHILDREN 2–11	21:49	23:31	20:10	21:20
	4TH QTR. 1993	1ST QTR. 1994	2ND QTR. 1993	3RD QTR. 1993

Source: Nielsen Media Research. *Television Audience 1994.* Reprinted by permission.

provide an effective vehicle for reaching working men and women. The programming is used for a wide variety of brands but is especially attractive for indulgence products and to corporations concerned about the national agenda.

Prime news is characterized by the high-profile network news programs and their star quality anchors. The strength of this daypart is generally perceived as providing extensive reach and affordable frequency against older segments of the adult population in a highly credible environment. The daypart is variously attractive to over-the-counter senior citizen brands, corporations with agenda concerns, and advertisers willing to accept a premium to reach adult males.

Late night, which includes films and action-adventure programs as well as the high-profile talk shows, is generally perceived as daytime for younger adults. Therefore, late night is accepted as a vehicle for generating high frequency against younger men and women. While late night programming experiences heavy clutter levels like those of daytime, it produces attentiveness levels comparable to those of prime time.

Weekend sports is a highly variable vehicle, as it tracks the sporting seasons and its advertising usage is often influenced by larger promotional strategies. Sports can be purchased on a scatter or program sponsorship basis. Sports are generally perceived as a highly promotable vehicle for establishing both reach and frequency against more upscale male consumers. The variety of sports and sports interests, however, also provides vehicles for tightly targeted segments of the population. The realities of supply and demand, combined with the unique interests of certain major advertisers, however, make sports vehicles an expensive investment.

TV SPORTS NO LONGER MOST EFFICIENT FOR MALES

Spiraling TV sports rights fees aren't just affecting stations, they're also having an impact on the bottom lines of advertising, according to the 1994 TV Sports Overview published by the BJK&E Media Group.

As a result, the analysis finds sports are no longer the most efficient way to reach adult male viewers.

In an analysis of weekend sports, prime time, early evening news and late-night daypart costs, BJK&E found that sports was the most efficient place to reach men ages 18 to 49 and men ages 25 to 54—the two primary demographic targets used by TV sports advertisers—in the 1989–90 TV season.

But by the 1993–94 TV season, only prime time remained a more expensive daypart to reach men 18 to 49 and men 25 to 54.

BJK&E attributed the rise primarily to the escalating costs of sports rights fees for the networks, which are passed on to advertisers.

The agency noted that efficiency is not always the primary reason advertisers buy TV sports programming.

Overall, broadcast and cable networks are now paying about $1.7 billion annually for rights to televise NFL, NBA, college football and basketball, and NHL hockey coverage, a 30% increase over the more than $1.3 billion spent annually under previous contracts.

The beneficiary of increased rights fees appears to be basic cable TV. In the nine year span from the 1984–85 to 1993–94 TV seasons, the number of hours the average household watched national TV sports increased 12% overall, but was up 86% on basic cable TV channels and declined 7% on broadcast networks and 37% in syndication.

SPORTS ARE NO LONGER THE MOST EFFICIENT PLACE TO REACH MEN

(sports indexed at 100).

| | Cost Index, by daypart | | | | | |
| | Households | | Men 18–40 | | Men 25–54 | |
Daypart	1989–90	1993–94	1989–90	1993–94	1989–90	1993–94
Weekend sports	100	100	100	100	100	100
Prime time	102	88	145	119	141	117
Early evening news	56	48	116	97	102	86
Late fringe	72	59	110	76	106	76

Source: BJK&E Media Group, network TV CPMs, June–May for indicated periods.

Source: *Advertising Age*, November 7, 1994. Reprinted by permission.

Weekend children's programming is often thought of as a pabulum-paved highway of cartoons. There are, however, many different kinds of children's programs available during each day of the week. The difference is that much of the most popular Saturday children's programming is distributed by the three broadcast networks and is capable of reaching all children. Weekday children's programming is distributed either by local stations or by cable networks. In either case, children's programming efficiently delivers both reach and frequency against its target audience.

CABLE TELEVISION

At one time unknown, and then a misunderstood stepchild, cable television has emerged as a major player in the television sweepstakes. More than 60 percent of television households now receive all of their television through a wire. Cable households tend to view television approximately ten hours more per week than unconnected households, and nearly equally divide almost 20 percent of their total viewing between pay television and advertiser-supported cable networks.

Three strategies have developed to characterize advertiser use of cable television networks and channels:

1. **Network compensation** strategies dedicate a certain percentage of every television buy to cable to insure the same reach and frequencies, or audience coverage, in cable households, that they once enjoyed when the three networks were the only national distribution system for television.

2. **Targeted** strategies focus on the more precisely defined audiences of certain cable networks and programming. In these instances, advertisers are seeking out either hard-to-reach segments of the general television audience, or unique program environments that are editorially tuned to the advertiser's message.

3. **Localization** strategies are pursued by regional advertisers who can take special advantage of the geographic interconnection of various cable systems, or by very local advertisers who can use cable system purchases as a means of affording television exposure.

For a national advertiser, none of these three typical strategies necessarily excludes the others. All three, in fact, can be pursued at the same time.

SYNDICATION

Barter syndication is extensively practiced (see Figure 9.3) by some national advertisers and avoided like the plague by others. In a typical barter syndication deal, a program distributor will sell an advertiser two or more minutes of advertising in a program and then attempt to distribute the program "free" to various stations. The distributor usually guarantees a certain degree of distribution, articulated as markets or as a certain percentage of television households. The local station makes its income from selling the remaining minutes in the program without the necessity of recouping the programming costs.

The advantages some advertisers perceive are controlled costs and controlled program environments. The disadvantages other advertisers perceive are the inability of the programs to clear as many markets as desired, limited program quality, the wide variation in the times the program airs from market to market, the closing cost differential from network, and shortfalls in the audience guarantees estimated by the distributors.

The driving force behind syndication, however, is neither sheer cost factors nor the poetry of program environment. Because local station viewing is increasing both as a result of changing demographics and as a result of the enhancements of cable distribution, syndication has enjoyed a decade of explosive growth. Its major advantages, however, go to those advertisers who have the clout to facilitate local clearances, who

FIGURE 9.3 GROWTH OF ADVERTISER SUPPORTED SYNDICATION

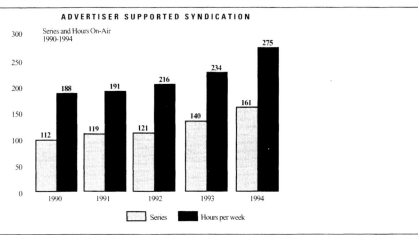

Source: Nielsen NSS Pocketpiece 4th Quarter each year. ASTA, 1994.

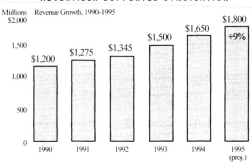

Source: Advertiser Syndicated Television Association, 1994.

have the programming smarts to spot winners and to be ahead of the crowd, and who have extensive staffs capable of monitoring and enforcing accountability.

MEDIUM AND VEHICLE EFFECTS

A key question is whether television programming environments have an impact on audience receptivity to various commercials. Most of the relevant research studies date from the 1960s and 1970s, and a definitive answer seems unavailable from the research community. Some general conclusions, however, can be implied from the existing data:

Program involvement has a measurable positive effect upon all measures of advertising response.

Involvement varies both by program and by demographic segments within a program's audience.

There are considerable differences in the effects of different programs within the same program type.

Different episodes of the same program can produce widely different advertising responses.

The Network Television Association released a study of audience involvement in September 1991. Its rather self-serving conclusion was that "prime time programs on the three broadcast networks provide greater value to advertisers because they deliver involved viewers who are more likely to be exposed and receptive to full commercial messages." Considering the way network television time has been bought and sold, however, there was considerable irony in another conclusion of the study, that "all rating points are not created equal."

There has been a long-held belief that the more involved consumers are with the various media, the more effective the vehicles will be for appropriate advertisers. Arriving at a consensus on how to quantify such involvement and to translate the information into media executions has proven to be a practical problem. This has been especially true of television where, in fact, the buying and selling of television time has treated all rating points as equal.

All of the advantages and disadvantages generally ascribed to television as an advertising vehicle are rooted in its technology and are expressed as the relative cost of producing reach and frequency. Television time has also been bought and sold as if all rating points were equal. Therefore, the prototypical strategic considerations in the utilization of television are: *Television provides the impact of sight, sound, and motion along with intrusiveness and demonstration ability that can be selectively scheduled by daypart and programming to deliver concentrations of the target audience efficiently and generate rapid awareness.*

If consumers are increasingly living in a solipsistic world of distinct lifestyles, this is supported (developed and reinforced) by their media choices, including their choices of television viewing. Given the absence of satisfying quantitative research, the only way to use this understanding as an accessible strategic tool is through an internal understanding of the individual programs and of the way a particular pattern of program viewing produces and supports a distinctive consumer psychology. For the present, however, this strategic understanding can only be individually understood, utilized, and expressed by following the imaginative processes previously articulated in this text. Conservative media planning, therefore, will continue to rely on the technical advantages of television during strategic considerations.

RADIO

Radio may be the most used medium in America. People wake up, travel, work, and retire with radio. Radio is our personal medium. It is our companion wherever we go, while we do whatever we are doing. That is why radio can fairly claim to reach more than 80 percent of the adult population on any given day, and 95 percent every week.

Technology

Radio, like television, is instantaneous and simultaneous because it is electronic. Radio, however, is not so much a mimetic avenue into experience as it is experience itself. Recorded music is music, direct and unadorned. Talk is sound shared. Because radio is experience, it is personal.

An advantage of radio's technology is the increasing inexpensiveness of its transmitting and receiving equipment. There are more AM and FM radio stations, and they continue to proliferate because they are both affordable and profitable. Nearly every automobile is equipped with a radio, and the average household has six working radios. The radio is small, unobtrusive, and portable.

The personal nature of radio's arts of music and talk, combined with the narrow segmentation, both sending and receiving, made possible by its affordable technology, makes radio ubiquitous and pervasive. The medium of radio may reach nearly everyone, but this total audience is developed almost one person at a time, like a pointillist painting.

Perceived Advantages

Radio is considered an important vehicle for building affordable frequency levels against tightly described target audiences. This advantage is derived primarily from programming design (Figure 9.4) and consumer use patterns. Radio's technology provides the medium's radical flexibility and cost advantages.

Targeting The dozen or more programming formats available in any marketing area enable an advertiser to reach more narrowly defined prospect groups more efficiently, than it can through most other media. This includes nearly every demographic or social interest grouping of any interest to advertisers.

Selectivity Radio's availabilities enable an advertiser to provide both national and local support in almost infinite combinations. Different prospect groups can be targeted in different markets or combined differently in different markets.

Flexibility Radio's use as a companion throughout the day offers advertisers unparalleled opportunities to insert messages coincident with the purchase decisions and usage occasions consistent with the lifestyle of the consumer. At the same time, messages can be tailored to different days, times of day, and market conditions on an immediate basis.

Cost Production expenses and the costs of time in radio are noticeably lower than in competitive media. These low cost characteristics provide a window of opportunity for

FIGURE 9.4 NARROWLY TARGETED RADIO FORMATS

SOME OF THE RECENT FORMATS ACTIVE, ALONG WITH NEWS, CLASSICAL, JAZZ, AND COUNTRY, AMONG THE 72 STATIONS IN THE NEW YORK MARKET.

C.H.R., for Contemporary Hit Radio. It is known as "Top 40," and plays the top pop hits of the day in every major style except country.

Churban. The nickname is a hybrid of CHR and urban. It concentrates on dance music, rap, and hip-hop by acts like Naughty by Nature, Silk, Arrested Development, and L.L. Cool J.

Alternative. Rock groups with large college audiences like R.E.M., Us, and Jesus Jones are the backbone of alternative rock.

Rock C.H.R. Focuses on rock singles by hard rock and metal bands like Metallica, Gun 'n' Roses, and Bon Jovi.

Adult C.H.R. Emphasizes ballads by singers like Whitney Houston and Michael Bolton and vocal groups like Shai and Boyz 2 Men.

A.O.R., for Album Oriented Rock. Mainstream rock acts like Van Halen and Bruce Springsteen are the meat and potatoes of A.O.R.

Classic Rock. Aimed at baby boomers, it concentrates on music from the late 1960s and 1970s by groups like Crosby, Stills and Nash and Led Zeppelin. Led Zeppelin's "Stairway to Heaven" is considered the ultimate classic rock cut.

A.C., for Adult Contemporary. Adult contemporary stations come in many stylistic shadings, but a typical one plays a mixture of current hit ballads and oldies by singers like Billy Joel, Barbra Streisand, and Linda Ronstadt.

Source: *The New York Times*, March 23, 1993. © 1993/94 by The New York Times Company. Reprinted by permission.

many advertisers and create a vehicle that can produce extensive frequency against target audiences for all advertisers.

Promotion Market-by-market and store-by-store promotion copy and tags can be combined with the merchandising that is almost always available to generate support from local merchants and distributors.

Perceived Disadvantages

Many of radio's disadvantages are simply the downside of its advantages. Some could be ameliorated by changes in industry practice, but others are inherent.

One Dimensional Radio is sound, and while some continue to believe that Rudolph Arnheim's "detour through the describing word" productively engages the imagination, most believe that it compares unfavorably with the options available to television.

Complexity The extraordinary number of constantly fluctuating radio formats on a market-by-market basis puts a premium on extraordinary levels of information and knowledge. This can have a negative impact both on planning and on purchasing. Use of the medium is often a more labor intensive endeavor than many agencies can absorb. Some industry efforts attempt to address these problems, but a permanent solution is not yet available.

Cost Moving beyond the confines of narrow targets and limited markets to national and broader-based consumer targets can rapidly escalate costs and erode the medium's advantages.

Background Transience Broadcast messages are transient by nature, but radio's effectiveness is further diminished by the fact that it is a background for other work or play activities.

Clutter The number of commercials aired per hour reduces the impact of all commercials. The combination of transience and clutter puts intense pressure on frequency and a premium on intrusive creative executions.

Radio's selectivity, flexibility, affordable frequency levels, and promotional characteristics make it a distinctive, and often primary, medium for many advertisers. The rising cost pressures of other media, especially during downturns in the economy, are encouraging may advertisers to rethink their use of radio.

Creative Intentions

Most of radio is recorded music. Any attempt, therefore, to fathom radio's creative intentions must begin with the intentions of the recording musicians. Music is the most physical of the arts and, yet, the most ephemeral. Music is both a method of inquiry and a method of expression. Much of classical music is an effort at understanding, and much of contemporary popular music is radical expressionism. What is remarkable about music, wherever it appears on this spectrum, is how much it is part of its aficionados' or fans' lives. Therefore, any effort to understand these people as consumers involves an effort to understand their music. It is part of imagining any prospect's communications situation and lifestyle. To be informed, the planner must listen.

Any station's music is selected from a variety of voices, arranged in a format, and fronted by a personality. The only way to do this successfully is through a psychographic (as opposed to a demographic) understanding of the potential audience. Therefore, the task for the media planner is to determine the combination of attitudes and motivations that add up to the prospects for whom this radio station's programming represents a comfort zone.

Any media planning attempt to reach beyond the numbers involves this kind of psychographic template. The planning questions then become: Does my brand require, or benefit from, these sets of attitudes and motivations? Does the situation require format compatible commercial executions, and are they available? The importance of each of these questions depends on the importance of image identification and peer acceptance to purchase and usage patterns.

What is true of music is also true of talk radio. People identify with the hosts of these programs and become actively involved in the discussions. Each station and personality represents a worldview—a perspective on life, its structures, and aggravations. The more dependent the brand is on the transfer of cultural values to establish loyalty, the more important it is to understand the character and possibilities of different talk radio formats and personalities.

Comedy talk, sports talk, and all-news formats are less compellingly different, easier to identify, and more readily accessible through demographics. Nevertheless, there are differences between them that might lead to the choice of one station over another.

SOCIAL FUNCTION

Even when people report that they first heard of a natural disaster or major political shock from a friend, the trigger is frequently radio. The reason is not so much that people rely on radio for information about their environment beyond traffic and weather, but that radio is such a widespread companion. Any understanding of radio's social function, therefore, must involve an attempt at understanding companionship.

A companion is a person who is frequently in our company and who shares common interests, ideals, experiences, and beliefs with us. Companions are not accidental associates, but people whose company we seek out. They are our chosen point of contact with social experience. In this context, radio's social function is to provide social contact and context for our lives. This is true whether the audience is older people seeking conversation through talk radio or teenagers acting out their lives to the beat of their different drummers.

Advertising Applications

Radio can be employed on either a national network or local market basis. In each instance the programming day is broken down into distinct elements:

A.M. Drive time	6–10 A.M.
Daytime	10 A.M.–3 P.M.
P.M. Drive time	4–7 P.M.
Evening	7 P.M.–Midnight
All Night	Midnight–6 A.M.

The character of the audiences delivered during these time periods is dictated by the broadcast format, but it is driven by the normal daily schedule of its consumers. Generally, A.M. drive time offers the largest audiences and includes teens as well as both male and female adults. Daytime provides an audience of women and older adults. The second largest audiences are provided during P.M. drive time and include all adult demographics and teens. Evening is mostly teen time, and all night radio adds adults to the continuing teen audience.

The strategic uses of radio can vary widely, perhaps more than any other medium.

Reach Although it can require the purchase of over 400 GRPs on multiple stations in a month to reach 75 percent of the audience, radio can be perceived as an affordable reach vehicle for local merchants, and as a necessary reach vehicle for larger advertisers dependent on communicating with light TV viewers—for example, males, teens, working women, and professional/managerial adults.

Frequency The converse of radio's slowly building reach curve is the rapid accumulation of frequency along the same curve. For example, in the process of building a 75 percent reach, it is common to produce an average frequency of five to seven impressions.

Affordability The relatively low costs of radio vis-à-vis other media enables it to be the frequent medium of choice for local advertisers, and to be a vehicle for increasing frequency for national advertisers who have satisfied their reach goals through television.

Compatibility There are many products, from films and music albums to 800-number direct response advertisers of insurance, books, and financial services, for whom radio's combination of direct talk and music are simply the most productive advertising environment.

Promotion Radio's purchase flexibility on both a national network and local station basis, combined with its ability to insert live copy instantly, enables advertisers to adjust and exert promotional pressure with local tags or line copy on a market-by-market or station-by-station basis. Not only does this provide an opportunity to insert unique support in weak markets, but it also provides the opportunity to craft local market trade promotions.

Timing Because radio is used as a companion to one's daily schedule, it offers extraordinary opportunities for scheduling advertising messages coincident with purchase and usage decision occasions. This can be of special importance for brands dependent on top-of-mind awareness (such as frequently purchased/low involvement products), or for brands anxious to increase usage in established and brand loyal categories.

None of these strategic uses of radio necessarily excludes the others, and they are often used in combination with considerable impact.

Medium and Vehicle Effects

People identify with their radio station choices and, consequently, can be identified by their choices. The dialogue of personal taste and peer support, which leads to these choices, produces a confidence level in the brand choices encouraged by advertising on these frequencies. Thus, brands that gain vitality from demographic and lifestyle identification gain a special impact from radio. Talk formats and hosts also produce a special loyalty and credibility. These programs can have the impact of family and the authority of a trusted advisor.

MAGAZINES

Magazines are persons with a specificity exceeding all other media. They are individual; have extended lives; and are capable of relationships. Consequently, they are a powerful advertising vehicle, but they require more subtlety of consideration and selection than do most other media.

Technology

Magazines are made of paper and ink, and they are bound, delivered and consumed one at a time. A magazine does not exist until it is printed. A magazine's circulation is dependent on its being printed over and over again, and then delivered by truck to a home or newsstand. These simple facts not only determine its costs, but also determine a magazine's use.

A magazine is a tangible product to be picked up and held in the hands. Consequently, a magazine must be chosen and, once chosen, it can be worked, played, debated, and dreamed with. Magazines also last virtually forever until they are physically shredded and destroyed.

The developments of offset and ink jet printing combined with new collating and binding equipment—all driven by computer technology—provide magazines with extensive flexibility and variations in their look and content. This flexibility of editions is never free from both the bounds and possibilities of ink and paper.

The key facts about magazines are derived from their foundations in print. The first is cost: Unlike any electronic vehicle, the distribution of magazines is always incremental. Every copy delivered to a reader represents an additional cost. The second is words: The printed word is a tool of thought and reflection, capable of high density information packaging. Consequently, for both publisher and consumer, every copy and every reader involves a price value decision. The publisher must make a decision about the value of the reader, and the reader must make a decision about the value of the information.

Perceived Advantages

Targeting Magazines generally reach more narrowly defined demographic, psychographic, and geographic prospect groups more precisely and thoroughly than any medium other than direct mail.

Managed Coverage Individual magazines can provide split runs of their circulation, and combinations of magazines can be utilized to develop a broad coverage of uniquely defined prospects efficiently.

Graphic Impact High quality color reproduction and the infinite design possibilities of magazines can provide both startling and contemplative visual attention and pleasure.

Flexibility Advertising copy can be of any length—long or short—that the message requires and it can be presented in a wide variety of space and combined units. Magazines can distribute samples, as well as offering spreads, gatefolds, and spectaculars.

Influence Many magazines are perceived as authorities by their readers, and these magazines can provide credibility or prestige to any message within their covers.

Extended Impact Magazines have a long shelf life in the home, are consulted frequently, and often are passed along to other readers, both inside and outside the home.

Perceived Disadvantages

Long Lead Time The closing dates for magazines vary from several weeks to three months, requiring advertisers to prepare materials far in advance of publication and of any immediate marketing demands.

Limited Flexibility Key magazine positions such as covers, center spreads, and editorial adjacencies may well be preempted by other advertisers. This possibility can also lead to pressure on longer lead times.

Delayed Reach Magazine audiences build slowly, both in terms of when primary readers get around to reading an issue, and in terms of pass-along exposures. The result is a lack of immediacy.

Cost The gross cost of broad-based magazines, or the cumulative cost of narrower circulation vehicles, can make extensive prospect reach unaffordable for many advertisers. For many advertisers, magazines are also viewed as an inefficient means of developing frequency.

Clutter Print vehicles attract many direct competitors, and magazines have few alternatives for providing competitive separation.

Creative Intentions

Since a magazine is a stand-alone product in a very competitive environment, more consumer and advertiser attention is focused on the defining mind of its creator. The general intentions available to rhetoricians for centuries were to inform, persuade, or entertain. Life in the magazine world, however, has become intensely complex, and the general categories of editorial intention have narrowed, combined, expanded, and interacted in distinctly individual ways.

People Weekly, for example, is identified as a newsweekly in Audit Bureau of Circulation (ABC) reports and, certainly, the magazine is full of news. The purpose and use of this information, however, may most clearly be entertainment. Furthermore, all of the reviews in the front of the magazine are clearly judgmental, and reviewers' judgments are often taken as persuasive by their readers.

Another way of looking at a magazine's editors' intentions is to ask: Are they trying to show me how to do something, to explain the meaning and character of events, to help me decide on a policy or purchase, or simply to provide me with a good time? These questions lead to the definition of editorial intent as "how-to," "service," "lifestyle," and "entertainment." A service magazine, however, may include not only a great deal of product information, but also instruction on how to use and enjoy the products. The variations are endless.

It is possible to classify magazines in various useful ways for various purposes, but each such construct has a certain degree of unreality built in. The ultimate fact is that magazines are individually created and individually consumed. It is a process of personal dialogue that can be best accessed through an understanding of the initiating editors' intentions and judgments.

Mirabella and *Martha Stewart Living*, two magazines named after their founding editors, are an excellent place to begin to understand the magazine dynamic. *Mirabella* contains a great deal of fashion editorial, reporting on the alternatives of current style. *Martha Stewart Living* is itself a fashion and tells you how to give a specific shape and form to your daily life. Grace Mirabella has described her magazine as a "terrific party, where the guests are funny, smart, provocative, and the conversation can range from Prague to lipstick. That's the fun of it for us," she concluded, "throwing that kind of party." That is the fun for her readers, as well. Each month Grace Mirabella invites her readers to share her urban chic lifestyle.

Martha Stewart invites us not only to share her suburban life, but even to follow her daily calendar as she lives out the seasons. To follow *Martha Stewart Living*, however, is to learn how to create the quality of life she lives, and to value her "basic premise that every task worth doing is worth doing well." Her magazine is about good housekeeping beyond urban boundaries, where the joy is in the doing. *Martha Stewart Living* wants us to know "how to throw the ultimate grown-up Halloween party," and *Mirabella* wants us to enjoy it after someone else has done the work.

William Shawn, for thirty-three years the editor of *The New Yorker*, once said that the idea and tradition of a magazine "exist in the minds of a group of writers, artists, editors and editorial assistants who have been drawn together by literary, journalistic, aesthetic and ethical principles they share." The same can be said of the magazine's readers. Consequently, the birth or death of a magazine is the birth or death of a particular kind of cultural life.

When the *Rolling Stone* generation grew up, for example, the magazine moved beyond rock and roll to include politics and movies. This evolution was a reflection of the evolution of a particular cultural life. This is what editors mean when they say that they are not editing for a demographic but for a sensitivity or mindset.

EXHIBIT 9.2 MIRABELLA ARTICULATES THE PERSONAL INTERESTS AND STYLE OF FOUNDER GRACE MIRABELLA

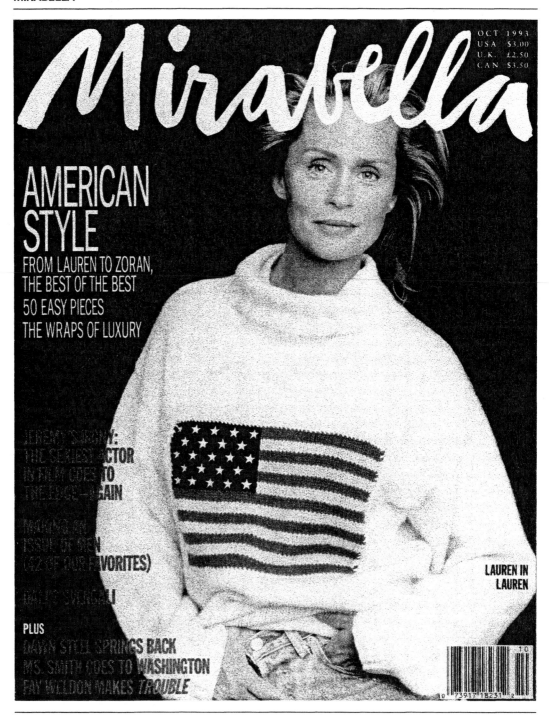

Source: Used with permission. Photo by Steen Sundland.

EXHIBIT 9.3 MARTHA STEWART LIVING IS ONE OF MANY MEDIA VEHICLES "BRANDED" WITH THE LIFESTYLE OF EDITOR-IN-CHIEF MARTHA STEWART

EXHIBIT 9.4 MAGAZINES REDEFINE THEMSELVES

THE NEW(EST) MCCALL'S

The December issue of McCall's features a redesign led by Axel Ganz, Gruner + Jahr's vice president of international magazine development. Publisher Barbara Litrell says the new McCall's is positioned to be "the inside source for women today." The redesign added 16 pages to the editorial well to allow broader coverage of fashion, beauty, food, home decorating and health, emphasizing service with tips, hints, recipes and inexpensive fashion and decorating ideas. Most pages showcase a four-column format, so they will be more text-heavy. Although the December cover features a celebrity, Kathie Lee Gifford, Litrell, says that Gruner + Jahr will be testing covers with an unknown model on the cover and another with a different logo on a regional basis. "Women are changing and we want to see where attitudes are going," she says. Since McCall's circulation is 89 percent subscription-based, G+J would like to boost newsstand sales, says Litrell to increase revenue and bring the readership age down. McCall's is without an editor since Kate White resigned last week to become the editor of Redbook. Possible replacements include McCall's executive editor Lynne Cusack and Sally Koslow, editor of Mary Emmerling's Country. Rumors also have Redbook executive editor Janet Chan under consideration and former Redbook editor in chief Annette Capone interested.

Looking for a newsstand boost.

Source: Inside Media November 2, 1994.

Editor Ellen Levine transformed *Redbook* from the pressured middle-class juggler of marriage, career, family, and home into an amusing, literate, confident friend who tells you everything. The purpose is to serve the woman who grew up reading *Cosmopolitan* or *Glamour*, got married, and had a baby. "She's still a sexy woman," Ms. Levine says, "She's not a grand matron yet."

Glamour has long been known for emphasizing serious issues and dealing directly with tough subjects like campus rape and women's reproductive rights. Like *Mademoiselle*, it is designed for young women who are too old for *Seventeen*, but it speaks in a different voice. *Mademoiselle* is chic, irreverent, and stylish in its subjects and tone of voice.

Any informed magazine observer could continue making these distinctions virtually forever in the process of analyzing thousands of magazines. What it tells us about magazines, however, is that each editorial voice represents a particular approach to life and defines a cultural perception. This is the foundation fact of magazines as a medium.

Social Function

Much of the vocabulary we use to describe mass media predates broadcast television and, in certain corners of our thought, our vocabulary hasn't caught up with reality. It is difficult, when we are confronted with television, to continue to think of magazines as simultaneously serving the mass media functions of environmental surveillance, correlation of judgments, cultural transmission, and general entertainment once ascribed to them. Simultaneously, some are inclined to think of magazines as so fragmented, distinct, and discriminating as to be of no egalitarian or democratic marketing interest.

The social functions of magazines have not so much been replaced by television as re-placed. *Life* magazine brought us World War II, and television has brought us all the wars since, with increasing immediacy. We no longer rely on magazines to provide us with the widest reports on social threats or opportunities, nor to provide our experience of them. Magazines, however, continue to provide our first reports on many things of broad significance and create a forum for our discussion of all events of importance. They also continue to entertain us all.

What television has accomplished is the liberation of magazines to do what they do best. Today, magazines are more distinctly definable than before as reflections of specific experiences and as specific reflections on experience—reporting and analyzing the odyssey of one personality through generalized experience. This explains how and why magazine readers develop such loyalty to their magazine choices for such long periods of their lives, identifying with and relying on one particular taste and perception.

Magazines share many of the characteristics of books in regard to what can be done with words and print. Books explore and capture what is deepest, least accessible, and least expressible in ourselves and by ourselves. Magazines, on the other hand, deal with what is less deep within us, and with what is almost accessible and expressible by ourselves. Because of this, we use magazines as our primary tool for the negotiation, selection, and confirmation of our lifestyle—the subculture through which we participate in the cultural life of society. Magazines help us define our social character. It is what we are trying to do when we pick up our favorite magazine.

Advertising Applications

Magazines are frequently thought of in very selective terms, but combinations of magazines often provide wide coverage of extensive target groups. Whether the target is broad or narrow, therefore, magazines—as a medium—can often achieve maximum reach among prospects with a consistent level of continuity.

Magazines build their reach more slowly than do broadcast vehicles, but they offer the compensating factor of providing longer-lasting messages, depending on their editorial format and frequency of issue. Weeklies build their readership most rapidly, maintain their reader interest for five weeks, and are generally referred to twice. Monthlies build their reach over twelve weeks and tend to be read and reread an average of four times. The perishability, complexity, and/or collectability of a magazine's editorial will influence these general rules of reader accumulation.

This reading process, combined with the nature of print, supports advertising messages that require detailed copy points and extensive information. They provide the advertiser room for explanation, and give the reader time for thoughtful consideration. These objectives are very difficult to achieve through other media.

Magazines offer both demographic and geographic editions. Therefore, magazines can deliver national, regional, or local groups of readers defined by age, sex, income, or professions such as doctors, business executives, and so on. Copy splits (that is, distributing different ads to different parts of a magazine's circulation) also enable advertisers to test different campaigns and promotional offers. Magazines also can generate trial through couponing or sampling and can support special promotions built around major events or holidays.

Magazines, then, can be utilized to maximize reach among broadly or narrowly defined targets while providing for extended copy and continuity. In constructing a magazine list for a campaign, planners frequently must go beyond the numbers representing cost and audience to consider editorial compatibility, positioning opportunities, and reproduction quality. A brand must also be in a position to absorb the slow-building reach of magazines.

Medium and Vehicle Effects

The conventional wisdom of media planning is that a reader's involvement with and attitudes toward a magazine can significantly influence the reader's reception and responsiveness to advertising within it. There is scattered research support for this conclusion, but more often it is a judgment call.

Both MRI and SMRB provide data on the percentage of a magazine's readers who cut out or used coupons, recipes, ads, and articles, sent for product information, or purchased advertised products. Although the data can have the persuasiveness of a news photo, it is very unstable and cannot be tied to any abstract principle with any certitude.

It appears that there is a correlation between the reason that readers purchase a particular magazine and the readers' responsiveness to similarly directed advertising.

To make a decision about why certain prospects select a particular magazine, however, and to match that with a decision about the character of a specific advertisement, often requires more judgment supported by self-confidence than most planners are prepared to exercise.

When constructing a strategy that might include magazines, planners generally note that magazines can reach a high concentration of targeted prospects. They conclude that magazines provide an editorial environment that enhances the effectiveness of the advertising, and they note that magazines provide the opportunity for especially appropriate copy.

NEWSPAPERS

When Americans first learned of the Declaration of Independence, they learned of it through a newspaper. Immediately following the famous signatures, the newspaper printed an advertisement. From then until now, newspapers have been at the core of our freedoms, seamlessly distributing news and advertising. Against all competition, newspapers continue to be our largest advertising medium.

Newspapers are both the brand name and the mass medium of their community. They are the universal cause and grounding of conversation, commerce, opinion, and decision. When journalists describe their work as "the first draft of history," they are describing newspapers. Newspapers are yesterday's diary and today's agenda.

Technology

Newspapers are print, and they are quick print. Even in the days when compositors were still using hot-metal linotypecasting machines, completely new editions came out each morning or afternoon, and when someone dramatically shouted "Stop the presses," a newspaper could be produced in hours.

New technologies, first introduced in the early 1970s, have enabled newspapers to be produced more quickly and efficiently, to be distributed more effectively, and to be designed more attractively. The basic technology consisted of minicomputer-based time-shared video terminals. This technology has led to an almost universal use of photo-typesetting, computer-aided composition, offset printing, and plastic printing plates.

The generally recognized and outstanding example of the effects of the application of these new technologies is *USA TODAY*, the national daily introduced by Gannett. This paper's distribution, however, also highlights the use of satellites and satellite printing plants. This means that complete newspapers can be distributed digitally across long distances and at little cost to local printing plants. This allows not only for cost efficient and time efficient national distribution, but also for the development of suburban editions of city newspapers.

The newspaper industry has been going through a great deal of anxious rethinking recently. One thought track leads to the creation of an entirely new range of information and marketing services, that is, new electronic media products. The other thought track attacks the basic printed newspaper product, from content and style to the way advertising is sold.

The purpose of redesigning newspapers, according to James K. Battern, chairman of Knight-Ridder newspapers, is to make readers "feel plugged-in and smart, touch their emotions, recognize their time poverty and help them with their lives." Newspapers always wanted to do most of these things. The truly new dimension is "time poverty." The pace of contemporary life, time/attention competition from other media, and the increasing number of women in the workforce have changed both newspapers and their readership patterns.

In the last ten years, many evening newspapers have either gone out of business or have metamorphosized into morning editions. Simultaneously, Sunday newspaper growth has accelerated (Figure 9.5). For consumers, the daily newspaper has, in a sense, become a weekly published on Sunday. The Sunday newspaper gains the greatest amount of reader attention and carries the lion's share of the week's advertising.

These same forces have encouraged many newspapers to produce themed or special section editions. Two important days, patterned to consumer needs and habits, are Wednesdays, when papers carry most of their food editorial and advertising, and Friday, which contains an entertainment guide for the weekend. This strategy is also driving newspapers to feature business and financial topics, health and fitness, fashion and style, and parenting or home improvement on different days.

Technology has enabled newspapers to respond to these market conditions. Technology has also enabled the introduction of color and other design factors that have helped readership. One purpose has been to capture readers' attention, but the more important objective has been to speed the reader through the newspaper with indices, visual cues, and shorter articles that never jump to continuations on another page.

The newspaper boy of American mythology may not look like technology, but a newspaper's distribution system can be perceived as part of its technology. Three out of four daily newspaper readers get home delivery. Retailers and other advertisers take advantage of this situation to distribute newspaper supplements. Supplements can be syndicated editorial such as *Parade* and *USA Weekend*, local editorial packages, or free-standing inserts.

As shopping malls and suburbs mushroomed around metropolitan centers, major discounters and retailers such as Kmart and J. C. Penney found it more economical to preprint advertising sections and to use a combination of city and suburban newspapers to distribute their mini-catalogues. This capacity has led some publishers to think of themselves as alternative delivery systems, competing with the U.S. Postal Service for direct response advertising.

The advent of desktop publishing has enabled hardworking entrepreneurs to compete for readers and advertising through weekly shoppers. These flyers contain little or no editorial content and have little or no overhead. Weeklies are also more economical to produce with new technology and can compete for attention by including pictures of church suppers and coverage of local town politics for which the major dailies do not

FIGURE 9.5 NEWSPAPER CIRCULATION IN MILLIONS OF COPIES

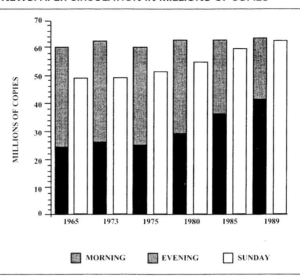

Source: Data from Editor & Publisher International Yearbooks, 1965–1990.

FIGURE 9.6 DECLINING CIRCULATIONS

Percentage change		Six months' circulation ended Sept. 1994
-7.26%	Newsday	693,556
-6.38%	San Francisco Chronicle	509,548
-3.30%	Chicago Sun-Times	518,094
-2.32%	The New York Times	1,114,905
-2.07%	Detroit Free Press	544,606
-1.85%	Chicago Tribune	678,081
-1.13%	Daily News, New York	753,024
-0.48%	Dallas Morning News	491,480
-0.22%	Washington Post	810,675

Source: Audit Bureau of Circulations

have space. One result of this kind of competition, rooted in new technology, is the encouragement it is giving publishers to think of their product not as editorial but as databased marketing (DBM) and their distribution system as audiotext or videotext.

The technological future of newspapers, as a printed product, appears to be here now. Most of the computer-based tools and techniques such as pagination, color scanning, manipulation of graphics, fax, and cellular phones are already in use. There may be a technological transfer to more local newspapers, and metropolitan dailies may continue to decline, but newspapers, it seems, will continue to be with us because people continue to find them useful in ways that other media technologies are not.

Perceived Advantages

Newspapers offer advertisers local mass market coverage and geographic identification with the immediacy and credibility of news. Consequently, they are a way of making things happen in the retail worlds of politics and marketing.

Market Coverage Newspapers are a mass medium that reaches most segments of society, and they are a local medium covering a specific geographic and socioeconomic area. Reading newspapers is a habit, and exposures build extensive reach and frequency in a short time. They also reach nearly everyone in a household who use the paper for various purposes on an as-needed basis.

Immediacy Newspapers are as current and timely as today's news, and this sense of immediacy extends to both issue-oriented and retail advertising. This sense of immediacy is enhanced by "quick closing" publishing, which enables the advertiser to craft or change copy almost minute by minute.

Flexibility (Geography) Individual newspapers and combinations of newspapers offer the advertiser national, regional, local, and specific zip code coverage as required.

Flexibility (Display) Because newspapers have many sections that are read selectively for what is personally interesting, advertising can be placed in environments most synergistic with its message. Furthermore, the advertising's physical dimensions can vary extensively and may feature either bold graphics or long and detailed copy.

Reader Involvement Newspapers are an active medium, and readers utilize them for comparison shopping. Since readers are involved shoppers, they clip, save, and use coupons and other reader response tools.

Local Traffic Because newspapers are a primary medium for creating retail traffic, many advertisers utilize them in a promotional strategy in concert with national awareness campaigns.

Perceived Disadvantages

Many of the newspaper medium's disadvantages are the flip side of its advantages. There are also economic structures and technical limitations that trouble many national advertisers.

Time Limits People read newspapers quickly and discard them quickly. Limited attention and limited life reduce newspapers to daily relevance, making it expensive to build a market or develop frequency.

Limited Coverage Younger consumers have not developed the newspaper habit and are not subscribers. Furthermore, metropolitan newspapers no longer blanket their market.

Reproduction Newspaper printing techniques are devoid of high fidelity reproduction. Many major newspapers also have limited or nonexistent color capabilities. When compared to television, newspapers are without the sounds and motions of life, and they cannot compensate for, or compete with, the outstanding printed graphics of magazines.

Clutter By responding to shopping patterns, both publishers and advertisers overload any individual edition with extensive and contiguous competitive advertising, which is perceived as reducing the impact of individual ads.

Expensive Both out-of-pocket and overhead costs are perceived as expensive by national advertisers. Most newspapers charge more for national than for local advertising, and buying space is complicated by the necessity of buying more than one vehicle with different page formats, rates, discounts, and billing practices.

Any marketer interested in generating retail traffic, and any advertiser interested in influencing grass-roots perceptions, must consider using newspapers. The more vital a newspaper is to its local community, the more important it is as an advertising vehicle. Journalism drives the process.

Creative Intentions

Most of us look upon news as an accurate report of a recent event and look upon newspapers as providing a full, sufficient, and satisfying package of current information.

Our demands, therefore, are that the editorial be fair, current, accurate, concise, balanced, and objective. These are also the goals and intentions of reporters and editors. It is not an easy task.

Every day other media, armed with electronic technology, leap forward to distribute the news before printing presses can roll. More and more, therefore, it has become the task of print journalists to define their work as going beyond the unvarnished who-what-when-where-why-how of the straight news story. They see their task as that of penetrating the reader's consciousness with a combination of facts and associated ideas that spotlight what is significant in events.

The goal of a well-written newspaper article is to recapture the vitality of the moment and to allow readers to relive the experience. Good journalism also provides readers with a vocabulary for their own expression. Thus, newspaper stories enable readers to experience the fulfillment of articulation. They enable readers to report the story to others and to enter into dialogue with other readers. Good newspaper journalism grounds our experience in a community experience.

James B. ("Scotty") Reston started out as a sports writer and publicist on his way to becoming the executive editor of the *New York Times*. He often expressed the belief that sports writing might be among the best training grounds for reporting world events.

For fans who weren't at an event, the best sports reports bring the event to them. For those who were at the event, the reporter's story confirms or denies that the game happened the way they experienced it. The precise and imaginative vocabulary enables the fan who was present and the fan who was not to experience the action again, to suffer through or glory in the experience. Good sports stories parse and enhance our often vicarious experience of challenge and achievement, or of risk and failure. They are superior journalism.

Our direct or vicarious experience of an event, however, is never equal to what actually happened. Good reporters strive to tell us about both the inside and outside of a moment of action. Good reporting tells us about the people involved and about those who chose not to get involved. It measures the event against other similar events and tells us what was going on around the event. Good reporting, therefore, expands our direct experience by adding detail and perspective.

Reporters are trying to penetrate life and deliver life. This understanding of a reporter's intentions enabled Ezra Pound to define literature as nothing more or less than "news that stays news."

Social Function

Daily papers are read by more than 113 million adults each weekday, or nearly two out of every three. Typically, they spend forty-five minutes reading these papers and sixty-two minutes on Sunday. Sixty-three percent of these readers usually read every page. A reader interested in as few as three in ten of a newspaper's editorial and feature categories tends to become a subscriber.

People simply find newspapers useful. Newspapers are useful for shopping, for comparing the offerings of goods, services, or ideas. Newspapers provide the information necessary for our daily participation in life. They also are essential to the creation of our sense of community identity. Newspapers are the vehicle through which a community perceives itself, converses with itself, and formulates its experience and judgments. Without a newspaper, most of us would notice our community only as represented by a tax bill, a school teacher, or a policeman.

Newspapers are Main Street, which is where the living is done.

Advertising Applications

The ten largest newspaper advertisers in the United States are department stores and discount chains (Figure 9.7). The prototypical and largest national advertisers are auto-

FIGURE 9.7 TOP 25 NEWSPAPER ADVERTISERS BY COMPANY

(Dollars are in millions)

1994

1.	Federated Department Stores	$320.8
2.	May Department Stores Co.	317.2
3.	Ford Motor Co. (dealers)	291.9
4.	Circuit City Stores	245.7
5.	General Motors Corp. (dealers)	244.5
6.	Valassis Communications	178.6
7.	Toyota Motor Sales USA (dealers)	172.8
8.	Sears, Roebuck & Co.	170.9
9.	News Corp.	163.1
10.	Dayton Hudson Corp.	136.4
11.	Kmart Corp.	118.8
12.	General Motors Corp.	109.8
13.	Chrysler Corp. (dealers)	106.7
14.	Broadway Stores	99.9
15.	AT&T Co.	99.5
16.	Nissan Motor Corp. (dealers)	98.9
17.	Dillard Stores	94.9
18.	Ford Motor Co.	92.3
19.	J. C. Penney Co.	89.5
20.	Montgomery Ward & Co.	79.0
21.	Walt Disney Co.	78.7
22.	Honda Motor Co. (dealers)	75.8
23.	Time Warner	69.4
24.	The Wiz	63.6
25.	Tandy Corp.	62.7

Source: Competitive Media Reporting and Publishers Information Bureau

mobile manufacturers and airlines. Like retailers, airlines use newspapers for market-specific price advertising. Automobile companies use newspapers for promotional events and tie-ins with local dealers.

When we combine these three outstanding types of newspaper advertisers with the fact that more than 80 percent of manufacturers' cents-off coupons are distributed through newspapers, we have a clear picture of how advertisers use newspapers. Newspapers are promotional vehicles used to build retail traffic and trade.

It is not surprising that the major shifts in newspaper advertising have resulted from major shifts in retailing practice. When major discounters and retailers moved from downtown centers to suburban shopping malls, they widened their marketing areas. Malls draw people from many miles away, and even from different states. This caused a shift to preprinted inserts, which functioned as weekly or monthly catalogues and could be distributed through multiple vehicles. These preprints are less costly than display advertising, and newspapers succumbed to advertiser pressure to distribute these preprints and at lower rates than for the conventional run-of-paper (ROP) advertising that they displaced.

Never large in recent decades, national advertising continues to erode. Local retail display advertising has also been declining, even though revenues have remained stable due to aggressive price increases. Classified advertising has become the industry's lifeblood, now accounting for 40 percent of total advertising revenues and a larger percentage of profits. These advertising patterns seem to have stabilized and will only change again if new electronic media somehow find a way to displace newspapers as the driving force of local sales.

Medium and Vehicle Effects

The key and singular fact about newspapers is that they are believable. Nearly 50 percent of consumers consistently select newspapers as the most believable advertising medium. Newspapers are information resources, and advertising is welcomed as part of the information flow.

Newspapers tell you who was elected and when the roads will be fixed; they tell you the price of pork chops and automobiles; who died and also who got married; what jobs are available and what houses are for sale; what's on television and at the movies; your future under the stars and the score of last night's baseball game under the lights; when the next game will be played and where to buy tickets. When a corporation is seeking a new chief executive, editors treat the fact as news. When the same corporation is searching for twelve lathe operators and four secretaries, the fact must be communicated through paid advertisements. To readers and consumers, however, these two information capsules are the same.

Newspaper advertising is effective because newspaper ads are information people can use. If they plan to make a purchase and have settled on a brand, 90 percent of consumers read newspaper ads for location, and if a brand is a possible choice, 78 percent will read the advertising before buying.

Newspapers are also a major influence on unplanned purchases. Of those who saw advertising before making an unplanned purchase, 60 percent saw the advertising in a newspaper. The effect of newspapers as news is that readers treat everything in the newspaper as news.

OUT-OF-HOME MEDIA

From the days, five thousand years ago, when Phoenician merchants painted their messages on the walls of cliffs for passing ships to see, through medieval guild signage, to the present, we have described this kind of promotion as **outdoor advertising**. With the arrival of railroads, subways, and buses, this same kind of promotion found a home as **transit advertising**. In recent years, the placement of promotion vehicles in health spas, doctors' offices, and university buildings has given currency to a business called **on-site advertising** (Exhibit 9.5). Outdoor advertising, transit advertising, and on-site advertising are all different, of course, but they have so much in common that it is not inaccurate to think of them as similar; they are called **out-of-home media**.

**EXHIBIT 9.5 THE VITALITY AND VARIETY
OF OUT-OF-HOME AND ON SITE MEDIA**

In New York, the state lottery prize hit the $40 million mark last week. For their part, out-of-home companies are eyeing another upcoming jackpot; the New York City bus stop shelter franchise, worth an estimated $150 million over the life of the current 10-year deal that expires in May 1995.

As the city prepares to reveal the much-talked about request for proposal, out-of-home companies have already begun the race to the finish line for what is again expected to be a 10-year ticket to the bus stop advertising. Contenders for the prize have begun sniping at incumbent Gannett, accusing the company of poor maintenance and other transgressions involving the 2,800 shelters in the five boroughs. Gannett acquired the franchise in 1987, when it bought out New York Shelter Media. "We were confronted with a program in shambles," says Joan Davidson, vice president, public affairs, at Gannett Outdoor Group, defending her company's role.

Now, seven years later, the contract goes up for a bid, which will give others a chance to present possible solutions to some of the problems Gannett has encountered. "We feel there is a lot of room for improvement," Davidson agrees.

A source at New York City's Department of Transportation has been trying to get the word out to out-of-home companies big and small. "I thought New York was the center of the universe, but people are coming out of the woodwork," he says.

One small, New York-based contender is SHF Communications, a $2 million company headed by Steve Feinberg, a former Gannett employee who was involved with the initial installation of the shelters. Patrick Media Group, the aspiring 800-pound gorilla of outdoor, has already asserted its intention to capture the franchise, while France's JCDecaux, which created the shelter concept in Europe, and Germany's Wall City Designs, an innovator in public toilet ads, both confirm that they will pursue the bus shelter contract.

In addition to the expected requests for suggestions for maintenance, designs, and other innovations, the RFP may require bidders to make use of the new, federal government-funded Intelligent Vehicle Highway System, which incorporates a bus-tracking system into the shelters that enables riders to call up arrival times.

Who will come out on top? The DOT source lends no clue, throwing out terms like "re-let [the contract]" in the same conversation as "[the franchise] could be better with a new company."

A critical part of the equation will no doubt come down to the city's cut of total ad revenues, which is currently at 22.2 percent. Some sources expect the city's take won't surpass 30 percent, although in a bidding war, that ratio could certainly climb higher.

Although the source can't say for sure when the RFP will hit the street, out-of-home executives anticipate that the real battle will be joined by mid-November.

Kiosk commitment. While outdoor companies are moving underground and into the transit scene, other out-of-home companies are making overtures to advertisers with innovative products like Ameri-Guide, an interactive kiosk system.

The privately-funded kiosk network, currently operating in three Branson, Mo. locations, is designed to aid visitors in their search for local restaurants and entertainment. The launch follows a six-week test according to Bill Stephenson, president of the Machesney Park, Ill.-based Ameri-Guide

Stephenson reports that the kiosks received almost 50,000 touches for 28 advertisers' messages over the first month. Advertisements are shown after every feature selected, and once every 10 minutes when the kiosks are not in use. Future Ameri-Guide applications may include delivery of theater tickets to one's hotel, triggered by phone.

"People love it," reports Brooks Whitmore, general manager at Branson Tower, a local luxury hotel housing one of the kiosks. He says that the Ameri-Guide machine, set up near the hotel's continental breakfast area, attracts groups of people every morning. "Mostly adults and seniors," he says, noting many are likely theatergoers previewing the shows' two-minute videos. Stephenson reports that Branson is home to more theater seats than Broadway, and the industry generated more than $10 million for the local economy. This was part of Stephenson's reasoning in selecting Branson, but there was another deciding factor, the lack of competition: "Time Warner would never think of going to Branson, Missouri," he says.

Although all current advertisers involved are local, Stevenson plans to appeal to national sponsors soon. Ameri-Guide Kiosks may soon be rolled out in Nashville and Myrtle Beach, S.C.

Sports bar spots. PROSTAR Entertainment Network, the subscription-based closed-circuit and pay-per-view distributor, has locked up two sponsorship deals for its national network of 700 sports bars, nightclubs, hotel lounges and taverns. Terry Cunningham, vice president of marketing at the Stafford, Texas-based company, reports that Turner Publishing and Nabisco Brands (for its A-1 steak sauce) have made national buys on the network that transmit 16 hours of satellite-delivered programming daily, including sports and news features, comic strips, a sports ticker, and trivia games encouraging patron interaction. In addition, PEN serves as an agent for the various establishments in terms of distributing and advertising PPV pro and college football, boxing and wrestling events.

Vivian Lawand, vice president of marketing at Turner Publishing, feels that the network is a good match for the 75th Anniversary NFL book the company is advertising. "The patrons of sports bars and hotels, that's our audience," says Lawand of the publication, which is being positioned as a holiday gift. "We're running [on PEN] through mid-December (the schedule kicked off in mid-October), and then we'll pick it back up again a couple of weeks before the Super Bowl." Asked if she was concerned about measurement, Lawand, who would not disclose the cost of Turner's buy, replies: "We know this is a captive audience. Everybody looks at ESPN while they're sitting there, so they're definitely going to watch this."

Source: *Inside Media,* November 2, 1994.

Perceived Advantages

All of these media share the fact that they are out-of-home and gain their relevance from their location.

Saturation Coverage Out-of-home media provide extensive reach of the mobile population and coverage of either the total adult population or all of those directly and immediately interested in certain products.

Flexibility Out-of-home advertising can be placed almost anywhere and everywhere an advertiser is interested in reaching consumers. Environmental concerns have established some limits, but inventive entrepreneurs have managed to develop alternatives.

Cost The relative cost-per-exposure of out-of-home vehicles is the lowest of all advertising media.

Impact The sheer size and multiplicity of out-of-home media translates into simple but spectacular impressions.

Perceived Disadvantages

Audience Measurement Out-of-home media provide the least satisfying accountability data of all the media.

Limited Messages The tradeoff for spectacular expression is the medium's resistance to anything but the simplest messages.

Distracted Attention The very nature of the exposures to most out-of-home vehicles limits the consumer's message recall.

Cost Although the relative cost-per-exposure can be expressed as very competitive, the out-of-pocket costs can be prohibitive.

Planning and Buying Production requirements make it necessary to commit six to eight weeks in advance. Purchasing requires negotiations with multiple companies and frequently requires travel for the purpose of selecting and verifying installations.

Advertising Applications

Aside from the interest of the motorist seeking motel signs late at night on a lonely road, it is difficult to perceive any direct consumer interest or involvement in out-of-home media. On-site advertising has developed editorial presentations, but they are read by people waiting for something else to happen. Thus, out-of-home media are advertiser driven. Some even believe outdoor advertising to be the only pure form of advertising.

The intention of out-of-home media is to interrupt the eye. This kind of advertising is primarily an attention-getting device. In this context, the advertising is pure and effective. It is an athletic medium, presenting itself as a presence that cannot be denied.

Presence is the essence of out-of-home media. It is a presence, and its creates presence. The simple message, the dramatic graphics, and the ubiquity of the medium support brand and package recognition.

TAKING OFF WITH HEAVY FLYERS

SAMSONITE'S SALES SOAR VIA
LEO BURNETT'S INTEGRATED, CAB-TO-CABIN MEDIA PLAN

Intuitively, it's about as simple as it can be: when you're advertising luggage, you place some of your media in airports and on airplanes. For several years Samsonite has done just that, with dioramas in airport walkways and ads in in-flight magazines. This past year, though, Leo Burnett's Samsonite work has really taken off, evolving from a few basic elements to a fully integrated, specifically targeted media plan that allows us to reach heavy flyers a number of times as they pass through the airport and onto the airplane—their home away from home.

Though we have broadened the basic concept of airport/airplane marketing into a full-scale, multidimensional program, we haven't gone overboard by placing messages on every baggage cart and cab top a traveler might see. We have selected those media opportunities that best meet our desire to home in on heavy flyers with as little wasted coverage as possible, and to repeatedly contact prospective luggage buyers.

Our plan is designed so that a flyer's trip—from the moment the cab door shuts outside the airport to when another is opened at the final destination—is filled with Samsonite messages.

After checking in, our heavy flyer heads down the terminal and spots a backlit Samsonite diorama. Because we know specifically who and where diorama viewers are, we can create copy that talks to them about their luggage needs when they fly and how Samsonite can meet those needs. For example, an ad for The Piggyback hardside wheeled suitcase extends sympathy and a solution to the weary traveler, giving hope that the compact, easy-to-pull Samsonite bag depicted along with the headline "Relieves Terminal Backache" will in fact do just that.

Similarly, the diorama for the Ultravalet Garment Bag speaks to those carrying overstuffed, insufficient bags with a picture of Samsonite's's large, compartmentalized garment bag and the headline, "If You're Leaving Town, Hold Everything." As flyers think of the wrinkled suit or dress inside their current bags, they might be tempted to dial Samsonite's displayed 800 number.

As the heavy flyer continues the journey toward the departure gate, he or she often comes across Samsonite again through one of our week-long display events like those held this fall in major airports in Chicago, Boston, Las Vegas, Raleigh/Durham, Philadelphia and Dallas. During these "sampling" events, travel-

ers interact with Samsonite sales representatives and over 30 Samsonite products. With this program, we go beyond even our feature-specific print and broadcast advertising to let consumers personally touch, feel, zip and even pack Samsonite's innovative products so they might gain full appreciation of the quality and functionality of the luggage. We believe this kind of one-on-one interaction with Samsonite's products is the ultimate brand contact. Based on the terrific results we have received, we're expanding the program in 1995 to include more airports and involvement in sporting and cultural events across the U.S.

After the packing demonstration, our flyer finally reaches the gate and encounters Samsonite again while watching CNN's Airport Network or reading USA Today. Because each exposure has featured a different product, by this time we have made our point about the breadth of Samsonite's product line.

As people board and take their seats, they enter into yet another phase of Samsonite's integrated plan: advertising in in-flight magazines such as United Airlines' Hemispheres. Although our competitors may also appear in these highly targeted magazines, for some these ads represent the only contact they have with consumers. For Samsonite, it way well be the third or fourth exposure that day, perhaps the one to change a prospect's mind about luggage brands. If still not entirely convinced, heavy flyers may use the 800 number or "bingo cards" provided in the in-flight magazines to request more information.

Finally, Samsonite sponsors "Road Warrior," a series of vignettes featuring business-travel themes on USA Today's Sky Radio. We suggested the idea for the show based on the USA Today column of the same name featuring a panel of travel experts answering reader questions. Not only is the audience another great fit for Samsonite, but the live-announcer format allows us to point out our in-airport sampling events, promotions and other advertising.

We recognize that Samsonite can't be all things to all people. Instead, we concentrate on the platform that's been successful to date—positioning Samsonite as the premier maker of innovative luggage for busy travelers. With this in mind, we avoid the temptation to overindulge in broad-reach media, instead choosing to focus on the best prospects (heavy flyers) and deluge them with Samsonite messages.

This type of highly targeted media planning wouldn't be possible without the trust, support and open-mindedness of our client. Paige Miller, director of marketing services, and all of the people at Samsonite continually encourage us to seek better ways to reach heavy flyers. This client understands that sometimes media—especially newer media—has to be based on "gut feel" as well as hard numbers.

And such support is paying off for Samsonite. With the in-airport "sampling" program, for example, we have created high purchase potential among consumers. While we are still awaiting results for the current year, in on-site evaluations conducted during 1993, a full 57 percent of travelers reported that they expected to be in the market for luggage within the next three months. Moreover, 51 percent of the respondents indicated that they planned to purchase luggage within the next three months as a result of the display. The most frequently asked question in each city: "How do I purchase one of these Samsonite products?" We can't hand them Samsonite's 800 numbers and copies of "Check Our Bags," Samsonite's new retail catalog fast enough!

And since Samsonite's sales are up significantly for the second year in a row while the overall luggage category is flat, we figure we must be doing something right. With these kind of results, it's no wonder that Samsonite's heavy traveler strategy continues to fly.

Source: *Inside Media,* November 2, 1994.

Out-of-home media are not often thought of by media planners faced by limited budgets, multiple tasks, and multiple media. These media are also often funded out of promotion budgets and are not perceived as an advertising task. Perhaps they should be thought of more often, because out-of-home media offer the advertiser continuous marketplace presence and can be used effectively in conjunction with other media forms.

Other forms of marketing communications, such as direct mail, telemarketing, video cassettes, and on-line computer services are not considered here, because they are not normally within the province of media planning or subject to media planning decisions. Often they are even located in a separate agency specializing in such services. We will consider these topics, however, when discussing the future of integrated marketing communications in the last chapter.

STRATEGY DECISIONS

The defining moment in which we can describe how media planners perceive themselves and in which we can also describe how their clients, superiors, and coworkers perceive them is in the construction and articulation of strategic media selection. This is the moment when we can determine if media planners actually and privately see themselves as number crunchers with green eyeshades. This is also the moment when we can determine if others perceive them as skilled back-room functionaries or as creative professionals and equal team members.

How can you tell? You will not be able to tell from a meeting in which the Media Plan is presented and accepted. You will not be able to tell from watching the daily activities, when the department is "in planning," as they say. You can only tell by discerning the logic of others' expectations and the logic of the planner's strategic decision process. When it comes to logic, the premises are everything.

Whenever a character in one of Lewis Carroll's Alice stories casually or arrogantly remarks: "It's logic!", we know it is time to laugh. We laugh because the claim will be the opposite of truth, even though the process of getting there was perfectly logical. The charm of Carroll's looking-glass world is that the perfectly rational is perfectly nonsensical. The only answer to "It's logic" is: "It's your assumptions!"

For our minds to act from both a certain and a creative foundation, we must begin with the history of the natural world or the facts of human behavior. Our concepts and mental constructs must remain as plastic, transformable, and combinable as human life. If, on the other hand, our hubris establishes a closed system based on limited perceptions, we will continue working inside it forever, driven by logic but cut off from reality.

Let's look at the alternatives.

FACILITATING INSTITUTIONS

The first set of premises and perceptions is that the advertising, or so-called "creative," is everything and that media are simply facilitating institutions. One prominent media planning text succinctly describes the effects of this premise: "Creative strategy is one of the most significant considerations in planning strategy. *In fact, it is often the starting place for all media planning.* 'Creative' indicates that some media are much more appropriate to the message than others." (Emphasis added.)

What works, what is substantive and significant, is the message, or creative, and all that planners have to determine is how to send it. The product and its packaging are the givens. What media planners do is to determine how it will get to its destination, and to insure its delivery. The mode of transportation is only significant as a facilitating institution, and it will be judged only by its physical compatibility and cost efficiency.

For example, if we were in the shipping business, we would first eliminate any transportation that did not have the technology to transmit the message package. (Print cannot transmit video.) Secondly, we would measure the size and weight of the package and compare the cost of shipping by plane, boat, truck, or railroad relative to time and destination. The vehicle and mode of transportation are otherwise irrelevant.

This is a perfectly logical way of treating media planning once based on the premise that the creative, or advertising message, is what advertising is all about. It is a circular system, although it may be operating with hollow logic.

What enables this logic to work smoothly, and apparently effectively, is that tradition has discovered and passed on the most appropriate and relevant message forms. Thus, those involved in initiating, creating, and selecting the advertising end up with the most relevant and effective forms out of habit or intuition. Following the same traditions, the media planners have been thinking the same thoughts and are planning compatible media even without seeing the advertising.

If a planner is caught in this type of system, almost all of the media considerations articulated in this chapter are irrelevant. Their only utility is in identifying efficient and compatible delivery systems and surrounding them with inspirational rhetoric. In this scenario, however, the media planner is functioning as, and is perceived as, a back-room facilitator. Under these circumstances media planners might just as well put on their green eyeshades. They are vice presidents of transportation, not media planners.

SCHEDULING IMPRESSIONS

The second set of premises and perceptions is that media planning consists of scheduling consumer impressions, but, in order to accomplish this in a complex multimedia world, media planners must be highly skilled practitioners. The job is to set reach, frequency, and continuity objectives, efficiently purchase the media required, report the results, and account for the money. Given all the money, data, and computers involved, you have to be pretty good to do the job well.

The partial reality behind these premises is learning theory and the communication effects model of advertising. The model is valid, and the task is real. Given the zero-sum game of reach, frequency, and continuity on an always limited budget, someone has to make significant judgments and do some planning. When we add the complexities of seasonality, purchase and usage patterns, pricing, brand awareness levels, media clutter, and so on, we can recognize the need for special intelligence and sophisticated planning.

This scenario, however, still accepts the primacy of the message and only adds a level of sophistication to the execution of its delivery. It also assumes a certain level of equivalency in media types. A sound knowledge of the various media alternatives and a facile knowledge of their advantages and disadvantages enable the planner to manipulate various combinations of media in order to discover the optimal media mix for achieving the desired reach and frequency.

In these circumstances, media planners certainly are planning, but they are planning the delivery of something created by others. They are highly skilled, but they are still back-room functionaries. Their role on the team is important and necessary but secondary. They are vice presidents of strategic purchasing.

In each of these first two scenarios, media planners need not know much about the media beyond the characteristics described under perceived advantages and disadvantages. In the first instance, they need to know very little. In the second, they need to know a lot more. In both scenarios, however, the media types have been preselected by others—whether creatives, clients, or both. Since accepted reach and frequency parameters imply effectiveness, the final measure of success will still be efficiency.

Media Imperatives

The easiest way to determine whether or not media planners are perceived as creative professionals and equal team members is to observe whether they have a significant voice in determining the physical or media characteristics of the message. If they do have a vote, it is the logical result of premises that accept the intrinsic dependence of advertising on media.

Creative media planners must first identify the dynamic of knowledge, attitudes, and decision involved in the consumer purchase. They must imagine the exchange and the communications consumption that led up to it. They must recognize how and why consumers use media as individuals and as members of society, in the process of arriving at practical judgments. The pattern is different for every consumer group and for every brand category.

If the marketing purpose of advertising is to transfer cultural values to a brand of which the consumer has been made aware, and if consumers derive their awareness and cultural values from their media dialogue, the identification of this dialogue is a necessary foundation for effective advertising.

If the first-place consumers answer the question "Why?"—at any stage of the consideration process—is in a media choice, and if these media are the conditions of the penultimate moment of decision and the necessary substrate of the marketing message, the characteristics of these media should determine the external characteristics of the message.

The purpose of media planning is to identify and manipulate this communication process. The process requires two things: First, it requires an understanding of how a medium works and why it works; an understanding of the medium's technology and its creators' intentions; an understanding of the medium's social function, how it is used and experienced by particular consumers; and an understanding of each particular medium's source effects. Second, it requires a detailed knowledge of past advertiser experience and a knowledge of all of the tools of measurement and control, such as research data and effective reach.

Strategic media planning is an inclusive form of thought. It involves all of the resources and working methods of the mind. It requires abstract command and imaginative control. The task is to make the delivery of advertising synchronous and compatible with the consumer's processes of awareness, consideration, and choice. The method is to use the dynamics of society communicating for the exploitive purposes of selling products, services, and ideas. It requires imaginative recognition of the process and technical skill in manipulation.

Successful advertising demands two separate but interacting strategies. The first examines the product and the consumer and asks: How can I best articulate the need and relevance fit of the two? The second examines the consumer and the communication process the consumer goes through and asks: How can I best communicate with this consumer? To communicate well, I may have to accommodate myself to the media. To articulate well, the strategic media may have to accommodate the message's production style. It is a dialogue of equal demands.

If a product group accepts these premises, media planners are creatives and creatives are media planners. They are both rhetoricians who should work in concert as copy and art directors do. If media planners are so empowered, the nature of their work is changed when they make the strategic decisions involved in media selection. It also puts greater demands on their talent and courage.

Media Selection Decisions

The process of making media selections and articulating their rationale depends upon the premises of the client and agency product groups. How planning is perceived will determine how planners act.

Facilitators In this instance media planners are required only to provide media planning's articulated support for the choices that have, in effect, already been made.

If the decision has been made, for example, that the advertising will be thirty-second television commercials, the recommendation of television is not at issue. The planner should then select appropriate points and language from the available list of perceived advantages and disadvantages. In this instance, the supporting language might read: "Television is being utilized for the impact of sight, sound, motion and demonstration ability." If creative in a second media form has been prepared, the planner would support it in a similar manner.

Since most of the actual work will be done at the tactical level, no more extensive strategic statements are required. It is not unknown, however, for planners to include all of the possible advantages of a medium as part of their rationale, even though some, or most, may be irrelevant to the circumstances.

At the tactical level of outlining the actual media purchases, efficiency will be the primary criterion. Weighting might be utilized to evaluate different television dayparts or to compare various print vehicles. These weighting norms might be articulated as part of the strategy, but usually are not.

Schedulers In this instance, planners are expected to be subtle calculators of reach and frequency. However, reach, frequency, continuity, seasonality, geography, and so on, have already been articulated in the planning format utilized here. The only issue, therefore, is media selection.

When it comes to media selection and rationale, the difference between schedulers and facilitators is that schedulers must include the reach, frequency, and/or continuity role a medium will perform. Thus, if television is the medium of choice or direction, the planner might add to the rationale that "prime time television will be considered for its high reach potential, and daytime television will be considered for its ability to develop high frequency among the target audience." If magazines are to be used, the planner would include the advantage of coverage of the target market (that is, reach) and add another strategic function such as: "Magazines also provide for affordable continuity throughout the year."

The practical relationship between prime time and daytime, or the number of magazines and the degree of coverage they actually provide at any time, would be left to tactical decision making. Some strategic direction has been provided, but most significant decisions will come when flowcharts are developed. The driving forces will be reach, frequency, continuity, and budgets, that is, the judgments contained in the media objective. The reach and frequency goals also would have been articulated earlier.

Communicators If media planners are perceived as professional communicators, and if their insights and judgments are perceived as relevant at every point of the marketing communications process, recommending a media selection strategy is the fulcrum of their work.

Recommending a media selection strategy requires the total engagement of the mind, all of its rational and imaginative capacities, and all of the marketing tools and insights available. In short, it invoices all of the territory and all of the details covered up to this point in this text.

The starting point is to imagine the marketing exchange and its motivations. The second step is to imagine the media dynamic that supported the knowledge, attitudes, and decisions involved in the exchange. The third step is to envision what pattern of media dialogue, emerging out of and reflecting the consumer's media consumption and use, will be required to effect future marketing exchanges for the brand. The more planners know about marketing, the more they know about communications, and the more they know about consumers, the better they will be at this task.

Once the planner has identified the relevant dynamic and perceived its operating gestalt, the next step is to place it next to the previously developed templates of reach, frequency, and continuity. The result will be an identification of the technical or rhetorical role that each element of the consumer's media dynamic must fulfill.

For example, prime time television may not be perceived as an important element of the consumer's media dynamic as it relates to the exchange. If it was significantly present in the consumer's media dynamic, however, it is likely that prime time television also would be assigned major responsibility for achieving reach.

Whatever the case, it is at this point that all of the elements of the media considerations described above become relevant. The technical characteristics, the creative intentions, and the sociocultural functions of each medium gain considerable importance. Thus, a medium's presence and role in a consumer's personal and social life is just as important as its perceived advantages and disadvantages as a delivery system and just as important as traditional advertiser experience and use. In fact, the more revolutionary the consumer behavior change required to effect an exchange, the more revolutionary the media selection strategy may appear.

The practical articulation of the media selection strategy in these circumstances includes the expected references to normally perceived advantages and disadvantages

EXHIBIT 9.6 NOVICE GUIDE TO DYNAMIC MEDIA SELECTION

Goal	Objective	Strategy	Medium
Reality	Awareness	Reach	Television
Impulse	Repetition	Frequency	Radio/TV Spot
Lifestyle	Consideration	Dialogue	Magazines
Sales	Traffic	Promotion	Newspapers

Goal is the arena of change the advertiser is attempting to influence.

Objective is the communication objective within the media planner's area of responsibility.

Strategy is the technical means the planner will implement.

Medium is the vehicle type that most likely will form the foundation of the plan's execution.

This exhibit provides the novice planner with an avenue of attack once the consumer and the basis of consumer decision are imaginatively understood.

of each medium, and their function in achieving reach, frequency, and continuity. The articulation, however, will also include a description of the consumer's communication dynamic and the role of each medium within it. The media selections, then, will be made based on the cognitive objectives and psychological goals required of the exchange.

Exhibit 9.6 outlines a crude example of this process that is intended to provide a simplified gestalt for the beginning planner. Imaginative insight requires imaginative expression, and facile articulation requires experience and practice. Therefore, we can only rely on the understanding of media and marketing achieved up to this point. Imaginative planners will always find their own poetic and useful expressions.

SUMMARY

* Advertisers are not only dependent on media to carry their messages, they are dependent on how the media work for the success of their messages.

* Media are the inescapable environment in which demand can be negotiated.

* Media strategy consists of designing the plan through which the marketer will utilize the means and momentum of society communicating so as to borrow value and effect a sale.

* Efficiency can be discovered through numbers, but effectiveness can only be discovered through imagination.

* Each of the many media perform different cultural functions in American society. Each communication type is experienced and used by consumers in a specific way.

* An understanding of how a medium works and why it works that way tells the planner what the medium is.

* What a medium is creates advertising possibility in terms of reach, frequency, efficiency, and awareness.

* How a medium is used and experienced determines how effective the medium will be in achieving advertising objectives relating to motivation and behavior.

* To make a prudent recommendation of the media types to be utilized for a campaign and to identify their role and purpose, a planner must consider five aspects of the media: (1) the components or functional characteristics of each medium (2) what the creators of the medium are doing when they do their job; (3) the medium's cultural role and how people use the medium in their lives; (4) advertiser understandings of the advantages and disadvantages of each medium; and (5) successful applications of each medium in solving marketing problems in the past.

* How media planners actually apply their knowledge of all aspects of the various media types depends on how their superiors, clients, and coworkers perceive the function and priorities of media in the advertising process.

* When recommending media types and their strategic role, planners may be responding to the perception that they are facilitators, schedulers, or communicators.

* Acting as a professional communicator requires the total engagement of the mind, all of its rational and imaginative capacities, and all of the marketing tools and insights available when making strategic recommendations.

QUESTIONS

1. What are the three steps in the imaginative process of making strategic recommendations an artistic act of informed judgment?
2. What are the five aspects of any media type that a professional media planner must know?
3. What is meant by "medium and vehicle effects"?
4. What factors influence the media planner's role in the selection and recommendation of media types?
5. What is the rationale for the case that media planners should have a role in determining the form the advertising message should take?

ASSIGNMENT

Develop a media selection strategy and rationale for the case you are working on or for another that is available to you.

Part Four

Tactical Planning and Execution

10

Media Work Plan: Part III— Tactical Planning

OVERVIEW

This chapter introduces and describes the third major step in the media planning process. Part III of the Media Work Plan articulates the tactical plan, describes its executional characteristics, and demonstrates how the tactics fulfill the objectives and strategies. It includes all the data necessary to support vehicle selections and to manage the budget.

REALITY CHECK

One of the more exasperating sentences heard by strategic planners in business, or professors in universities, is the sentence that begins "But, in the real world . . . ." Businesspeople say it to academics and operations people say it to corporate planners. You know that what they mean is the same thing that students are communicating when they say, "Get real!" You also know that it will be difficult, if not impossible, to change their minds.

The moment when this attitude is most likely to surface in relation to the media planning process is the point we are calling Part III of the Media Work Plan. In this context, "real" means that media planning, in fact, is all about media buying. If you get a job in an agency of any size, other than a full service mega agency, the argument goes, you will be a media buyer, and if you get a job in a big agency, your first function will probably be media buying. Therefore, teach media buying. That is why so many people begin their discussion of media planning with the math and definitions of media sales and purchase. It is their view of reality.

Reality checks are worthwhile, but they are dangerous when they reflect mythology. There is a significant difference between planning and buying. A plan is a detailed description of actions to be taken. The details of a Media Plan are descriptions of media or vehicles that will be purchased and when they will be purchased, supported by estimates of what the purchases will cost and what they will deliver. The plan assumes that some change is inevitable. The dollars associated with vehicles are not actual numbers based either on negotiations or on completed purchases. They should be realistic, but they are not real. A plan is not a "buy."

The identification of media buying with media planning is contained in the belief that the singular function of media planning is to find and select vehicles that reach a large number of target prospects at the most cost-efficient price. Vehicle delivery and unit pricing, therefore, are the essential elements of the planning design (strategy). Hypothetical buys are the foundation of media planning. Therefore, buying is both the beginning and end of media planning, and it is the place to start understanding the planning process.

Another version (which is usually propagated by account executives in any size agency) is that what the client is interested in is outcome, not process. The outcome of the media planning process is what you plan to buy, and buying it. Both of these outcomes will, in fact, be judged by standards of efficiency. Therefore, they argue, get on with it, and save us the poetry of all that "strategizing." The strategy is the plan; the plan is the buy; and the buy will be judged by how much you got for how little.

One analogy for these approaches to media planning is the idea that the best approach to architecture is carpentry or bricklaying. Architecture is building, the analogy would continue, and building is beams and bricks. Therefore, when an architect is designing, he is using a trowel and hammer, and when a planner or planning group is "in planning," they are, in fact, stringing together media and vehicle purchases. It wouldn't be so sad if it weren't so often true.

PLANNING TACTICS

The media plan is the conscious and specific design of a combination of vehicle purchases that will embody and express the recommended media strategies. A plan outlines and describes the activities required for the implementation of a strategy. The Media Plan is the tactical translation of the media strategies. It is the proposed method for carrying out the strategic design.

Since a plan is the design of executions, it must vibrate with virtual reality. It is common practice for architects to photograph a realistic model of their proposed building and superimpose it on a photograph of the building site and its surroundings. The final photograph looks real, but actually it is what a future reality might look like. The Media Plan performs a similar function: It proposes a future reality.

To create a realistic plan, the media planner must be fully aware of vehicle performance, current unit prices, and probable delivery. The planner must know broadcasting audience trends and the profile of individual magazine readerships. In short, a planner needs to know many of the same things required to make media purchases, just as smart shoppers are informed about prices and product promotions by a specific supermarket when they are making up their shopping lists.

A supermarket shopping list or a Christmas gift list is not always judged by the lowest cost, however. A special meal may require special and costly purchases, just as certain Christmas gifts will. The meal and the gifts will be judged by effectiveness. Faced by a limited budget, however, the shopper will continually rearrange the list until the best combination, which fits within the budget, is arrived at. The list is a realistic plan that might change in the market when you get there.

Developing a media plan is no different. It inevitably involves a degree of juggling as the general idea of what you want to do encounters estimated costs. Media vehicles must be juggled to fit delivery demands, and estimated costs must be juggled to fit the budget. It can be a frustrating process, but computers are there to help.

Computers enable the planner to look at thousands of media combinations and reams of vehicle audience data. Unfortunately, the process can be endless. Only a strategy that establishes the guidelines and parameters can contain the process and bring it to a satisfactory conclusion. Ironically, strategy is the most practical tool on the media planner's desk.

THE MEDIA PLAN

Part III of the Media Work Plan articulates the plan and its executional characteristics (Exhibit 10.1). It demonstrates how the plan matches and fulfills the objectives and strategies. It summarizes the allocation of the budget and provides all the data necessary to support individual market and vehicle selections.

The three essential elements are:

Flowcharts: A fifty-two-week calendar indicating all media purchases and their expected delivery

Budget Summary: An articulation of the money to be spent by quarter and by medium, and the cumulative totals

Delivery Summary: An articulation of what the budget will buy. It is expressed in audience delivery terms of gross rating points, reach, and frequency. It is broken down by quarter and medium.

These may become the most handled and discussed pages of any Media Work Plan. In some instances, the flowchart, budget summary, and delivery summary are all that the client wishes to see.

Plan Discussion/Presentation

The larger the budget and the more sophisticated a client is, the more likely it is that a flowchart will not be adequate. Furthermore, if the plan is to be presented verbally,

EXHIBIT 10.1 MEDIA WORK PLAN: SECTION III

The Plan

•Flowchart

•Budget Summary

•Delivery Summary

Plan Discussion/Presentation

•Plan Description

•Scheduling Details

•Media Purchase Guidelines/Limitations

•Media Mandatories

•Plan Delivery vs. Goals

•Changes vs. Year Ago

Plan Support—open-ended

---

the media planner must be prepared to explain it. Both circumstances require elaboration, which could include:

Plan Description A capsulized overview of the media plan with paragraphs that review the plan relative to the objectives and strategies and to the budget, geography, seasonality, and media selection. It parallels the transcript of the speech a planner might give if she had time only to show the flowchart in a new business presentation.

Scheduling Details Included in or separate from the plan description, there are paragraphs that highlight what is happening when and why on the flowchart.

Media Purchase Guidelines/Limitations, or executional guidelines. These are very important in making the plan useful and meaningful to the buying function. These paragraphs describe any positioning requirements for print, and they state the ideal programming environment for broadcast purchases. Special scheduling requirements (for example, weekends only, best food days, morning drive time, and so on) must be articulated.

Media Mandatories Also important to the buying function are client mandates relating to violence on television, or brands that can only be advertised in certain dayparts.

Plan Delivery vs. Goals A side-by-side comparison demonstrating how the plan delivers against key strategies and communication goals.

Change vs. Year Ago Provides a historical perspective and identifies any strategic shifts in budget, target audience, media types, and so on.

All of these elements are intended to be either persuasive descriptions or purchase prescriptions. They should bring the plan to life for anyone looking mostly at a flowchart. They should bring the strategy to life for thoughtful marketers who have been tracking and participating in the planning process. They should provide all the necessary information for the negotiators executing the plan.

Plan Support

The extent of the supporting documentation required of a plan presentation varies a great deal and depends on the level of client involvement and sophistication. Some of the possible data analyses are:

Spot Market Analysis A geographical media analysis of all relevant broadcast markets showing sales, percent population, CDI/BDI, relative CPMs, and so on. The selected markets and the criteria for selection are highlighted.

TV Daypart Analysis A data description of costs and delivery of each television daypart against primary and secondary targets. The data may also include a quintile analysis of the target's viewing habits or preferences.

Magazine Considerations A list of all the magazines considered, their relevant data, and an identification of those magazines selected and why they were selected.

These and similar support elements are often included in an Appendix or treated as Exhibits. Their purpose is to demonstrate both thoroughness and rationality. The more sophisticated and involved a reviewer is, therefore, the more important these elements become.

BUILDING THE PLAN

The flowchart is a graphic description of intended purchases and estimated delivery for every week of the year. Therefore, it is expressed in media purchase terms. For broadcast media this means gross rating points by daypart, and for print vehicles this means the identification of specific vehicles and page sizes. The flowchart is not only the final plan, it is also the template of plan construction.

In the previous chapter, we observed that how a planner approaches media selection and rationale as a strategic discipline depends, in fact, on how media planners are viewed by themselves and others. We introduced this chapter with some similar observations on planning and buying. Both discussions are directly relevant to how a planner approaches the process of building a flowchart.

There are three basic approaches to the execution of a Media Plan. Ideally, you are specifying the tactics that will articulate the strategy you developed in Part II of the planning process. Your choice of executional approach under any circumstances, however, will depend on how you approached the strategy process. We identified the three typical approaches as facilitator, scheduler, and communicator.

When putting the plan together, the facilitator will be primarily directed by the budget; the scheduler will be primarily directed by reach and frequency; the communicator will be primarily directed by the strategy. Each will use the same tools. They differ only in their approach to the process.

The tools involved in developing a plan are rate cards of media costs, research estimates of media and vehicle delivery, and various formulas for calculating reach and frequency. Cost estimates, audience profiles, and reach/frequency projections are generally available as computer models or published tables from syndicated media research firms, media suppliers, or an agency's own system. The larger the agency, the more certain you can be that all the necessary information is already loaded and programmed. Your task will be to access the data. Since the computer calculations can be expressed as tables, we will utilize tables to illustrate the process.

Facilitator

The facilitator begins with the decisions that have been made about quarterly budget allocations and have already been adjusted for the variable media costs. This planner then determines how many impressions, or GRPs, these budget decisions will allow by quarter. Since the communication strategy is being driven by creative, the planner already knows which media to cost out. Once the planner knows how many impressions, or GRPs, the budget will purchase by quarter by medium, the planner then divides them into four-week periods or whatever smaller time frame is called for. The planner then "buys" the most efficient vehicles.

EXAMPLE

The budget for your product is $30 million. Your target is adults 18+. For various marketing reasons, you have decided (or, been directed) on an allocation of your funds by quarter of 30%, 20%, 15%, and 35%.

Step 1: You begin by determining the available dollars by quarter. In this instance: $9 million, $6 million, $4.5 million, and $10.5 million.

Step 2: You then identify what each quarter's allocation could purchase in various dayparts or media by using the grids and rate cards. If you are working with TV commercials, you would use published cost-per-points tables or agency estimates for network and spot.

For the purposes of illustration, we will focus only on network television for a brand in national distribution. By dividing the cost per point (CPP) into the quarterly budget, you can determine how many impressions you can purchase (Exhibit 10.2).

$9 million ÷ $8,975 = 1003 prime time GRPs in 1st qtr.

$9 million ÷ $2,957 = 3044 daytime GRPs/1st qtr.

Step 3: You then determine the potential effect of these GRP levels on a four-week basis, or whatever basis is appropriate.

1003 GRPs ÷ 3 = 334 GRPs/month

3044 GRPs ÷ 3 = 1015 GRPs/month

Step 4: After you have determined the monthly GRP possibilities, you translate them into reach and frequency. To do this, you consult the reach tables (Exhibit 10.4) to determine the percentage of adults reached at the GRP level and then divide the GRPs by the estimated reach to determine the average frequency.

The reach estimates in the scenario we are following would be:

334 prime time GRPs = 73 reach

334 GRPs ÷ 73 reach = 4.6 avg. frequency

1015 daytime GRPs = 50 reach

1015 GRPs ÷ reach = 20.3 avg. frequency

Step 5: To a facilitator, efficiency is the name of the game. Therefore, the next step would be a comparison of CPMs. These can be calculated, or roughly estimated from industry reports. Currently, these estimates report:

	Network TV	Spot TV
Daytime	$2.55	$4.10
Early News	5.50	4.75
Prime Time	8.65	11.85
Late News	—	9.25
Late Evening	6.17	6.25

EXHIBIT 10.2 NATIONAL TV HOUSEHOLDS: COST PER POINT (CPP)*

Daypart	1st Qtr. ($)	2nd Qtr. ($)	3rd Qtr. ($)	4th Qtr. ($)
Early A.M.	3,650	4,405	3,985	4,460
Daytime	2,957	3,569	3,229	3,841
News	4,835	5,835	5,729	6,279
Prime Time	8,975	10,832	9,800	11,657
Late Night	6,650	8,026	7,262	8,638
Kids	5,876	7,092	6,483	7,632
CATV	3,580	4,321	3,909	4,650
Syndication	5,040	6,083	5,503	6,546 ·

*Author estimates based on background interviews with several agencies and media services.

EXHIBIT 10.3 SPOT TV HOUSEHOLDS: COST PER POINT (CPP)*

Market	U.S. HHS (%)	Day ($)	News Avg. ($)	Prime Access ($)	Prime ($)	Fringe Avg. ($)
New York	7.04	323	676	654	1263	535
Los Angeles	5.18	365	727	673	1468	524
Chicago	3.25	173	352	384	584	231
Philadelphia	2.81	162	327	345	653	245
San Francisco	2.36	178	474	491	781	349
Boston	2.21	165	389	370	687	255
Washington, D.C.	1.97	121	289	361	576	236
Dallas-Ft. Worth	1.91	97	306	241	477	147
Detroit	1.83	97	178	157	338	141
Atlanta	1.64	64	158	166	362	102
Mkts.1–10	30.21	1,745	3,673	3,799	7,188	2,764
(+) 11–20	43.99	2,521	5,536	5,418	9,188	3,927
(+) 21–30	53.55	3,123	6,789	6,657	11,968	4,854

*Author estimates based on background interviews with several agencies and media services.

Clearly, daytime at a $2.55 CPM is more efficient than prime time at an $8.65 CPM. This doesn't necessarily mean that you would choose daytime because, in doing so, you would be sacrificing reach.

Step 6: This is the initial decision point. Having established the basic parameters of budget and delivery, you must now develop a combination that provides the best of both worlds.

A: If you are in a high frequency category, you will probably start by choosing daytime. However, you may then reduce your daytime GRPs in order to purchase prime time spots to increase your reach. Since daytime's reach curve builds so slowly and adding a second daypart normally accelerates reach, a good starting place might be to sacrifice 515 daytime GRPs and set the daytime base at 500 GRPs. This would enable you to buy 170 prime time GRPs, equaling a 60% reach in prime time while retaining 500 daytime GRPs

EXHIBIT 10.4   ADULTS REACHED IN FOUR WEEKS

4 Week GRPs (Adults)	Daytime (W18+)	Prime Access (A18+)	Prime Time (A18+)	Late Fringe (A18+)
50	26%	32%	33%	26%
75	31	41	42	31
100	35	48	49	35
125	38	53	54	37
150	40	57	58	39
175	41	60	62	41
200	42	63	65	42
300	46	70	72	45
400	47	75	77	47
500	48	78	80	48

*Author estimates based on background interviews with several agencies and media services.

and a reach of 48%. These reach estimates must be combined. The kind of random combination formula frequently used for this purpose can be simulated in a table (see p. 233).

To use the table, identify the prime time reach (higher of the two) on the horizontal line and follow it down to the point where it intersects with the estimated reach of the second medium. Using this table for our example produces an estimated reach of 79% (60 intersects with 48 at 79) and retains a respectable 8.4 average frequency.

To estimate the reach if a third medium (for example, radio or magazines) is added, use the new combined reach (79 in this instance) on the top horizontal line and track it down to the estimated reach of the added or third medium. The addition of an entirely new medium, however, requires a different type of frequency calculation, which we will describe in a subsequent example (see p. 235).

Step 7: The budget allocations clearly indicate the acceptance of the shrinkage of either reach or frequency in the third quarter. A consultation of the same tables would suggest the choice of a 47R/9.9F using only daytime, or 58R/2.6F using only prime time. Your objectives will determine your choice of reach over frequency, or vice versa. One solution is to turn to local television markets, which make a significant contribution to sales, and to utilize spot television in these markets in a pattern similar to that which you chose for the first quarter national effort. Flighting during the third quarter might also enable you to continue using a combination of prime and day.

Summary   The facilitator is only required to find the best combination of vehicles in the medium for which the message has been created. The task requires the consultation of several tables, or punching up a few combinations on a computer, but it is a rather straightforward process. A modest degree of experience will eliminate most of the trepidation, and it is clear that one does not need an advanced degree to perform the task.

Scheduler

Strategic scheduling is rooted in the communication effects model of advertising and the learning-forgetting curve. Consequently, the scheduler is primarily interested in

EXHIBIT 10.5 RANDOM COMBINATION TABLE

		Reach of First Medium													
Reach of Second Medium	25	30	35	40	45	50	55	60	65	70	75	80	85	90	95
25	46	47	51	55	59	62	66	70	74	77	81	85	89	92	95
30	–	51	54	58	61	65	68	72	75	79	82	86	90	93	95
35	–	–	58	61	64	67	71	74	77	80	84	87	90	93	95
40	–	–	–	64	67	70	73	76	79	82	85	88	91	94	95
45	–	–	–	–	70	72	75	78	81	83	86	89	92	94	95
50	–	–	–	–	–	75	77	80	82	85	87	90	92	95	95
55	–	–	–	–	–	–	80	82	84	86	89	91	93	95	95
60	–	–	–	–	–	–	–	84	86	88	90	92	94	95	95
65	–	–	–	–	–	–	–	–	88	89	91	93	95	95	95
70	–	–	–	–	–	–	–	–	–	91	92	94	95	95	95
75	–	–	–	–	–	–	–	–	–	–	94	95	95	95	95
80	–	–	–	–	–	–	–	–	–	–	–	95	95	95	95
85	–	–	–	–	–	–	–	–	–	–	–	–	95	95	95
90	–	–	–	–	–	–	–	–	–	–	–	–	–	95	95
95	–	–	–	–	–	–	–	–	–	–	–	–	–	–	95

* Use of this table is described on page 232.

effective reach and continuity. It is this point of view that distinguishes a scheduler from a facilitator. In both instances, the planner is working only with the media for which advertisements have been (or planned to be) made. The scheduler, however, is more focused on effectiveness and is generally working in an environment that has computer facilities that can generate frequency distributions on the various media and media combinations.

EXAMPLE

The budget for your product is $30 million. Your target is adults 18+. Your goal is to maximize effective reach at 3 + frequency (?/3+).

Step 1: The first thing you must establish is your foundation in reach. You know that for most consumer brands with an adult target, prime time network television is the outstanding reach vehicle. For other products or targets the first choice could be another medium. Whatever the case, you are first looking for reach or coverage.

A consultation of the table of four-week reach for scattered schedules in television will tell you that you need 270 prime time GRPs to reach 70% of adults. Consulting the cost-per-point tables informs you that this will cost approximately $2,423,250 per flight. Ten flights would exhaust your budget and would produce an average frequency of only 3.85. Since the frequency is only an average, you know that the demands of a frequency distribution (Exhibit 10.6) will leave you far short of your effective reach goals.

Step 2: Your next question is: Where do I look to increase my frequency? Radio would be a possibility since it is perceived as an affordable high-frequency medium. The two possible problems are: a) It works less well as the demographics get older, and b) more often than not, it is not available for creative reasons.

What you are probably looking for, therefore, is a less expensive network television daypart with a slow building reach curve. This describes both daytime and late evening. Daytime is eliminated because it is primarily effective with adult women, and your target is total adults.

Consulting the tables would suggest that 200 GRPs in late evening programming would provide an average frequency of approximately five (4.76). Given an average cost per point of $6,650, the required funds would be $1.33 million, or $13,300,000 for ten flights.

The inevitable conclusions from these first two steps are: a) That you will probably end up with a combination of prime and late evening, and b) That you will have to reduce the number of flights.

Step 3: Continuity will be the next concern of planners, who are primarily concerned with effects and the learning/forgetting curve, when they confront a budget which will require the shrinkage of a flighting schedule. Your question is: What will I do about continuity? Reflection on the perceived advantages for the various media will recall that magazines are perceived as providing continuity. Experience, or the consultation of magazine reach tables, suggest that two or three magazines will provide a four-week reach of 50 to 60%.

EXHIBIT 10.6 **EFFECTIVE REACH AT CONSTANT HHs GRPs**

	GRPs	+Prime	R/F	Reach @3+	Reach @6+
Daytime	200	—	49/4.1	25	12
Early Fringe	200	—	65/3.1	31	9
Prime Access	200	—	68/3.0	31	9
Prime	200	—	69/2.9	32	8
Late Fringe	200	—	50/4.0	26	12
Daytime	100	100	70/2.9	31	8
Early Fringe	100	100	74/2.7	32	6
Prime Access	100	100	74/2.7	32	6
Late Fringe	100	100	70/2.8	31	8

* Use of this table is described on page 232.

For the initial purpose of making a rough estimate, a review of magazine rate information for a newsweekly and a dual audience magazine would suggest that approximately $1.5 million could purchase a page in ten issues of both magazines. Assuming the availability of magazine creative, or copy, the planner would then set aside this amount of money for continuity. The total budget for broadcasting, then, would be $28.5 million, to be divided between late evening and prime time in as many flights as possible.

Step 4: Now the planner must find the right balance between the two television dayparts. The planner would note that the cost relationship between the two dayparts is such that every reduction of 50 GRPs in prime time will enable you to afford 80 GRPs in late evening.

A consultation of the reach tables would indicate that prime time's accumulation of reach begins to flatten out between 100 and 125 GRPs. Since two broadcast dayparts increase reach and your goal is to maximize the frequency distribution, you would start with the lower goal for prime time. 125 prime GRPs provides a 53% reach. This would make up to 300 late evening GRPs affordable, and they would contribute a 45% reach. Purchasing both would cost approximately $4.2 million, provide a combined reach of 73 and an average frequency of 5.8.

Entering these numbers into a computer would confirm an effective reach of 50% at the 3+ frequency. On the cost side, a little division would confirm the affordability of 6.8 flights. Given cost fluctuations by quarter, you now know that, with a little further manipulation of the combinations, you will probably be able to afford seven flights, which will enable you to cover the year adequately, especially when seasonality is taken into consideration. Therefore, you have discovered the parameters for the basic outline of a plan.

Step 5: You have set money aside in order to use magazines for continuity. These magazines will have a significant impact on reach and little on frequency, because the magazine readers that you will be reaching tend to be lighter viewers of television. If the magazines you choose provide a coverage, or reach, of 50% of your adult target, you will increase your overall reach to 86% with an average frequency of 5.5.

Your final delivery numbers with this plan structure, therefore, will look like an 86/5.5 R/F, with an effective reach of over 50% at the 3+ level. These are quite acceptable base numbers.

Conclusion Both the questions, and how they go about the process, are different for a scheduler than they are for a facilitator, but a great deal of the work is the same. The scheduler generally has a little more flexibility in media choices and generally is supported by computer programs. The similarity becomes more apparent when the scheduler has arrived at the basic parameters of a plan and proceeds to manipulate costs and delivery not only to arrive at the proper fit, but also to increase efficiency.

Communicator

The communicator approaches the construction of a Media Plan with a clear image of the marketing exchange and its motivations. The hard work has already been done in the development of a media strategy. The planner has a distinct understanding of the prospect's learning gestalt, or the media dynamic that has supported the prospect's knowledge, attitudes, and decisions in the past. The planner also has already decided on the pattern of media dialogue that will be required to effect future marketing exchanges for the brand. When it comes to building a plan, the planner is working from a rather complete set of architectural drawings.

EXAMPLE

The strategy calls for a combination of prime time television to create product consciousness, magazines to create lifestyle identification, and radio to propel purchase. The budget is $30 million. The target is adults 18+, and the reach/frequency goal is 70/3+.

Step 1: The issue is where to begin. The starting point is the medium that is determined to be the most critical to consumer motivation and/or is the least flexible of the media in the strategic mix. In this instance that medium is magazines. They will form the foundation of the plan.

Step 2: If you had been following the planning process—fueled by the cognitive imagination—described in this text, you already would have imagined either specific magazine titles or, minimally, one or more magazine categories such as newsweeklies, women's service, sports, epicurean, and so on. In either instance, they tell you what to look for. By consulting the appropriate cost data, plus either the magazine grid, SMRB, or computer files, you identify the top five magazines significantly used by your consumers. You will also determine (hypothetically) that it will cost you approximately $312,000/month and produce a reach of 60%. On a quarterly basis, therefore, you are projecting a $900,000 budget for magazines.

Step 3: If you start with a foundation of magazines, the addition of network television will result in an extension of reach to light magazine readers and the multiplication of frequency for the 60% of your core prospects whom you are already reaching. Nevertheless, television will be the guarantor of reach, or timely presence, during important sales periods.

Your next step, therefore, is to identify the number of prime time GRPs required to deliver the expected reach. Consulting the grids or a computer informs you that 275 GRPs are required for a 70% reach at an average cost of $2.8 million. Two flights per quarter would produce an annual cost of approximately $22.4 million.

Step 4: A continuation of this approach would produce an annual cost for magazines and television of approximately $26 million and a typical R/F of 88/3.4. Radio is intended to increase these frequency numbers, but the remaining $4 million may not allow the purchase of sufficient radio. Your first task, however, is to find out what can be achieved.

Step 5: A consultation of the appropriate network radio tables will inform you that the CPP is approximately $3,000 and that a combined purchase of 100 GRPs in A.M. and P.M. drive time will provide a reach of 65%. When used in conjunction with both television and magazines, this will increase your reach to 95%. When used with magazines alone, it will produce a reach comparable to the combination of magazines and television.

With an available budget of $4 million and a radio cost per flight of $300,000, you can afford between 13 and 14 radio flights.

Step 6: The basic parameters are in place, and they appear to be generally affordable. You know what a basic plan might look like, but you have not provided any subtlety in the magazine list, you haven't adjusted for seasonality, you haven't fine-tuned frequency distribution, and you haven't tested the alternatives for efficiency. This is the point, therefore, at which you can work on tactical variations of your strategy. You have proven out the basic practicality of the proposed strategy, and now you are free to make executional adjustments within it.

For example, you may want to evaluate the possible reliance on magazines and radio while eliminating television in weaker sales quarters. This would enable you to apply the money to increased TV announcements and additional magazine titles in stronger sales quarters.

Final Words

No experienced media planner relies exclusively on one approach or another, and the availability of computer data and programs offers a great deal of flexibility. Furthermore, no experienced media planner is without awareness of these approaches, their options, and the budgetary implications when developing their strategies. They are far from approaching the plan with the same blank slate as a novice.

Nevertheless, everyone must get to planning sometime, and when they do, they must begin someplace. That means that they must begin by selecting one of the approaches outlined above. The choice of initial approach is up to the planner, but it is often dictated by the corporate culture in which the planner is functioning.

The frightening fact is that the differing starting points seldom result in the same ending points. The questions asked and the sequence in which they are asked tend to dictate different conclusions. An enlightened client and a wise agency should know what they are doing, therefore, when they act to shape the culture in which planners will work.

SUMMARY

* There is a significant difference between planning and buying.
* The media plan is the conscious and specific design of a combination of vehicle purchases that will embody and express the recommended media strategies.
* A media plan inevitably involves a degree of juggling, as the general idea of what you want to do encounters estimated costs.
* The three essential elements of the media plan are the flowchart, budget summary, and delivery summary.
* All other elements of plan presentation are intended to be either persuasive descriptions or purchase prescriptions.
* The flowchart is a graphic description of intended purchases, with estimated delivery and costs, for every week of the year.
* The flowchart is expressed in media purchase terms.
* The tools involved in developing a plan are agency estimates or rate cards of media costs, research estimates of media and vehicle delivery, historical brand experience, and various formulas for calculating reach and frequency.
* The choice of executional approach will depend on how the planner approached the strategy process.
* Cost estimates, audience profiles, and reach/frequency projections are generally available as computer programs or published tables from syndicated media research firms, media suppliers, or an agency's proprietary systems.
* A facilitator is primarily directed by efficiency, a scheduler by reach and frequency, and a communicator by strategy.
* The questions asked and the sequence in which they are asked in plan development tend to dictate the conclusions articulated in the finished flowchart.

QUESTIONS

1. What is the difference between planning and buying?
2. What is a media plan?
3. Why could the development of a flowchart be described as a juggling act?
4. What are the tools generally available for the development of planned media executions?
5. Does the approach a planner takes to building a plan make any significant difference in the final product? Explain.

ASSIGNMENT

Develop a flowchart and other Media Plan elements for the case you are working on or for another that is available to you.

MEDIA WORK PLAN—PART III: BUDGET GOURMET

Overview

The plan makes extensive use of lifestyle/life stage programming and editorial environments on a national basis, but geographic concentrations of the target also require a heavy focus on spot television. National media establish the cultural utility of the brand, while local television produces trial building frequency.

Network television dayparts include broadcast prime and late night. Cable network usage is heavy in prime, news, and late night. Programming is comedy and entertainment oriented: for example, *Seinfeld, Larry King, Nick-at-Nite*.

Prime broadcast is utilized as a reach vehicle and in conjunction with cable generates 95 GRPs/week during launch periods October through December, and again during September after summer hiatus. Late night broadcast and cable networks are flighted from January through April at 85 GRPs/week. Total network television GRPs achieve the goal of 2,000 GRPs generally required to generate 15% trial for a new product introduction.

Local overlays in key category and brand markets coincide with national flighting in late news and prime access. Together the vehicles generate 3,000 GRPs (150/wk.), which is generally required to generate 20% trial for a new product introduction.

National magazines are scheduled to provide continuity throughout the key consumption periods. Weekly magazines are scheduled to provide a foundation of extensive reach at the beginning of each television flight. Two groupings of monthly magazines—Music/Entertainment and Lifestyle (fashion, health, food)—are scheduled to overlap television flights. The print schedule adds 702 GRPs to the campaign.

Vehicle Guidelines

Network television purchases will be in programming whose comedic point of view reflects a growing-up interest in the wondrous absurdities of relationships, coupled with an identification with the tumescent innocence that gets us all into relationships in the first place. This point of view is reflected in a sample of programs that show high performance against the key life stage segments.

Program	Index
Seinfeld	129
Growing Pains	123
Wonder Years	121
Roseanne	114
Cheers	113

This point of view contrasts with an attitude of thoughtful concern colored by anguish at the experiential costs represented by *Northern Exposure*, which also performs well against the target. The key comedic optic slides easily into the hip but romantic silliness of *David Letterman* and *Saturday Night Live*.

Late Night Video (158) performs extremely well and is consistent with preferred cable network programming

Network	Index
MTV	171
VH-1	162
BET	152
Nick-at-Nite	119
USA	106

This preferred television programming reinforces and satisfies the lifestyle/life stage interests and attitudes of the target audience. This POV is also seen in six magazines:

Title	Index
Spin	246
Rolling Stone	210
Gentlemen's Quarterly	183
Glamour	155
US	149
Sports Illustrated	132

These vehicles illustrate the editorial franchise sought in all media purchases. It is a distinct point of view.

Local Plan Overlay

The purpose of the local plan is to increase communication levels by more than 50% over the national plan in especially productive markets.

The recommended dayparts are late news and prime access, which have two advantages. First, they provide message delivery when prospects are considering buying or consuming the product. Second, both dayparts allow brand connection with the same editorial franchises as network: for example, film and concert reviews, *Entertainment Tonight*, and so on.

Media usage varies from market to market. Therefore, these plan intentions may be modified to adjust to local conditions.

FIGURE 10.1 FLOW CHART: NATIONAL/LOCAL OVERVIEW

BUDGET GOURMET
PROTOTYPICAL 1992-1993 MEDIA PLAN

	Oct.	Nov.	Dec.	Jan.	Feb.	Mar.	Apr.	May	Jun.	Jul.	Aug.	Sep.	$(000)
	28 5 12 19	26 2 9 16 23	30 7 14 21 28	4 11 18 25	1 8 15 22	1 8 15 22	29 5 12 19	26 3 10 17 24	31 7 14 21	28 5 12 19	26 2 9 16 23	30 6 13 20 27	
NATIONAL													
NETWORK TV													
CABLE PRIME (:30)	25	25	25	25		25	25					25	$1,590.0
CABLE NEWS (:30)	15	15	15	15		15	15					15	$1,171.1
CABLE LATE NIGHT (:30)	15	15	15	15		15	15					15	$662.9
PRIME (:15)	40	40	40									40	$3,277.9
LATE NIGHT (:15)				30		30	30					25	$825.3
TOTAL NETWORK	95	95	95	85		85	85					95	$7,527.2
PRINT	247			231			133					91	$4,217.9
TOTAL NATIONAL													$11,707.7
LOCAL													
LATE NEWS (:30)	25	25	25	30		30	30					25	$3,208.4
PRIME ACCESS (:30)	30	30	30	35		35	35					30	$3,050.5
TOTAL LOCAL	150	150	130	150		150	150					150	$6,258.9
DEFENSE													
OUTDOOR													$1,996.0
GRAND TOTAL													$20,000.0

FIGURE 10.2 FLOW CHART: PRINT VEHICLES

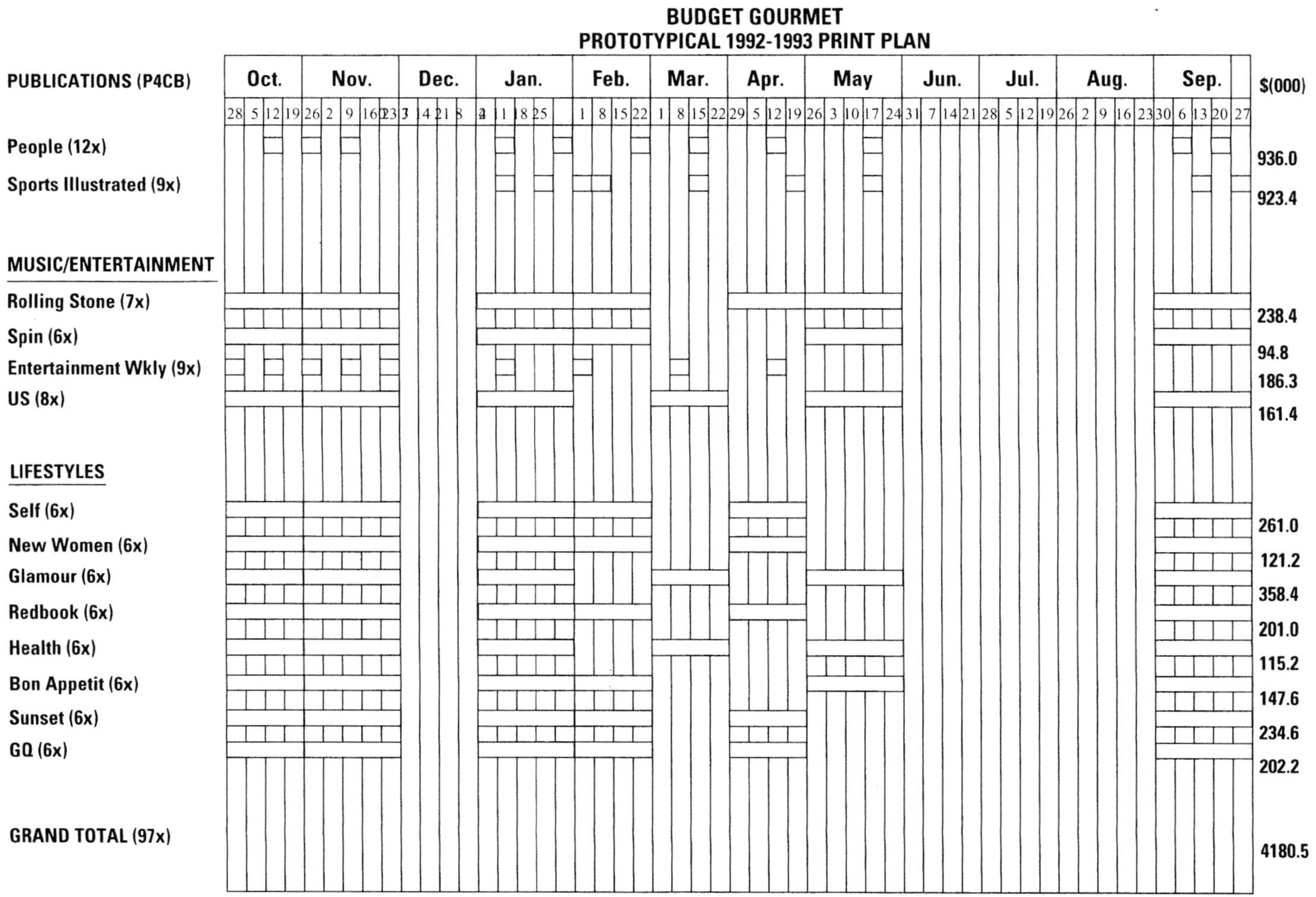

BUDGET GOURMET
PROTOTYPICAL 1992-1993 PRINT PLAN

PUBLICATIONS (P4CB)	Oct.	Nov.	Dec.	Jan.	Feb.	Mar.	Apr.	May	Jun.	Jul.	Aug.	Sep.	$(000)
People (12x)													936.0
Sports Illustrated (9x)													923.4
MUSIC/ENTERTAINMENT													
Rolling Stone (7x)													238.4
Spin (6x)													94.8
Entertainment Wkly (9x)													186.3
US (8x)													161.4
LIFESTYLES													
Self (6x)													261.0
New Women (6x)													121.2
Glamour (6x)													358.4
Redbook (6x)													201.0
Health (6x)													115.2
Bon Appetit (6x)													147.6
Sunset (6x)													234.6
GQ (6x)													202.2
GRAND TOTAL (97x)													4180.5

Defensive Plan

A defensive plan will be implemented in order to combat competitive erosion in the top five volume markets: Los Angeles, San Diego, San Francisco, New York, and Boston. Heavy competitive activity is anticipated during fourth quarter 1992.

Each of these high volume markets is a heavy commuter environment. Therefore, out-of-home media—billboards, transit, bus shelters, and so on—will provide a strong and continuous presence in support of local broadcast activity.

FIGURE 10.3 FLOW CHART: LOCAL OVERLAY

PROTOTYPICAL LOCAL PLAN

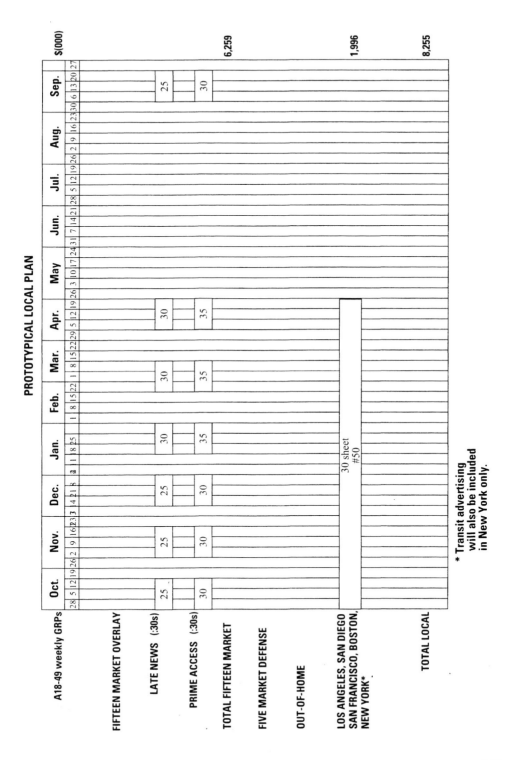

A18-49 weekly GRPs	Oct.				Nov.				Dec.				Jan.				Feb.				Mar.				Apr.				May				Jun.				Jul.				Aug.				Sep.				$(000)
	28	5	12	19	26	2	9	16	23	3	14	21	8	4	1	1	8	25	1	8	15	22	1	8	15	22	29	5	12	19	26	3	10	17	24	31	7	14	21	28	5	12	19	26	2	9	16	23	30	6	13	20	27	
FIFTEEN MARKET OVERLAY																																																							
LATE NEWS (:30s)	25				25				25				30						30				30																													25			
PRIME ACCESS (:30s)	30				30				30				35						35				35																													30			
TOTAL FIFTEEN MARKET																																																						6,259
FIVE MARKET DEFENSE																																																						
OUT-OF-HOME																																																						
LOS ANGELES, SAN DIEGO SAN FRANCISCO, BOSTON, NEW YORK*										30 sheet #50																																												1,996
TOTAL LOCAL																																																						8,255

* Transit advertising
will also be included
in New York only.

245

11

Tactical Resources and Skills

OVERVIEW

This chapter identifies the typical data resources utilized in the planning and purchase of media vehicles. The sources for audience and cost estimates are described, and their applications are explained, using the necessary media math.

DATA DEPENDENCE

Planners need to plan realistic purchase and performance parameters. Only market-place negotiations, however, establish real prices, and vehicle performances can only be measured in the past tense. It is in no one's interests, under these fragile and some-what mercurial circumstances, to misjudge radically or to overpromise. Consequently, planners, buyers, and vehicle representatives are all in the same boat, and they use the same resources in the same way.

It is very easy for planners, juggling gross rating points and reach estimates against budgets, to lose all sense of reality about the communication dynamics and the probable negotiated facts represented by the numbers. Knowing how the numbers are derived and used is critical not only as a reality check, but as an essential element of the creative imagination. The creative imagination is concrete and never fanciful.

Media planners are not only investment counselors, they are also stewards of the client's, resources. They are responsible for accounting as well as spending. Given this dual responsibility, the price/value judgments involved in post-buy analysis and per-formance accounting involve the same databases and interpretive skills as those involved in planning and purchase.

At every step of the planning process, therefore, it is important to know what the numbers are, where they come from, and how to manipulate them. It is also important to know what they mean, but their meaning is often hidden in estimates and formulas, and it can only be discovered and understood through experience.

TELEVISION

Network Data Sources

The Nielsen Television Index (NTI) is the accepted measuring instrument of network broadcasting. NTI employs a people meter, which is connected to its computer in Florida and automatically reports whether the sample household's television set is turned on, what station it is tuned to, and the demographic characteristics of each person viewing the program. The information is available on-line to subscribing agencies and in various printed publications.

The Pocketpiece predates on-line computer access and is the best-known and oldest NTI report. It is produced fifty-two weeks a year (Exhibit 11.1) and reports the ratings, viewing levels, shares, and demographics for both network television programs and time periods. *The Pocketpiece* also reports quarter-to-date program averages, premiere-to-date program averages, program type averages, and VCR contribution by program.

Perhaps the second most used Nielsen data source is the National Audience Demographics (NAD) report, which is issued twelve times each year (Exhibit 11.2). This two-volume report provides elaborate cross-tabulated demographic information on network programs on both a household and per-person basis. The planner/buyer can identify audiences by county size, household income, education, presence of nonadults, and so on. Consequently, network advertising schedules can be designed and evaluated according to the complex, multidimensional criteria required by most sophisticated marketers.

It is important to recognize that the information reported weekly by NTI and monthly by NAD are only directly useful to post-buy analysis and accounting. In order to evaluate proposed advertising/program schedules and negotiate their cost, it is necessary to accumulate the data from these reports, to identify the apparent trends, and to project future performance. Nielsen provides much of this information in NTI's Planner Report (Plan), Household and Persons Cost per 1000 (CPT), Household Tracking Report (HTR) and Persons Tracking Report (PTR). In addition to its eleven basic services (Exhibit 11.3), NTI provides many supplemental and special reports, custom analyses, and PC-based services. In short, a planner, buyer, or steward can know nearly anything they need or want to know about network television viewing and are willing to pay for.

Qualitative data on network television programs is provided by TvQ, a service of Marketing Evaluations, Inc. These reports provide measures of the audience's familiarity with a program and its attitudes toward it. This information can be used to judge audience involvement and its possible affect on future audience behavior or its impact on advertising messages. TvQ is a possible measure of a program's "source effect," to the extent that one believes in such effects in a television context and has confidence in the data.

EXHIBIT 11.1 NTI POCKETPIECE

Nielsen **NATIONAL TV AUDIENCE ESTIMATES**   **EVE.THU. JUL.20,1995**

TIME	7:00	7:15	7:30	7:45	8:00	8:15	8:30	8:45	9:00	9:15	9:30	9:45	10:00	10:15	10:30	10:45		
HUT	46.7	46.9	46.6	47.2	48.0	49.4	50.2	52.0	53.5	55.2	56.4	57.0	56.0	54.9	54.2	53.2		

ABC TV
HHLD AUDIENCE% & (000)
TA% AVG. AUD. 1/2 HR   %
SHARE AUDIENCE   %
AVG. AUD. BY 1/4 HR   %

CBS TV
HHLD AUDIENCE% & (000)
TA% AVG. AUD. 1/2 HR   %
SHARE AUDIENCE   %
AVG. AUD. BY 1/4 HR   %

NBC TV
HHLD AUDIENCE% & (000)
TA% AVG. AUD. 1/2 HR   %
SHARE AUDIENCE   %
AVG. AUD. BY 1/4 HR   %

FOX TV
HHLD AUDIENCE% & (000)
TA% AVG. AUD. 1/2 HR   %
SHARE AUDIENCE   %
AVG. AUD. BY 1/4 HR   %

INDEPENDENTS
(INCL. SUPERSTATIONS
EXCEPT TBS)
AVERAGE AUDIENCE
SHARE AUDIENCE   %

PBS
AVERAGE AUDIENCE
SHARE AUDIENCE   %

CABLE ORIG.
(INCLUDING TBS)
AVERAGE AUDIENCE
SHARE AUDIENCE   %

PAY SERVICES
AVERAGE AUDIENCE
SHARE AUDIENCE   %

1. Between 8:00 and 8:15, 48 percent of all TV households were watching television (HUT); 2. "Mad About You" had a quarter hour rating of 9.2, and a 19 share, with an average program rating of 8.9; 3. Between 9:00 and 9:30 CATV programming had a 16.5 rating with a 30 share.

Source: Nielsen Hispanic Television Index TV Audience Report. Used with permission.

Basic Terms and Calculations

The basic social assumption, it would appear, is that everyone in America owns a television set and that most Americans are watching television most of the time. Neither assumption is true, although more than 98 percent of our homes are equipped with a television set.

Advertisers and their agents are realists. They care about how many people can see, will see, and did see their commercials. Their basic concern, therefore, is with how many homes are using television at any given moment. That is where all their planning assumptions begin.

Households Using Television (HUT) The percentage of all TV households with one or more sets in use during a specific time period. Viewing levels vary throughout the day, week, month and year. Whether it is summer or fall, for example, daytime

PROGRAM AUDIENCE ESTIMATES (By Time Periods)   JUL.17-23,1995

AVERAGE MINUTE AUDIENCE %

DAY / TIME / NETWORK PROGRAM NAME	HOUSE HOLDS	TOTAL PERS 2+	WORKING WOMEN 18+	WORKING WOMEN 18-49	LOH 18-49 W/CH <3	WOMEN TOTAL	WOMEN 18-34	WOMEN 18-49	WOMEN 25-54	WOMEN 35-64	WOMEN 55+	MEN TOTAL	MEN 18-34	MEN 18-49	MEN 25-54	MEN 35-64	MEN 55+	TEENS TOT 12-17	TEENS FEM 12-17	CHILDREN TOT 2-11	CHILDREN TOT 6-11
THURSDAY EVENING																					
6.00-6.30PM TVU	43.1	23.9	18.6	17.0	22.3	27.5	19.3	20.2	21.4	24.8	43.2	22.0	15.6	16.5	17.4	20.5	37.0	19.7	22.2	21.5	23.9
6.30-7.00PM TVU	45.1	25.5	20.4	16.2	23.0	29.1	19.7	20.8	22.6	26.6	46.6	25.2	16.9	19.0	20.1	21.3	42.0	19.1	20.1	20.7	23.2
7.00-7.30PM TVU	46.8	27.0	23.1	20.4	23.2	31.3	21.7	23.2	25.3	29.3	47.9	26.7	18.0	20.7	22.4	27.3	42.1	20.7	20.3	20.4	21.9
7.30-8.00PM TVU	46.9	27.8	25.2	22.4	24.1	32.5	23.2	24.6	26.9	31.0	48.4	26.0	20.5	22.8	24.6	28.6	41.6	20.7	20.7	19.3	21.3
8.00-8.30PM TVU	48.7	29.0	28.1	26.0	27.8	34.1	26.0	27.2	28.9	33.0	48.3	29.5	22.1	24.4	26.6	30.2	42.4	22.2	23.4	18.8	21.6
A MATLOCK	6.4	3.4	3.4	2.5	2.9^	4.8	1.7	2.6	3.2	4.8	9.2	3.4	1.4	1.7	2.2	3.6	7.6	1.4^	1.9^	1.0^	1.0^
C BURKE'S LAW	6.2	3.3	3.3	2.9	2.0^	5.1	1.9	2.8	3.3	4.9	10.3	2.8	1.0^	1.7	1.9	2.9	6.2	1.2^	1.6^	.8^	.6^
N MAD ABOUT YOU-THU	9.2	4.8	7.3	7.4	6.0	6.6	7.3	6.8	3.3	6.1	6.1	2.1	4.1	4.0	4.8	4.3	3.7	4.3	5.8	1.9	2.5
F MARTIN	5.4	3.5	3.2	3.6	5.8	3.1	5.4	4.0	3.3	2.1	1.5	2.6	3.8	3.3	2.7	2.0	1.4^	5.4	5.4	4.0	4.6
F UNDER THE HELMET-THU>	6.0	3.5	3.5	3.8	6.4	3.3	5.6	4.2	3.4	2.3	1.8	2.8	4.1	3.5	2.8	2.2	1.5^	6.4	6.4	4.3	5.2
8.30-9.00PM TVU	51.1	30.8	30.2	28.3	29.4	35.8	28.1	29.3	31.0	34.9	49.3	31.6	23.9	26.6	29.1	32.7	44.4	25.0	25.8	19.0	21.6
A MATLOCK	6.6	3.8	3.5	2.7	2.3^	5.2	2.0	2.9	3.5	5.3	9.7	3.5	1.4	1.8	2.2	3.6	8.0	1.7^	1.8^	1.1	1.1^
C BURKE'S LAW	6.2	2.4	3.4	3.0	2.3^	5.1	1.9	2.9	3.4	4.8	9.9	2.9	1.1^	1.7	2.0	3.1	6.4	1.1^	1.8^	1.3	1.3^
N HOPE & GLORIA	9.8	5.1	8.1	8.3	7.3	7.0	7.9	7.4	7.4	6.6	6.0	4.6	4.0	4.0	5.5	4.7	3.8	4.1	5.6	2.0	2.6
F LIVING SINGLE	6.0	3.5	3.8	4.2	6.2	3.6	6.1	4.6	3.8	2.6	2.1	2.6	3.6	3.2	2.7	2.1	1.3^	7.2	7.0	3.6	4.1
9.00-9.30PM TVU	54.3	32.6	33.8	32.1	31.9	36.1	31.3	32.8	34.7	37.7	49.2	34.2	26.7	29.5	32.3	35.1	46.3	25.6	24.7	18.6	20.7
A MCKENNA	5.2	3.1	3.6	3.0	2.6^	4.3	2.0	2.9	3.8	4.8	6.6	2.8	1.2	1.8	2.0	3.0	5.5	.9^	1.0^	1.6	1.6^
N SEINFELD	15.5	8.5	12.4	12.9	14.2	10.8	12.1	11.9	11.8	10.7	8.8	8.7	9.5	9.2	10.2	8.7	6.8	6.8	7.5	3.1	3.9

1. "Mad About You" was viewed by 9.2 household rating, 24.8 persons rating, and a 6.6 rating among all adult women; 2. The demographic rating for men 18–34 was 4.1.

EXHIBIT 11.3 A.C. NIELSEN TELEVISION REPORTS

Code	National Reports	Item	Sta & Cov	Type by Pgm	US Avg Aud %	US Avg Aud Share	Terr/CS/Cable · HH size/A of NA · Income/Sel Demo · Race/VCR · Ed of HOH	Share	Tot Pers	LOH	Work Wom	Tot & 18-34	15-24	18-24	21+ · 21-49 · 21-54 · 25-49	18-49 & 25-54	35-64	55+	Respond Charac	Teens Tot	Teens Fem	Teens Tot	Children Tot	Children 6-11	6-8	9-11
NSS	Pocketpiece	Usage			%																					
		Programs	X	X	⊗Ⓐ	%																				
		Pgm Types			%																					
NTI	Pocketpiece	Usage			%																					
		Programs	X	X	⊗Ⓐ	ⓤ%																				
		Pgm Types			%																					
NSS	National Audience Demographics	Usage																								
		Programs		X	%A		%V		%AV	%AV	%AV	%AV	%AV	%AV	%AV	%AV	%AV	%AV	%AV	%AV♦	%AV♦	%AV♦	%AV♦	%AV♦	%AV	%AV
		Pgm Types			%A				%AV	%AV	%AV	%AV	%AV	%AV	%AV	%AV	%AV	%AV	%AV	%AV♦	%AV♦	%AV♦	%AV♦	%AV♦	%AV	%AV
NAD	National Audience Demographics Volume 1	Usage			U%A																					
		Programs		X	%A				%AV	U%AV	U%AV*	U%AV	U%AV	U%AV	U%AV	U%AV	U%AV	U%AV		U%AV♦	U%AV♦	U%AV♦	U%AV♦	U%AV♦	U%AV	U%AV
		Pgm Types			%A			%	%AV	%AV*	%AV†	%AV	%AV	%AV	%AV	%AV	%AV	%AV	%AV	%AV♦	%AV♦	%AV♦	%AV♦	%AV♦	%AV	%AV
NAD	National Audience Demographics Volume 2	Usage			U%		U%V		U%V		U%V	U%V			U%V	U%V	U%V	U%V		U%V	U%V	U%V	U%V	U%V	U%V	U%V
		Programs		X	U%		U%V		U%V		U%V	U%V			U%V	U%V	U%V	U%V		U%V	U%V	U%V	U%V	U%V	U%V	U%V
		Pgm Types			U%		U%V		U%V		U%V	U%V			U%V	U%V	U%V	U%V		U%V	U%V	U%V	U%V	U%V	U%V	U%V
UFBG	Up-Front Buying Guide	Usage			%	%																				
		Networks			$A	%					V	V			V	V	V	V		V		V	V			
CPT	Household & Persons	Programs		X	$A						$A	$A			$A	$A	$A	$A		$A	$A	$A	$A	$A		
		Pgm Types			$A	%					$A	$A			$A	$A	$A	$A		$A	$A	$A	$A	$A		
HTR	Household Tracking Report	Usage			%																					
		Programs			%	%																				
PTR	Persons Tracking Report	Usage	cov'g only						V		V	V			V	V	V	V		V	V	V	V			
		Programs		X	%A					V		V	V			V	V	V	V		V	V	V	V			
PLAN	Planner's Report	Usage																								
		Pgm Types																								
NHTI	Hispanic National Television Audience Report	Agg Viewing			%A				%AV		%AV	%AV			%AV	%AV				%AV	%AV	%AV	%AV	%AV	%AV	%AV
		Programs		X	%A				%AV		%AV	%AV			%AV	%AV				%AV	%AV	%AV	%AV	%AV	%AV	%AV
		Pgm Types			%A			%AV	%AV		%AV	%AV			%AV					%AV		%AV	%AV	%AV	%AV	%AV

Demographics are reported for most tables and vary to better match the target audiences used by the marketplace for individual dayparts. Overall, over 25 persons demographics are reported.

Key

- ▢ Gross Average Audience
- % Rating
- A Projected Audience
- V Viewers Per 1000
- U○ Average Hours
- ‧ Also Quarter-to-Date & Premiere-to-Date Averages
- X Data Reported
- $ Persons Characteristics Within Households
- • Cost Per Comm'l/30" & Cost Per 1000
- · Total: 18–34, 18–49, 25–54, 35–54, 55+
- ♦ Also Male
- ♦ Also Age 2–5
- ♦ Also Age 25–34 & 35–49
- ♦ Also Male & Female
- ♦ Also Teens 12–14 & 15–17

viewing Monday through Friday builds to about 25 percent of TV households. At 9:00 P.M. in February, however, nearly 70 percent of TVHHs are viewing television, while in July that number drops to 50 percent (Figure 9.1).

Share   The percent of Households Using Television (HUT) that are tuned to a specific program or station at a specific time. Shares always equal 100 percent of all viewing taking place, regardless of the amount of total viewing at that time. Since viewing levels change hour by hour throughout the day and season, share is the primary competitive measure examined by network and station executives. For media planners and buyers, share can be used to indicate a station's or network's overall strength. More important, however, is the role share and HUT levels play in predicting future performance and the possible value of a proposed broadcast schedule.

Rating   The percentage of any demographic and market universe which is viewing a specific station or program. It is the estimated percentage of all TV households or persons tuned to a specific schedule. Ratings are always historic, in the past tense. The projection of future ratings is a factor of estimated HUTs and shares.

$$\text{Rating} = \text{HUT} \times \text{Share}$$
$$\text{Share} = \text{Rating} \div \text{HUT}$$
$$\text{HUT} = \text{Ratings} \div \text{Share}$$
$$\text{Total Ratings} = \text{HUT}$$

EXAMPLES

If at 9:00 P.M. on Wednesday a program enjoys a 40 share and the HUT level is 65, what is the program's rating?

$$.65 \times .40 = .26$$

The program's rating is 26.

If a program's rating at 9:00 P.M. on Friday is 18 and the HUT level is 68, what is the program's share?

$$.18 \div .68 = .26$$

The program's share is 26.

If a program's rating is 9 at 10:00 A.M. on Tuesday and it has a share of 33, what is the HUT level at that time?

$$.09 \div .34 = 26$$

The HUT level at that time is 26.

Persons Using Television (PUT) or Persons Viewing Television (PVT)   The percentage of people in any universe who are viewing television at a given time. It accounts for the different number of people in a household and for multiset viewing. The same terms and calculations utilized in relationship to HUTs can be applied to PUTs. Computer programs or conversion tables provided by research suppliers enable a planner to translate any household rating into demographic or persons data.

An understanding of these sources, definitions, and the modest arithmetic involved are sufficient for a planner to project performance, evaluate schedules, and perform a post-buy analysis. A great deal of the action, however, occurs at a local, rather than network, level.

Local Market and Station Data

Since the recent retreat of Arbitron, Nielsen provides the remaining standard source of local market television data. The service is called the Nielsen Station Index (NSI).

The **daypart summary** section of these reports (Exhibit 11.4) enables the planner/buyer to evaluate the cumulative audience reach of each local station for the various time periods; to analyze the station's ability to cover the market area, and to compare a station's present share of audience to its past performance.

The **program averages** section (Exhibit 11.5) provides data for the evaluation of audiences on a program basis, and for the evaluation of individual week ratings and share trends.

The **time period** section (Exhibit 11.6) supports post-buy analyses on a four-week average audience basis. It also enables the planner/buyer to estimate average audiences during station breaks and to evaluate time period viewing levels.

The **persons/share** section (Exhibit 11.7) enables the planner/buyer to project demographic ratings using the share and PUTs provided, and to evaluate a station's growth or decline in share among specific audiences.

After all else is said, a planner is proposing the achievement of a certain number of impressions, or a certain level of reach and frequency. What a buyer is purchasing, however, are rating points as reported by Nielsen. Consequently, media plans usually call for a specific number of gross rating points (GRPs) per week by daypart and in total. For example, a one-week planned schedule might call for:

Daypart	GRPs/Wk.	%/Daypart	Budget
Early Fringe	50	33	?
Prime Access	30	20	?
Late News	50	33	?
Late Fringe	20	14	?
Total	150	100	?

Cost is the obvious missing link in this example, and, as in all the other budget and buying situations of life, it is in neither the planner's nor the buyer's interest for there to be a major disconnect between the planner's estimate of cost and the actual cost at the time of purchase.

EXHIBIT 11.4 NSI DAYPART SUMMARY REPORT

PHILADELPHIA, PA

DAYPART SUMMARY

METRO HH R/G	METRO HH S/F	DAYPART TIME (ETZ) STATION	DMA HOUSEHOLD RTG	SHR	IN SRT	SHARE TREND MAY '95	FEB '95	NOV '94	JUL '94	DMA RATINGS PERSONS 2+	12-24	12-34	18-34	18-49	21-49	25-54	35+	35-64	50+	WOMEN 18+	12-24	18-34	18-49	25-49	25-54	WKG	MEN 18+	18-34	18-49	21-49	25-49	25-54	TNS 12-17	CHILD 2-11	6-11	PERCENT DISTRIBUTION MET	HOME DMA	ADJACENT DMA #1	#2	#3	TV HH RATINGS IN ADJACENT DMA'S #1	#2	#3
1	2		7	8	9	10	11	12	13	15	17	18	19	20	21	22	23	24	25	26	27	28	29	31	32	34	35	36	37	38	39	40	41	42	43	44	45	46	47	48	49	50	51
		MON.-FRI. 6:00P-8:00P																																									
7	14	KYW N	7	13	19	14	13	13	13	4	2	2	3	3	3	4	5	4	7	5	2	3	4	4	4	5	4	2	2	2	2	3	2			71	96	2	1	1			
5	9	WCAU C	4	8	11	10	10	10	10	2	1	2	1	2	2	2	3	3	4	3	1	2	2	2	3	2	2	1	1	2	2	2	2			80	97	2	1				
<<		WFMZ I	<<				NR		NR																											3	86	3	10	1			
3	6	WGBS I	3	6	8	6	8	9	8	2	3	2	2	2	2	1	1	1	1	2	5	2	2	2	2	1	1	2	1	1	1	1	4	3	4	81	98	2					
<<		WGTW I	<<			1		1	1																											93	100						
1	2	WHYY P	1	2		2	2	2	2	1							1	1	1	1							1									61	88	12	1				
<<		WLVT P	<<																																	43	98		2				
<<		WNJS+ P	<<																																	66	84	16					
4	7	WPHL I	3	7	10	8	8	8	7	2	4	3	3	2	2	3	2	2	2	2	4	3	2	2	2	2	2	3	3	3	3	3	4	1	1	64	89	3	2	5			1
18	33	WPVI A	18	32	47	33	31	33	35	9	3	4	5	6	6	7	15	10	21	13	4	5	7	7	8	9	9	4	5	5	6	6	2	2	2	70	96	1	1	2		1	1
4	7	WTXF IF	3	6	9	7	9	10	8	2	3	3	3	2	2	2	1	2	1	2	3	3	2	2	2	2	2	4	3	3	3	3	3	2	2	72	86	2	1	2			
1	1	WTBS T	1	1		1	1	1																																			
<<		WWOR I	<<			NR	NR																																				
<<		AEN	<<						1																																		
2	4	CNN	2	4		3	6	1	1	1				1	1	1	2	2	3	1	1	1	1	1	1	1	2		1	1	1	1											
<<		DSC	<<					1																																			
<<		ESP	<<			1	1	1	1																																		
1	3	HBO	1	2		2	1	2	NR			1	1			1					1	1	1	1	1									1	1								
1	1	LIF	1	2		1	1	1	1								1	1		1			1	1	1	1																	
1	1	MTV	1	1		1	1	1			1	1									1							1					1										
2	4	NIK	2	4		3	4	4	2	1	1	1									1	1											1	6	5								
1	2	TNT	1	1		1	1	1											1																								
<<		TWC	<<			NR		NR																																			
1	1	USA	1	1		1	1	1													1	1																					
52		H/P/T.*	61		35	54	63	60	50	30	23	24	24	25	24	27	37	32	48	36	27	27	27	27	28	29	30	21	22	22	23	25	23	20	21								
		7:00P-7:30P																																									
		7:30P-8:00P																																									
9	17	KYW N	8	16	26	17	18	18	18	5	4	4	4	4	4	5	7	6	8	7	4	5	6	6	6	7	5	3	3	3	3	4	4	1	1	70	94	3	1	1			
5	10	WCAU C	4	8	13	10	10	9	9	2	3	3	3	2	2	3	3	3	4	3	3	4	3	3	4	3	2	2	2	2	2	2	3			80	96	2	1				
<<		WFMZ I	<<				NR	1	NR																											3	74		23	3			
3	6	WGBS I	3	5	8	6	8	8	8	2	3	2	2	2	2	1	1	1	1	1	4	2	2	2	2	1	1	2	2	1	1	1	3	2	2	75	95	4		1			
1	1	WGTW I	<<			1	1	2	1																											92	100						
2	5	WHYY P	2	4		3	4	4	5	1							2	1	3	1						1	1									68	87	12		1			
<<		WLVT P	<<																																	62	95		5				
<<		WNJS+ P	<<			1	1	1																												68	80	10					
3	7	WPHL I	3	6	10	8	7	7	7	2	1	2	2	2	2	2	2	2	2	2	1	2	1	1	2	1	3	2	2	2	3	3	2	1	1	64	87	5	2	6			1
13	26	WPVI A	13	26	40	25	26	28	26	8	3	4	4	5	5	6	12	7	17	11	5	5	5	6	6	6	7	3	4	4	4	4	4	3	3	63	94	2	2	2		1	2
3	6	WTXF IF	3	5	8	7	8	8	10	2	3	2	2	2	2	2	1	2	1	2	3	2	2	2	2	1	2	2	2	2	2	2	3	2	2	78	95	2		3			
<<		WTBS T	<<			1	1	1																																			
<<		WWOR I	<<			NR	NR																																				
<<		AEN	<<																																								
2	3	CNN	2	3		2	4	2	2	1				1	1	1	2	1	2	1	1	1	1	1	1	1	1				1	1											
<<		DSC	1	1		1	1	1								1		1									1			1	1	1											
1	1	ESP	1	1		1	1	2	1																																		
2	3	HBO	1	3		2	2	2	NR	1		1	1	1	1	1	1	1	1	1		1	1	1	1	1	1	1	1	1	1	1	1	1	1								
1	1	LIF	1	1			1	1											1																								
1	1	MTV	1	1		2	1	1			1																						1										
2	4	NIK	2	4		3	3	4	2	1											1	1											1	6	5								
2	3	TNT	1	2		2	1	1		1	1						1		1	1	1					1	1	1															
<<		TWC	<<			NR		NR																																			
1	2	USA	1	2		2	2	1	1	1	1	1	1	1	1	1				1	1	1	1	1	1	1	1	1		1	1	1											
53		H/P/T.*	52		33	57	65	62	52	31	24	24	24	25	25	28	39	33	49	38	27	28	28	28	30	32	30	20	22	22	23	25	25	19	21								
1	2		7	8	9	10	11	12	13	15	17	18	19	20	21	22	23	24	25	26	27	28	29	31	32	34	35	36	37	38	39	40	41	42	43	44	45	46	47	48	49	50	51

#1=NEW YORK	6,716,020
#2=WILKES BARRE-SCRANTON	554,780
#3=HARRISBURG-LNCSTR-LEB-YORK	577,980

Source: Nielsen Station Index, July 1995. Used with permission.

The vocabulary both planner and buyer share is **cost per point (CPP)**, used by the planner in planning and the buyer in negotiation. CPP represents the estimated cost of purchasing rating points during specific time periods within a given market. CPPs are the basis for estimating what it will cost to buy a certain number of rating points

EXHIBIT 11.5 NSI PROGRAM PROGRAM AVERAGES REPORT

PHILADELPHIA, PA

WK1 7/06-7/12 WK2 7/13-7/19 WK3 7/20-7/26 WK4 7/27-8/02

PROGRAM AVERAGES

METRO HH RTG	METRO HH SHR	STATION DAY PROGRAM	DMA HH RATINGS WEEKS 1	2	3	4	MULTI-WEEK AVG RTG	MULTI-WEEK AVG SHR	HUT	PERSONS 2+	18+	12-24	12-34	18-34	18-49	21-49	25-54	35+	35-64	50+	WOMEN 18+	12-24	18-34	18-49	21-49	25-49	25-54	50+	WKG	MEN 18+	18-34	18-49	21-49	25-49	25-54	TNS 12-17	CHILD 2-11	6-11
1	2		3	4	5	6	7	8	14	15	16	17	18	19	20	21	22	23	24	25	26	27	28	29	30	31	32	33	34	35	36	37	38	39	40	41	42	43
2		R.S.E. THRESHOLDS 25+%	3	3	3	3	1			1	1	5	3	3	2	2	1	1	2	2	1	7	6	2	2	3	2	3	3	2	6	3	3	3	8	10	6	9
1		(1 S.E.) 4 WK AVG 50+%	1	1	1	1	LT			LT	LT	1	1	1	LT	1	LT	LT	1	LT	LT	2	1	1	1	1	1	1	1	LT	1	1	1	1	1	3	2	3
		7:00PM																																				
1	1	WGTW MON HILL ST BLUES	1	1	1	<<	<<		54																			1	1									
1	1	TUE HILL ST BLUES	1	1	<<	<<	<<		51																				1									
<<		WED HILL ST BLUES	<<	<<	<<	<<	<<		62																													
1	1	THU HILL ST BLUES	<<	<<	1	<<	<<		53																													
1	1	FRI HILL ST BLUES	1	1	1	<<	1	1	49																													
1	1	AVG HILL ST BLUES	1	1	<<	<<	<<		52																													
1	1	SAT WRLD-KICKBOXNG	<<	1	<<	<<	<<		44																													
<<		SUN PAID PROGRAM		<<	<<		<<		48																													
3	5	WPHL MON REAL-HWY PATRL	3	3	3	3	3	6	53	2	2	1	2	3	3	3	3	2	3	2	2	1	4	3	3	3	3	2	3	3	2	2	3	3	4		1	1
3	5	TUE REAL-HWY PATRL	4	2	4	3	3	6	51	2	2	2	2	2	2	2	3	2	3	2	2	3	1	2	2	1	2	2	2	2	2	3	3	3	3	3		
3	6	WED REAL-HWY PATRL	2	4	4	3	3	7	52	2	2	2	2	3	2	2	3	2	3	2	2	3	3	3	2	2	2	2	2	3	2	2	2	3	3	1		
4	7	THU REAL-HWY PATRL	4	3		4	4	7	53	2	2	1	1	1	1	2	3	3	3	3	2		1	1	1	1	2	2	1	3	1	2	2	2	4	2	2	3
3	7	FRI REAL-HWY PATRL	2	5	3	3	3	6	49	2	2	1	3	4	3	3	3	2	2	2	2	2	3	2	2	2	2	1	2	3	5	3	4	4	4			
3	6	AVG REAL-HWY PATRL	3	3	4	3	3	6	51	2	2	1	2	3	2	2	3	2	3	2	2	2	3	2	2	2	2	2	2	3	2	2	3	3	4	1	1	1
3	7	SAT FRESH PRINCE		4	3		4	8	45	1	1	2	1	1	1	1		1		1	1	2	1	1	1	1	1			1						3		
1	1	SAT HI SCHOOL FTBL				1	1	2	46									1		1								1										
6	13	SAT PHILLIES-SAT	7				7	14	47	4	4	4	4	5	3	3	2	4	3	6	3	2	3	2	2	1	1	4	2	7	7	6	4	5	4	2	1	
3	8	SUN RENEGADE	2	3	3	4	3	8	50	1	2		2	3	2	2	3	1	1	1	2		3	3	3	4	3	1	3	1	2	1	2	2	2			
16	29	WPVI MON JEOPARDY	15	15	16	17	16	30	53	9	11	4	4	5	6	6	6	14	10	20	13	6	7	7	7	7	8	23	10	9	3	4	4	4	6	2	3	4
15	29	TUE JEOPARDY	14	14	17	16	15	30	51	9	11	4	5	5	5	5	7	14	10	20	13	7	7	7	7	7	8	23	10	8	3	4	4	4	6	4	2	3
15	28	WED JEOPARDY	14	14	14	16	14	28	52	8	10	2	3	4	5	5	6	13	9	19	11	3	4	5	5	6	7	21	9	8	4	4	4	5	5	2	2	2
16	29	THU JEOPARDY	18	14	13	17	16	29	52	9	11	5	4	5	6	6	6	13	9	19	13	5	6	6	6	6	7	23	9	9	5	5	5	5	5	2	3	5
15	29	FRI JEOPARDY	15	15	13	17	15	31	49	9	11	3	3	3	5	5	6	14	10	21	13	4	4	6	6	6	8	24	9	8	2	4	4	4	5	3	2	3
15	29	AVG JEOPARDY	15	14	15	16	15	30	51	9	11	4	4	5	5	5	6	14	10	20	13	5	6	6	6	6	7	23	9	8	3	4	4	4	5	2	3	3
5	10	SAT CHILDREN-ALONG		4			4	9	46	3	2		2	3	2	2	2	2	2	4	4		3	2	2	2	2	7	3	1	3	2	2	2	2		4	
8	18	SAT PRIME TIME	6		7	8	7	16	43	4	5		1	1	2	2	2	6	4	10	6		2	3	3	3	3	10	4	4	1	1	1	1	1		1	1
10	20	SUN AMER-VIDEO-ABC	10	10	10	10	10	20	49	8	8	8	8	8	8	8	9	7	7	7	8	9	9	9	9	9	9	8	8	6	7	7	7	7	8	10	12	13
5	9	WTXF MON SIMPSONS	4	5	5	4	4	8	53	3	2	6	6	4	3	4	3	1	2	1	2	4	2	2	2	2	2		2	3	6	5	5	4	4	6	3	3
6	12	TUE SIMPSONS	5	5	6	5	5	10	51	4	3	5	6	6	4	4	4	2	3	1	3	7	5	4	4	4	3	1	3	4	6	6	6	5	4	5	4	6
6	11	WED SIMPSONS	5	5	5	6	5	10	52	4	3	7	6	6	5	4	3	2	2		2	4	3	3	3	3	3		2	4	9	6	6	5	4	7	6	6
6	11	THU SIMPSONS	4	6	6	6	6	10	52	4	3	8	7	6	4	4	3	1	2	1	2	8	5	4	4	3	3	1	3	3	7	4	4	4	4	11	5	5
6	12	FRI SIMPSONS	4	6	6	5	5	11	49	4	4	6	6	7	5	5	4	2	2	1	3	6	5	4	4	3	3	1	3	5	10	7	7	6	6	4	4	5
6	11	AVG SIMPSONS	4	5	5	5	5	10	51	4	3	6	6	6	4	4	3	2	2	1	2	6	4	3	3	3	3	1	2	4	8	5	5	5	4	7	5	6
4	9	SAT STAR TK DS9-AS	3	4	4	3	4	8	44	2	2	3	3	3	3	3	3	2	3	1	2	2	1	2	2	3	3	1	2	3	4	4	4	4	4	4	1	
4	7	SUN SLIDERS SU-FOX	3	4	2	3	3	6	50	2	2	1	3	4	3	2	3	1	1	1	2	1	3	2	2	2	2	2	2	2	6	3	3	3	3		1	1
		7:30PM																																				
10	18	KYW MON HARD COPY	9	9	8	10	9	17	55	5	6	5	5	5	5	5	6	7	6	8	8	4	7	7	7	7	8	9	8	5	4	3	3	3	4	3	1	1
10	18	TUE HARD COPY	9	8	7	10	9	17	52	5	6	4	4	3	4	4	5	7	6	10	7	5	5	5	5	8	6	10	7	5	2	2	2	2	3	4		
9	17	WED HARD COPY	9	8	8	8	8	16	52	5	6	3	3	3	4	4	5	7	6	8	7	2	4	5	6	6	6	9	7	4	2	3	3	3	3	4	1	2
9	16	THU HARD COPY	9	7	8	8	8	16	53	4	5	2	3	3	4	4	6	7	6	8	6	3	4	5	5	6	6	8	7	4	3	3	3	3	4	2	1	1
9	17	FRI HARD COPY	8	8	8	9	8	17	49	6	6	6	5	4	5	4	5	7	6	8	7	6	5	6	5	6	6	9	7	5	3	4	3	3	4	6		
9	17	AVG HARD COPY	9	8	8	9	8	16	52	5	6	4	4	4	4	4	6	7	6	8	7	4	5	6	6	6	6	9	7	5	3	3	3	3	4	4	1	1
5	9	WCAU MON EXTRA	3	4	5	4	4	7	55	3	3	3	3	3	3	3	3	3	3	3	3	1	3	3	3	3	3	3	4	3	4	3	4	3	3	2	1	1
5	9	TUE EXTRA	3	3	4	4	4	7	52	2	3	2	3	3	2	2	3	2	2	3	3	2	4	3	3	4	4	2	3	2	3	1	2	1	1	2		
6	12	WED EXTRA	4	5	6	6	5	10	52	3	3	3	3	3	2	2	3	3	3	5	4	3	4	3	3	3	4	6	4	2	2	2	2	2	2	4		
5	9	THU EXTRA	6	4	4	3	4	8	58	3	3	3	3	4	3	2	3	3	3	3	4	4	5	4	3	3	4	3	3	2	2	2	2	2	3	2	1	
5	10	FRI EXTRA	5	4	4	4	4	9	48	2	2	2	2	2	2	2	2	3	2	4	3	4	3	2	2	2	3	4	2	2	1	1	1	2	2	4		
5	10	AVG EXTRA	4	4	5	4	4	8	52	2	3	3	3	3	2	2	3	3	3	4	3	3	4	3	3	3	4	4	3	2	2	2	2	2	2	3		
3	6	WGBS MON FAMILY MATTERS	3	3	2	4	3	6	55	2	1	3	2	1	1	1	1	1	1		1	4	2	2	2	2	2	1	1	1	1	1	1	1	1	5	3	4
3	6	TUE FAMILY MATTERS	3	2	2	3	3	5	52	2	1	2	1	1	2	2	2	1	2	1	2	4	1	2	2	2	2	1	1	1		1	1	2	1	3	2	1
3	6	WED FAMILY MATTERS	3	2	3	2	3	5	52	1	1	2	3	3	2	2	2	1	1		2	3	4	3	2	3	2		2	1	1	1	1	2	1	2	1	2
3	6	THU FAMILY MATTERS	3	3	4	2	3	5	53	2	2	3	3	3	2	1	1	1	1	1	1	5	1	1	1	1	1	2	1	2	4	3	1	1	1	4	3	3
3	6	FRI FAMILY MATTERS	3	2	3	2	3	5	49	2	2	3	2	2	2	2	1	1	1	1	2	4	2	2	2	1	1	1		2	2	2	2	1	1	2	2	1
3	6	AVG FAMILY MATTERS	3	2	3	3	3	5	52	2	1	3	2	2	2	2	1	1	1	1	1	4	2	2	2	2	2	1	1	1	2	2	1	1	1	3	2	2
2	5	SAT FAMLY MATTRS W	1	2	2	2	2	4	44	1		2	1	1	1							3	1	1	1											2	1	2
2	4	WPHL MON TOP COPS	1	3	3	2	2	4	55	2	2	1	2	3	2	2	3	2	2	2	2	2	2	2	2	1	2	2	1	2	3	2	2	2	3		1	2
9	16	TUE PHILLIES BSBL		9		8	8	14	60	4	6	2	3	4	4	4	4	7	6	9	4		2	2	2	3	3	7	2	7	6	6	5	5	5		1	1
2	5	TUE TOP COPS	2	2	4		2	5	51	2	2	3	2	1	2	2	2	2	2	1	1	2	2	2	2	2	1	1	1	2	1	2	2	3	3	5		
9	16	WED PHILLIES BSBL		9			9	15	60	5	5	7	5	3	4	4	4	6	5	7	4	5	2	3	3	3	3	6	2	6	3	6	5	6	6	14	2	
6	11	WED THIS WK-BSBL		4			4	9	49	2	2	4	4	2	2	2	2	2	2	3	1		2	1	1	1	1	2	1	3	3	3	3	4	3	6		
3	7	WED TOP COPS	3		3	4	3	6	53	1	2		2	3	2	2	2	1	1	2	1	1	2	1	2	2	2	1	1	3	4	3	3	3	3	1		
10	17	THU PHILLIES BSBL	9	10			10	18	62	5	6	1	2	2	3	3	4	7	6	10	4	1	1	2	2	2	2	8	2	7	4	4	4	5	6	2	3	4
2	5	THU TOP COPS			2	3	2	4	50	1	2	1		1			1	2	2	3	1						1	2	1	2	1	1		1	2			
8	14	FRI PHILLIES BSBL		7			7	13	55	4	4	1	1	1	3	3	3	6	5	8	3	2	1	2	1	2	1	5	2	6	2	3	4	4	6	1	1	
2	5	FRI TOP COPS	2		2	2	2	4	48	1	2	1	1	2	2	2	2	1	2	1	1	3	2	2	2	1	1	1	1	2	1	2	2	2	3	1	1	1
8	15	AV4 PHILLIES BSBL	8	8		8	8	15	60	5	5	3	3	3	3	3	4	7	6	8	4	1	1	2	2	2	2	7	2	7	4	5	5	5	6	3	2	3
9	15	NOR PHILLIES BSBL	9	9		8	9	15	61	5	5	3	3	3	3	3	4	7	6	9	4	2	1	2	2	2	2	7	2	7	4	5	5	6	6	3	2	3
3	5	AVG TOP COPS	2	2	3	3	2	5	52	1	2	1	2	2	2	2	2	2	2	2	1	2	2	1	2	1	2	1	1	2	2	2	2	2	3	1		1
3	7	SAT SAT CINEMA 17		4	3		3	7	51	3	3	3	2	1	2	2	3	4	4	4	3		1	2	2	3	3	3	3	3		2	2	2	2	6	1	1

Source: Nielsen Station Index, July 1995. Used with permission.

for a planned schedule. Either the planner receives this information from the buyer during the planning process, or both use syndicated or trade sources that report and provide estimates for them.

The buyer, however, will still need a certain degree of flexibility. The solution, in so far as one exists, rests in the fact that the planner has a fixed budget for achieving fixed objectives, which will be evaluated in both gross and relative terms. This means that the planner needs a certain number of impressions, or reach and frequency, and is ultimately concerned about the absolute and comparative cost of the package.

EXHIBIT 11.6 NSI TIME PERIOD REPORT

PHILADELPHIA, PA

WK1 7/06-7/12 WK2 7/13-7/19 WK3 7/20-7/26 WK4 7/27-8/02

The exhibit is a Nielsen Station Index (NSI) Time Period Report table for Thursday 6:30PM – 8:30PM, showing DMA Household Ratings (Weeks 1–4, Multi-Week Avg, Share Trend), DMA Ratings for Persons, Women, Men, and Child across numerous demographic age columns, by station and program. Stations listed include KYW, WCAU, WGBS, WGTW, WHYY, WLVT, WNJS+, WPHL, WPVI, and WTXF with programs such as NBC Nitely News, CBS Eve News, Family Matters, I Dream-Jeannie, MacNeil&Lehrer, Nite Bsnss Rpt, Married-Children, Phillies Day, ABC-World News, M*A*S*H, Ent Tonight 30, Amercn Journal, Roseanne, Hill St Blues, NJN News, Real-Hwy Patrl, Jeopardy, Simpsons, Hard Copy, Extra, Are You-Served, Travels-Europe, NJ Live, Phillies Bsbl, Top Cops, Wheel-Fortne, Coach, Mad Abt U-Thu, Burkes Law-Thu, Mystery Movie, Prime Movie, On Waterways, Talk2 Reprsntv, This Old House, Motor Week, Babylon 5, Gettn Ovr-ABC?, Matlock-ABC, ABC Mv Sp Thu, and Martin-Fox, along with HUT/PUT/TOTALS rows.

Source: Nielsen Station Index, July 1995. Used with permission.

This is the point at which cost per thousand (CPM) enters the broadcast picture. CPMs are the standard industry measure of how much it costs an advertiser to reach a thousand persons or homes. Since audience estimates in the rating books are shown in thousands, you simply divide the cost by the reported number of homes or persons reached. By setting CPM limits, which restrict the overall relative cost of a schedule, the agency planner achieves an accountable use of the budget, while the buyer achieves a degree of flexibility in the purchasing negotiation. CPM parameters enable both buyer and seller to mix more expensive spots and dayparts with less expensive spots and dayparts so as to achieve an acceptable competitive cost.

EXHIBIT 11.7 NSI PERSONS/SHARE REPORT

PHILADELPHIA, PA

4-WEEK TIME PERIOD AVERAGES

TIME STATION PROGRAM	WOMEN 18+					WOMEN 18-34					WOMEN 18-49					WOMEN 25-54					WOMEN WKG					WOMEN 12-24					PERSONS 12-24				
	RTG	SHR	MAY '95	FEB '95	JJ '94	RTG	SHR	MAY '95	FEB '95	JJ '94	RTG	SHR	MAY '95	FEB '95	JJ '94	RTG	SHR	MAY '95	FEB '95	JJ '94	RTG	SHR	MAY '95	FEB '95	JJ '94	RTG	SHR	MAY '95	FEB '95	JJ '94	RTG	SHR	MAY '95	FEB '95	JJ '94
	28	77	78	79	80	26	81	82	83	84	23	85	86	87	88	32	89	90	91	92	34	93	94	95	96	27	97	98	99	100	17	101	102	103	104

MONDAY-FRIDAY (CONTINUED)

7:00P

KYW ENT TONIGHT 30	8	17	14	13	17	5	18	14	10	13	5	18	13	11	15	6	19	14	13	17	6	19	14	13	16	2	8	7	8	10	2	9	8	5	10
WCAU AMERCN JOURNAL	3	8	9	10	10	1	5	3	4	14	2	7	5	7	12	3	9	5	8	12	1	5	6	9	11	1	2	3	2	13	2	7	3		11
WGBS ROSEANNE	2	5	8	7	9	3	9	12	15	18	2	7	12	10	14	2	6	11	7	12	1	5	8	8	10	4	14	13	19	18	2	10	10	13	11
WGTW HILL ST BLUES																																			
WHYY NITE BSNSS RPT																																			
WLVT NITE BSNSS RPT																																			
WNJS+ NJN NEWS																																			
WPHL #REAL-HWY PATRL	2	6	6	8	5	3	9	9	12	8	2	8	8	11	7	2	8	8	9	6	2	7	7	8	6	2	7	5	12	10	1	6	8	10	20
WPVI JEOPARDY	13	34	35	32	37	6	20	23	21	18	8	22	25	25	23	7	25	28	25	25	9	30	30	30	28	5	19	22	19	18	4	15	19	17	14
WTXF SIMPSONS	2	6	7	7	7	4	14	19	14	11	3	12	14	13	11	3	9	9	11	11	2	8	9	11	10	6	21	27	18	9	6	25	30	27	12
PUT	37		40	48	37	28		32	35	27	28		32	37	29	30		33	40	31	31		34	39	31	27		33	33	26	25		27	33	25

7:30P

KYW HARD COPY	7	19	18	17	19	5	18	14	11	15	8	20	16	14	18	6	21	17	17	20	7	23	17	18	17	4	14	7	10	13	4	16	5	9	16
WCAU EXTRA	3	9	11	9	11	4	13	12	7	11	3	11	11	8	11	4	12	10	10	13	3	10	10	10	13	3	10	13		9	3	12	10	5	8
WGBS FAMILY MATTERS	1	4	6	6	8	2	7	9	13	16	2	6	10	10	13	2	6	9	8	10	1	3	7	7	8	4	14	17	17	20	3	13	16	16	14
WGTW HILL ST BLUES																																			
WHYY VARIOUS	1	4	3	4	4				3					3	3			2	3	3	1	2	3	4	2								2		
WLVT VARIOUS																																			
WNJS+#NJ LIVE																																			
WPHL #TOP COPS	2	4	5	6	6	2	7	6	9	8	1	6	7	8	6	2	5	7	7	6	1	4	6	8	6	1	5	4	9	6	1	6	6	8	7
WPVI WHEEL-FORTNE	11	31	29	28	29	5	17	19	19	16	5	19	18	20	17	6	21	21	19	17	8	24	23	23	23	5	18	17	21	19	3	14	16	16	16
WTXF COACH	2	6	7	7	8	2	8	13	14	13	2	7	11	12	13	2	6	8	8	13	1	4	8	8	12	3	12	15	17	11	3	11	15	20	16
PUT	38		42	52	39	28		32	39	27	28		33	41	30	30		34	44	33	32		36	43	31	27		30	33	26	24		24	32	23

PERSONS SHARES

12:00M

KYW TONITE SHW-NBC	3	19	16	15	14	2	14	9	5	5	2	13	12	7	8	3	16	13	13	11	2	12	15	10	10	2	18	14		3	2	13	9	4	6
WCAU D LETTRMAN-CBS	4	22	19	23	22	4	24	25	27	29	4	24	22	27	23	4	25	21	32	21	3	23	19	30	19	3	22	21	15	23	3	22	19	28	25
WGBS HUNTER	1	7	10	8	15	1	7	11	8	17	1	5	8	7	14	1	5	6	6	15	1	8	5	9	12	2	12	15	7	16	1	7	14	5	17
WGTW MIDNIGHT MOVIE																																			
WHYY #CHARLIE ROSE																																			
WLVT VARIOUS																																			
WPHL #TOP COPS	1	4	10	13	4	1	4	10	20	3	1	4	10	15	4	1	4	10	7	3			6	17				9	28	6			8	20	4
WPVI #MILLN$MOV12M1D	2	14	19	16	20	2	14	14	14	19	2	12	14	14	19	2	11	16	11	19	2	16	17	9	26	1	9	13	18	20	1	5	7	11	14
WTXF NASH	1	8	6	8	6	1	8	7	5	1	1	7	8	4	10	1	7	9	9	1	1	6	7	4	1	1	9	10	12	1	1	11	14	10	15
PUT	17		19	20	20	15		19	20	19	15		19	18	20	17		19	16	20	14		18	15	18	13		13	18	18	12		13	14	15

12:30A

KYW #C O'BRIEN-NBC	1	14	15	13	10	1	10	14	12	4	1	13	18	10	6	2	16	18	13	11	1	14	19	14	10	2	10	19		3	1	1	8	14	13
WCAU TOM SNYDER-CBS	1	15	16	18	20	1	9	14	14	23	1	12	14	18	21	1	14	15	19	18	2	18	9	25	22	1	3	12	15	19		8	10	21	
WGBS RICHARD BEY-R	1	12	10	7	26	3	25	6	6	30	2	16	8	4	28	1	12	7	8	22	1	12	7	8	22	9	53	10	10	33	5	40	14	6	29
WGTW MIDNIGHT MOVIE																																			
WHYY CHARLIE ROSE																																			
WLVT VARIOUS																																			
WPHL #CONSUMR CORNR2			5	5	4			9	5	5			7	7	4			8	7	5			8		6				8	6				7	
WPVI #MILLN$MOV12M1D	2	18	24	22	13	2	17	22	28	6	1	13	18	21	10	1	16	17	12	16	2	16	20	18	18	1	9	22	36		1		18	21	
WTXF NIGHT COURT				8					5	13					10					4					12	1	8			19	2	18		16	18
PUT	10		13	14	14	11		14	13	14	10		12	12	14	9		11	12	13	10		10	10	12	18		11	12	18	13		10	12	12

1:00A

KYW #C O'BRIEN-NBC	1	18	19	10	10	1	15	24	8		1	16	26	8		1	15	26	9	12	1	17	26	10		2	19	25			1	13	20	24	
WCAU TOM SNYDER-CBS	1	11	15	17	19	1	14	8		26	1	11	9	17	17	1	14	10	20	10	1	15		22	22	1	5		7	33					31
WGBS RICHARD BEY-R	1	12	8	36		2	21	8	9	43	1	17		41	1	8		7	35	1	12	11	7	30	6	54	14	15	44	4	45	21	8	42
WPHL #CONSUMER CORNR																																			
WPVI #MILLN$MOV12M1D	1	20	31	28	15	1	17	33	34	7	1	16	28	28	14	1	19	27	16	19	1	17	26	20	23	1	6	30	62				18	29	
WTXF HAWAII 5-0										7					7					7					7					7				15	
PUT	8		8	10	10	8		8	8	9	7		8	8	10	7		8	8	8	11		7	8	11	8		8	8	8	

| 28 | 77 | 78 | 79 | 80 | 26 | 81 | 82 | 83 | 84 | 23 | 85 | 86 | 87 | 88 | 32 | 89 | 90 | 91 | 92 | 34 | 93 | 94 | 95 | 96 | 27 | 97 | 98 | 99 | 100 | 17 | 101 | 102 | 103 | 104 |

Source: Nielsen Station Index, July 1995. Used with permission.

Estimating Ratings

One of the most important steps in the buying process is the pre-buy analysis, which provides estimates and establishes program values. Forecasting ratings is not a job for amateurs. To estimate future ratings, a buyer must make subjective judgments based on historical activity in the market. Competitive circumstances will establish relative prices (CPP) in the negotiation with station representatives, but the ratings estimate will determine gross costs, because it determines what will be purchased—or what each side agrees is being purchased—as well as performance accountability.

The two necessary resources are research reports on share trends and HUT/PUT trends. The planner or buyer must study historical shares for each station and each program type in the time period (Exhibit 11.8). It helps when the program types, if not the programs themselves, remain the same. Life, however, is seldom so simple. Whatever the case, the buyer must estimate share-of-viewing for the various programs under consideration for a future quarter. If the station representative does not agree, buyer and seller must negotiate a resolution.

The next step is to determine a HUT/PUT for each program time period. The planner/buyer can use the same quarter from the previous year, or use an average of the same quarter over a number of years. Using an average of several years' worth of HUT/PUT levels tends to stabilize the viewing levels and is generally a more accurate way of forecasting the future. Once a HUT level is determined and a share agreed upon, a simple multiplication will provide the ratings estimates.

These numbers were always remarkably stable until the arrival of cable television and the other new media. In today's environment, HUT/PUT levels have a tendency to rise from year to year, while station shares decline. Since most of the nation is now wired for CATV, some stability has returned and projections are easier to formulate than they were a decade ago. Demographic trends, plus the rambunctiousness of new media developments, however, can quickly change the situation. Consequently, it is imperative that buyers stay on top of the news (programming, technologies, penetrations, and so on) so that they can remain ahead of the wave.

Negotiations are an intricate and sensitive process and usually take place immediately following the pre-buy analysis. A season of political campaigns and Olympics, or the peculiarities of a particular market situation, may produce a **closed negotiation**, in which the buyer is faced with a "take it or leave it" price. More often, both buyer and seller are faced with an **open negotiation**, in which both sides put all their cards on the table (in other words, budget, GRP goals, CPPs, program estimates, CPM objectives, and so on) and try to come to an equitable consensus. After all, it is in neither side's interest to misjudge either broadcast performance or the commodity marketplace.

RADIO

There are more than nine thousand commercial radio stations in the United States and, on average, nearly 80 percent of their revenue comes from local advertisers. Networks exist, but radio's revenue picture is rooted in local broadcasts.

Local Market and Station Data

Radio reality is primarily measured by Arbitron (Exhibit 11.9), which has recently announced a 70 percent increase in its sample size for continuously metered markets. This increase is in response to the statistical axiom that "the smaller the phenomenon to be measured, the larger the sample must be." Because of the staggering number of

EXHIBIT 11.8 SHARE TRENDS IN ONE TV MARKET

	Programming: Mon–Fri. 7:30–8:00 P.M.			Share Trends		
Station	Nov.	Feb.	May	Nov.	Feb.	May
A	Sitcom	Adventure	Adventure	17	18	17
B	Talk/Ent.	Talk/Ent.	Talk/Ent.	30	27	35
C	Game Show	Game Show	Western	22	26	15
D	Game Show	Game Show	Sitcom	18	16	20

radio choices, listened to by over 95 percent of the population over twelve years of age, any individual station's audience is minuscule by television standards. Consequently, radio is necessarily a niche medium that requires elaborate and detailed data to unlock its potential for buyers increasingly interested in highly targeted audiences. The Arbitron rating book for a medium sized market can easily include two hundred pages or more. In all, the pricing, packaging, and purchasing of radio is a challenge to both buyers and sellers.

Network Data

There are more than twenty-nine radio networks defined by their programming format and their clearance pattern by market and station. Mostly, these networks are delivered via satellite transmission, but they may be distributed by wire or on audiotape. Some network formats effectively program a station's total broadcast day. Others are broadcast only during limited time periods, or only on specific days.

Network radio audiences are measured by RADAR (Radio's All Dimension Audience Research), which issues reports in the spring and fall of each year (Exhibit 11.10). Data is collected through daily recall interviews with respondents age twelve or older to determine their listening for a seven-day period. Respondent answers are matched with the program and commercial clearance schedules prepared by the networks and are combined to provide ratings for the individual networks in the past six months. RADAR reports the average number of stations cleared, their average audience, and the total audience accumulated over a five-day period.

Evaluations

Radio data generally measures station activity rather than program performance. **Average audience** reports how many people are listening during a particular quarter hour during a particular daypart. **Cumulative audience** is a measure of how many different people will hear at least some of the station's programming during a specific daypart, throughout the day, or during a week.

Because radio ratings are so small, cumulative audience measures are much more important than a quarter-hour average audience for advertisers interested in market or demographic target coverage and/or in developing satisfactory reach and frequency

EXHIBIT 11.9 ARBITRON RADIO REPORT FOR PHILADELPHIA

Target Audience
PERSONS 18-34

	MONDAY-FRIDAY 6AM-10AM				MONDAY-FRIDAY 10AM-3PM				MONDAY-FRIDAY 3PM-7PM				MONDAY-FRIDAY 7PM-MID				WEEKEND 10AM-7PM			
	AQH (00)	CUME (00)	AQH RTG	AQH SHR	AQH (00)	CUME (00)	AQH RTG	AQH SHR	AQH (00)	CUME (00)	AQH RTG	AQH SHR	AQH (00)	CUME (00)	AQH RTG	AQH SHR	AQH (00)	CUME (00)	AQH RTG	AQH SHR
KYW METRO	221	1823	1.8	6.3	45	652	.4	1.2	67	987	.5	2.2	16	390	.1	1.2	37	673	.3	1.9
TSA																				
WBEE METRO	165	978	1.3	4.7	286	1032	2.3	7.8	184	1109	1.5	6.2	49	604	.4	3.6	90	791	.7	4.6
TSA																				
WDAS METRO				.1	4	50		.1	1	19				19			12	127	.1	.6
TSA																				
WDAS-FM METRO	170	892	1.4	4.9	219	1079	1.8	6.0	182	1116	1.5	6.1	136	822	1.1	9.9	150	881	1.2	7.6
TSA																				
WFLN METRO	34	164	.3	1.0	50	184	.4	1.4	36	205	.3	1.2	14	102	.1	1.0	11	79	.1	.6
TSA																				
WGMP METRO	7	49	.1	.2	5	57		.1	8	99	.1	.3	3	70		.2	8	149	.1	.4
TSA																				
WHAT METRO	5	52		.1	14	45	.1	.4	9	45	.1	.3	11	44	.1	.8	5	37		.3
TSA																				
WIBF METRO	98	904	.8	2.8	154	1289	1.2	4.2	129	1419	1.0	4.3	70	986	.6	5.1	104	1164	.8	5.3
TSA																				
WIOQ METRO	156	1148	1.2	4.5	200	1450	1.6	5.4	174	1557	1.4	5.8	84	1095	.7	6.1	140	1226	1.1	7.1
TSA																				
WIP METRO	186	978	1.5	5.3	174	773	1.4	4.7	147	836	1.2	4.9	49	568	.4	3.6	39	376	.3	2.0
TSA																				
WJJZ METRO	49	407	.4	1.4	91	386	.7	2.5	71	443	.6	2.4	21	292	.2	1.5	53	349	.4	2.7
TSA																				
WMGK METRO	152	1097	1.2	4.3	221	1290	1.8	6.0	175	1452	1.4	5.9	65	819	.5	4.7	144	1125	1.2	7.3
TSA																				
WMMR METRO	325	1794	2.6	9.3	402	1779	3.2	10.9	278	2004	2.2	9.3	82	1039	.7	6.0	145	1433	1.2	7.4
TSA																				
WNAP METRO	2	17		.1	4	67		.1	* 2	35		.1					* 3	51		.2
TSA																				
WOGL METRO	85	545	.7	2.4	105	554	.8	2.9	57	544	.5	1.9	22	353	.2	1.6	50	465	.4	2.5
TSA																				
WPEN METRO	6	28		.2	7	58	.1	.2	6	38		.2	4	45		.3	5	47		.3
TSA																				
WPLY METRO	257	1687	2.1	7.3	309	1726	2.5	8.4	278	2043	2.2	9.3	112	1384	.9	8.1	157	1572	1.3	8.0
TSA																				
WUSL METRO	256	1461	2.0	7.3	309	1671	2.5	8.4	269	1756	2.2	9.0	257	1535	2.1	18.7	218	1415	1.7	11.1
TSA																				
WWDB METRO	46	242	.4	1.3	80	395	.6	2.2	74	503	.6	2.5	16	229	.1	1.2	29	236	.2	1.5
TSA																				
WXTU METRO	117	736	.9	3.3	122	623	1.0	3.3	104	769	.8	3.5	34	401	.3	2.5	77	628	.6	3.9
TSA																				
WYSP METRO	665	2333	5.3	19.0	266	1851	2.1	7.2	140	1328	1.1	4.7	36	680	.3	2.6	78	911	.6	4.0
TSA																				
WYXR METRO	158	1167	1.3	4.5	214	1173	1.7	5.8	202	1595	1.6	6.8	114	1290	.9	8.3	128	1119	1.0	6.5
TSA																				
WZZD METRO	10	108	.1	.3	4	62		.1	12	105	.1	.4	4	60		.3	6	74		.3
TSA																				
WABC METRO	2	12		.1	5	36		.1	4	12		.1								
TSA																				
WCHR METRO	4	33		.1	4	70		.1	3	69		.1	4	21		.3	2	32		.1
TSA																				
WFMZ METRO	1	35			2	26		.1	3	44		.1		17			1	27		.1
TSA																				
WJBR-FM METRO	13	109	.1	.4	21	88	.2	.6	12	105	.1	.4	4	59		.3	11	112	.1	.6
TSA																				

Footnote Symbols: * Audience estimates adjusted for actual broadcast schedule. + Station(s) changed call letters since the prior survey - see Page 58.

ARBITRON

PHILADELPHIA   36   WINTER 1995

1: During the average quarter hour between 6:00 A.M. and 10:00 A.M. 17,000 persons listened to WDAS-FM for a minimum of five minutes; 2: During these hours a total of 89,200 different persons listened; 3: This produced an average quarter hour persons rating of 1.4; and 4: a share of 4.9 of adult 18–34 years old.

Source: Arbitron Radio Market Report. January 5–March 29, 1995. Used with permission.

EXHIBIT 11.10 RADAR NETWORK RADIO REPORT. (USED WITH PERMISSION)

108   RADAR 30 - FALL 1988

AUDIENCE ESTIMATES FOR XXX RADIO NETWORK
AUDIENCES TO ALL COMMERCIALS
NUMBER OF PERSONS IN THOUSANDS

MONDAY-FRIDAY PROGRAMS

PROGRAM TITLE (DAYS & DURATION)	AVG NUM PERS 12+	TOTAL ADULTS 18+	MEN TOTAL	MEN 18-49	MEN 25-54	MEN 25+	MEN 35+	WOMEN TOTAL	WOMEN 18-49	WOMEN 25-54	WOMEN 25+	WOMEN 35+	TEENS 12-17
9U0A HOURLY NEWS (M-F 5:00) 382													
AVG PER BROADCAST	1792	1784	721	206	311	696	610	1063	385	446	1046	912	•
5 DAY WEEKLY CUME	5159	5138	2216	858	1054	2091	1015	2922	1198	1279	2847	2420	•
FREQUENCY PER WEEK	1.74	1.74	1.63	1.30	1.48	1.66	1.70	1.82	1.61	1.74	1.84	1.88	•
10U0A HOURLY NEWS (M-F 5:00) 375													
AVG PER BROADCAST	1797	1788	701	201	341	671	558	1087	413	482	1072	918	•
5 DAY WEEKLY CUME	4934	4908	2163	912	1066	2045	1698	2746	1174	1255	2675	2260	•
FREQUENCY PER WEEK	1.92	1.82	1.62	1.54	1.60	1.64	1.67	1.96	1.76	1.92	2.00	2.03	•
11U0A HOURLY NEWS (M-F 5:00) 377													
AVG PER BROADCAST	1609	1585	606	276	318	573	465	979	357	412	968	850	•
5 DAY WEEKLY CUME	4756	4666	2040	946	1038	1698	1532	2628	1106	1163	2577	2179	90
FREQUENCY PER WEEK	1.69	1.70	1.49	1.46	1.53	1.51	1.52	1.88	1.61	1.74	1.88	1.97	•
12U0A HOURLY NEWS (M-F 5:00) 378 ①													
AVG PER BROADCAST	1318	1296	474	195	219	441	364	822	323 ②	369	815	692	•
5 DAY WEEKLY CUME	3938	3859	1557	683	735	1453	1178	2302	989	1087	2273	1911	79
FREQUENCY PER WEEK	1.67	1.68	1.52	1.45	1.37	1.52	1.54	1.79	1.63	1.70	1.79	1.81	•
1U0P HOURLY NEWS (M-F 5:00) 368													
AVG PER BROADCAST	1320	1305	476	225	256	447	350	829	318	368	819	708	•
5 DAY WEEKLY CUME	4126	4068	1634	779	787	1501	1206	2434	1016	1173	2385	2054	58
FREQUENCY PER WEEK	1.60	1.60	1.46	1.44	1.50	1.49	1.45	1.70	1.56	1.57	1.72	1.72	•

1. This network was carried by 378 stations during its 12:00 newscast with an average audience of 1,318,000 and a total of 3,938,000 during five days. The average person listened 1.67 times.

2. The same newscast generated on average of 323,000 women 18–49 and a cume of 989,000 of these women with an average frequency of 1.63.

relationships. Coverage is a direct function of share. Having a noticeably higher share either of the total audience, or of a specific demographic target's listening, increases the likelihood that a station will be essential to market coverage, or to any reach/frequency formulation.

The dynamics of radio are such that, although ratings and station average ratings are important, the number of stations purchased and the dispersion of announcements across different dayparts are critical to reach and frequency.

To obtain rapid reach for a time-constrained promotional strategy, the planner/buyer will naturally focus on the handful of stations with the highest average ratings. This strategy provides the highest possible reach in the shortest possible time, and it parallels television planning and purchase patterns.

To increase reach, however, the planner/buyer will have to increase the number of stations purchased. To increase frequency the planner will have to schedule more commercials per planning period. Since the cost of commercial time on a long list of lower-rated stations is less than on the higher-rated stations, it becomes affordable to increase the number of commercial announcements to increase frequency at the same time that a longer list of stations is being purchased to increase reach. This is a much more complicated set of considerations and computations than that required in broadcast television, even though the vocabulary, mathematics, and look of the numbers are the same.

MAGAZINES

To the degree that magazine titles are more permanent and less ephemeral than television programs, the research data available about magazines is more tangible and predictable.

Reader Profiles and Dynamics

The primary data sources for magazines are published by Simmons Market Research Bureau (SMRB) and Mediamark Research Inc. (MRI), both of which were described in chapter 4 as part of our discussion of resources for marketing information. We cautioned, at that point, that the planner resist the temptation of jumping ahead too rapidly to vehicle selection, or of matching vehicles and target markets. The appropriate point in the process for doing just that, however, is the moment of tactical planning that we are currently examining.

SMRB and MRI use different research techniques, but of most significance to media planners is the data both provide and the fact that they utilize similar formats. Both SMRB and MRI provide magazine total audience reports, reader accumulation and duplication data, and cross-tabulations with product user information. The questions they enable the planner to answer about any magazine or combination of magazines are:

1. What is their delivery of demographic targets?
2. What is their delivery of product user targets?

3. What is their delivery of psychographic targets?
4. What strategic relationship do they articulate and what degree of target duplication do they represent?

The planner must evaluate the importance of these various information streams to specific brand strategies and weight them in proportion to cost efficiencies.

The services' Magazine Audience Reports (Exhibit 11.11) quantify the demographic characteristics of each magazine's readership for an average issue. Thus it is possible to determine the sex, age, education, employment, household income, the presence of children by age, and so on, for hundreds of consumer magazines. These reports also tabulate the basic arithmetic of magazine readership. They identify a magazine's **coverage**, or the percentage of any demographic group accounted for by the publication's readership. They report each magazine's **composition**, or the percentage of a publication's readers who fall within certain demographic parameters. Finally, they provide an **index** that compares the incidence of a given demographic characteristic among a publication's readers with the population as a whole.

Coverage, when used to describe magazine readers, is the equivalent of reach. A magazine's coverage is the percentage of any target population reached by an average issue of the magazine. The handful of megacirculation magazines almost invariably will provide the highest reach of a wide variety of demographic groups. At the same time, however, they will often include many thousands of consumers outside of the prospect definition. In this context, reach potential must always be modified by relative costs, generally calculated on a CPM basis.

Composition represents the density of a target population within a magazine's readership. The higher the composition for a desired prospect, the lower will be the percent of populations outside of the target. Consequently, and to the extent that all other factors are equal, magazines with the highest composition of the target reader will also have a relative cost advantage.

Cost is never the end of the discussion, however, especially in regard to magazine selections. Composition, or the density of the prospect population within the magazine's readership, is also a measure of a magazine's authority and the intensity of its attraction to the prospect's interests. The magnetic energy of higher compositions may well be judged worth higher relative costs in reaching the prospects through such a vehicle.

Composition is especially significant in the evaluation of prospects along the user/nonuser axis (Exhibit 11.12). Since composition is a reflection of the editorial franchise and consumer interests, the magnetic field of editor/reader dialogue, it follows that they share a gestalt of values and understandings that a brand must penetrate and absorb as part of its own personality, if it is to be successful.

The rational approach to unlocking the mystery of consumer motivation includes various lifestyle and psychographic studies, especially VALS 2. Presumably, a planner could derive a useful answer from a sensitive and imaginative reading of the relevant magazines but few have demonstrated the courage to try. Fortunately, because the research services have provided an alternative (Exhibit 11.13), each magazine's readers can be measured in relationship to identifiable psychographic motivations and buying styles.

EXHIBIT 11.11 SIMMONS MAGAZINE REPORT

	TOTAL U.S. '000	ADULTS A '000	B %DOWN	C %ACROSS	D INDX	MALES A '000	B %DOWN	C %ACROSS	D INDX	FEMALES A '000	B %DOWN	C %ACROSS	D INDX	PRINCIPAL SHOPPERS A '000	B %DOWN	C %ACROSS	D INDX
TOTAL	187747	187747	100.0	100.0	100	90070	100.0	48.0	100	97676	100.0	52.0	100	115901	100.0	61.7	100
AMERICAN BABY	1600	1600	0.9	100.0	100	325	0.4	20.3	42	1275	1.3	79.7	153	1154	1.0	72.1	117
AMERICAN HEALTH	1577	1577	0.8	100.0	100	448	0.5	28.4	59	1129	1.2	71.6	138	1228	1.1	77.8	126
ARCHITECTUAL DIGEST	2016	2016	1.1	100.0	100	800	0.9	39.7	83	1216	1.2	60.3	116	1396	1.2	69.2	112
AUDUBON	1057	1057	0.6	100.0	100	549	0.6	51.9	108	508	0.5	48.1	92	644	0.6	60.9	99
BARRON'S	940	940	0.5	100.0	100	728	0.8	77.4	161	213	0.2	22.6	43	511	0.4	54.3	88
BETTER HOMES AND GARDENS	16430	16430	8.8	100.0	100	2752	3.1	16.8	35	13678	14.0	83.2	160	12833	11.1	78.1	127
BON APPETIT	3071	3071	1.6	100.0	100	739	0.8	24.1	50	2332	2.4	75.9	146	2323	2.0	75.6	123
BRIDAL GUIDE	809	809	0.4	100.0	100	**61	0.1	7.6	16	748	0.8	92.4	178	480	0.4	59.4	96
BRIDE'S & YOUR NEW HOME	905	905	0.5	100.0	100	**100	0.1	11.1	23	804	0.8	88.9	171	466	0.4	51.5	83
BUSINESS WEEK	2938	2938	1.6	100.0	100	2112	2.3	71.9	150	826	0.8	28.1	54	1452	1.3	49.4	80
CAR AND DRIVER	2916	2916	1.6	100.0	100	2652	2.9	90.9	190	264	0.3	9.1	17	1255	1.1	43.0	70
CAR CRAFT	1616	1616	0.9	100.0	100	1369	1.5	84.7	177	*247	0.3	15.3	29	610	0.5	37.8	61
COLONIAL HOMES	1070	1070	0.6	100.0	100	225	0.3	21.1	44	844	0.9	78.9	152	809	0.7	75.6	123
CONDE NAST SELECT (NET)	18453	18453	9.8	100.0	100	4541	5.0	24.6	51	13912	14.2	75.4	145	12357	10.7	67.0	108
CONDE NAST TRAVELER	1324	1324	0.7	100.0	100	558	0.6	42.1	88	766	0.8	57.9	111	895	0.8	67.6	109
CONSUMERS DIGEST	2933	2933	1.6	100.0	100	1682	1.9	57.4	120	1250	1.3	42.6	82	1835	1.6	62.6	101
COSMOPOLITAN	6929	6929	3.7	100.0	100	1055	1.2	15.2	32	5873	6.0	84.8	163	4715	4.1	68.0	110
COUNTRY HOME	2600	2600	1.4	100.0	100	588	0.7	22.6	47	2011	2.1	77.4	149	1967	1.7	75.7	123
COUNTRY LIVING	6629	6629	3.5	100.0	100	1581	1.8	23.8	50	5049	5.2	76.2	146	5002	4.3	75.5	122
DISCOVER	1721	1721	0.9	100.0	100	954	1.1	55.4	116	767	0.8	44.6	86	991	0.9	57.6	93
EATING WELL	1004	1004	0.5	100.0	100	231	0.3	23.0	48	773	0.8	77.0	148	817	0.7	81.4	132
EBONY	7951	7951	4.2	100.0	100	2872	3.2	36.1	75	5079	5.2	63.9	123	5294	4.6	66.6	108
ELLE	1439	1439	0.8	100.0	100	*153	0.2	10.6	22	1286	1.3	89.4	172	985	0.8	68.4	111
ENTERTAINMENT WEEKLY	2494	2494	1.3	100.0	100	954	1.1	38.2	80	1540	1.6	61.8	119	1553	1.3	62.3	101
ENTREPRENEUR	708	708	0.4	100.0	100	456	0.5	64.4	134	*252	0.3	35.6	68	378	0.3	53.4	87
ESQUIRE	1057	1057	0.6	100.0	100	721	0.8	68.2	142	336	0.3	31.8	61	611	0.5	57.8	94
ESSENCE	3915	3915	2.1	100.0	100	1073	1.2	27.4	57	2842	2.9	72.6	140	2762	2.4	70.6	114
FAMILY CIRCLE	13442	13442	7.2	100.0	100	1446	1.6	10.8	22	11995	12.3	89.2	172	11076	9.6	82.4	133
FAMILY CIRCLE/MCCALL'S (NET)	19540	19540	10.4	100.0	100	1877	2.1	9.6	20	17663	18.1	90.4	174	16153	13.9	82.7	134
THE FAMILY HANDYMAN	2439	2439	1.3	100.0	100	1765	2.0	72.4	151	674	0.7	27.6	53	1239	1.1	50.8	82

1: The average issue audience of *Better Homes & Gardens* is estimated to be 16,430,000. 2: This represents 8.8 percent of the 187,747,000 adults in the U.S. 3: Its average issue audience includes 2,752,000 men, or 3.1 percent. 4: 17 percent of *BH&G*'s audience are men, but men are 48.0 percent of the total population. 5: This index means that *BH&G*'s male composition is 65 percent less than the total population.

Source: Simmons Market Research Bureau, Inc. Used with permission.

In a planning world dominated by reach, frequency, and cost considerations, the buying style of a magazine's readers is seldom determinative. This is especially true since many question the validity of the self-administered/self-appraisal methodology involved in generating the data. The result is that most often this data is utilized as a tie-breaker or to suggest a vehicle that might merit heavier investment.

Strategic decisions concerning the relative importance of reach and frequency are also of major significance in magazine selection. We have discussed relative costs only with reference to target reach, but certain degrees of reach may have to be sacrificed to achieve a motivational frequency, or a strategy may call for both extensive reach and heavy frequency. In either context, the mix of vehicles is significant.

Both SMRB and MRI provide research data on the turnover and accumulation of magazine audiences (Exhibit 11.14). With this data, the planner can estimate the reach and frequency of any specific magazine schedule. The data reports on turnover, or the percentage of an average issue audience that will not be reached by a second issue. It also reports on audience accumulation, or the number of different people who will be reached by the same two issues. By cross-referencing magazines in cells that show the number of readers of both vehicles of a pair, and the percentage of each magazine's readership that is accounted for by the duplicated audience, a schedule's reach and frequency can be determined.

EXHIBIT 11.12 MEDIAMARK MAGAZINE REPORT (USED WITH PERMISSION)

BASE: WOMEN	TOTAL U.S. '000	(1) A '000	(2) ALL B % DOWN	(3) C % ACROSS	(4) D INDEX	HEAVY MORE THAN 7 A '000	B % DOWN	C % ACROSS	D INDEX	MEDIUM 3-7 A '000	B % DOWN	C % ACROSS	D INDEX	LIGHT LESS THAN 3 A '000	B % DOWN	C % ACROSS	D INDEX
All Women	98070	52646	100.0	53.7	100	13212	100.0	13.5	100	18961	100.0	19.3	100	20473	100.0	20.9	100
American Baby	4059	2744	5.2	67.6	126	738	5.6	18.2	135	1110	5.9	27.3	141	896	4.4	22.1	106
American Health	2906	1709	3.2	58.8	110	*393	3.0	13.5	100	689	3.6	23.7	123	627	3.1	21.6	103
American Hunter	*545	*372	.7	-	-	*72	-	-	-	*136	.7	-	-	*164	.8	-	-
American Legion	1608	677	1.3	42.1	78	*142	1.1	8.8	66	*265	1.4	16.5	85	*270	1.3	16.8	80
American Rifleman	810	*493	.9	60.9	113	*118	.9	14.6	108	*224	1.2	27.7	143	*151	.7	18.6	89
American Way	409	*208	.4	50.9	95	*27	.2	6.6	49	*74	.4	18.1	94	*106	.5	25.9	124
American Way/SW Spirit (Gr)	733	*311	.6	42.4	79	*39	.3	5.3	39	*141	.7	19.2	99	*130	.6	17.7	85
Architectural Digest	2927	1439	2.7	49.2	92	*264	2.0	9.0	67	497	2.6	17.0	88	678	3.3	23.2	111
Atlantic	486	*197	.4	40.5	76	*5	-	1.0	8	*48	.3	9.9	51	*144	.7	29.6	142
Audubon	997	456	.9	45.7	85	*85	.6	8.5	63	*197	1.0	19.8	102	*174	.8	17.5	84
Automobile	*517	*377	.7	-	-	*127	1.0	-	-	*69	.4	-	-	*180	.9	-	-
Baby Talk	2645	1843	3.5	69.7	130	*542	4.1	20.5	152	568	3.0	21.5	111	734	3.6	27.8	133
Barron's	*430	*171	.3	-	-	*34	.3	-	-	*11	.1	-	-	*125	.6	-	-
Bassmaster	619	*399	.8	64.5	120	*148	1.1	23.9	177	*185	1.0	29.9	155	*67	.3	10.8	52
Better Homes & Gardens	27750	15036	28.6	54.2	101	3521	26.7	12.7	94	5250	27.7	18.9	98	6264	30.6	22.6	108
BHG/LHJ Combo (Gr)	45166	24561	46.7	54.4	101	6017	45.5	13.3	99	8772	46.3	19.4	100	9772	47.7	21.6	104
Black Enterprise	1334	826	1.6	61.9	115	*147	1.1	11.0	82	*419	2.2	31.4	162	*260	1.3	19.5	93
Bon Appetit	4172	2037	3.9	48.8	91	*326	2.5	7.8	58	741	3.9	17.8	92	970	4.7	23.3	111
Bridal Guide	2899	1941	3.7	67.0	125	*579	4.4	20.0	148	633	3.3	21.8	113	729	3.6	25.1	120
Bride's	3001	1923	3.7	64.1	119	*518	3.9	17.3	128	*663	3.5	22.1	114	743	3.6	24.8	119
Business Week	1835	888	1.7	48.4	90	*162	1.2	8.8	66	*382	2.0	20.8	108	*344	1.7	18.7	90
Byte	*531	*260	.5	-	-	*67	.5	-	-	*129	.7	-	-	*64	.3	-	-
Cable Guide/Total TV (Gr)	6994	4186	8.0	59.9	111	1104	8.4	15.8	117	1640	8.6	23.4	121	1442	7.0	20.6	99
Car and Driver	732	*375	.7	51.2	95	*161	1.2	22.0	163	*106	.6	14.5	75	*108	.5	14.8	71
Car Craft	*374	*312	.6	-	-	*41	.3	-	-	*196	1.0	-	-	*75	.4	-	-
Colonial Homes	2056	952	1.8	46.3	86	*148	1.1	7.2	53	*333	1.8	16.2	84	471	2.3	22.9	110
Compute	*411	*173	.3	-	-	*87	.7	-	-	*42	.2	-	-	*44	.2	-	-
Conde Nast Select (Gr)	49850	27963	53.1	56.1	104	5799	43.9	11.6	86	10149	53.5	20.4	105	12017	58.7	24.1	115
Conde Nast Traveler	1669	770	1.5	46.1	86	*94	.7	5.6	42	*197	1.0	11.8	61	479	2.3	28.7	137
Consumers Digest	3345	1895	3.6	56.7	106	*261	2.0	7.8	58	950	5.0	28.4	147	684	3.3	20.4	98
Cooking Light	3836	1683	3.2	43.9	82	*307	2.3	8.0	59	585	3.1	15.3	79	791	3.9	20.6	99
Cosmopolitan	13031	7597	14.4	58.3	109	1618	12.2	12.4	92	2875	15.2	22.1	114	3105	15.2	23.8	114
Country America	2354	1349	2.6	57.3	107	*272	2.1	11.6	86	*520	2.7	22.1	114	*557	2.7	23.7	113
Country Home	6813	3674	7.0	53.9	100	696	5.3	10.2	76	1539	8.1	22.6	117	1439	7.0	21.1	101
Country Living	10073	5540	10.5	55.0	102	948	7.2	9.4	70	2306	12.2	22.9	118	2286	11.2	22.7	109
Country Music	3860	2530	4.8	65.5	122	*661	5.0	17.1	127	988	5.2	25.6	132	881	4.3	22.8	109
Delta's SKY Magazine	645	*285	.5	44.2	82	*35	.3	5.4	40	*96	.5	14.9	77	*154	.8	23.9	114
Discover	2441	1296	2.5	53.1	99	*328	2.5	13.4	100	*365	1.9	15.0	77	602	2.9	24.7	118
Disney Channel Magazine	6082	3616	6.9	59.5	111	805	6.1	13.2	98	1403	7.4	23.1	119	1407	6.9	23.1	111
Easyriders	*402	*211	.4	-	-	*74	.6	-	-	*105	.6	-	-	*32	.2	-	-
Eating Well	1798	896	1.7	49.8	93	*120	.9	6.7	50	*413	2.2	23.0	119	*363	1.8	20.2	97
Ebony	6569	4342	8.2	66.1	123	1612	12.2	24.5	182	1506	7.9	22.9	119	1224	6.0	18.6	89
Elle	3519	1841	3.5	52.3	97	*227	1.7	6.5	48	834	4.4	23.7	123	780	3.8	22.2	106
Endless Vacation	848	*442	.8	52.1	97	*100	.8	11.8	88	*169	.9	19.9	103	*173	.8	20.4	98
Entertainment Weekly	3619	2243	4.3	62.0	115	*453	3.4	12.5	93	926	4.9	25.6	132	864	4.2	23.9	114
Entrepreneur	1374	842	1.6	61.3	114	*122	.9	8.9	66	*278	1.5	20.2	105	*442	2.2	32.2	154
Esquire	1362	856	1.6	62.8	117	*202	1.5	14.8	110	*426	2.2	31.3	162	*228	1.1	16.7	80
Essence	4446	2939	5.6	66.1	123	897	6.8	20.2	150	1208	6.4	27.2	141	833	4.1	18.7	90
Family Circle	24271	13487	25.6	55.6	104	3361	25.4	13.8	103	5240	27.6	21.6	112	4887	23.9	20.1	96

1: An estimated 15,036,000 female cola drinkers read *Better Homes and Gardens.* 2: This represents 28.6 percent of all female cola drinkers. 3: 54 percent of the magazine's female readers are cola drinkers. 4: This index means that the *BH&G* female reader is slightly more likely to be a cola drinker than are her sisters in the general population.

Source: Mediamark Research Inc. Used with permission.

The services also provide cross-referenced data on other media vehicles, such as television programs, so that, with computer capability, a planner can cross-tabulate target audiences by media vehicle to develop a composite analysis. This process, however, can become an endless search for the ideal set of alternatives, considering reach, frequency, and cost. In order to limit this odyssey rationally, the computer assisted planner should make the same initial analysis as the pencil-assisted planner. If the strategy calls for frequency, the planner should be seeking out vehicles with heavily duplicated audiences. In short, the strategy objective dictates what the planner is looking for and forms the basis on which vehicles are further explored with or without a computer.

Circulation: Verification and Meaning

Estimates, after all, are only estimates salespeople have been known to overstate their delivery in order to get a signature on a contract. That is why the Audit Bureau of Circulations (ABC) was formed in the early days of advertising, when thousands of

EXHIBIT 11.13 SIMMONS BUYING STYLES REPORT

	TOTAL U.S. '000	ECONOMY-MINDED				EXPERIMENTERS				IMPULSIVE				AD BELIEVERS			
		A '000	B % DOWN	C % ACROSS	D INDX	A '000	B % DOWN	C % ACROSS	D INDX	A '000	B % DOWN	C % ACROSS	D INDX	A '000	B % DOWN	C % ACROSS	D INDX
TOTAL FEMALES	97676	39950	100.0	40.9	100	28039	100.0	26.7	100	21240	100.0	21.7	100	23906	100.0	24.5	100
AMERICAN BABY	2004	761	1.9	38.0	93	581	2.2	29.0	109	550	2.6	27.4	126	584	2.4	29.2	119
AMERICAN HEALTH	1913	818	2.0	42.8	105	464	1.8	24.2	91	389	1.8	20.4	94	442	1.8	23.1	94
ARCHITECTUAL DIGEST	1760	782	2.0	44.5	109	434	1.7	24.7	93	464	2.2	26.4	121	422	1.8	24.0	98
AUDUBON	667	245	0.6	36.7	90	*205	0.8	30.6	115	*129	0.6	19.3	89	*82	0.3	12.3	50
BARRON'S	277	*143	0.4	51.6	126	*120	0.5	43.1	162	*111	0.5	40.1	184	**79	0.3	28.4	116
BETTER HOMES AND GARDENS	18583	8086	20.2	43.5	106	4891	18.8	26.3	99	3964	18.7	21.3	98	4644	19.4	25.0	102
BON APPETIT	3301	1455	3.6	44.1	108	970	3.7	29.4	110	686	3.2	20.8	96	742	3.1	22.5	92
BRIDAL GUIDE	1106	482	1.2	43.6	107	367	1.4	33.2	124	*323	1.5	29.2	134	362	1.5	32.7	134
BRIDE'S & YOUR NEW HOME	1255	556	1.4	44.3	108	344	1.3	27.4	103	421	2.0	33.5	154	386	1.6	30.8	126
BUSINESS WEEK	1628	687	1.7	42.2	103	451	1.7	27.7	104	282	1.3	17.3	80	364	1.5	22.3	91
CAR AND DRIVER	395	*156	0.4	39.4	96	**59	0.2	14.9	56	**64	0.3	16.2	74	**110	0.5	27.8	114
CAR CRAFT	*280	**96	0.2	34.4	84	**133	0.5	47.6	178	**112	0.5	40.0	184	**164	0.7	58.6	240
COLONIAL HOMES	1183	516	1.3	43.6	107	248	1.0	21.0	79	231	1.1	19.6	90	182	0.8	15.4	63
CONDE NAST SELECT (GROSS)	32222	13433	33.6	41.7	102	9409	36.1	29.2	110	7999	37.7	24.8	114	8419	35.2	26.1	107
CONDE NAST TRAVELER	1078	469	1.2	43.5	106	322	1.2	29.8	112	338	1.6	31.4	144	232	1.0	21.6	88
CONSUMERS DIGEST	1890	788	2.0	41.7	102	548	2.1	29.0	109	359	1.7	19.0	87	462	1.9	24.5	100
COSMOPOLITAN	9329	3369	8.4	36.1	88	2955	11.3	31.7	119	2015	9.5	21.6	99	2798	11.7	30.0	123
COUNTRY HOME	2696	1407	3.5	52.2	128	650	2.5	24.1	90	551	2.6	20.4	94	574	2.4	21.3	87
COUNTRY LIVING	6773	2976	7.4	43.9	107	1825	7.0	26.9	101	1363	6.4	20.1	93	1571	6.6	23.2	95
DISCOVER	1349	561	1.4	41.6	102	347	1.3	25.7	96	298	1.4	22.1	101	327	1.4	24.3	99
EATING WELL	1154	530	1.3	45.9	112	355	1.4	30.8	115	249	1.2	21.5	99	353	1.5	30.5	125
EBONY	6338	2572	6.4	40.6	99	2046	7.9	32.3	121	1550	7.3	24.5	112	1865	7.8	29.4	120
ELLE	2171	800	2.0	36.9	90	732	2.8	33.7	126	764	3.6	35.2	162	643	2.7	29.6	121
ENTERTAINMENT WEEKLY	2389	1069	2.7	44.8	109	562	2.2	23.5	88	595	2.8	24.9	115	593	2.5	24.8	101
ENTREPRENEUR	598	*253	0.6	42.3	103	*219	0.8	36.5	137	**71	0.3	11.9	55	**128	0.5	21.4	87
ESQUIRE	737	377	0.9	51.2	125	316	1.2	42.8	161	*152	0.7	20.6	95	*205	0.9	27.8	114
ESSENCE	3744	1619	4.1	43.2	106	1157	4.4	30.9	116	970	4.6	25.9	119	1146	4.8	30.6	125
FAMILY CIRCLE	15990	7184	18.0	44.9	110	4334	16.6	27.1	102	3096	14.6	19.4	89	3869	16.2	24.2	99
FAMILY CIRCLE/MCCALL'S (GRS)	28237	12823	32.1	45.4	111	7929	30.5	28.1	105	5630	26.5	19.9	92	7079	29.6	25.1	102
THE FAMILY HANDYMAN	763	386	1.0	50.6	124	*216	0.8	28.3	106	*199	0.9	26.0	120	*145	0.6	19.0	78
FIELD & STREAM	1540	648	1.6	42.0	103	551	2.1	35.8	134	333	1.6	21.6	99	334	1.4	21.7	88
FIELD & STREAM/OUTDOOR LIFE (GROSS)	2636	1127	2.8	42.8	105	902	3.5	34.2	128	531	2.5	20.1	93	579	2.4	22.0	90
FINANCIAL WORLD	255	**108	0.3	42.3	103	**55	0.2	21.5	81	**48	0.2	18.9	87	**45	0.2	17.5	72
FIRST FOR WOMEN	2356	996	2.5	42.3	103	819	3.1	34.8	130	570	2.7	24.2	111	716	3.0	30.4	124
FOOD & WINE	1562	710	1.8	45.4	111	454	1.7	29.1	109	368	1.7	23.5	108	402	1.7	25.7	105
FORBES	999	453	1.1	45.4	111	372	1.4	37.2	140	187	0.9	18.7	86	*206	0.9	20.6	84
FORTUNE	914	370	0.9	40.5	99	204	0.8	22.3	84	*198	0.9	21.7	100	*202	0.8	22.1	90
GQ/GENTLEMEN'S QUARTERLY	1069	493	1.2	46.2	113	395	1.5	36.9	139	334	1.6	31.3	144	322	1.3	30.1	123
GLAMOUR	6854	2653	6.6	38.7	95	1925	7.4	28.1	105	1597	7.5	23.3	107	1805	7.6	26.3	108
GOLF DIGEST	1049	483	1.2	46.0	113	*191	0.7	18.2	68	267	1.3	25.5	117	273	1.1	26.0	106
GOLF MAGAZINE	697	234	0.6	33.5	82	*159	0.6	22.7	85	*124	0.6	17.9	82	**134	0.6	19.2	78
GOOD HOUSEKEEPING	17602	7969	19.9	45.3	111	4885	18.8	27.7	104	3450	16.2	19.6	90	4353	18.2	24.7	101
GOURMET	1973	915	2.3	46.4	113	502	1.9	25.4	95	401	1.9	20.3	93	454	1.9	23.0	94
GUNS & AMMO	741	*332	0.8	44.8	109	*275	1.1	37.1	139	**129	0.6	17.4	80	*242	1.0	32.7	134
HACHETTE MAG. NETWORK (GRS)	22897	10312	25.8	45.0	110	6556	25.2	28.6	107	5345	25.2	23.3	107	5537	23.2	24.2	99
HACHETTE MEN'S PACKAGE (GRS)	2759	1093	2.7	39.6	97	899	3.5	32.6	122	661	3.1	24.0	110	565	2.4	20.5	84
HARPER'S BAZAAR	2029	794	2.0	39.1	96	602	2.3	29.7	111	531	2.5	26.2	120	635	2.7	31.3	128
HEARST HOME BUY (GROSS)	14198	6211	15.5	43.7	107	3634	14.0	25.6	96	3089	14.5	21.8	100	3562	14.9	25.1	102
HOME	2591	1111	2.8	42.9	105	755	2.9	29.1	109	685	3.2	26.4	122	651	2.7	25.1	103
HOME MECHANIX	389	*207	0.5	53.2	130	**108	0.4	27.7	104	**84	0.4	21.7	100	**144	0.6	37.0	151
HOT ROD	415	*177	0.4	42.7	104	**95	0.4	22.9	86	*101	0.5	24.2	111	**104	0.4	25.0	102
HOUSE BEAUTIFUL	3974	1778	4.4	44.7	109	971	3.7	24.4	92	864	4.1	21.7	100	1171	4.9	29.5	120
HUNTING	422	*202	0.5	47.9	117	*138	0.5	32.7	123	**90	0.4	21.4	98	**123	0.5	29.2	119
INC.	408	*217	0.5	53.3	130	**74	0.3	18.2	68	**35	0.2	8.5	39	**23	0.1	5.6	23
INSIDE SPORTS	*243	**69	0.2	28.3	69	*101	0.4	41.5	156	**50	0.2	20.5	94	**122	0.5	50.2	205
JET	4938	1831	4.6	37.1	91	1663	6.4	33.7	126	1197	5.6	24.2	111	1424	6.0	28.8	118
KIPLINGER'S PERS FINANCE MAG	599	224	0.6	37.3	91	*125	0.5	20.9	78	*135	0.6	22.6	104	**78	0.3	13.0	53
LADIES' HOME JOURNAL	13233	5819	14.6	44.0	108	3504	13.5	26.5	99	2836	13.4	21.4	99	3419	14.3	25.8	106
LIFE	6028	2360	5.9	39.1	96	1796	6.9	29.8	112	1159	5.5	19.2	88	1495	6.3	24.8	101
LOS ANGELES TIMES MAGAZINE	1738	637	1.6	36.7	90	521	2.0	30.0	112	365	1.7	21.0	97	441	1.8	25.4	104
MADEMOISELLE	4102	1656	4.1	40.4	99	1323	5.1	32.3	121	1171	5.5	28.5	131	1187	5.0	28.9	118
MCCALL'S	12247	5639	14.1	46.0	113	3595	13.8	29.4	110	2534	11.9	20.7	95	3210	13.4	26.2	107
MEN'S FITNESS	*208	**61	0.2	29.3	72	**93	0.4	44.8	168	**48	0.2	22.8	105	**45	0.2	21.5	88
MEN'S HEALTH	276	**122	0.3	44.2	108	**97	0.4	35.2	132	**72	0.3	26.2	120	**90	0.4	32.5	133
MONEY	2929	1385	3.5	47.3	116	850	3.3	29.0	109	590	2.8	20.2	93	724	3.0	24.7	101
MOTOR TREND	*195	**49	0.1	25.3	62	**46	0.2	23.6	89	**30	0.1	15.6	72	**43	0.2	22.0	90
MUSCLE & FITNESS	796	203	0.5	25.6	62	194	0.7	24.4	91	*169	0.8	21.2	98	*260	1.1	32.7	134
NATIONAL ENQUIRER	11447	4682	11.7	40.9	100	3414	13.1	29.8	112	2647	12.5	23.1	106	3152	13.2	27.5	112
NATIONAL ENQUIRER/STAR (GRS)	19294	7908	19.8	41.0	100	5770	22.2	29.9	112	4593	21.6	23.8	109	5397	22.6	28.0	114
NATIONAL EXAMINER	2384	935	2.3	39.2	96	556	2.1	23.3	87	457	2.2	19.2	88	636	2.7	26.7	109
NATIONAL GEOGRAPHIC	11028	4522	11.3	41.0	100	3088	11.9	28.0	105	2302	10.8	20.9	96	2661	11.1	24.1	99
NATIONAL GEOGRAPHIC TRAVELER	791	325	0.8	41.1	101	190	0.7	24.1	90	*177	0.8	22.3	103	*96	0.4	12.1	50
NATURAL HISTORY	680	285	0.7	41.9	102	*149	0.6	21.9	82	*145	0.7	21.4	98	*89	0.4	13.1	54
NEWSWEEK	8566	3288	8.2	38.4	94	2409	9.2	28.1	105	1541	7.3	18.0	83	2204	9.2	25.7	105
NEW WOMAN	2713	1123	2.8	41.4	101	723	2.8	26.6	100	644	3.0	23.7	109	722	3.0	26.6	109
NEW YORK	722	269	0.7	37.3	91	183	0.7	25.4	95	*123	0.6	17.1	78	*161	0.7	22.3	91
THE NEW YORKER	1573	660	1.7	42.0	103	433	1.7	27.5	103	359	1.7	22.8	105	354	1.5	22.5	92
THE N.Y. TIMES DAILY	1565	741	1.9	47.3	116	425	1.6	27.1	102	469	2.2	30.0	138	449	1.9	28.7	117
THE N.Y. TIMES MAGAZINE	1984	857	2.1	43.2	106	539	2.1	27.2	102	506	2.4	25.5	117	492	2.1	24.7	101
OMNI	713	273	0.7	38.3	94	*170	0.7	23.8	89	*158	0.7	22.2	102	*183	0.8	25.6	105
ORGANIC GARDENING	1447	714	1.8	49.3	121	467	1.8	32.3	121	305	1.4	21.1	97	408	1.7	28.2	115
OUTDOOR LIFE	1095	479	1.2	43.8	107	*351	1.3	32.1	120	*198	0.9	18.1	83	*246	1.0	22.4	92

newspapers were the primary medium, and publishers were often guilty of inflating their delivery. Today there is far less chicanery, due in part to ABC's existence. Consequently, audit reports are currently more often used for analysis than for verification.

EXHIBIT 11.14 SIMMONS AUDIENCE DUPLICATION REPORT

0301 M 3 PAGE 31	DUPLICATION OF AVERAGE ISSUE AUDIENCES SUMMARY / ADULT FEMALES	0301 M 3 PAGE 31

ROWS - MADEMOISELLE TO POPULAR MECHANICS   (IN THOUSANDS)   COLUMNS - POPULAR SCIENCE TO SESAME STREET MAGAZINE

	U.S. TOTAL	POPULAR SCIENCE	PRE-VENTION	READER'S DIGEST	REDBOOK	ROAD & TRACK	ROLLING STONE	SASSY	SCIEN-TIFIC AMERICAN	SELF	SESAME STREET MAGAZINE
SINGLE ISSUE AUD.	97676	744	5184	21661	9087	579	2338	1513	599	2500	2637
COVERAGE	100.0	0.8	5.3	22.2	9.3	0.6	2.4	1.5	0.6	2.6	2.7
TWO ISSUE NET AUD.	97676	1108	7134	26875	12800	741	3240	2205	890	3367	3300
COVERAGE	100.0	1.1	7.3	27.5	13.1	0.8	3.3	2.3	0.9	3.4	3.4
NET UNDUPLICATED											
MADEMOISELLE	5888	4793	8881	24930	12357	4643	6004	5166	4648	6064	6639
MCCALL'S	16947	12870	16217	29397	18211	12686	14124	13477	12793	14227	14353
MEN'S FITNESS	274	951	5372	21796	9273	784	2538	1711	807	2696	2840
MEN'S HEALTH	478	1002	5448	21843	9346	853	2582	1776	875	2761	2911
MONEY	3680	3528	7631	23595	11642	3427	5180	4365	3502	5266	5400
MOTOR TREND	361	931	5367	21814	9246	745	2501	1707	789	2686	2825
MUSCLE & FITNESS	1175	1523	5902	22253	9773	1336	3004	2225	1394	3098	3334
NATIONAL ENQUIRER	15295	12077	15959	29957	19084	11917	13270	12674	12044	13502	13586
NAT. ENQUIRER/STAR (NT)	19318	15762	19453	32616	22263	15611	16898	16300	15762	17036	17159
NATIONAL EXAMINER	3319	3091	7335	23210	11061	2915	4551	3841	2979	4761	4888
NATIONAL GEOGRAPHIC	14486	11480	14964	28251	18720	11354	12965	12443	11396	13261	13184
NATIONAL GEO. TRAVELER	1077	1507	5858	22147	9784	1347	3100	2304	1374	3235	3399
NATURAL HISTORY	975	1403	5793	22109	9687	1258	3000	2192	1224	3146	3305
NEWSWEEK	11914	9100	12807	27385	16487	8957	10536	9940	9049	10651	10933
NEW WOMAN	4022	3417	7570	23596	11256	3261	4903	4089	3296	4746	5273
NEW YORK	1038	1465	5859	22230	9731	1300	3018	2216	1289	3177	3345
THE NEW YORKER	2356	2297	6565	22797	10485	2147	3803	3052	2121	4020	4162
THE N.Y. TIMES DAILY	2168	2281	6647	22974	10476	2127	3800	3057	2120	4026	4192
THE N.Y. TIMES MAGAZINE	2714	2708	7050	23281	10805	2554	4216	3427	2524	4373	4593
OMNI	1038	1450	5830	22109	9664	1290	3019	2208	1236	3174	3343
ORGANIC GARDENING	1909	2154	6382	22503	10364	2015	3749	2949	1997	3913	4019
OUTDOOR LIFE	1544	1745	6172	22317	9947	1593	3403	2601	1652	3539	3657
PARADE MAGAZINE	49122	41577	44048	52804	46203	41502	42357	41987	41447	42360	42664
PARENTING	3878	3449	7779	23714	11381	3242	4935	4174	3321	5105	4836
PARENTS	6969	5565	9897	25245	13071	5390	6971	6310	5443	7103	6821
PENTHOUSE	614	1173	5591	21980	9388	955	2732	1943	1035	2892	3005
PEOPLE	27904	19948	23103	35650	25813	19810	20884	20513	19908	21032	21415
PETERSEN'S 4WHEEL & O-RD	440	1068	5489	21884	9336	841	2650	1826	918	2810	2923
PLAYBOY	1494	1716	6175	22367	9966	1498	3265	2538	1632	3491	3573
POPULAR MECHANICS	1116	1295	5851	22139	9699	1235	3081	2267	1352	3224	3349
DUPLICATED											
MADEMOISELLE	2316	54	404	833	832	39	436	449	53	538	100
MCCALL'S	7547	121	1213	4511	3123	141	461	282	53	520	531
MEN'S FITNESS	143	2	20	73	22	4	8	10	0	13	6
MEN'S HEALTH	75	19	12	94	17	3	32	13	0	16	3
MONEY	1979	146	481	995	374	82	87	77	26	164	166
MOTOR TREND	28	8	11	42	35	30	32	0	5	9	7
MUSCLE & FITNESS	417	18	77	203	110	40	131	84	2	198	99
NATIONAL ENQUIRER	7600	115	672	3151	1450	110	515	286	2	446	499
NAT. ENQUIRER/STAR (NT)	11029	156	905	4219	1998	143	614	387	11	638	651
NATIONAL EXAMINER	1449	37	233	834	410	48	171	56	4	123	132
NATIONAL GEOGRAPHIC	7571	293	1248	4438	1395	254	401	98	231	267	481
NATIONAL GEO. TRAVELER	505	29	116	305	94	24	29	0	17	57	29
NATURAL HISTORY	385	22	71	232	79	2	17	1	55	34	12
NEWSWEEK	5218	211	943	2842	1166	189	368	140	117	415	270
NEW WOMAN	1405	41	327	778	544	32	148	138	16	468	77
NEW YORK	405	1	46	153	77	1	42	18	32	45	14
THE NEW YORKER	790	20	191	436	174	5	108	34	51	53	47
THE N.Y. TIMES DAILY	962	29	102	251	176	17	104	21	44	39	10
THE N.Y. TIMES MAGAZINE	1255	21	118	364	266	10	106	70	59	111	29
OMNI	389	8	67	265	136	3	33	18	77	40	8
ORGANIC GARDENING	985	37	248	604	169	11	36	11	49	34	65
OUTDOOR LIFE	646	95	107	439	235	81	30	7	42	57	75
PARADE MAGAZINE	33214	336	2304	10025	4051	245	1149	694	320	1309	1141
PARENTING	1592	31	140	682	441	73	138	74	13	130	536
PARENTS	2807	68	174	1303	904	78	255	91	44	285	704
PENTHOUSE	259	7	29	117	135	61	42	6	0	44	68
PEOPLE	11039	268	1552	5482	2745	241	925	472	163	940	693
PETERSEN'S 4WHEEL & O-RD	210	1	20	102	75	64	13	12	6	15	39
PLAYBOY	583	67	48	333	160	120	111	13	6	48	102
POPULAR MECHANICS	418	217	99	288	155	112	23	13	14	43	54

The Audit Bureau of Circulations reports on both magazines and, newspapers, and their audited circulations are the authority upon which advertising rates are based. To become a member of ABC's consumer magazine group, a magazine must demonstrate that at least 70 percent of its circulation is paid circulation. ABC issues three different reports: a twice-yearly publisher's statement; a summary compilation of these statements, called FAS-FAX; and an annual audit report on each magazine. The publisher's statement and the annual ABC audit report follow the same format (Figure 11.1).

The first reported data identifies the magazine's circulation and verifies whether or not the magazine has met its promised rate base. The data, however, immediately raises analytical questions since the statement reports the number of subscriptions and single copy sales. Some would argue that subscriptions describe loyal, committed, involved readers, and others would argue that single copy sales demonstrate immediacy, relevance, wantedness, and utility. Both arguments are sound, and it is up to the planner to weight the significance of these characteristics to a brand's marketing circumstances, and then to use the information in comparing competitive magazines.

There is less argument over the meaning of how subscriptions are sold. The assumption is that the greater the percentage of subscriptions sold at full price, without premiums, with longer commitments, and with a high renewal rate, the greater the value of the magazine to the reader. Of course, all subscriptions are sold at a price discounted from newsstand costs. The deeper the discount, the more reliant on premiums, the shorter the subscription time, and the lower the renewal rate for a magazine, the more a planner is convinced that the magazine's circulation is soft and the publication is in trouble.

Finally, the reports provide detailed information on geographic distribution. This data can be issued to compare a magazine's regional strengths with the brand's geographic strategy. It also enables the planner to compare and contrast various possible magazine selections on the same strategic grounds.

Editorial Composition

Hall's Magazine Editorial Reports (Exhibit 11.15), published by Russell Hall, is the primary source for comparing the editorial content of magazines. Competitive presentations by magazine representatives and the planner's own reading familiarity are supportive sources of information. Hall's, however, provides the view of an objective observer who uses a consistent vocabulary across magazine categories. Not only do these reports enable the planner to deliver on the often promised "compatible editorial" but, like circulation analysis, the editorial profile reflects why consumers choose to read the magazine. A higher competitive editorial profile for food, or travel, or health, or fashion might easily encourage a planner to choose one magazine in a service class over another.

NEWSPAPERS

The Audit Bureau of Circulations, as already noted, provides the most basic and credible circulation data on newspapers. Many of the same evaluation concepts are utilized in

FIGURE 11.1 PROTOTYPE ABC STATEMENT

MAGAZINE PUBLISHER'S STATEMENT
For 6 months ended Month, Year

Audit Bureau
of Circulations

PROTOTYPE
CITY, STATE ZIP CODE

Subject to audit by the Audit Bureau of Circulations, 900 N. Meacham Road, Schaumburg, IL 60173-4968

Class, Industry or Field Served: General interest.

1. AVERAGE PAID CIRCULATION

		% of Total
Total Average Paid Circulation:	**404,790**	
Advertising Rate Base:	400,000	
% Above/Below Rate Base (+/−)	+1.2	
Total Average Analyzed Non-Paid Circulation:	16,427	
Total Average Non-Analyzed Non-Paid Circulation:	12,050	
Subscriptions: Individual	295,069	72.9
Single Copy Sales:	109,721	27.1
		100.0

NOTE: This publication also provides an ABC Publisher's Statement analyzing its non-paid circulation.

1a. AVERAGE PAID CIRCULATION of Regional, Metro and Demographic Editions

Edition & number of issues		Edition & number of issues		Edition & number of issues	
Eastern (6)	149,772	Central (6)	161,916	Western (6)	93,102

2. PAID CIRCULATION by Issues

Issue	Subscriptions	Single Copy Sales	Total Paid	Issue	Subscriptions	Single Copy Sales	Total Paid
July	285,960	116,637	402,597	Oct.	301,738	105,764	407,502
Aug.	297,181	107,749	404,930	Nov.	290,590	109,495	400,085
Sept.	300,315	102,700	403,015	Dec.	294,630	115,979	410,609

PROTOTYPE

Magazine Publisher's Statement

For 6 months ended Month, Year

FIGURE 11.1 PROTOTYPE ABC STATEMENT (CONT.)

PROTOTYPE

ANALYSIS OF TOTAL NEW AND RENEWAL SUBSCRIPTIONS

Gross subscriptions sold during 6 month period ended Month, Year

3.	AUTHORIZED PRICES:		%
	(a) Basic Prices: Single Copy: $1.50.		
	Subscriptions: 1 yr. $12.00; 2 yrs. $22.00; 3 yrs. $30.00.	69,431	35.0
	(b) Higher than basic prices:	None	
	(c) Lower than basic prices: 1 yr. $7.00, $8.00, $8.99; 2 yrs. $13.99	128,924	65.0
	(d) Association subscription prices:	None	
	Total Subscriptions Sold in Period	198,355	100.0

4.	DURATION OF SUBSCRIPTIONS SOLD:		
	(a) One to eleven months (1 to 11 issues)	12,486	6.3
	(b) Twelve months (12 issues)	161,643	81.5
	(c) Thirteen to twenty-four months	1,861	0.9
	(d) Twenty-five months and more	22,365	11.3
	Total Subscriptions Sold in Period	198,355	100.0

5.	CHANNELS OF SUBSCRIPTION SALES:		
	(a) Ordered by mail-and/or direct request (may include direct mail, renewal mail, insert cards, television and direct mail agents, etc.)	138,101	69.6
	(b) Ordered through salespeople:		
	1. Catalog agencies and individual agents	17,444	8.8
	2. Publisher's own and independent agencies' salespeople	30,093	15.2
	3. Members of schools, churches, fraternal and similar organizations	12,717	6.4
	(c) Association members	None	
	Total Subscriptions Sold in Period	198,355	100.0

6.	USE OF PREMIUMS:		
	(a) Ordered without premium	186,434	94.0
	(b) Ordered with material reprinted from this publication, See Par. 11(a)	5,791	2.9
	(c) Ordered with other premium, See Par. 11(b)	6,130	3.1
	Total Subscriptions Sold in Period	198,355	100.0

ADDITIONAL CIRCULATION INFORMATION

7.	POST EXPIRATION COPIES INCLUDED IN PAID CIRCULATION (PAR. 1):		%
	(a) Average number of copies served on subscriptions not more than three months after expiration, See Par. 11	2,673	0.9

8. VARIANCE REPORT:

Latest Released Audit Report Issued for 12 months ended Month, Year
Variation from Publisher's Statements

Audit Period Ended	Rate Base	Audit Report	Publisher's Statements	Difference	Percentage of Difference
06-30-(Year)	335,000	343,600	342,900	700	0.2
06-30-(Year)	325,000	328,881	330,700	-1,819	-0.6
06-30-(Year)	325,000	331,446	335,207	-3,761	-1.1
06-30-(Year)	325,000	303,611	302,912	699	0.2
06-30-(Year)	(a)	308,402	309,601	-1,199	-.0.4

(a) Effective 01/01/(Year) changed from 300,000 to 325,000

9. U.S. PAID CIRCULATION BY ABCD COUNTY SIZE for the Month, Year Issue

Month, Year issue used in establishing percentages.

Data for coterminous 48 states.

County Size	% of U.S. Households	Total Circulation	% of Total Circulation	% Circulation/ % Households
A	41	145,969	37.6	92
B	30	124,561	32.1	107
C	15	67,439	17.3	115
D	14	50,588	13.0	93

County Size Group Definition by the A.C. Nielsen Company

FIGURE 11.1PROTOTYPE ABC STATEMENT (CONT.)

---

10. **GEOGRAPHIC ANALYSIS OF TOTAL PAID CIRCULATION** for the Month, Year Issue

Paid circulation of this issue was 0.7% greater than the total average paid circulation.

STATE	Subs.	Single Copy Sales	TOTAL	% of Circ.
Maine	2,144	619	2,763	
New Hampshire	2,016	588	2,604	
Vermont	1,037	352	1,389	
Massachusetts	6,750	2,512	9,262	
Rhode Island	1,087	432	1,519	
Connecticut	4,907	1,345	6,252	
NEW ENGLAND	**17,941**	**5,848**	**23,789**	**6.1**
New York	18,594	6,688	25,282	
New Jersey	8,834	3,121	11,955	
Pennsylvania	15,153	4,502	19,655	
MIDDLE ATLANTIC	**42,581**	**14,311**	**56,892**	**14.6**
Ohio	14,500	4,017	18,517	
Indiana	7,598	2,178	9,776	
Illinois	17,086	3,531	20,617	
Michigan	12,654	3,882	16,536	
Wisconsin	8,402	2,189	10,591	
EAST N. CENTRAL	**60,240**	**15,797**	**76,037**	**19.4**
Minnesota	8,018	1,916	9,934	
Iowa	6,341	1,345	7,686	
Missouri	5,470	1,630	7,100	
North Dakota	1,393	356	1,749	
South Dakota	1,287	317	1,604	
Nebraska	2,344	507	2,851	
Kansas	3,914	973	4,887	
WEST N. CENTRAL	**28,767**	**7,044**	**35,811**	**9.2**
Delaware	857	248	1,105	
Maryland	5,013	1,638	6,651	
District of Columbia	426	338	764	
Virginia	5,520	2,376	7,896	
West Virginia	1,994	580	2,574	
North Carolina	5,889	1,586	7,475	
South Carolina	2,616	941	3,557	
Georgia	5,106	1,753	6,859	
Florida	10,803	5,289	16,092	
SOUTH ATLANTIC	**38,224**	**14,749**	**52,973**	**13.6**

STATE	Subs.	Single Copy Sales	TOTAL	% of Circ.
Kentucky	3,166	774	3,940	
Tennessee	4,383	1,420	5,803	
Alabama	3,012	899	3,911	
Mississippi	1,729	735	2,464	
EAST S. CENTRAL	**12,290**	**3,828**	**16,118**	**4.1**
Arkansas	2,060	447	2,507	
Louisiana	3,733	1,374	5,107	.
Oklahoma	4,922	1,553	6,475	
Texas	16,243	6,845	23,088	
WEST S. CENTRAL	**26,958**	**10,219**	**37,177**	**9.5**
Montana	1,479	491	1,970	
Idaho	1,587	503	2,090	
Wyoming	1,056	330	1,386	
Colorado	5,470	2,222	7,692	
New Mexico	1,964	753	2,717	
Arizona	4,047	1,452	5,499	
Utah	1,665	886	2,551	
Nevada	1,371	610	1,981	
MOUNTAIN	**18,639**	**7,247**	**25,886**	**6.6**
Alaska	815	436	1,251	
Washington	6,272	2,549	8,821	
Oregon	3,353	1,252	4,605	
California	36,154	14,264	50,418	
Hawaii	668	455	1,123	
PACIFIC	**47,262**	**18,956**	**66,218**	**16.9**
Miscellaneous				
Unclassified				
UNITED STATES	**292,902**	**97,999**	**390,901**	**100.0**
U.S. Circ. Percent of Grand Total				95.9
Poss. & Other Areas	284	38	322	0.1
U.S. & POSS., etc.	**293,186**	**98,037**	**391,223**	**96.0**
Canada	7,438	6,327	13,765	3.4
Foreign	873	1,236	2,109	0.5
Unclassified				
Military or Civilian Personnel Overseas	241	164	405	0.1
GRAND TOTAL	**301,738**	**105,764**	**407,502**	**100.0**

Geographic Distribution of % Circulation ÷ % Population

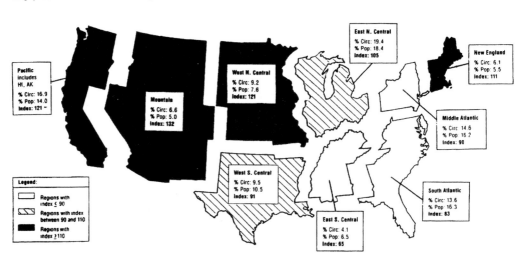

East N. Central
% Circ: 19.4
% Pop: 18.4
Index: 105

New England
% Circ: 6.1
% Pop: 5.5
Index: 111

Pacific includes HI, AK
% Circ: 16.9
% Pop: 14.0
Index: 121 ~

West N. Central
% Circ: 9.2
% Pop: 7.6
Index: 121

Mountain
% Circ: 6.6
% Pop: 5.0
Index: 132

Middle Atlantic
% Circ: 14.6
% Pop: 16.2
Index: 90

West S. Central
% Circ: 9.5
% Pop: 10.5
Index: 91

South Atlantic
% Circ: 13.6
% Pop: 16.3
Index: 83

East S. Central
% Circ: 4.1
% Pop: 6.5
Index: 65

Legend:
☐ Regions with index ≤ 90
▨ Regions with index between 90 and 110
■ Regions with index ≥ 110

FIGURE 11.1 PROTOTYPE ABC STATEMENT (CONT.)

11.	EXPLANATORY:

(a) Par. 6(b): A book entitled "Prototype's Greatest Articles," which consisted of articles reprinted from previous issues, with no advertised or stated value, was offered with 1 yr. subscriptions at $12.00.

(b) Par. 6(c): A duffelbag, with no advertised or stated value, was offered with subscriptions sold at basic prices.

(c) A sweepstakes contest was conducted during this statement period in which prizes worth $10,000.00 were awarded.

(d) A sweepstakes collection contest was conducted during this statement period in which cash and merchandise prizes were offered with 3,604 paid-in-full subscriptions.

Total expirations during 12 months May 1, (Year) - April 30, (Year)	236,219
Total renewals of these expirations	171,602
12-month renewal percentage	72.6%

Post Expiration Copies - Under ABC Rules, copies served to paid subscribers may be reported as paid circulation, provided the issues served are consecutive within three months of expiration.

ABC Publisher's Statement - This report has not been audited but has been compiled by the publisher in a format approved by ABC. An audit of the publisher's records will be issued by ABC reflecting differences, if any, from the Publisher's Statement.

12.	**FIVE YEAR ANNUAL TRENDS:** Total average paid circulation as reported in June and December Publisher's Statements

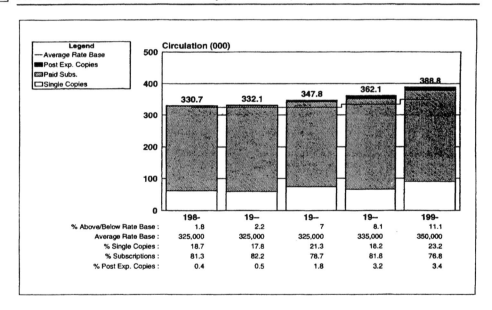

	198-	19—	19—	19—	199-
% Above/Below Rate Base :	1.8	2.2	7	8.1	11.1
Average Rate Base :	325,000	325,000	325,000	335,000	350,000
% Single Copies :	18.7	17.8	21.3	18.2	23.2
% Subscriptions :	81.3	82.2	78.7	81.8	76.8
% Post Exp. Copies :	0.4	0.5	1.8	3.2	3.4

We certify that to the best of our knowledge all data set forth in this Publisher's Statement are true and report circulation in accordance with Audit Bureau of Circulations' Bylaws and Rules.   04-0000-0

PROTOTYPE, published by Company Name, Address, ZIP Code.

NAME	NAME	<u>Sales Offices:</u>
Title	Title	New York 212-555-0000
Date Signed,		Chicago 312-555-0000
		Los Angeles 415-555-0000

EXHIBIT 11.15 HALL'S MAGAZINE EDITORIAL REPORTS

COMPARATIVE REPORT

JANUARY-APRIL 1995

PAGE #	MAGAZINES	# ISSUES	HOME FURNISHING			SPORTS, HOBBIES RECREATIONS			TRAVEL & TRANSPORTATION			WEARING APPAREL			CULTURE/ HUMANITIES		
			LINES	PAGES	%	LINES	PAGES	%	LINES	PAGES	%	LINES	PAGES	%	LINES	PAGES	%
42	VOGUE	4	12641	30.1	5.0	1898	4.5	0.8	5336	12.7	2.1	128603	306.2	51.0	23793	56.7	9.4
43	W	4	11603	17.0	3.4	5254	7.7	1.5	21791	31.9	6.4	153663	224.7	45.0	12810	18.7	3.8
44	DETAILS	4	4746	11.3	2.7	9022	21.5	5.1	6176	14.7	3.5	48453	115.4	27.4	57541	137.0	32.5
45	ESQUIRE	4	840	2.0	0.5	10095	24.0	6.0	4805	11.4	2.8	27822	66.2	16.5	48767	116.1	28.9
46	GENTLEMEN'S QUARTERLY	4	2555	6.1	1.3	29478	70.2	15.4	9004	21.4	4.7	57538	137.0	30.0	16202	38.6	8.5
47	MENS' HEALTH	3	780	1.9	0.8	10354	24.7	10.4	4659	11.1	4.7	6166	14.7	6.2	16993	40.5	17.1
48	PLAYBOY	4	6072	14.5	2.6	7257	17.3	3.1	3571	8.5	1.5	13032	31.0	5.5	45464	108.2	19.2
49	COLONIAL HOMES	2	39569	94.2	53.0	146	.3		3940	9.4	5.3				7994	19.0	10.7
50	COUNTRY LIVING	4	64615	153.8	41.7	805	1.9	0.5	8876	21.1	5.7	420	1.0	0.3	7211	17.2	4.7
51	BETTER HOMES & GARDENS	4	39221	93.4	22.7	70	0.2	0.2	1767	4.2	1.2	1240	3.0	0.8	2887	6.9	1.9
52	BH&G SIP BUILDING IDEAS	1	6532	15.6	17.6												
53	BH&G SIP DECORATING	1	35886	85.4	49.3										621	1.5	1.4
54	BH&G SIP DO IT YOURSELF	1	10255	24.4	25.3												
55	BH&G KITCHEN&BATH IDEAS	1	25649	61.1	65.2				858	2.0	1.0	429	1.0		105	.3	0.2
56	BH&G REMODELING IDEAS	1	7679	18.3	19.6												
57	AMERICAN HOMESTYLE	2	25098	59.8	37.8										5754	13.4	6.6
58	ELLE DECOR	2	55394	129.1	63.9	420	1.0	0.3							910	2.2	0.9
59	HOME	3	45601	108.6	44.3		1.0			2.0	1.0		1.0	0.5	6732	16.0	4.7
60	HOUSE BEAUTIFUL	3	73641	175.3	51.1	1144	1.0	0.3	4628	11.0	3.2	459	1.1	0.3	462	1.1	0.7
61	METROPOLITAN HOME	2	33801	78.8	51.8	1144	2.7	1.1	1750	4.1	2.7				2788	6.5	2.6
62	MARTHA STEWART LIVING	4	28514	66.5	26.7	1144	2.7	1.1	715	1.7	0.7	1452	3.4	1.4	7763	18.5	4.5
63	SOUTHERN LIVING	4	20309	48.4	11.8	2157	5.1	1.3	42491	101.2	24.8				2579	6.1	1.9
64	SUNSET	3	5160	12.3	3.8	4392	10.5	3.2	30044	71.5	22.0						
65	NEW CHOICES FOR RET LIV	3	2055	4.9	2.8	173	0.4	0.2	10934	26.0	14.8	610	1.5	0.8	16093	38.3	21.8
66	READER'S DIGEST	4	1300	7.1	1.1	2839	15.6	2.4	2234	12.3	1.9				39792	218.6	33.3
67	ARCHITECTURAL DIGEST	4	114978	273.8	54.5	1057	2.5	0.5	4907	11.7	2.3				10329	24.6	4.9
68	CONDE NAST TRAVELER	4	330	0.8	0.2	3865	9.2	2.2	123929	295.1	71.3				9569	22.8	5.5
69	GOURMET	4	4412	10.5	0.2	1775	4.2	1.2	59876	142.6	39.0	4983	11.9	2.9	4415	10.5	2.9
70	FOOD & WINE	4	13392	31.9	12.3	1482	3.5	1.4	11811	28.1	10.8				114	0.3	0.1
71	LIFE	4				10492	25.0	9.6	4445	10.6	4.1	4592	10.9	4.2	21943	52.2	20.0
72	NATIONAL GEO TRAVELER	2				8755	20.8	10.7	54982	130.9	67.5				5111	12.2	6.3
73	OUTSIDE	4	174	0.4	0.1	59683	142.1	40.5	23679	56.4	16.1	4400	10.5	3.0	18653	44.4	12.7
74	TRAVEL HOLIDAY	3				3194	7.6	3.2	63709	151.7	64.1				14043	33.4	14.1
75	TRAVEL & LEISURE	4	2672	6.4	1.6	10940	26.0	6.5	120495	286.9	71.9		7.9	2.0	6536	15.6	3.9
76	TOWN & COUNTRY	4	15416	35.9	9.1	6275	14.6	3.7	22367	52.1	13.2	3325	72.4	18.3	19333	45.1	11.4
77	VANITY FAIR	4	5041	12.0	2.5	3615	8.6	1.8	3360	8.0	2.0	31081	3.1	0.6	40832	97.2	20.1
78	VICTORIA	4	46850	111.5	31.6	1563	3.7	1.1	6818	16.2	4.6	13303	31.7	9.0	16522	39.3	11.2
79	FIELD & STREAM	4	235	0.6	0.2	64599	153.8	55.1	8676	20.7	7.4	351	0.8	0.3	5826	13.9	5.0
80	OUTDOOR LIFE	4	210	0.5	0.1	71969	171.4	60.8	11104	26.4	9.4	1759	4.2	1.5	3011	7.2	2.5
81	SPORTS AFIELD	4	60	0.1	0.1	65281	155.4	59.5	5591	13.3	5.1	3185	7.6	2.9	7088	16.9	6.5
82	FAMILY HANDYMAN	4	12793	30.5	13.8				4961	11.8	5.4				192	0.5	0.2
83	HOME MECHANIX	4	6123	14.6	8.5				11081	26.4	15.4						
84	POPULAR MECHANICS	3	12003	28.6	8.6	18399	43.8	13.2	44195	105.2	31.8	35	0.1	0.0	9388	22.4	6.8
85	POPULAR SCIENCE	4	16237	38.7	15.1	8263	19.7	7.7	30552	72.7	28.5	74	0.2	0.1	17281	41.1	16.1

272

Source: Hall's Magazine Reports, May, 1995. Used with permission.

analyzing newspapers as magazines. The major difference is that heavy newspaper advertisers are almost always most vitally interested in a newspaper's coverage of very specific geographic areas. Retailers know the towns and zip codes of their trading area and are vitally interested in gaining at least a 60 percent coverage of this pinpointed geography. Distributors know which counties are important to them. Thus, the ABC statement is heavily utilized to provide these locally oriented businesses with household coverage data.

ABC does not report demographic data. It is possible to imply this data from *Sales Management* or *Editor and Publisher* market reports, but in the end this process is not satisfying. In fifty-one major television markets, however, Scarborough's Newspaper Ratings Study (Exhibit 11.16) provides extensive demographic data not available in circulation audits. The report also provides unduplicated readership estimates on a two-issue and five-issue basis.

A research report of special interest to local retailers examining newspaper coverage, as well as to direct marketers, is PRIZM (Potential Rating Index of ZIP Markets), which has been keeping continuous records, developed from census data and consumer purchasing records, since 1983 on 37,000 ZIP code populations. They have classified each of these small geographic areas by psychographic and lifestyle characteristics with over forty symbolic names (for example, Blood Estates, Shotguns and Pickups, and so on). These clusters can then be correlated with newspaper circulations in the process of executing rather precise marketing strategies.

There are other widely available research resources, such as Monroe-Mendelsohn, which provides SMRB-like data on affluent households with income over $60,000, and ClusterPLUS, which provides PRIZM-like data. Researchers are also quite excited by the possibilities of consumer behavior research based on electronic checkouts at supermarkets, correlated with more precise media behavior data based on the same consumer's accessing of the electronic super highway. At the moment, however, the planner has many quite effective tools for projecting vehicle audiences and correlating these consumers with marketing's prospect data.

Costs and Vehicle Requirements

At the end of the day, planned advertising must be physically delivered to a vehicle's production center in a form the medium can utilize and in time for inclusion. The primary source of this information is Standard Rate and Data Service (SRDS). This source provides consumer data, organized by television markets, on household income, and expenditures in a manner similar to *Sales & Marketing Management Survey of Buying Power* and *Editor and Publisher Market Guide* (see chapter 4). The primary use of SRDS volumes, however, is for current cost information and mechanical requirements of nearly every available media vehicle. Some of SRDS's most useful volumes are:

EXHIBIT 11.16 1994 SCARBOROUGH REPORT

1994 Scarborough Report

NEW YORK MARKET   NA–2A   PAGE 1

PROJECTED NUMBERS IN HUNDREDS (00)

BASE: ADULTS IN NEW YORK DMA

BASIC DEMOGRAPHIC CHARACTERISTICS OF NEWSPAPER AUDIENCES

▀▀▀▀▀ SUNDAY NEWSPAPER AUDIENCES ▀▀▀▀▀

▀▀▀ AVERAGE ISSUE AUDIENCE ▀▀▀   ▀▀▀ 4 ISSUE CUME ▀▀▀

		TOTAL	NEWS	TIMES	NEWS-DAY	RECORD	STAR-LEDGER	NEWS	TIMES	NEWS-DAY	RECORD	STAR-LEDGER	ANY WEEKDAY	ANY SUNDAY
TOTAL		143752	31425	38107	25517	6411	18763	44795	52442	33929	8252	24124	100940	112316
	COVERAGE	100%	21.9	26.5	17.8	4.5	13.1	31.2	36.5	23.6	5.7	16.8	70.2	78.1
	COMPOSTN	100.0	100.0	100.0	100.0	100.0	100.0	100.0	100.0	100.0	100.0	100.0	100.0	100.0
SEX														
ADULT MEN		67599	14572	19365	11973	3079	9261	20944	25968	16264	4155	12083	50651	53356
	COVERAGE	100%	21.6	28.6	17.7	4.6	13.7	31.0	38.4	24.1	6.1	17.9	74.9	78.9
	COMPOSTN	47.0	46.4	50.8	46.9	48.0	49.4	46.8	49.5	47.9	50.4	50.1	50.2	47.5
	INDEX	100	99	108	100	102	105	99	105	102	107	107	107	101
ADULT WOMEN		76153	16853	18744	13546	3332	9502	23850	26483	17670	4100	12043	50289	58960
	COVERAGE	100%	22.1	24.6	17.8	4.4	12.5	31.3	34.8	23.2	5.4	15.8	66.0	77.4
	COMPOSTN	53.0	53.6	49.2	53.1	52.0	50.6	53.2	50.5	52.1	49.7	49.9	49.8	52.5
	INDEX	100	101	93	100	98	96	101	95	98	94	94	94	99
AGE														
18 – 24		18640	4233	3258	3227	568	2367	6331	5229	4238	816	3227	11489	13092
	COVERAGE	100%	22.7	17.5	17.3	3.0	12.7	34.0	28.1	22.7	4.4	17.3	61.6	70.2
	COMPOSTN	13.0	13.5	8.5	12.6	8.9	12.6	14.1	10.0	12.5	9.9	13.4	11.4	11.7
	INDEX	100	104	66	98	68	97	109	77	96	76	103	88	90
25 – 34		31247	6267	7937	5230	1260	3731	9245	10858	7212	1761	4918	20425	23302
	COVERAGE	100%	20.1	25.4	16.7	4.0	11.9	29.6	34.7	23.1	5.6	15.7	65.4	74.6
	COMPOSTN	21.7	19.9	20.8	20.5	19.6	19.9	20.6	20.7	21.3	21.3	20.4	20.2	20.7
	INDEX	100	92	96	94	90	91	95	95	98	98	94	93	95
35 – 44		30417	5641	9045	5580	1419	4074	8585	12636	7593	1764	5278	21697	24174
	COVERAGE	100%	18.5	29.7	18.3	4.7	13.4	28.2	41.5	25.0	5.8	17.4	71.3	79.5
	COMPOSTN	21.2	18.0	23.7	21.9	22.1	21.7	19.2	24.1	22.4	21.4	21.9	21.5	21.5
	INDEX	100	85	112	103	105	103	91	114	106	101	103	102	102
45 – 54		23228	5213	7084	4552	1258	3285	7634	9542	6101	1631	4000	17198	18764
	COVERAGE	100%	22.4	30.5	19.6	5.4	14.1	32.9	41.1	26.3	7.0	17.2	74.0	80.8
	COMPOSTN	16.2	16.6	18.6	17.8	19.6	17.5	17.0	18.2	18.0	19.8	16.6	17.0	16.7
	INDEX	100	103	115	110	121	108	105	113	111	122	103	105	103
55 – 64		16448	4237	4711	2961	771	2175	5413	5983	3704	931	2840	12487	13671
	COVERAGE	100%	25.8	28.6	18.0	4.7	13.2	32.9	36.4	22.5	5.7	17.3	75.9	83.1
	COMPOSTN	11.4	13.5	12.4	11.6	12.0	11.6	12.1	11.4	10.9	11.3	11.8	12.4	12.2
	INDEX	100	118	108	101	105	101	106	100	95	99	103	108	106
65 AND OVER		23773	5835	6074	3967	1137	3131	7630	8226	5086	1357	3865	17645	19315
	COVERAGE	100%	24.5	25.5	16.7	4.8	13.2	32.1	34.6	21.4	5.7	16.3	74.2	81.2
	COMPOSTN	16.5	18.6	15.9	15.5	17.7	16.7	17.0	15.7	15.0	16.4	16.0	17.5	17.2
	INDEX	100	112	96	94	107	101	103	95	91	99	97	106	104
MEDIAN AGE		42.1	44.2	43.7	42.6	44.7	43.0	42.8	42.9	42.1	43.8	42.2	43.5	43.1
MARITAL STATUS MARRIED		74701	15001	21496	14731	4019	10566	20929	28686	18905	4824	13200	55616	61515
	COVERAGE	100%	20.1	28.8	19.7	5.4	14.1	28.0	38.4	25.3	6.5	17.7	74.5	82.3
	COMPOSTN	52.0	47.7	56.4	57.7	62.7	56.3	46.7	54.7	55.7	58.5	54.7	55.1	54.8
	INDEX	100	92	109	111	121	108	90	105	107	112	105	106	105
SINGLE (NEVER MARRIED)		41837	9737	10713	6358	1347	4832	14057	15371	8799	2004	6491	27348	30621
	COVERAGE	100%	23.3	25.6	15.2	3.2	11.5	33.6	36.7	21.0	4.8	15.5	65.4	73.2
	COMPOSTN	29.1	31.0	28.1	24.9	21.0	25.8	31.4	29.3	25.9	24.3	26.9	27.1	27.3
	INDEX	100	106	97	86	72	88	108	101	89	83	92	93	94
DIVORCED OR SEPARATED		15509	3840	3502	2426	587	1806	5743	5038	3489	801	2502	10007	11252
	COVERAGE	100%	24.8	22.6	15.6	3.8	11.6	37.0	32.5	22.5	5.2	16.1	64.5	72.6
	COMPOSTN	10.8	12.2	9.2	9.5	9.2	9.6	12.8	9.6	10.3	9.7	10.4	9.9	10.0
	INDEX	100	113	85	88	85	89	119	89	95	90	96	92	93
WIDOWED		11706	2848	2397	2003	459	1561	4065	3359	2750	639	1941	7970	8929
	COVERAGE	100%	24.3	20.5	17.1	3.9	13.3	34.7	28.7	23.5	5.5	16.6	68.1	76.3
	COMPOSTN	8.1	9.1	6.3	7.8	7.2	8.3	9.1	6.4	8.1	7.7	8.0	7.9	7.9
	INDEX	100	111	77	96	88	102	111	79	100	95	99	97	98

Source: Scarborough Research Corporation. Used with permission.

Newspaper Rates and Data, which profiles 1,600 local and national newspapers and newspaper groups (Exhibit 11.17). The listings report advertising rates and discount structures, mechanical requirements, closing dates, and other contract limitations.

Consumer Magazines and Agri-Media, which lists more than 1,500 consumer magazines and 400 farm publications (Exhibit 11.18). Magazines are arranged according to their editorial focus, and their mechanical formats, costs, discount structures, and closing dates are reported. The volumes also contain extensive media advertising through which magazines provide reader profiles and marketing information. Other volumes cover more than 4,500 business, trade, and technical publications.

EXHIBIT 11.17 NEWSPAPER RATES AND DATA

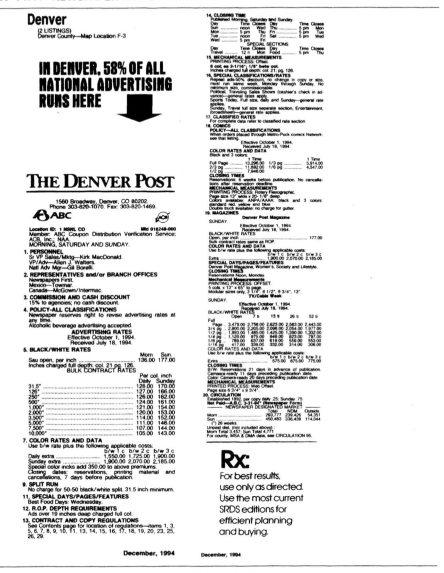

Source: Standard Rate and Data Service. December, 1994. Used with permission.

SRDS also publishes volumes on spot television and radio. These publications are not as useful as before in today's market, since radio and television time sales is a commodity business in which rates change daily. Increasingly, magazine rates are negotiable, but their rate cards still have some meaning. Other volumes report on direct mail lists available for rental, sources of cooperative advertising, and print production requirements. As a result, SRDS is often used as frequently by traffic and marketing departments as by media planners.

EXHIBIT 11.18 CONSUMER MAGAZINES AND AGRI-MEDIA

49 Women's

NEW WOMAN—cont

COLOR RATES:
2-Color:

	1 ti	3 ti	6 ti	9 ti	12 ti
1 page	17,010.	16,670.	16,330.	15,990.	15,480.
4-Color:					
1 page	18,190.	17,830.	17,460.	17,100.	16,550.

CIRCULATION:
6-30-94—267,872.

CUSTOM REGIONALS
MINIMUM BLACK AND WHITE RATES:
1 page .... 12,580.
MINIMUM COLOR RATES:
2-Color:
1 page .... 13,820.
4-Color:
1 page .... 15,000.
Minimum cost is for 1st 100,000 circulation.
Additional thousands of circulation (over 100,000) at 19.00 per thousand regardless of coloration.

15. GENERAL REQUIREMENTS
Also see SRDS Print Media Production Source.
Specifications effective with March 1995 issue:
Printing Process: Web Offset Full Run Cover
Trim Size: 8 x 10-1/2; No./Cols. 3.
Binding Method: Perfect.
Colors Available: Black and white; Black and one color; 4-color process; 5th cylinder.
Covers: Black and one color; 4-color process.

AD PAGE DIMENSIONS

Sprd	15 x	10	1/3 v	2-1/4 x	10
1 pg	7 x	10	1/3 sq	4-5/8 x	5
2/3 v	4-5/8 x	10	1/6 v	2-1/4 x	5
1/2 v	3-1/2 x	10	Digest	4-5/8 x	6-1/2
1/2 h	7 x	5			

16. ISSUE AND CLOSING DATES
Published monthly.

Issue:	On sale	Closing	Issue:	On sale	Closing
Jan/95	12/20	11/1	Jul	6/13	4/26
Feb	1/24	11/29	Aug	7/18	5/30
Mar	2/21	1/3	Sep	8/15	6/27
Apr	3/21	1/31	Oct	9/19	8/1
May	4/18	2/28	Nov	10/24	9/5
Jun	5/16	3/28	Dec	11/21	10/3

17. SPECIAL SERVICES
A.B.C. Supplemental Data Report released march 1990 issue.

18. CIRCULATION
Established 1970. Single copy 2.50; per year 15.97.
Summary data—for detail see Publisher's Statement.
A.B.C. 6-30-94 (6 mos. aver.—Magazine Form)

Tot. Pd.	(Subs)	(Single)	(Assoc)
1,316,771	771,384	545,387	...

Average Non-Analyzed Non-Paid Circulation (not incl. above):
Total 46,200
TERRITORIAL DISTRIBUTION 5/94—1,318,820

N.Eng.	Mid.Atl.	E.N.Cen.	W.N.Cen.	S.Atl.
76,185	212,479	203,826	81,856	221,011
E.S.Cen.	W.S.Cen.	Mtn.St.	Pac.St.	Canada
62,354	106,079	75,006	1,231,662	72,899
Foreign	Other			
10,447	3,812			

Publisher states: "Effective with January 1994 issue, rates based on a circulation average of 1,300,000."
(D-C2)

PARENTING
A Time Inc. Ventures Publication
ABC MPA

Location ID: 8 MLST 49 **Mid 039706-000**
Published 10 times a year by Time Inc. Ventures, 301 Howard St. 17th Flr., San Francisco, CA 94105-2252. Phone 415-546-7575. Fax 415-546-0578

PUBLISHER'S EDITORIAL PROFILE
PARENTING is aimed at an audience of educated and worldly parents. The magazine covers all the issues relevant to raising children from 0-12, with in-depth coverage of issues relevant to families -- from day-to-day matters like discipline and diet, to more global concerns such as the day care crisis, reinventing education, developing self-esteem in girls, and more. Regular features focus on age-specific child development, education, health, family activities, food, travel, toys and games, fashion and beauty. Each issue also includes essays. Rec'd 11/16/94.

1. PERSONNEL
Pres—Carol Smith.
Editor—Steven Reddicliffe.
Pub—Diane Oshin.
Grp Ad Dir—Deborah Mignucci.

2. REPRESENTATIVES and/or BRANCH OFFICES
New York 10036—Lori Fromm, Assoc Pub (Baby Talk), Barbara Friedmann, Mktg Dir; Freda London, Susan Schwartzman, Robert Acquaotta, Amelia Cooper, Julie Arkin, Karen Levine, Hilary Van Kleeck, Acct. Execs.; Grace Chung, Dir/Direct Response Adv; 25 W. 43rd St. Phone 212-840-4200. FAX: 212-827-0019.
San Francisco, CA 94105—Eileen Sherman, Western Reg Dir., 301 Howard St. Phone 415-546-7575. Fax 415-546-0578.
Chicago, IL 606111—Kathy Goodman, Midwestern Adv. Mgr., Myrna James, Claudia Casey, Acct. Execs., 303 East Ohio. Phone 312-321-7996. Fax 312-321-7980.
Bloomfield Hills, MI 48304—Katie Kiyo, Detroit Adv Mgr., Bloom Wood Centre, 1577 N. Woodward Ave., Ste. 200. Phone 810-988-7795. FAX 810-988-7925.
Los Angeles, CA 90025-6538—Donna Castorino, Los Angeles Adv Mgr, 11766 Wilshire Blvd.Phone: 310-268-7405. FAX: 310-268-7605.
Dallas, TX 75240—Tierney & Co.

3. COMMISSION AND CASH DISCOUNT
15% to recognized agencies. No cash discount. Net 30 days.

4. GENERAL RATE POLICY
Cigarette advertising not accepted.

ADVERTISING RATES
Effective January 1, 1995. (Card 11)
Rates received October 31, 1994.

5. BLACK/WHITE RATES

	1 ti	6 ti	12 ti	18 ti	24 ti
1 page	34,600.	32,870.	31,140.	29,410.	27,680.
2/3 page	26,990.	25,640.	24,290.	22,940.	21,590.
1/2 page	23,185.	22,025.	20,865.	19,705.	18,545.
1/3 page	17,300.	16,435.	15,570.	14,705.	13,840.
1/6 page	10,380.	9,860.	9,340.	8,825.	8,305.

	30 ti	40 ti
1 page	25,950.	22,490.
2/3 page	20,245.	17,545.
1/2 page	17,390.	15,070.
1/3 page	12,975.	11,245.
1/6 page	7,785.	6,745.

DISCOUNT POLICY
Maximum discount is 35%. To earned volume discounts, advertisers may add either category or discounts, whichever is higher. Qualifying insertions may also earn additional Facing Page, Coupon Backing or Consecutive Page Discounts which apply only within maximum discount limitations.

VOLUME DISCOUNTS

6-11 pages	5%	24-29 pages	20%
12-17 pages	10%	30-39 pages	25%
18-23 pages	15%	40+ pages	35%

MATCHING DISCOUNT
1995 Advertisers who match 1994 volume will be eligible to earn an additional 5% discount over their earned rate on all qualified spending.

FACING PAGE DISCOUNT
Subject to availability. National full-page advertisers committing in advance to face another advertiser's full-page ad will earn an additional 20% discount over their earned rate for that insertion.

COUPON BACKING DISCOUNT
Subject to availability. Advertisers committing in advance to have their advertisement backed by an ad carrying a removable coupon or other clippable material will receive an additional 10% discount over their earned rate for that insertion. Maximum total discount: 35%.

CONSECUTIVE PAGE DISCOUNT
10% for 4 or more pages. Booklets and inserts do not qualify.

CATEGORY DISCOUNTS
Food 15%
Beauty 10%
Travel 10%
Mass Merchant (100 or more stores) 10%
Direct Response, Publisher's, Retail 25%

6. COLOR RATES

	1 ti	6 ti	12 ti	18 ti	24 ti
2-Color:					
1 page	41,090.	39,035.	36,980.	34,925.	32,870.
2/3 page	32,050.	30,450.	28,845.	27,240.	25,640.
1/2 page	27,530.	26,155.	24,775.	23,400.	22,025.
1/3 page	20,545.	19,520.	18,490.	17,465.	16,435.

	30 ti	40 ti
1 page	30,820.	26,710.
2/3 page	24,040.	20,835.
1/2 page	20,650.	17,895.
1/3 page	15,410.	13,355.

	1 ti	6 ti	12 ti	18 ti	24 ti
4-Color:					
1 page	43,250.	41,090.	38,925.	36,765.	34,600.
2/3 page	33,735.	32,050.	30,360.	28,675.	26,990.
1/2 page	28,980.	27,530.	26,080.	24,635.	23,185.
1/3 page	21,625.	20,545.	19,465.	18,385.	17,300.

	30 ti	40 ti
1 page	32,440.	28,115.
2/3 page	25,305.	21,930.
1/2 page	21,735.	18,835.
1/3 page	16,220.	14,060.

7. COVERS

	1 ti	6 ti	12 ti	18 ti	24 ti
4-Color:					
2nd cover	49,735.	47,255.	44,765.	42,280.	39,790.
3rd cover	47,575.	45,200.	42,820.	40,440.	38,060.
4th cover	56,225.	53,415.	50,605.	47,795.	44,980.

	30 ti	40 ti
2nd cover	37,305.	32,330.
3rd cover	35,685.	30,925.
4th cover	42,170.	36,550.

8. INSERTS
Inserts, gatefolds and insert cards available.

9. BLEED
No charge.

11. CLASSIFIED/MAIL ORDER/SPECIALTY RATES
DISPLAY CLASSIFICATIONS:
PARENTING BY MAIL
Published 10 times a year. Payment must accompany order.
Black/White Rates:

1 page	20,760.	1/6 page	4,150.
2/3 page	16,195.	1/12 page	2,335.
1/2 page	13,910.	1 inch	900.
1/3 page	6,920.		

Frequency Discounts:
6-9 times .... 5% 10+ times 10%
Matching Discount:
1995 advertisers who match or exceed their 1994 volume will be eligible to earn an additional 5% discount over their earned rate on all qualified spending.
Maximum Discount:
The maximum discount possible on any given ad is 35% off the general rate card.
Color Rates:

2-color:			
1 page	24,655.	1/3 page	12,325.
2/3 page	19,230.	1/6 page	7,395.
1/2 page	16,520.		
4-color:			
1 page	25,950.	1/3 page	12,975.
2/3 page	20,240.	1/6 page	7,785.
1/2 page	17,390.		

2-color consists of black plus 1 process color (yellow, magenta or cyan). Any other colors will be matched with process and charged as 4-color.
General Requirements:
Ad Page Dimensions

1 page	7 x 8-7/8
2/3 page v	4-5/8 x 8-7/8
1/2 page h	7 x 4-3/8
1/2 page v	3-3/8 x 8-7/8
1/3 page v	2-1/4 x 8-7/8
1/3 page sq	4-5/8 x 4-3/8
1/6 page v	2-1/4 x 4-3/8
1/6 page h	4-5/8 x 2-1/4
1/12 page	2-1/4 x 2-3/8
1 inch	2-1/4 x 1

Issue and Closing Dates:
Published 10 times a year.

Issue:	On-Sale	Closing
Feb	1/23	11/15
Mar	2/20	12/15
Apr	3/20	1/13
May	4/24	2/15
Jun-Jul	5/22	3/15
Aug	7/24	5/15
Sep	8/21	6/15
Oct	9/18	7/14
Nov	10/23	8/15
Dec-Jan/96	11/20	9/15

14. CONTRACT AND COPY REGULATIONS
See Contents page for location—items 1, 2, 3, 8, 12, 14, 18, 20, 21, 22, 24, 25, 26, 27, 30, 32, 35, 36, 42.

15. GENERAL REQUIREMENTS
Also see SRDS Print Media Production Source.
Printing Process: Web Offset Full Run
Trim Size: 8 x 10-1/2; No./Cols. 3.
Binding Method: Perfect.
Colors Available: 4-color process; Matched.
Covers: 4-color process.

AD PAGE DIMENSIONS

Sprd	14 x	10	1/3 v	2-1/4 x	10
1 pg	7 x	10	1/3 sq	4-5/8 x	4-7/8
2/3 v	4-5/8 x	10	1/4 sq	3-3/8 x	4-7/8
2/3 h	7 x	6-1/8	1/6 v	2-1/4 x	4-7/8
1/2 v	3-3/8 x	10	1/6 h	4-5/8 x	2-1/4
1/2 h	7 x	4-7/8	Digest	4-5/8 x	7

16. ISSUE AND CLOSING DATES
Published 10 times a year.

Issue:	On sale	Closing	(**)
Feb '95	1/23	11/15	11/1
Mar	2/20	12/15	12/1
Apr	3/20	1/13	1/2
May	4/24	2/15	2/1
Jun-Jul	5/22	3/15	3/1
Aug	7/24	5/15	5/1
Sep	8/21	6/15	6/1
Oct	9/18	7/14	6/30
Nov	10/23	8/15	8/1
Dec-Jan '96	11/20	9/15	9/1

(**) Regional closing date.

REVISIONS—INSERT MATERIALS AT QUAD:
Feb-12/20, Mar-1/20/, Apr-2/17, May-3/24, Jun/Jul-4/21, Aug-6/23, Sep-7/21, Oct-8/18, Nov-9/22, Dec-10/20.

SPECIAL FEATURE ISSUES
Feb/95—Parenting's Second Annual Video Magic Awards.
Mar/95—The New American Family.
Apr/95—The Second Annual Parenting Achievement Awards.
May/95—Kids In Crisis.
Jun-Jul/95—Summer Fun.
Aug/95—Can Your Hospital Handle a Pediatric Emergency?
Sep/95—Parenting's Annual Special Back-to-School Issue: Early Learning Strategies, Dealing with Learning Disabilities, Public Schools.
Oct/95—Family Finance.
Nov/95—Best Toys of the Year; Parenting's Annual Roundup.
Dec-Jan/95—Winter Fun; Kids and Religion.

17. SPECIAL SERVICES
A.B.C. Supplemental Data Report released November 1990 issue.

18. CIRCULATION
Established 1987.
Summary data—for detail see Publisher's Statement.
A.B.C. 12-31-94 (6 mos. aver.—Magazine Form)

Tot Pd	(Subs)	(Single)	(Assoc)
865,019	810,732	45,287	...

A.B.C. 12-31-94 Analyzed Non-Paid (6 mos. aver.)

Total	Direct Request	Other	Bulk
71,319	31,409	39,910	...

Total Non-Analyzed Non-Paid Circulation (not incl. above):
Total 84,747
TERRITORIAL DISTRIBUTION 11/94—928,618

	N.Eng.	Mid.Atl.	E.N.Cen.	W.N.Cen.	S.Atl.
Paid	50,341	130,496	139,367	57,993	141,835
Non-Pd	3,392	16,522	10,841	4,505	12,859
	E.S.Cen.	W.S.Cen.	Mtn.St.	Pac.St.	Canada
Paid	40,884	75,697	50,730	147,089	18,480
Non-Pd	4,268	7,309	3,782	9,257	2
				Foreign	Other
Paid				428	2,435
Non-Pd				...	206

Publisher states: "Effective with February 1995 issue, rates based on an average circulation of 1,000,000."
(D-C2, C-C2)

Parents
America's #1 Family Magazine
A Gruner & Jahr USA Publishing Publication
ABC MPA

Location ID: 8 MLST 49 **Mid 001289-000**
Published monthly by Parents Magazine, A div. of Gruner & Jahr USA Publishing, 685 Third Avenue, New York, NY 10017. Phone 212-878-8700. Fax 212-286-2656
For shipping info., see Print Media Production Source.

PUBLISHER'S EDITORIAL PROFILE
PARENTS Magazine is edited for young women 18-34 with growing children. Editorial coverage emphasizes family formation and growth, focusing on the day-to-day needs and concerns of today's woman as a mother and as a woman. Regular departments include Beauty, Food, Fashion, Home, As They Grow (age by age child

Source: Standard Rate and Data Service. December, 1994. Used with permission.

Space and Time/Before and After

The end-point of a plan is execution. Media plans are executed through the purchase of time and space in media vehicles. The end-point of execution is accountability. Media accountability consists of determining not only that the advertising appeared as ordered, but also that the exposures and cost efficiencies delivered by the vehicle fulfilled the plan. The same research resources are utilized for both buying and accountability.

The basic broadcast purchase unit is thirty seconds. This unit can be doubled or halved, but it must always be a factor of the basic unit of sale so that both commercials and programs can be consistently scheduled.

During the "Golden Age of Television," when advertisers and agencies typically owned and produced television programs, commercial time generally was the result of program sponsorship. Agencies produced programs, and the advertiser, who owned the copyright, occupied all of the commercial time. The benefits of this tactic were that it insured a certain quality of television programming and that it provided advertisers with an appropriate program environment for their commercial messages.

Program sponsorship had several disadvantages. The first was that the advertisers took all the risk. Second, program sponsorship limited the advertiser's prospect reach while increasing frequency to the point of diminishing returns. *Lux Playhouse* or *Goodyear Theater* might attract a large and loyal audience, but they were mostly the same people week after week, and the advertiser addressed them with the same message seven times each half hour. Even if the advertiser had a large enough budget to produce many programs in a week on three network channels in order to increase commercial reach, the frequency obtained went well beyond any motivational requirement. Advertisers with extensive product lines could mitigate this problem by scheduling different brand messages in any program they owned, but, overall, it soon became apparent that program sponsorship was inefficient as a regular way of doing business.

At the same time, the networks were becoming increasingly restless about program ownership. Now that advertisers had taken many of the risks in establishing television, the networks preferred to take all the programming risks, as well as the profits that would accrue from competitive bidding for their commercial time. Public interest advocates were also uncomfortable with the idea of advertisers owning so much network programming and controlling so much of the network schedule.

The results today are that few advertisers pursue program ownership, and most commercial time is purchased from the networks on a scatter basis. **Scatter buying** is the tactic of purchasing time on at least two networks and spread over various programs. For example, if the plan calls for the purchase of 200 GRPs per week, the buyer would achieve this goal by buying schedules on two networks (perhaps 95 GRPs on one network, and 105 GRPs on another) representing eight different programs on one network, and ten different programs on the other, spread over several days of the week.

For promotional and competitive reasons, certain advertisers will purchase program exclusivities, program sponsorships, or fractions (quarters or halves) of sponsorships. This tactic is especially prominent in the purchase of sports programming by beer, auto, and tire manufacturers. Hallmark Cards's use of holiday-oriented dramatic specials is more a strategic use of program ownership than is the regular tactical competition between male-oriented sponsors of sporting events. The many opportunities and narrower audiences provided by cable television, however, have led many advertisers to revisit the advantages of program development and program sponsorship as part of their basic media strategy.

Advertisers will, on occasion, attempt to achieve not only reach, but also simultaneous prospect coverage through a **road blocking** tactic. This tactic involves purchasing commercial time on all the available networks for airing at precisely the same time. In earlier television advertising, this tactic often was used for the introduction of new products or new automobile styles. It was difficult and expensive to execute when the advertiser was dealing with only three broadcast networks, but in today's world of five or six broadcast networks and ten or more cable and pay networks, successful road blocking is a near impossibility on a practical level. Therefore, it is seldom attempted.

Scatter plans have the advantages of achieving broad prospect reach and, frequently, with price guarantees by the networks. What scatter plans sacrifice are narrowly targeted reach and guaranteed program environments. The alternative purchasing tactic is **selected-program schedules**. The advertiser preselects certain programs across a network or station schedule and negotiates for the purchase of this designated schedule. The advertiser obtains compatible program environments and narrower targets, but sacrifices in higher costs and audience guarantees. Larger advertisers with the leverage of larger budgets, however, can achieve many of the advantages of program selection through the tough negotiation of scatter buys on the networks.

Similar tactics can be executed in print vehicles. Advertisers can seek impact (Figure 11.2) through the purchase of magazine covers or newspaper back pages, through spreads, through positions opposite certain editorial features, or in special sections. Advertisers can seek to capture attention through gatefolds, sequential advertising, or carefully placed partial spaces that produce a pattern on the page. Each of these tactics, however, generally involves a trade-off of cost for impact.

Whatever physical media unit is purchased, however, the intention and value of the purchase is defined by the number of prospect impressions to be made and the cost of those impressions. The purchase is made with the expectation of a particular marketing communication profit. These buyer projections (and, frequently, seller guarantees) are established by existing research.

We have discussed at various points in this and other chapters, however, that media research is intrinsically limited. Each research database includes an admitted margin of error. There are continuing efforts to limit or eliminate such research fragility. For example, many advertisers are looking forward to the implementation of Passive People Meters, which will use heat-detecting technology to record how many different people are actually watching a television commercial. Media exposures are increasingly capable of being tracked with retail sales through checkout scanners coded to the same individuals as is the media research. All the new two-way technologies of cyberspace also promise more precise and less fallible data.

FIGURE 11.2 PRINT PURCHASE ALTERNATIVES

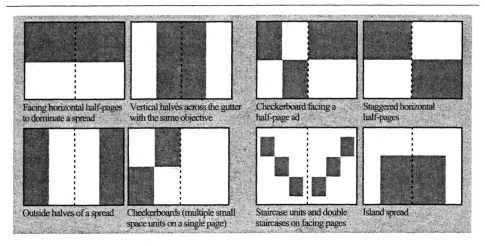

Media planners, however, will always be required to make decisions without perfect data and absolute knowledge. *Hamlet*, if you will, will still be pertinent in cyberspace. The only conclusion is that whatever research exists and is agreed upon is the "coin of the realm" for media planning and purchase.

SUMMARY

This chapter has provided a brief description of the resources available for vehicle audience analysis, vehicle and marketing correlations, and vehicle purchasing with an eye to logical progression. It is in everyone's interest to make the process of placing and accounting for advertising as easy as possible. Complexity is caused only by the complexity of the communications each medium initiates.

Two final notes: First, any business more than likely has a supportive trade association. Media are no different; therefore, a novice planner can always call upon one of these associations to provide data and procedural orientation on the purchase of its members' products. Second, with so much money at stake, it is likely that some kind of data exists on any medium or vehicle a planner contemplates. If it has not been reported in this text, feel confident that it is, nevertheless, available and attainable.

The creative imagination is always concrete and practical. The experience of living with all the available data enhances the creative imagination, but this is true only if the imagination is not bogged down in the existential process of simply buying and selling. Data is there to be commanded and used.

12

Negotiating the Future: Media Sales and Purchase

OVERVIEW

This chapter provides a framework for the negotiated selection of media vehicles. Weighting is described and explained. The future of integrated marketing communications and the media planner's role are examined.

NEGOTIATION

Media planning is the anticipation of a negotiation at two levels. The first, which has been the focus of much of our discussion, is the consumer's negotiation of a lifestyle in the marketplace of ideas, articulated by the media, and in the marketplace of goods and services, represented by advertising distributed through the media. The second is the negotiation between the buyers and sellers of media vehicles, which is the endgame of media planning and results in specific consumer exposures.

There is a fundamental difference between broadcast and print, television and magazines, in the media marketplace. Some argue that print products are sold but that broadcast products are purchased. Their point is that broadcast products, especially television, are a commodity without much vehicle differentiation. They are also a commodity for which demand often almost exceeds supply. For many national brands, print is not perceived as a required medium, and the existence of many distinguishable printed products, especially magazines, requires strong representation to insure the perception of their values and distinctions.

The future, however, may not replicate the past. Broadcast television is experiencing an annual decrease in its share of consumer viewing time. Most people in America now receive their television through cable, which also delivers an increasing number of alternative networks. These networks are developing personalities and loyalties with some similarities to those regarding magazines. Decreasing shares and the shattering of commodity sameness will undoubtedly require that video products be sold and not simply negotiated with a smile, a shine, and a price.

Newspapers are a printed product that has enjoyed some of the demand characteristics of network television. For the local retailer, they have been not only the basic mass medium of their communities, but also a proven traffic builder. Newspapers, however, have been experiencing a declining readership as well as a fragmentation resulting from the creation of more narrowly defined products, such as the suburban press. Future cable services, however, not only will increase the number of dedicated shopping channels, and reduce the cost of producing and presenting commercials, but also will deliver a variety of direct response retail options. Thus, even local print products will have to be sold more vigorously in a newly competitive environment.

This inevitable future suggests that media planners have a serious and growing need to understand purchasing and selling. For many this will be a new experience. Media representatives, on the other hand, have a serious and growing need to understand the meeting point of marketing and communications, which is the responsibility of media planners. They will be selling in a new environment in which knowledge will be the root of persuasion.

BUYING AND SELLING

All media are products that are sold and vehicles that are purchased. There are four critical elements in the media sales and purchase equation: **market, medium, product**, and **price**. The buyer and seller have somewhat different perspectives, but they define their relationship in terms of these four elements.

Market

Every vehicle creates an audience, which is a market.

Seller The seller argues that this vehicle audience represents a substantial number of people with buying power.

Buyer The buyer must determine whether this audience consists of the right people for my brand and whether it is large enough to be sales productive as a singular vehicle or when combined with another vehicle I can consider.

It is the seller's responsibility, in the continuing dialogue of sales calls, promotions, and press coverage, to insure that all relevant planners and decision makers are aware of the market power they represent. Media planners have the responsibility to survey all available research data, and to be open to the salesperson's ability to bring these numbers alive. The planner has clear responsibilities to be knowledgeable and aware of the possibilities, but it is the salesperson's direct responsibility to insure that the planner perceives the real consumers represented by the numbers.

Medium

Every vehicle is an expression of its medium and is perceived as the medium is perceived.

Seller The second premise, permeating every sales message, is that this vehicle is an example of a medium that is experienced and used by consumers in a specific and useful way.

Buyer The fundamental planner inquiry is whether the message and persuasive task at hand need, or are helped to be effective by, this medium's kind of consumer use' and experience.

All salespersons must sell their medium. There is a point in every consumer product's life cycle in which it must sell the value and utility of its product category (for example, ibuprofen). For many products, such as beer, every brand advertisement helps sell the category. Media selling constantly lives in both of these worlds.

The beginning point of this dialogue is the generally perceived set of advantages and disadvantages of each medium (see chapter 9). These checklists can work for or against the vehicle's sales message. In either case, however, it is the task of buyer and seller to help one another to get beyond these categories to the dynamics of the social role and creative tension represented by this vehicle's expression of the medium.

Product

Every communications vehicle is a unique product. Magazines have always known this. Radio stations and cable television channels are aware of this. Even broadcast networks, which generally sell schedules rather than programs, must fight for larger shares of the advertiser's investments on the basis of the unique environments their programs provide.

Seller and Buyer In the instance of product analysis and perception, both buyer and seller have the same considerations. The questions are:

> How good is this vehicle as an example of the medium?
>
> How important is this vehicle in the lives of its users?
>
> Where does this vehicle fit into the lives of its users?
>
> How does this vehicle compare with competitive products within the same medium and reaching the same market?
>
> How vital a marketing vehicle has this vehicle proven to be?

These are the questions of quality that are critical to closing a vehicle sale. The answers to these questions are not generally available through syndicated research.

Therefore, it is the responsibility of the producer or publisher to research these subjects and to find ways of articulating them. The buyer should not act without such knowledge, and if the information is not generally available, the buyer must form a judgment about these subjects before investing. The only way to do this is through creative insight, which should also form the background for creative listening to sales presentations.

Price

Understood as a marketing strategy, pricing is a different issue than cost.

Seller   Must insure that price is defined in terms of value, both in fact and in perception. This involves comparisons to both direct and indirect competition. Indirect competition is primarily represented by other media and, therefore, involves selling the medium. Direct competition is generally derived from within the medium's community of products and, therefore, is generally dependent on the seller having presold the vehicle as an outstanding expression of the medium's possibilities.

Buyer   The investment counselor is constantly questioning whether he or she can tell a good enough story to persuade others of the value for the price.

The buyer must be sold, but the buyer must also sell the investment to clients, to superiors, and to the product group. The seller must keep these dual audiences in mind and make sure that the planner, who may be convinced easily, has all the data, language, and presentation tools necessary to convince others who may not be so easily persuaded.

PURCHASE CONSIDERATIONS

All information is entertaining and all entertainment is information. We may look upon a television sitcom or *People* magazine as pure entertainment, but their viewers and readers are absorbing information on morals and mores, styles and lifestyles, which they will accept or reject in their own lives. We may look upon *Meet the Press* or *Fortune* as pure information, but the viewers and readers find themselves engaged and refreshed. Whether observers categorize media products as entertainment or as information, media as a whole are experienced as an activity that occupies a significant amount of time and involves a significant amount of enjoyment.

Editorial Franchise

All successful media products have a focus or an element of specialization that is common to most of their consumers, attractive enough to occupy a great deal of their time, and significant enough to affect their lifestyle. The planner's job is to understand this core element of successful media products. The planner must comprehend what news agenda, information, judgments, instruction, dramatic experiences, or comedy premises of the media vehicle are sufficiently serious and common to attract an audience and influence or confirm their attitudes and actions. This magnet is the product's **editorial franchise**.

The vehicle's advertising franchise is derived from its reader/viewer franchise, which is derived from the editorial franchise, and the editorial franchise is derived from the media product's reason for existence. These are the central existential facts that we first addressed conceptually in chapter 1 and then strategically in chapter 9. It is the mutual responsibility of both media planners and media representatives to understand the dynamics of this franchise and utilize this knowledge to solve marketing problems.

Relevance and Practicality

When presenting print plans, media planners have a habit of saying that the advertisements "will be placed opposite compatible editorial" without ever describing what they mean by "compatible editorial." When asked, they suggest that they mean "dog food opposite pet editorial," or "cosmetics opposite beauty editorial." Such answers are both too specific and too generic: too specific because they describe column inches rather than a magazine, and too generic because they make the point of view and content of the specific article irrelevant.

When proposing television purchases, some planners will go so far as to designate program types such as action-adventures or situation comedies. Most do not, only indicating GRP requirements and CPM parameters. Both approaches suggest that there is no source effect inherent in television programs. Either all GRPs are equal, or all situation comedies are the same and of equal value as an advertising environment for a specific brand message.

Practical demands cannot be overlooked, however. A planner who takes his or her judgments about the character of specific magazines too seriously and refuses to consider alternatives with slightly different editorial franchises will invariably be blind to efficiencies. This can develop into a particularly serious problem for products that are one brand among many that the client has in the marketplace. In these instances, the client often makes corporate purchases that produce major discounts, which could not be achieved without balancing the benefits of editorial environment with the benefits of cost efficiencies. What is required is both a practical point of view and a practical procedure (Exhibit 12.1).

It is not the practicality of efficiencies, however, that is most often overlooked, but the vitality of program and editorial source effects. What is most needed, therefore, is a practical procedure for ensuring the proper consideration of both. Such a procedure includes:

1. Consideration of the objective and strategies
2. Articulating the relevance of editorial
3. Weighting the choices
4. Flexibility

EXHIBIT 12.1   CASE: YOU PAY YOUR MONEY AND YOU TAKE YOUR CHOICE

Question: Which is more important to someone on a tight budget: a medium with a better audience match at $25,000, or a medium priced at $22,000 with a less favorable match and which is available at a negotiated price well below normal?

Discussion: The first issue is whether the planner is sincerely open to considering the less expensive but less targeted medium. The answer is the planner should be open. The second issue is how great is the relative cost (or CPM) between the two media based on the target audience reached. The greater the spread in favor of the less targeted medium, the more it should be considered. The third issue is how significant are the environmental concerns to the brand. A brand such as a moisturizing soap may be so inappropriate to a newsweekly and so dependent on an environment of beauty editorial, that the relative cost question may be moot. The final answer is that it is a judgment call and great deal will be dependent on the client's value system.

Strategic Use

Relevance is not always that relevant. If the only media objective is to make the whole world aware of my brand at the least cost, editorial considerations may be virtually irrelevant. Furthermore, every media type and every vehicle selection need not carry the full burden of the media plan. After all, media mix is a strategy that inherently recognizes different roles for different media.

The planner must keep the objectives in mind. The persuasive task (based on product loyalty, pricing strategies, position in the life cycle, and other considerations) may make top-of-mind awareness among large consumer segments the primary objective. Tonnage strategies are intelligent and, when the planner executes them, editorial relevance is more a means to efficiency than to cultural transfer. This approach could be equally valid within a proposed media mix in which one medium is utilized for broad awareness, while another is utilized for establishing value and cultural transfer.

The planner's first task, therefore, is to be both reflective and candid about the tasks that the medium and vehicle are intended to perform. This implies that the planner is always prepared to make cost/benefit tradeoffs.

Articulating Relevance

A larger problem faced by planners is their need to accurately and usefully articulate the editorial and its relevance. Too few planners can honestly articulate the difference between two closely competitive magazines, and too many are at a complete loss in trying to describe the different comic premises of two popular television programs. The degree to which the persuasive task requires the transfer of cultural values to the brand is the degree of importance the planner must place on compatible editorial.

The issue here, we must recall, is execution, or vehicle tactics and purchasing. A thorough strategy analysis has previously identified the target audience's preferences in media types, and has identified the role each medium must play. The immediate issue, therefore, is selecting between vehicles within the same medium and the importance of editorial compatibility to these selections.

The Hall Reports are the basic source for assisting the planner in analyzing and articulating the editorial design of magazines reaching the same demographic audience (Exhibit 12.2). Among those magazines generally perceived as reaching young women, 'Teen clearly puts more emphasis on beauty and grooming than Seventeen, which puts twice as much emphasis on apparel and accessories. Mademoiselle, however, provides the most balanced coverage of the two topics.

Mademoiselle also competes against Cosmopolitan. Comparing their editorial profiles (Exhibit 12.3) argues that Mademoiselle is three times more focused on apparel and accessories, but this can be misleading. If the brand's target market are "women who bought activewear," Cosmopolitan could be perceived as having advantages (Figure 12.1) in coverage and relative cost. When it comes to activewear, the core lifestyle gestalt of Cosmopolitan is of greater editorial influence than are the number of column inches dedicated to apparel. Everything depends not only on how you define your market, but also on how you understand the motivations of its consumers.

The relevance of editorial to vehicle selection is entirely dependent on the brand's persuasive purpose and the plan's strategic intent. If the plan's target audience, for whatever reason, is adults who have traveled domestically on business in the previous twelve months, it is significant, but not decisive, that United Airlines's inflight magazine, Hemispheres, has such a high composition of this demographic that you can assert a sense of identity between the editorial and your target market (Exhibit 12.4). Reader and editor clearly share an interest that would suggest that they must be interested in what is being advertised. The CPM is relatively high and the reach relatively small, but the sense of identity with the needs your product satisfies may be so great that effectiveness will compensate for the cost.

At the opposite end of the spectrum of strategic choices is Time B, which is the same newsweekly editorial everyone receives but is distributed only to businesspeople, so that advertising can be limited to this circulation. There is no sense of identity between the business traveler and Time's broad editorial stance. Rather, it just so happens that, for a variety of external circumstances, business travelers also read Time. For extensive reach and low CPM, however, the magazine offers significant opportunities.

Cases could also be made for The Wall Street Journal and Conde Nast Traveler on the basis of probable interest in the advertising message, or compatible editorial tone, or male/female skew or balance. If low-cost reach is the only issue, Time B is the clear choice, but if the strategy did not require print for long copy purposes, it would be even more efficient to gain reach through televised sports or news. On the other hand, if it is important to expose a directly responsive nerve, or to wrap the persuasive message in certain cultural values, the plan will tilt strategically to one or the other more vertical magazines and will, most probably, include Hemispheres on the selected magazine list.

These ideas can be transferred to television. Most often, television is purchased on the coincidental basis that a large number of the target audience just happen to be viewers. However, there are increasing opportunities for identity in television programs, from commercials for entertainment products on MTV to ads for fishing reels on ESPN. When planners recommend action-adventure programming, or situation come-

EXHIBIT 12.2 YOUNG WOMEN'S MAGAZINES—EDITORIAL PAGES BY SUBJECT CATEGORY

	Seventeen		Glamour		Mademoiselle		YM		Sassy		'Teen	
	Pages	% of Total	Pages	% of Total	Pages	% of Total	Pages	% of Total	Pages	% of Total	Pages	% of Total
Issues	12		12		12		10		11		12	
Classifications												
400 Beauty & Grooming	179.9	16.8%	215.2	13.6%	274.3	20.2%	121.7	15.4%	69.0	10.8%	231.3	28.8%
600 Business & Industry	15.4	1.4%	39.1	2.5%	42.2	3.1%	23.3	2.9%	9.4	1.5%	20.2	2.5%
900 Food & Nutrition	40.3	3.8%	66.2	4.2%	36.0	2.7%	3.3	0.4%	6.5	1.0%	15.9	2.0%
1000 Health & Med. Science	26.2	2.5%	98.8	6.3%	34.9	2.6%	8.2	1.0%	26.8	4.2%	31.8	4.0%
1100 Home Furnishings & Mgmt.	21.1	2.0%	50.5	3.2%	14.7	1.1%	2.1	0.3%	10.5	1.6%	6.6	0.8%
1400 Apparel & Accessories	323.6	30.3%	446.0	28.2%	444.6	32.7%	252.9	32.0%	160.8	25.3%	100.5	12.5%
1500 Culture/Humanities	178.4	16.7%	320.2	20.3%	227.5	16.8%	169.5	21.4%	138.8	21.8%	148.6	18.5%
1508 Personal Relations	36.9	3.5%	142.9	9.0%	121.2	8.9%	76.0	9.6%	38.2	6.0%	47.6	5.9%
1509 Self-Improvement	11.7	1.1%	83.8	5.3%	43.7	3.2%	28.0	3.5%	14.5	2.3%	40.2	5.0%
1800 Fiction	56.1	5.3%	10.5	0.7%	35.5	2.6%	0.0	0.0%	28.6	4.2%	50.4	6.3%
Sub-Total	841.0	78.8%	1,246.5	78.9%	1,109.7	81.7%	581.0	73.5%	448.6	70.5%	605.3	75.4%
All Other Editorial	226.8	21.2%	332.8	21.1%	248.1	18.3%	210.0	26.5%	187.9	29.5%	197.2	24.6%
Total Editorial	1,067.8	100.0%	1,579.3	100.0%	1,357.8	100.0%	791.0	100.0%	636.5	100.0%	802.5	100.0%

Source: Hall's Editorial Reports, December 1990.

EXHIBIT 12.3 FASHION & LIFESTYLE MAGAZINES—EDITORIAL CONTENT ANALYSIS

	Cosmopolitan		Glamour		Madamoiselle		Self		Vogue	
	Pages	%	Pages	%	Pages	%	Pages	%	Pages	%
Culture/Humanities	444.0	27.2%	268.4	18.3%	196.1	15.8%	155.6	13.5%	175.7	9.8%
Amusements	223.6	13.7%	41.8	2.8%	52.3	4.2%	16.4	1.4%	159.4	8.9%
Apparel/Accessories	201.7	12.3%	412.3	28.1%	452.3	36.6%	161.5	14.0%	822.8	46.0%
Fiction	141.2	8.6%	10.7	0.7%	33.0	2.7%	0.0	0.0%	5.8	0.3%
Beauty & Grooming	127.8	7.8%	232.6	15.8%	260.0	21.0%	267.5	23.3%	163.1	9.1%
Food & Nutrition	88.5	5.4%	50.9	3.5%	24.3	2.0%	113.0	9.8%	41.6	2.3%
General Interest	72.6	4.4%	69.5	4.7%	43.0	3.5%	84.2	7.3%	59.5	3.3%
Health/Medicine	72.4	4.4%	106.3	7.2%	62.5	5.1%	161.6	14.1%	48.2	2.7%
Home Furnishings	67.8	4.1%	37.2	2.5%	2.1	0.2%	47.8	4.2%	74.5	4.2%
Business & Industry	62.6	3.8%	55.9	3.8%	37.6	3.0%	32.4	2.8%	14.2	0.8%
Miscellaneous	50.2	3.1%	49.3	3.4%	43.0	3.5%	57.1	5.0%	58.6	3.3%
Sports/Recreation	29.9	1.8%	8.0	0.5%	9.1	0.7%	9.4	0.8%	21.2	1.2%
National Affairs	19.6	1.2%	55.5	3.8%	9.7	0.8%	18.4	1.6%	31.2	1.7%
Travel/Transportation	17.5	1.1%	46.9	3.2%	5.0	0.4%	9.7	0.8%	63.3	3.5%
Children	10.0	0.6%	14.5	1.0%	7.3	0.6%	6.5	0.6%	2.6	0.1%
Foreign Affairs	2.5	0.2%	0.6	0.0%	0.0	0.0%	2.7	0.2%	27.3	1.5%
Gardening & Farming	1.2	0.1%	4.1	0.3%	0.0	0.0%	1.9	0.2%	13.8	0.8%
Building	1.1	0.1%	3.3	0.2%	0.2	0.0%	4.0	0.3%	5.1	0.3%
Total Pages	1,634.2	100%	1,468.1	100%	1,237.3	100%	1,149.7	100%	1,787.7	100%

Source: Hall's Magazine Report, January–December 1991.

FIGURE 12.1 SHARE OF MARKET— WOMEN WHO BOUGHT ACTIVEWEAR

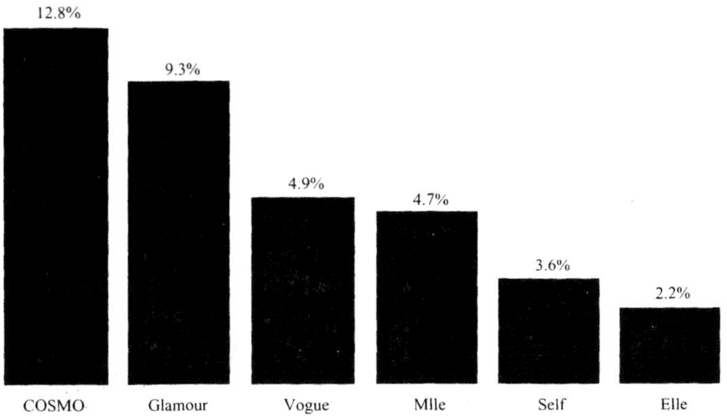

Source: 1982 Spring MRI

dies, they are, in fact, reflecting a judgment about the ambience of the program environment. To the extent that these editorial value ideas are appropriate to television, as well as magazines, there is no reason why a planner should not consider and include them in broadcast buying guidelines.

WEIGHTING

Weighting is one of the more problematic tools of media planning, but it has major practical advantages. Weighting may be puzzling and questionable, but it is also handy, efficient, and guiltless.

Weighting is a popular tool in media planning. It clearly addresses the question "What am I actually getting for my money?" Weighting also satisfies the intellectual quest for social science certitudes in communications, while gratifying all the number crunchers who are secretly afraid of the responsibilities of judgment and the shadow of their imaginations.

MEDIA MATH

Weighting is a method of assigning values to raw numbers. In effect, it is a method for marking up, or discounting, the importance of one or more factors you are considering. Weighting might be called the "power factor." It is a method of adjusting numbers to reflect the value you believe they have in a specific context.

To weight a number, multiply the number by the percent representing the value ascribed, and treat the resulting percentage as a real number.

EXHIBIT 12.4 ADULTS 18+—ANY DOMESTIC BUSINESS TRAVEL PAST 12 MONTHS

Vehicle	Open Rate 1/3Pg 2C	Aud. (000)	Comp.	Cvg. Rtg.	2C CPM	Audience %Male	%Fem.
Hemispheres	$14,530	576	41.2%	2.8%	$25.23	64.2	35.8
The Wall Street Journal	28,651	1,314	32.7	6.4	21.80	74.3	25.7
Conde Nast Traveler	13,460 .	587	32.1	2.9	22.93	56.6	43.4
Time B	30,700	2,878	15.2	14.1	10.67	65.3	34.7

EXAMPLES

Three different media planners at three different agencies representing three different automobile nameplates are comparing the same two magazines.

1. One planner is informed that women have only half the influence that men have in the purchase of the high-performance automobile his agency represents. Which magazine would he favor?

	Magazine A			Magazine B		
	Male	Female	Total	Male	Female	Total
Readers (000)	3,200	3,700	6,900	1,700	5,800	7,500
Weighted %	100%	50%		100%	50%	
Weighted Audience (000)	3,200	1,850	5,050	1,700	2,900	4,600

This planner would prefer Magazine A because of its male skew.

2. a. A second planner is informed that men only have half the influence in the purchase of the hatchback, get-about automobile her agency represents. Which magazine would she favor?

	Magazine A			Magazine B		
	Male	Female	Total	Male	Female	Total
Readers (000)	3,200	4,800	8,000	1,700	5,800	7,500
Weighted %	50%	100%		50%	100%	
Weighted Audience (000)	1,600	4,800	6,400	850	5,800	6,650

This planner would prefer Magazine B because of its female skew.

2. b. The third planner is informed that men and women have an equal influence on the purchase of the family sedan his agency represents. This planner would favor Magazine A because of the more balanced dual audience and greater number of total readers.

EXERCISES

1. If the agency and client have agreed that women 18–34 have an index value of 100 for their product, women 35–54 a 75 index value, women 55+ a 50 index value, and that adult men have zero value, which of the two broadcast audience packages would best serve the client's advertising goals?

	Package A	Package B
Women 18–34	150,678	134,626
Women 35–54	122,232	156,374
Women 55+	97,842	101,238
Men 18+	278,700	257,132
Total Adults 18+	649,452	649,370

Ans. _____

2. You have concluded that adults 35+ are only 60% as significant as adults 18–34 to your brand. Rank the following three magazines using this scale.

Magazine	Adult Readers	18–34	35+	Weighted Readers
A	7,454,232	33%	67%	_____
B	6,167,832	40%	60%	_____
C	5,900,500	49%	51%	_____

Applications

Weighting is used for two purposes: to measure exposures to advertising and to evaluate the value of those exposures. The first issue is that not every vehicle exposure is an advertising exposure. Audience research proposes to measure how many people looked at a vehicle, but it makes no claims that all of these people saw—to say nothing of recalling—all the advertising in the vehicle. This disconnect between vehicle exposure and advertising exposure has been known for over thirty years, long before the advent of "zapping" and "surfing" with the help of remote controls.

The second issue addresses advertising effects. The argument is that television in its various forms has varying impacts, as do the various forms of print. Advertising executions also vary in their effectiveness. Weighting is used to account for either or both of these variables. Exposures are evaluated on everything from time of day to length or size of the advertisement (Exhibit 12.5).

Exposures and Effects Not all GRPs are equal, media ratings are not advertising ratings. Relying on various kinds of research, many advertising agencies and their clients have concluded that it is only logical to weight Nielsen ratings, or SMRB/MRI

EXHIBIT 12.5 HOW MEDIA DIRECTORS RATE THE MEDIA

	Index
Prime (30)	100
Day (30)	48
Early Fringe (30)	83
Late Fringe (30)	63
Mags (P4C)	70

In the spring of 1993, Ed Papazian asked 50 agency media directors to rate the exposure and impact value of different media. (A medium's advertising value is the product of its "probability of exposing the average ad" and its "contribution to the impact of the message.") The results were published in his newsletter, "Media Matters." The data are a fair representation of how media planners would say they rate the advertising value of different media.

Source: The newsletter Media Matters

coverage ratings, according to their beliefs about the audience's attentiveness to advertising.

In almost all instances, this results in a downscaling of advertising ratings. Researchers will argue, for example, that only 80 percent of the reported prime time network television audience actually sees a specific commercial. This exposure percent drops to about 55 percent for daytime, 40 percent for radio, and 35 percent for newspapers. Following this arithmetic, a 15 program rating in prime time is discounted to a 12 advertising rating. The result for a single announcement, of course, is less extensive reach. Weighting a schedule of commercials, therefore, will affect both the reported reach and estimated frequency, while producing a different perception of relative cost.

Many advertisers also discount this advertising exposure rating further. They may have proprietary research from the testing of their commercials, for example, which tells them that only 45 percent of the people who see these commercials can recall the brand's selling proposition. Following the case above, this would mean that only 45 percent of the people represented by the 12 advertising exposure rating were affected. Thus, they would discount their reach accordingly to 5.4 percent of the target. The case for this approach is quite simple: Let's be realistic about what will happen when we advertise.

In lieu of this proprietary research, agencies can access Starch, Burke, Gallup and Robinson, and other research services for indices of advertising recall for commercials in their brand category. The numbers they derive are then applied just as proprietary recall numbers are.

Another approach to weighting uses the numbers from studies that focus on a medium's history. In this instance, research from multiple brand categories over time is utilized to determine the general effectiveness of 60-second television commercials versus 30-second commercials, or full-color back cover magazine advertisements versus a single black-and-white page inside the magazine.

This approach could result in weighting a page upward. For example, if an agency assumes that the typical magazine advertisement is noted by only 55 percent of readers, but that a back cover performs better (that is, it indexes at 135), the planner would conclude that the brand's back cover advertisement will be noted by 74.25 percent (55×1.35) of the magazine's reported readers.

Occasionally, all three weighting approaches are utilized together. Circulation is weighted by an exposure factor, by a recall factor, and by a media placement factor.

Problems A planner has to admit that this all sounds pretty good and the vast majority of major advertising agencies utilize weighting in one form or another, based on one or more research inputs. At the same time, most agencies would admit that the process poses major problems and may, in fact, resolve very little.

What are the problems?

There is insufficient data to substantiate the exposure assumptions being made. The real exposure number could just as easily be higher or lower than the formula weight used.

Recall scores for individual advertisements, for a category of advertisements, or across brand categories, are inappropriate to media evaluations, because the research was designed to measure message communications.

Each marketing communication and Media Plan situation is entirely different, and it is impractical to pursue equally unique data.

It is too difficult to defend any specific weighting procedure if the planner is questioned by the product group, the media representatives, or clients.

The extensive manipulation of the numbers involved gets to no practical end and is often not appreciated by clients.

Uses and Abuses Advertisers purchase circulations or ratings, which are translated into reach and frequency. Whenever advertisers or agencies discount these numbers to account for their estimate of actual advertising exposure and/or effectiveness, they have no alternative but to purchase more GRPs in order to increase their estimated actual reach and frequency to acceptable levels. In short, weighting is often a rationale for higher advertising budgets.

Some believe that weighting for actual exposure or effectiveness will help them in negotiating with the media, but they are dreaming. The parameters and pricing flexibility built into the cost of television seconds or printed inches is built on manufacturing, distribution, and marketing costs, plus profit, as modified by supply and demand. If the industry could agree on lower exposure numbers as the reference point for competitive pricing, the only result would be higher costs per point as the new competitive vocabulary. They will add up to the same out-of-pocket cost per time or space purchased.

Weighting, however, can be utilized to compare one proposed execution to another, or simply not to inflate the expected sales impact of an advertising schedule. In the process, a planner should be cautious in giving the weights more credibility than they deserve. After all, weighting is a judgment call that can be balanced by other equally valid judgments. The fact that a weight is a number only masks the fact that it is also a judgment without definitive data support.

Advocates of weighting often misinterpret the planning process. An understanding of the research background relating to exposures and recall has already been integrated into much of the strategy planning process. The data has informed the media selection and rationale, as well as being incorporated in considerations of motivational frequency. In short, weighting has already taken place, often in a more sensitive and sophisticated way than is possible with cumbersome executional formulas.

Clients who often do a great deal of commercial research will frequently exercise greater candor than will their agencies. These clients do not insist on altering the planning process; rather, they accept it as it is. They do, however, recognize whether the agency's creative product is less effective than normally reported recall scores. If they are running such commercials, they may increase their budgets to compensate. They will not do that very often, however, and these agencies are made very aware of the costs of their less successful creative efforts.

Some advertisers and agencies see great possibilities in computer modeling. The method is to obtain extensive data on the results of a specific campaign. They will have sales data, recall data, actual ratings, and so on. They will then go through a process of applying differing weights to all the communication elements, until the weighting produces the actual sales and recall results. This weighting formula is the model.

Once an agency has a model for a specific brand, it can play "What if" games against various advertising schedules. When used by professionals, these models are recognized as applying to only one brand in specific circumstances. They are not unsophisticated enough to apply the model across brands. The other limitation of these models is that history never repeats itself. Everything from competition to the character of the media available changes from year to year. Therefore, these models must be used with caution when they are used to create future plans. However, they can be very informative and can generate significant insights.

CONTINUING DIALOGUE

Neither the media planner, who is crafting a tactical outline, nor the media buyer, who is constructing or selecting a schedule of vehicles, is ever alone. Media representatives are their constant companions.

The key word in any relationship is "dialogue." Media planners and buyers may occasionally perceive themselves as monarchs of all they survey, but the facts contradict their inflated self-importance. Planners cannot advertise without budgets, which are useless without media vehicles to buy. Furthermore, no one knows everything, especially not planners functioning in a constantly changing media and marketing world. Planners are reliant on the self-interested and radically focused research and information brought to them by media representatives in order to do their job responsibly. Planners and vehicle, salespeople have mutual and interdependent interests that can only be realized through continuous dialogue.

INTEGRATED MARKETING COMMUNICATIONS

Integrated Marketing Communication (IMC) is one of the hot topics struggling to become the managing idea of the future. Integrated Marketing Communications presents itself as responsive to the growing numbers of media and to fragmenting consumer markets. IMC also promises control and efficiency. Taken at face value, it is a hard concept to resist. Most assuredly, we will hear a great deal more about it in the years to come.

The facts we are currently experiencing and the future facts we are facing mirror one another. Any major advertiser today finds itself utilizing a proliferating number of media at rapidly increasing costs. The natural outcomes are an insistence on greater accountability, a desire for more persuasive impact per communication, and a continuing hope for productivity in synergism. These circumstances and motivations can only be intensified by future media and marketing developments. Integrated Marketing Communications proposes to address these very urgencies.

Integrated Marketing Communications can be defined as the intentional employment and management of all the applicable tools of consumer communication to insure a seamless message strategy and produce maximum sales impact. IMC is a management concept aimed at both efficiency and effectiveness. This concept has been used in the past, but history and technology make it new.

Historically, direct mail, public relations, and product promotions, although recognized as marketing communications, were treated as separate activities, provided by separate suppliers. Advertising agency growth, which had been stimulated by expansion into international markets, had apparently stalled in the 1970s. Led by Young & Rubicam, agencies sought expansion by acquiring other agencies that had specialized in direct mail, public relations, and product promotions. These mega agencies promoted one-stop shopping for all these services, promising cost-saving management efficiency and strategic communications effectiveness. Young & Rubicam called this proposition "The Whole Egg."

At the same time, marketing science was developing elaborate models of consumer behavior that proposed the ability to perform a cost/benefit analysis of all marketing variables, including communication variables. One major limitation, however, was research data. The combination of scanners at supermarkets and ever more targeted communication opportunities appeared to bridge a major portion of the research gap.

Meanwhile, the media were experiencing the double threats of economic recession and growing competition. In order to compete more effectively for the available dollars, the various media vehicles—especially magazines—began offering what they called "added value" packages. This meant providing mailings to consumers or retailers. It also meant sponsoring specially designed promotions. The result was not only further encouragement to recognize the advantages of integrated marketing communications, but also a growing list of market test examples for everyone to study and learn from.

We are now at the moment when the energy behind these various business tides is converging. Everyone is getting into the act. None of these efforts, however, has a necessary or obvious direct link to the way media planners do their jobs. On the other hand, planners must be aware of the changing environment and ever more alert to synergistic opportunities.

Data Requirements

Integrated Marketing Communications is especially reliant on extraordinary databases. We may like to believe that supermarket scanners and interactive media will make a great deal of data available and accessible in the near future. So they might, but the data will be expensive, perhaps more expensive than most advertisers can afford. The data will be expensive because of its quantity, its proprietary nature, and the need for its extensive manipulation.

Judgment and imagination will become obvious needs in the face of proliferating databases. If the marketing and communications futures we project prove to be true, they will be built on greater and greater individuality. Not only will this help make research more expensive (because of the need for larger samples verging on a census), but it also will make the conclusions more fragile. This fragility will increase as the research reports are combined in order to form the foundation of useful strategies. There will be more numbers to see through, and more connections to be found. Consequently, there will be a premium on judgment and imagination.

Management Issue

Integrated Marketing Communications, however, is mostly a management issue. All of the elements of integrated marketing exist today, but they exist in different companies with competitive agendas. The integration of these disciplines and businesses will require an imaginative grasp of each, and judgment in their strategic application.

But can it happen? It can, if we recognize that we already operate with accountability and synergism in the media planning process. Developing strategies from a cognitive imagination of communications in people's lives will be required in an Integrated Marketing Communications system, and what this text encourages today. If we recognize that we already have integrated marketing communications and that the future only proposes an increase in media and media data, we can exercise the talents today that we will require in the future. If we do not see the present as dynamic, we will sink rather than swim in the future's data inundation and demands for integration.

IMAGINING THE FUTURE

The future continues to enchant us, confuse us, encourage us, and frighten us. We can say with absolute certitude that we will see the development of new media, new products, and new consumers in the future. We can be certain that the future will look no more like today than today looks like 1939 and the Pavilion of the Future at that year's World's Fair.

Nearly every magazine we read over the coming years will be reporting new mergers and acquisitions among media companies, describing exciting technological developments, and publishing assertive essays about the home or office of the future. It is probably foolish to believe that any particular one of these new companies will survive, that any particular one of the new technologies will become dominant, or that communications in the home or office will be configured as we speculate about it today; the 1939 Fair should have taught us that. In the present, however, we will have to experiment with all of the new possibilities on the way to creating whatever future will become reality.

Cyberspace

Communications technology, which developed parallel with industrialization, supported the growth of mass society from the early decades of the nineteenth century and, most intensively, from the 1870s to the 1970s. Since then, technology has been facilitating demassification in society and industry. The so-called Information Superhighway, or World Wide Web, is the most radical current example of this recent historical trend.

The history of media from printing to broadcast television is, in many ways, the history of technology. The emerging media revolution is, at its roots, a digital revolution. Pictures from life, the sounds of voices and printed words can now be reduced to so many ones and zeroes. Transmission can be accomplished via satellites, which are distance insensitive, and fiber optics, which are capacity insensitive. The result is that anything and everything can now move with the speed of light to anywhere and everywhere. All that has been needed to complete the revolution is receivers. They now exist, not only in the miniature satellite dishes, CD players, and modem-equipped personal computers but, most especially, in the growing number of people—citizens and consumers—who insist on plugging into the possibilities and becoming receivers.

The Internet is a vast collection of mainly private computer networks, connecting millions of users in an estimated 150 countries. More than half of the users are outside of the United States. There are more than seventy thousand private computer bulletin board systems in the United States, and an uncounted number of private business networks. Private commercial computer networks, such as America Online, CompuServe, and Prodigy Services, have nearly six million subscribers.

To access these systems, after accumulating the necessary home equipment, a consumer must pay for the installation of a line into the home and then pay a monthly fee for service, much as they now do for telephone service. Today, on-line subscriptions carry a base cost of approximately $25 per month.

To become an information provider, a publisher usually contracts with an access service. Setup fees vary from $4,000 to $15,000, depending on the graphic sophistication involved. Monthly maintenance charges range from $200 to $2,000, depending on usage and update frequency.

According to Leslie Laredo, director of marketing development for Ziff-Davis Interactive, their service has already surpassed 45,000 paid circulation. Through the service, readers of *PC Magazine* can access supplemental information, or interact with other readers. The on-line network is sponsored by the publisher and suppliers such as Prodigy and America Online. That means that, for the moment, the service is free.

Advertising Applications

Someone eventually will have to sponsor much of the Information Superhighway, many argue, because publishers are ultimately dedicated to profits and consumers will seek relief from the mounting user costs. Some experts predict that these consumer fees, without advertising or sponsorship, will rise to $1,000 per month.

Some current experimental applications are:

Advertisers are experimenting as information providers.

> AT&T provides tours of famous museums around the world (Figure 12.2) in ways not dissimilar to a CD-ROM tour of the Louvre.

> Miller Beer offers participation in a virtual pub, Tap Room, where the gossip and chat covers music, fashion, sports, and food (Figure 12.3).

> Digital Equipment Corp. offers a "test drive" of its Alpha computer with customer success stories of applications.

> Ragu has introduced "Mama's Cucina" to the Web, and she offers information about Ragu products and Italian cooking and culture. Ragu announces promotional offers from cookbooks to T-shirts and requests marketing data from its purchasers about themselves and their eating habits (Figure 12.4).

Agencies are using the network to extend their services or to display their expertise.

> Bernard Hodes Advertising offers Career Mosaic, where job seekers can search for opportunities in a variety of businesses (Figure 12.5)

> Ogilvy & Mather Direct/Interactive Marketing Group offers advice on "the responsible participation of marketers on the Internet" as part of its self-promotion (Figure 12.6).

Media Companies, both old and new, are repositioning themselves as electronic publishers.

> *Wired* magazine went on-line with Hot Wired in November 1994. One area is called "Coin of the Realm," featuring advertising from AT&T, IBM, MCI, Coors Brewing Co., and Volvo.

> *U.S. News and World Report* has joined *PC Magazine* and an expanding number of other magazine and newspaper publishers experimenting with electronic editions.

> Global Network Navigator provides a rationalized entry site to the Internet (Figure 12.7) and mixes advertising and other content as a new kind of catalogue publisher.

These few examples, in fact, are only the tip of the iceberg. Few publishers would claim not to be experimenting; few advertisers disclaim interest, and few major agencies have not announced their developing expertise.

FIGURE 12.2 AT&T OFFERS ART ON THE INTERNET

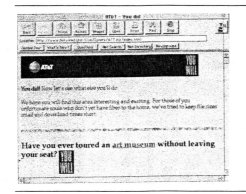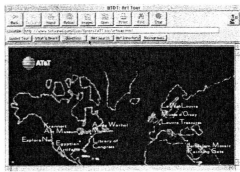

FIGURE 12.3 MILLER BEER'S VIRTUAL PUB

FIGURE 12.4 RAGU HAS INTRODUCED MAMA TO THE INTERNET

EXHIBIT 12.5 AN AGENCY CREATES ITS OWN AD MEDIUM

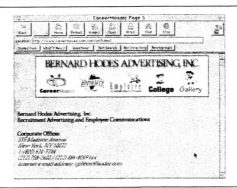

EXHIBIT 12.6 OGILVY & MATHER DIRECT PROMOTES ITS SKILLS

EXHIBIT 12.7 GLOBAL NETWORK NAVIGATOR HELPS FIND OTHER PUBLICATIONS

EXHIBIT 12.6 CYBERSPACE PUBLISHING AND ADVERTISING

U.S. NEWS BREAKS DOWN WALLS

U.S. News and World Report is bringing its advertisers onto CompuServe. What's noteworthy is not the quality of the campaigns, but that this is the first "advertising" content to reside outside the walls of the service's Electronic Mall.

Saab and DeBeers Diamonds, using distinctly different approaches, are the first to go on line. Both advertisers can be accessed from the "Offers & Promotions" selection of the U.S. News and World Report editorial menu on CompuServe. Three or four other advertisers are in different stages of development and may be added to the area by the beginning of next year. U.S. News Publisher Tom Evans says no more than 12 advertisers would be featured at any one time.

Saab has opened an electronic showroom offering photographic images of various models, standard features and prices and selected complimentary quotes from auto buff magazines. The experience is more like a slide show than an interactive tour. The "jazziest" feature is a dealer locator. Enter the two-letter state abbreviation and locations appear. The initial plan, developed in conjunction with Saab agency Angotti, Thomas & Hedge, New York, called for an engineer or other expert to field online questions. But that person became unavailable when the campaign went live at summer's end.

The DeBeers campaign, meanwhile, is a six-week promotional appearance running through Nov. 14. It ties directly to a sweepstakes that appeared in the Oct. 10 print issue of U.S. News & World Report. Entrants are invited to guess the number of diamonds on a jewelry-iced birthday cake to "win a diamond bracelet valued at approximately $4,000 for the woman you love." (A bit of a gender assumption here.)

It takes some time—about 8 minutes at 9600 baud—to watch a photographic image of the cake bake. (And CompuServe never warns just how long the process will be.) Yet by the third week, U.S. News had collected "thousands," rather than the hundreds of online entries anticipated. Fine print in the magazine ad instructed readers they could use CompuServe as an entry vehicle instead of the U.S. Mail.

Such literal translation of a print promotion to the online medium hardly exploits the capabilities. In discussion are much sexier applications for DeBeers that may or may not ever make it to CompuServe. (Our personal favorite: Design your own diamond ring.)

Later this year, DeBeers will run an interactive guide by buying diamonds on the Sports Illustrated Almanac on CD-ROM, says Matt Schwach, senior vice president, planning director for The Media Edge. It will include basic information about carats along with such lighthearted fare as "favorite proposal lines." This educational information may also wind up on CompuServe.

Meanwhile, the new initiative from U.S. News is causing CompuServe to rethink how it positions its advertising. Keith Arnold manages The Electronic Mall,

which currently houses about 135 advertisers. He says a "pseudo rate card" was created for the U.S. News advertisers that limits the area to not more than 10 screens
and five or six pictures. Price is $7,500–10,000 per quarter rather than the annual
contracts written for the Mall—typically starting at the six-figure level. These are
highly customized and allow for much more scope and capability. So does that mean
a U.S. News advertiser wishing to mount something more ambitious will have to go
through the Mall?

"Nothing is set in stone, it's all still very fluid at this point," says Arnold.

A bridge may be developed in The Mall that links the commercial area to the
U.S. News Offers & Promotions. So a shopper looking for information about Saab,
who doesn't know it resides in U.S. News, will still be able to find it.

U.S. News' assumption is that adjacency to editorial content adds value to the
online advertising. Susan Riker, director of editorial business development for U.S.
News, notes that for its online College Fair it's logical to make a direct link to financial advertisers to that students can calculate their projected costs. There are also
plans to survey online readers to understand who is using it and how. The overall
U.S. News area is attracting an average 70,000 visitors per week.

Source: Inside Media, November 2, 1994, Vol. 6, No. 21

Issues

The ultimate question is: Will the Information Superhighway become a Marketing
Superhighway? Several central issues currently are being hotly debated and will have
a major impact on the "If" and "How" of advertising on the interactive networks.

Access   The first issue facing advertisers in the emerging digital environment is
access. The driving philosophy behind advertising is that economic communications
should be integrated wherever social communications are occurring. Advertisers
believe—to put it more biblically—that wherever two people are gathered together to
communicate, advertising should be there among them. This explains car cards on
subways as well as commercials on television, and point-of-purchase displays as well
as magazine spreads.

Advertising has always been a secondary communication, and advertisers have
been happy to pay much of the cost of transmission and reception of primary communications in order to be seen and heard. Writers create readers and audiences;
advertisers do not. Advertising is the price people have been willing to pay to reduce
their out-of-pocket costs for information and entertainment. This consumer perception
(or, cost-benefit analysis), however, may change radically for users of the digital
Information Superhighway.

Much of the current dialogue on the Internet expresses either skepticism or out-
rage over the very idea of advertising invading the user's private space. Many claim to

be on the World Wide Web to escape commercialization and any media pollution of information. Consequently, access will become a continuing debate, and no one yet knows how or if an accommodation will be reached (Exhibit 12.7).

Style   The second critical issue is: What rhetorical form should or will advertising take when it goes on-line? We are not referring here only to rhetoric as persuasion. Rather, we are referring to rhetoric as the foundations and rules of the formulation of marketing communications.

The search for an effective and acceptable rhetoric explains much of the experimentation going on today. Most advertisers are not excited by and will not pay much for the privilege of having their name at the bottom of the screen or their logo in an upper corner. Advertisers want their presence to be impressive and meaningful. They also want new media to perform marketing communications functions that they find difficult or impossible in a contemporary environment.

Advertisers welcome any opportunity to speak only to the most narrowly targeted consumers and to carry on a direct conversation. Beyond the question of whether consumers will welcome such advertiser access, however, is the question of what the advertiser will have to say and how the advertiser will say it in order to hold the consumer's attention and satisfy the consumer's quest for information. At the current moment, no one knows.

Whose Job?   The third issue is: What role, if any, will traditional advertising agencies play? Some think that the combination of cyberspace options and integrated communication strategies will force traditional agencies into the role of general contractors, overseeing and coordinating the work of others' trades or boutiques. Others believe that if advertising is going to have a role on the World Wide Web, it will be as information, not persuasion, and the barrier between editorial and advertising will dissolve. If that is to be the case, who needs an agency? Client product information and promotion departments currently handle these tasks and are certainly better equipped and equally positioned to perform these functions as agencies.

Known and Unknown

If no one knows the precise shape of the future, what, then, do we know? We know that there will be a quantum leap in available information and entertainment. We know that there will be a quantum leap in the speed of communications. We know that there will be a quantum leap in our individual means of access. We know that the media will be increasingly demassified and increasingly interactive. We know that a radically different communications environment will be in place long before most of those who read this book retire from their professional careers.

We also know that consumers will change. The new media will change consumer attitudes and lifestyles. It happened before, and it will happen again. Most likely, the eclectic nature of experience and isolation of decision made possible by the new media will produce many cultures, kaleidoscopic subsets of values and motivations. It will be

EXHIBIT 12.7 CYBERSPACE COALITION

CONTENT PROVIDERS JOIN TOGETHER TO EXAMINE ADVERTISING STANDARDS, POLICIES AND TECHNOLOGY

Cyberspace content providers are forming their own trade association to help standardize elements of their emerging industry.

The Cyberspace Content Coalition will have major cyberspace content providers pooling their time to discuss and format issues concerning advertising standards, policies and technology. Members include Time Warner, Hearst New Media, Tribune Interactive Network Services, The Washington Post, Reuters New Media, Advance Publication's Newhouse Newspapers and Wired magazines HotWired Web site.

CCC will be the equivalent to what the Coalition for Advertising Supported Information and Entertainment [CASIE] is for advertisers and ad agencies. That organization recently put together a summit in New York to discuss issues concerning new media, including interactive TV and Internet services.

"Advertisers and content providers are anxious for ways to play in the new media that gives them some efficiency so that you are not creating differently for every platform that you are on or for every provider you work with," says Kathryn Creech, general manager of Hearst New Media's HomeArts.

The CCC, for instance, will form one committee to examine different kinds of advertising on the Internet and on the commercial online services. Subsequently, it will recommend standardizing, say, the size of advertiser logos.

"There aren't many standards in the marketplace," says Creech. "Everyone is trying something new and we'd like to all share that information so we can learn from each other."

Another committee will look at "click-stream," and other online measuring software. Clickstream measures the flow and duration of Internet users as they move from home pages or Web sites to other areas. They'll be another committee surveying Web browser technology.

Andrew Anker, president of HotWired, the Internet version of Wired Magazine, is one of the forces behind the Coalition. Unlike CASIE, though, CCC, as yet, will not hold an in-person summit. Instead, it'll most likely conduct its discussion among members in—what else—cyberspace.

"This is not-the-bureaucratic committee approach," says one executive about the coalition. "It's 'Lets get some guys together who have enough clout so maybe others will follow.' We are all going to comply [will some standardizing]."

The group hopes to meet with CASIE, as well as individuals at major ad agencies and advertisers. It will then convene with the online services. "We think then there'll be a lot of pressure for AOL [America Online], Prodigy, and CompuServe to [go along with CCC's recommendations]," says the source.

So far, other members of the coalition include Walter Isaacson, editor, New Media for Time Inc., Charles Brumback, chairman, chief executive officer, and president of The Tribune Company, and Steven Newhouse, editor in chief of The Jersey Journal. Newhouse has been the point person for Newhouse Newspapers for online technology.

Source: Inside Media, March 29, 1995.

a major challenge to comprehend this consumer marketplace and to discover the clusters of connections among consumers that will enable marketing communications to retain its efficiency and effectiveness.

Perhaps we need not know many more specifics at this point, because we will be participants in the future. The question, then, is: Are we prepared for greater speed, information, entertainment, interactivity, isolation, and individuality? The only tools responsive to these conditions are strategy and imagination. These are the tools that we should be using in the present. If we do this, we will be prepared.

SUMMARY

* Negotiations between buyers and sellers of media vehicles is the endgame of the media planning process.
* In the mercurial world of evolving media all media representatives will have to work at becoming marketing partners as well as salespeople.
* Media sales and purchase are the result of a continuing dialogue.
* The key elements of the sales and purchase equation are: market, medium, product, and price.
* The market, from both buyer and seller points of view, is created by the vehicle's editorial franchise.
* The degree of relevance of the editorial franchise to the brand's selling proposition is dependent on the strategic use to which the vehicle will be put.
* The planner, as well as the salesperson, must be capable of articulating the editorial franchise and its possible relevance.
* Weighting is a problematic but often useful tool in the evaluation of media and media vehicles.
* Attentive and imaginative listening are key tools for both players in the sales and purchase dialogue.
* Integrated Marketing Communication is a promising management concept, facing significant obstacles.

* Many advertisers, agencies, and media companies are involved in experiments with digital and interactive media.
* No one is now certain if advertising will be welcomed on the World Wide Web, what form it will take, or who will be directly responsible for its creation and placement.
* Any scenario for the future of communications must include concomitant changes in consumer culture.
* The skills of imaginative understanding and prudent judgment required today will be in even greater demand in the future.

QUESTIONS

1.   Why do media planners need a dialogue with media representatives?
2.   What are the key elements in the sales and purchase equation? Explain the point of view of the buyer and seller on each of these elements.
3.   Why will media representatives be increasingly required to become marketers as well as salespersons?
4.   What is an editorial franchise, and how is it relevant to advertising?
5.   How do planners utilize weighting in the media planning process? What limitations should the planner be aware of in applying media weights?
6.   Why is listening well one of the more significant skills of superior media representatives? Is listening an equally important talent for media planners and buyers? Why?
7.   What, if anything, can be said with certitude about the future landscape of communications?
8.   Describe Integrated Marketing Communications.
9.   What are the major issues facing the future of advertising on the World Wide Web?
10. Why will the exercise of your cognitive imagination today be the best preparation for managing future communication opportunities?

EXERCISE

You represent a popular family dessert brand that is utilizing print advertising featuring ease of preparation and recipes. The print strategy is to use general interest magazines to establish reach and awareness, and to use vertical interest family and food magazines to create frequency and cultural confirmation. You have a magazine budget of $2,500,000.

1.   Create a 12-month flowchart identifying the magazines and issues you recommend purchasing. The brand experiences virtually no seasonality in sales or usage.
2.   Explain how you selected the magazines identified on the flowchart: What did you consider; what criteria did you use; how did you weight the criteria, etc.?

3.   What "added value" package would you expect the magazines to provide?

4.   In class discussion, attempt to persuade your classmates of the validity and creativity of your plan.

MAGAZINE ANALYSIS W25-54 W/KIDS < 18; HHI $25M+

Publication	Rate Base (000)	P4CB Cost	Avg. Aud. (000)	Composition %	Rank	Coverage %	Rank	CPM $	Rank
Working Mother	625	$17,722	1,346	53.4	1	6.0	4	13.17	3
Sesame St. Mag.	1,225	$37,044	2,143	49.6	2	9.5	2	17.29	5
Child	500	$14,700	1,013	49.3	3	4.5	6	14.51	4
Parents	1,725	$29,805	3,922	48.7	4	17.4	1	7.60	1
Disney Channel Mag.	5,150	$41,212	1,625	46.7	5	7.2	3	25.36	6
Parenting	630	$15,665	1,334	43.6	6	5.9	5	11.74	2
Reader's Digest	16,250	$82,500	6,743	24.0	5	29.8	1	12.23	2
TV Guide	15,800	$73,731	6,224	24.6	4	27.5	2	11.88	1
People	3,150	$81,775	5,806	28.3	3	25.7	3	14.08	3
Cable Guide	7,100	$51,093	3,232	29.3	2	14.3	4	15.81	4
Soap Opera Digest	1,300	$20,000	1,212	19.1	6	5.4	5	16.50	5
Ebony	1,750	$36,008	1,028	17.3	7	4.6	6	35.03	7
Entertainment Wky.	650	$17,645	635	35.5	1	2.8	7	27.79	6
Food & Wine	800	$29,975	541	30.6	1	2.4	4	55.41	5
Eating Well	350	$6,850	329	30.6	2	1.5	5	20.82	1
Cooking Light	900	$16,875	805	30.6	3	3.6	2	20.96	2
Bon Appetit	1,200	$28,175	1,047	25.7	4	4.6	1	26.91	3
Gourmet	750	$29,849	582	23.7	7	2.6	3	51.29	4

ASSIGNMENT

1.   Prepare comparison tables or other exhibits that describe both the media and the vehicles you have considered for your plan. Identify your criteria for the choices you finally recommend.

2.   Using Nielsen data and cost-per-point tables, prepare a schedule of broadcast announcements which delivers the number of GRPs by daypart required in your plan. Would a station or network initially offer this same schedule? If not, what would they offer? Could you reach a compromise or must your schedule be executed?

ANSWERS TO CHAPTER 12: EXERCISES

Page 290

1. Package B because it has a weighted audience of 302,525. Package A has a weighted audience of 291,273.

2. A) 5,456,498
   B) 4,687,552
   C) 4,696,645

GLOSSARY

A

ABC statement—An independent audit of a print vehicle's circulation. *See also* Audit Bureau of Circulations.

Ad/edit ratio—The ratio of percentage of advertising pages to percentage of editorial pages in a print vehicle.

ADI (Area of Dominant Influence)—A geographical market as defined by Arbitron. Every broadcast station is assigned to just one ADI.

Adjacency—A commercial time immediately preceding or following a scheduled broadcast program. In print, refers to a advertising contiguous with editorial.

Advertising impression—A possible exposure of an advertising message to one member of a vehicle audience.

Advertising to sales ratio—The percentage of a marketer's or industry's gross sales that is generally allocated to advertising.

Advertising weight—The amount of dollars supporting a brand during a specific period of time. Also, the number of impressions delivered during a specific period of time.

Advertorial—Advertising material that is designed to look and read like the editorial material of a specific print vehicle. Most publications require the copy to be labeled so as not to deceive the reader.

Affidavit— A notarized statement from a broadcast station that a commercial or commercial schedule in fact aired at the time shown on the station's invoice.

Affiliate—A broadcast station under contractual obligation to carry network-originated programming and commercial announcements at specifically scheduled times in return for monetary compensation.

Afternoon drive—A radio daypart, usually between 3:00 P.M. and 7:00 P.M. Also called P.M. drive time.

Agate line—A newspaper advertising space that is one fourteenth of an inch high and one column wide. There are fourteen agate lines to a column inch; they can be set in any shape. Mostly obsolete as unit of sale. *See also* Standard Advertising Unit.

Agency commission—Usually 15 percent, allowed to advertising agencies by the media and retained by the agency on all advertiser purchases of time or space. This traditional method of agency compensation is eroding in favor of a fixed fee system of client-agency compensation.

Agency of Record (AOR)—An advertising agency or media buying service that purchases and coordinates media placements on behalf of one or more agencies serving the same client for an agreed-upon compensation.

Air check—Recording of a broadcast to serve as archival proof of performance.

Allotment—The number and type of outdoor panels in a unit of sale. *See also* Showing.

Announcement—An advertising message in broadcast media, aired during or between programming elements. *See also* Spot.

Area of Dominant Influence—*See* ADI.

Arrears—Subscribers to a print vehicle whose subscriptions have expired but who continue to receive the publication without charge. This circulation is identified in an audit.

As it falls—A method for simulating a national media plan in a test market that reflects the media weight the market would receive if the national plan were executed *See also* Little America.

Audience—The number of people or households exposed to a media vehicle. Most strictly used in reference to broadcast vehicles, but also applied to print and to other media.

Audience composition—A vehicle audience described in terms of demographics or other characteristics.

Audience duplication—An estimated measurement of the number of persons or households exposed to more than one media vehicle in a specific period of time, or exposed more than once to the same vehicle.

Audience flow—The changes in the audience of a broadcast program, or in a station broadcast schedule, as the program or schedule is broadcast.

Audience, Primary—*See* Primary Readers.

Audience turnover—The average number of times a broadcast program, or station programming schedule, receives a "new" audience in a specific period of time. It is a ratio of total cumulative audience to average audience.

Audimeter—A device developed by A. C. Nielsen that automatically records television set tuning and usage on a minute-by-minute basis, and that provides raw data for television ratings.

Audit Bureau of Circulations (ABC)—A nonprofit organization established by media owners, advertisers, and ad agencies to audit the circulations of its member newspapers and magazines.

Availability—A specific commercial position in a program, between programs, or in a broadcast schedule that is open and offered for purchase to an advertiser. Also called avails.

Average audience—The number of homes or persons that are tuned to an average minute of a broadcast program. In print, represents the number of people who are exposed to an average issue of a publication.

Average frequency—An estimate of the average number of times that a household or individual is exposed to an advertisement in a media schedule during a specific period of time.

Average net paid circulation—The average paid circulation (subscribers plus news-stand sales) of a print vehicle's issues published during a specific period of time.

B

Back of book—The concluding section of a magazine. Also, the pages that follow the main editorial section.

Back to back—Two or more commercials or programs aired in immediate succession.

Backlit—An outdoor vehicle display in which the advertising is printed on a transparent surface and illuminated from behind.

Barter—The acquisition of media time or space in exchange for merchandise or other considerations, as opposed to cash purchases.

Barter syndication—The offering of programming to stations at no cost, but premised on the stations' airing the commercials integrated into the program. The station may sell the remaining advertising time for its own profit.

Basic prospect designation—*See* Source Generator.

Basic rate—*See* Open Rate.

Best food day—The day, usually preceding a community's primary grocery shopping day, when newspaper publishers feature special food sections to attract retail promotions and other advertising of packaged goods.

Billboard—In broadcasting, a brief eight- and ten-second announcement at a program break that identifies the major sponsor(s) of the program. Also an outdoor advertising sign.

Billings—The dollar amount of media placements handled by an agency on behalf of its advertiser clients.

Bind-in care—A promotional or response card inserted in a magazine and bound in with the printed pages. *See also* Tip-in.

Black-and-white page—An advertisement printed with black ink on white paper (or in reverse type), generally abbreviated as B/W, or PB/W.

Bleed page—An advertisement in print media in which the copy/artwork extends to the borders, utilizing the entire available space without margins. Generally sold at a premium.

Blow-in card—A loose promotional card randomly inserted between magazine pages.

Bonus circulation—Circulation delivered by a print vehicle that exceeds the publication's guaranteed rate base.

Brand Development Index (BDI)—The percentage of a brand's sales volume relative to a market's percentage of national or regional population. Used to evaluate brand strength, weakness, or opportunity on the premise that equal populations should evidence equal sales.

Broadcast calendar—An accepted calendar used for accounting purposes in which each quarter contains thirteen weeks, and each month begins on a Monday. Available through Standard Rate and Data Service, Inc.

Broadcast coverage area—The geographic area within which a broadcast station signal can be received.

Broadsheet—Full-size standard newspaper page, as opposed to tabloid page.

Buy—The advertising time or space purchased from a medium or media vehicle and the process of negotiating, ordering, and confirming a purchase.

Buying service—An independent company established to execute the media planning and purchasing function of a client's marketing communications. Comparable to a creative boutique, and distinct from a full-service agency.

c

Campaign—A coordinated advertising promotion following a specific strategy for a specific period of time for a particular brand or service.

Car card—An advertising unit offered in a bus, subway, or other transit vehicle.

Case allowance—Discount provided to retailers on each case of product with the assumed agreement that the retailer will advertise and promote the product.

Cash discount—A discount on media costs granted to an advertiser in return for prompt payment, generally within ten to thirty days.

Category Development Index (CDI)—The percentage of a product category's sales in a specific market, in relation to that market's percentage of the relevant population.

Center spread—An advertisement appearing on facing pages in the exact center of a magazine and usually printed as a single unit.

Chain break—The time between network programs during which local affiliated stations sell advertising and promote themselves.

Checking copy—A copy of a print publication sent to an advertiser or agency to verify that an advertisement ran as ordered.

Circulation—In print media, the number of copies of a publication distributed on a single occasion, or for an average issue. In broadcast, the number of households that tune to a station at least once during a rated period of time. In outdoor, the number of people passing an advertising display with an opportunity to see it.

City zone—A geographic area designated for auditing newspapers. A distinction is made between circulation in the center city and contiguous areas of the city limits, and suburban circulation.

Clearance—The number of broadcast stations carrying a network or syndicated program. Also, the percentage of U.S. households represented by the station markets.

Closing date—The absolute deadline set by a publication for the receipt of copy and artwork, with a supporting contract, for an advertisement to appear in a particular issue.

Combination rate—A discount rate offered to advertisers who purchase space in two or more publications owned by the same media company.

Commercial pool—The group of radio or television commercials that are strategically relevant and available for use for brand advertising at any given time. *See also* Rotation.

Commercial protection—The amount of time separating a client's commercial and that of a competitive brand, guaranteed by a broadcaster as part of the purchase agreement.

Competitive report—An internal report that compiles and compares the media spending/usage of all products or services in a specific category.

Consumer profile—A demographic (and often psychographic) description of the persons or households considered prime prospects for a particular product or service

Continuity—A scheduling strategy that seeks to maintain a constant and consistent level of advertising during a season or year.

Controlled circulation—The restricted and free distribution of publications that are made available only to specific professions or demographics.

Conversion factor—A percentage applied to household rating points in order to estimate persons or demographic rating points.

Cooperative advertising—Retail advertising contracted for by a local merchant, but paid for in whole or part by a manufacturer, distributor, or national advertiser.

Cost per Rating Point (CPP)—The cost of achieving advertising exposure before 1 percent of a target audience. Used to estimate in advance the cost of purchasing time for a proposed media schedule, or for comparing alternatives.

Cost per Thousand (CPM)—The cost of advertising exposure before one thousand households or persons through a particular medium, media vehicle, or schedule. Used to make cost-benefit comparisons between communication options.

Coverage—In print media, the percentage of a geographic market or target population delivered by a publication. This percentage is often treated as a rating point for evaluating mixed-media schedules.

Cover position—Premium priced advertising space on the covers of magazines. First cover = outside front cover; second cover = inside front cover; third cover = inside back cover; fourth cover = outside back cover.

Cumulative rating—A broadcast term for the net unduplicated audience of a station or network during two or more time periods, usually over four weeks. In Nielsen jargon, called cume. Also, the number of different households or persons reached by an advertising schedule during a specific period of time.

Cut-in—The insertion of a different commercial or copy at the local station level to replace the national commercial, purchased by the same advertiser and running at the same time on the network.

D

Daily Effective Circulation (DEC)—The gross audience that has an opportunity of seeing an outdoor display during a twenty-four-hour period.

Daypart—Specific broadcast time periods throughout the broadcast day (e.g., prime time, late night) with relative pricing structures.

Dealer tie-in—A national advertisement that carries, on a national or market-by-market basis, the names and addresses of local dealers or distributors.

Demographic editions—Unique issues of national publications, distributed only to specific, precisely defined audiences, that can carry unique advertising.

Demographics—The quantitatively measurable characteristics of a population, such as age, gender, education, and income, used to describe target markets and vehicle audiences.

Designated Market Area (DMA)—A geographical market, as defined by A. C. Nielsen. Every broadcast station is assigned to just one DMA.

Diorama—A backlit outdoor display, frequently located in transit terminals and sports arenas.

Direct Broadcast Satellite (DBS)—A satellite transmission that delivers programming directly to a receiving antenna (dish) at a home or business. Used for corporate conferences and sporting events, or as an alternative to cable and pay television in the home.

Direct mail advertising—Advertising materials sent through the mail directly to consumers.

Direct response advertising—Any form of advertising that enables the consumer to conclude a sale with the manufacturer or distributor without an intervening retailer.

Directory advertising—Advertising that appears in a buying guide or directory; especially Yellow Pages displays.

Double truck—A two-page spread in a magazine or newspaper that runs across the gutter of the binding fold.

Downscale—A general description of a prospect market, or vehicle audience, indicating lower demographic characteristics and interests.

Drive time—The morning and afternoon periods of radio broadcast day when most commuters in a market are on their way to or from work. *See also* Afternoon Drive.

Duplication—The numbers or percentage of a population exposed more than once to the same vehicle, or to more than one vehicle during the same specific period of time. Also, prospects exposed to an advertisement more than once during a campaign schedule.

E

Early fringe—A television daypart, usually between 4:00 P.M. and 7:30 P.M. EST.

Early morning—A television daypart, usually between 6:00 A.M. and 10:00 A.M. EST.

Effective frequency—*See* Motivational Frequency.

Effective reach—The percentage of a population exposed to an advertisement at the designated motivational frequency for a campaign schedule.

Efficiency—A general term for the cost of reaching prospects with advertising messages; most often used in reference to the relative costs of competitive media or vehicles.

Eight-sheet poster—An outdoor display, measuring 5 feet by 11 feet.

Error Rate—*See* Standard Deviation.

Estimation—The calculation of the probable cost of a future media schedule.

Exposure—A person's visual and/or auditory contact with an advertisement.

F

Fixed position—In broadcast advertising, the premium rate attached to broadcast time that cannot be preempted by another advertiser.

Fixed rate—In newspaper advertising, a base cost not subject to discounting.

Flighting—A method of scheduling advertising so that a period of advertising activity is followed by an advertising hiatus, followed by a period of advertising activity, etc., in a designed pattern.

Flowchart—A graphical presentation summarizing advertising activity during a calendar period, and including media types, vehicles, costs, and estimated delivery.

Four-color page—Black and three colors (usually blue, yellow, and red) of ink used in printing for realistic or dramatic effect. Also called P4-C.

Freestanding insert—A preprinted advertisement of one or more pages inserted loosely as an independent element among newspaper sections.

Frequency—The number of times that an average household or person is expected to be exposed to an advertisement during a campaign schedule.

Frequency distribution—A full array of reach according to the frequency delivered to each percentage of the population.

Fringe time—*See* Early Fringe and Late Fringe.

G

Gatefold—A special magazine advertising unit, consisting of a folded page that, when unfolded, is larger than the publication's ordinary page.

Gross Rating Points (GRPs)—The sum of all the ratings delivered by an advertising schedule, including duplication. It is the result of multiplying reach by frequency, and is often used to evaluate the expected impact of a plan.

Guaranteed circulation—The circulation level of a print publication on which advertising rates are based. The advertiser is assured a cost adjustment if this base level is not achieved.

H

Homes Using Television (HUT)—The percentage of homes in a geographical area in which television sets are turned on and in presumed use. HUT × Share = Rating.

Horizontal half page—An advertising unit across one-half of two facing pages of a print publication.

I

Impressions—The gross total of all exposures to a media schedule, including duplication.

Index—A percentage that relates numbers to a base; used to show positive or negative deviation, for purposes of comparison.

Infomercial—A long-form advertising message, ranging from two minutes to thirty minutes, used to provide extensive information on the product and its uses, and frequently involving direct response solicitations.

Insertion order—The form sent to a media vehicle that details information relating to an advertisement's placement, size, rate, frequency, etc.

In-store media—Vehicles offered by companies that have contracted with supermarkets for display locations in aisles, on shopping carts, and at checkout counters.

Integration cost—A charge to advertisers to cover the expense of including a commercial in a program, or for substituting one commercial for another.

Interconnect—Two or more cable systems linked together, forming a mini network, for the purposes of simultaneous programming and commercial opportunities.

Issue life—The length of time it takes a publication to accumulate its total measurable readership.

K

Key—A code within an advertisement; used to facilitate the identification of the source of a direct response inquiry or order.

Keyline—*See* Mechanical.

L

Late fringe—A broadcast television daypart following prime time, usually 11:00 P.M. to 1:00 A.M. EST.

Leading National Advertiser (LNA)—A research supplier of competitive media reports.

Lead-in/Lead-out—Broadcast programs positioned immediately before and after a specific program, and used to project or identify audience flow.

Lifestyle—Describes the nondemographic behavioral characteristics of a population group, and the values represented by such behavior.

List broker—An agent who collects, compiles, and sells prospect lists for direct mail applications.

Little America—A method of test market media planning that equalizes the local media weight with the average media weight that would be delivered to markets in a hypothetical national plan. Also called Little U.S.A. *See also* As It Falls.

M

Makegood—Advertising space or time offered in compensation for a commercial or advertisement that did not run as ordered, or was improperly reproduced.

Marketing mix—The particular combination of marketing efforts utilized in a strategy.

Market segmentation—A strategy, based on demographic or lifestyle characteristics, that offers different products or promotions to different segments of the population.

Mean—The sum of all items in a set, divided by the number of items in the set; the average.

Media buyer—The person responsible for negotiating and purchasing vehicle time or space.

Median—The middle number in a set of numbers.

Mechanical—A camera-ready pasteup of all the elements of a print advertisement, including photography, artwork, and copy type, on a single artboard. Also called keyline.

Media mix—The strategy of utilizing more than one media type for the distribution of advertising messages. Also, the actual combination of media resulting from such a strategy.

Media planner—The person responsible for determining the appropriate strategy and tactics in the use of media to fulfill a marketing strategy.

Merchandising—Promotional activities that are designed to complement an advertising effort, and are offered by media vehicles, at little or no cost, to enhance the purchase of time or space in the vehicle.

Motivational Frequency—The minimum number of exposures—normally within a four week period—considered necessary to motivate the average prospect in the target audience in order to accomplish a specific advertising objective. Some call this "effective frequency."

N

Net unduplicated audience—*See* Reach.

Network—An integrated grouping of media vehicles.

Newsstand sales—Copies of a publication that are sold at full price and purchased as single copies at retail outlets.

O

O and O—A station owned and operated by a broadcast network.

On-air test—A test that inserts a commercial (to be evaluated for recall, attitude generation, or purchase interest) into an actual station broadcast before the audience is surveyed.

Open rate—The highest, undiscounted rate at which advertising space is offered for sale. Also called one-time rate, or basic rate.

Orbit—A method of rotating an advertiser's message through a broadcast schedule with special consideration of program type or theme.

Outdoor advertising—Billboards, posters, signs, and other advertising displays placed outside along highways, railroads, etc.

Overnights—Nielsen household ratings from metered markets that are available the morning after a broadcast.

P

Paid circulation—The number of magazines purchased through subscription or newsstand, and constituting a circulation segment reported by the ABC.

Painted bulletin—An outdoor advertising display on which advertising is either painted directly on a structure, or preprinted on vinyl and stretched across the structure. Also called paint.

Panel—A single outdoor advertising unit.

Passalong readers—Readers of a publication who were not its initial purchasers. Also called secondary audience.

Perfect binding—A process of binding that uses glue, rather than staples, and results in a square spine.

Per inquiry advertising—A method of paying broadcasters or publishers on the basis of the number of responses or sales generated by the advertising, rather than a flat fee for the time or space. Also called PI.

Plant operator—The owner of an outdoor advertising company operating in a specific city or area.

Point-of-Purchase (POP) Display—Advertising and promotions displayed within retail stores.

Post analysis—An evaluation of the performance of a broadcast schedule after it has run. Also called postbuy.

Positioning—A statement of how a marketer intends consumers to perceive a brand relative to competition.

Primary readers—Readers who purchase a specific magazine, and other readers in the immediate household.

Prime access—The television daypart immediately preceding prime time, in which local stations are required to broadcast their own programming. Usually 7:30 P.M. to 8:00 P.M. EST.

Prime time—The broadcast daypart that attracts the largest audiences. Usually 8:00 P.M. to 11:00 P.M. EST.

Product/benefit segmentation—*See* Market Segmentation.

Psychographics—A method of describing groups of people based on their motivations and values.

Public Service Announcement (PSA)—An advertisement or information broadcast free of charge to nonprofit organizations.

Publishers Information Bureau (PIB)—A research service that reports about magazine advertising space.

Pulsing—A scheduling strategy that features intermittent bursts of increased advertising from a base of continuous activity over a specific period of time.

Purchase cycle—The pattern of the length of time between purchase and repurchase of an item.

Q

Quintile—An analysis of populations that divides individuals into five equal-sized groups, ranging from the heaviest to the lightest amount of exposure or usage.

R

Rate card—A listing of a vehicle's advertising costs, discount structures, closing dates, and mechanical requirements.

Rating—The percentage of households or persons tuned to a broadcast program at a specific time. Also, the percentage of households or persons consuming a media vehicle.

Reach—The percentage of a population exposed to an advertisement at least once during a campaign schedule. Also called net unduplicated audience.

Readers-per-Copy (RPC)—The average number of people who normally read an individual copy of a publication.

Rep—Slang term for media sales representative.

Retail Trading Zone—The area from which city zone merchants attract a significant number of customers.

Roadblocking—An advertising placement tactic that purchases precisely the same time on various networks or broadcast stations to insure maximum immediate reach, or to counter channel switching.

Roll-out—A marketing strategy that introduces a product into a progressively larger group of markets to the point of national distribution.

Rotation—The schedule of use of different commercials for the same brand during the specific period of time of a broadcast purchase.

Run-of-Paper (ROP)—Advertising space that is contracted to run anywhere in a publication. Also called Run-of-Press.

Run-of-Station (ROS)—A sales and scheduling tactic by which commercials are aired throughout the broadcast day.

S

SAU—*See* Standard Advertising Unit.

Scatter—Time purchased on broadcast networks or stations without specific airing restrictions. Can refer to any purchase made outside of the preseason, up-front annual package, negotiated by an advertiser. Also called scatter buy.

Secondary audience—*See* Passalong readers.

Secondary research—Analysis or reworking of data resulting from research conducted and published elsewhere.

Self-liquidating premium—A promotional item with an apparently radically discounted price that actually will recover the costs of manufacture.

Share—The share of audience; the percentage of total viewing at a specific time that is attentive to a particular network, station, or program. *See also* Homes Using Television.

Share of market—Percentage of category sales attributable to an individual brand.

Share of voice—The percentage of total competitive advertising conducted by an individual brand.

Shopper—A newspaperlike publication that primarily contains advertising and is frequently distributed free to homes in a retail area.

Showing—The number of outdoor displays required to reach the equivalent of 100 percent of a market population during a specific period of time. *See also* Gross Rating Points.

Signature—The designation of a printed sheet as it comes off the press. Also, the eight, sixteen, or thirty-two pages it becomes after folding and trimming.

Source generator—The part of the marketing strategy statement which broadly defines the consumer group who will be prospects for the plan.

Spill-in/Spill-out—The viewing of a broadcast station from an adjacent market and identified as in or out in accordance with the issue to be resolved. For example, protecting the purity of a test market, or paying for out of market exposures, etc.

Split run—The testing of two pieces of different advertising copy in the divided circulation of a print vehicle so that no one market or person sees both advertisements.

Sponsorship—The purchase of a significant percentage of commercials to be broadcast during one program.

Spot—The purchase of broadcast time on a selective market basis. The word can refer to the purchase process (spot buying), the commercial time purchased, or the announcements to be run.

Standard Advertising Unit (SAU)—Prescribed space units common to all newspapers, whether the publication is of tabloid or standard size.

Standard deviation—A measure of the variance of individual values from the reported mean of a group of values. The higher the standard deviation, the greater the spread of accuracy in survey scores.

Station break—The time between broadcast programs in which local stations identify and promote themselves, as well as selling commercial time. Considered a major contributor to the perception of network clutter.

Store check—An in-field visit to a retail outlet in order to evaluate product distribution, shelf presentation, consumer behavior, and sales.

Strategy—A plan for action intended to achieve an objective.

Superstation—An independent television station whose signal is consciously exported to other markets via satellites and cable television systems, and with the intention of selling this added national or regional audience to advertisers.

Supplement—A newspaper section in a magazine format, not distributed in every issue.

Sweep—The time period during which local market broadcast ratings are gathered. Conducted four times each year in most markets, and usually accompanied by high profile competitive programming.

Syndication—A method of program distribution that is dependent on market-by-market sales.

T

Tabloid—A newspaper smaller than the standard size, and about the size of a broadsheet folded in half.

Tactics—For media planners, the implementation through specific vehicles, at specific costs, of the media strategy.

Tag—A local dealer identification added, on a market-by-market basis, to a broadcast commercial.

Target market—The geographic region or demographic group that is the object of an advertising campaign.

Tear sheet—A page of a printed publication, containing advertising, and sent to the advertiser for approval, or as proof of performance.

Telephone coincidental—A research survey conducted through random phone calls at the same time that a program is being broadcast in order to identify audience size, characteristics, or preferences.

Test market—One or more markets selected in order to test new product acceptability or various promotional strategies.

Thirty-sheet poster—An outdoor advertising display measuring approximately 10 feet by 22 feet. The name is derived from the traditional number of panels required to be pasted together to form the display.

Tip-in—A preprinted advertisement pasted along one edge to a bound-in page of a print publication.

Tonnage strategy—A media strategy which puts a premium on the greatest possible number of impressions at the lowest relative cost, regardless of the media environment of program, time period, or station.

Total audience—The number of different households of persons tuned to a broadcast program for six minutes or longer.

Trade paper—A specialized publication designed to serve the interests of a specific industry or profession.

Transit advertising—Advertising that is placed within mass transit vehicles. Also, posters placed within terminals or stations.

U

Up-front—A method for purchasing quantities of network television time before a season or quarter begins.

Upscale—A description of an audience exhibiting high-class socioeconomic characteristics.

V

Vehicle—A particular example of a media class, such as a magazine title or television program.

Vertical publication—A print publication designed to serve the specific interests of those who engage in a particular activity.

W

Wastage—The percentage of a vehicle audience that falls outside the marketer's target group, but that nevertheless is reached by the advertising.

Wear out—The level of frequency of exposure to an advertisement at which it loses its ability to communicate.

Weighting—An arithmetic method for giving added value, or discounted value, to one or more numbers.

Women's service magazine—Publication designed to appeal to women interested in homemaking.

Y

Year-to-date—The base used for measuring sales or expenditures from the first day of the calendar year, or first day of the fiscal year, to the present. In some research data bases, refers to the fifty-two weeks prior to the present week, regardless of the calendar year in which the weeks occur.

Index